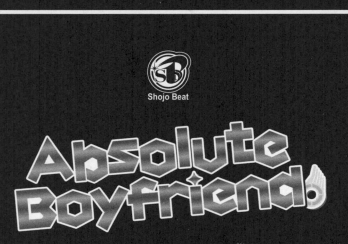

Absolute Boyfriend

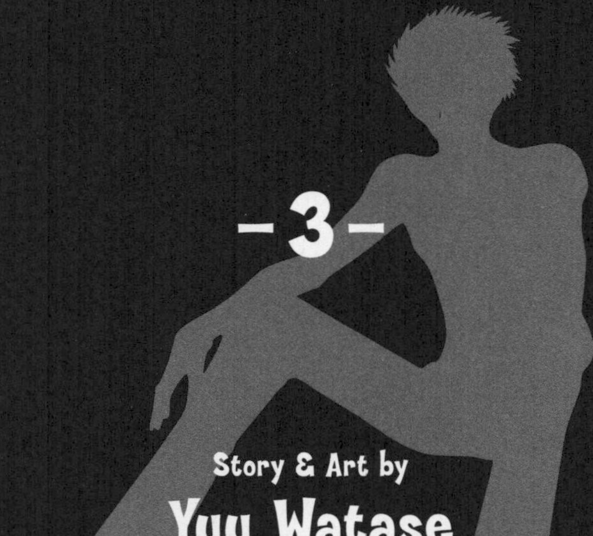

-3-

Story & Art by
Yuu Watase

Shojo Beat

Absolute Boyfriend

CAST

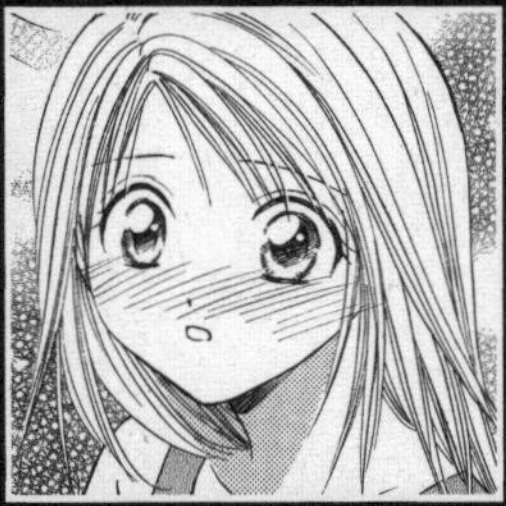

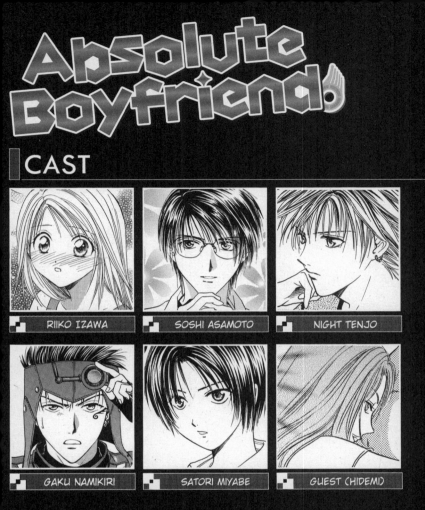

RIIKO IZAWA

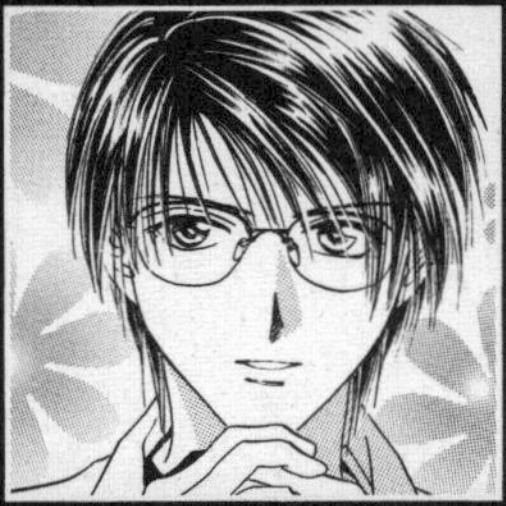

SOSHI ASAMOTO

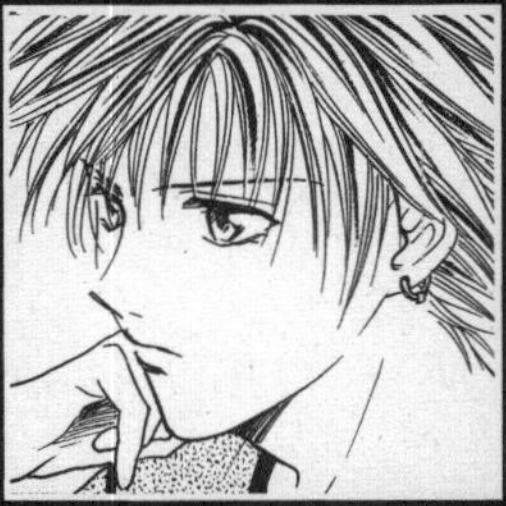

NIGHT TENJO

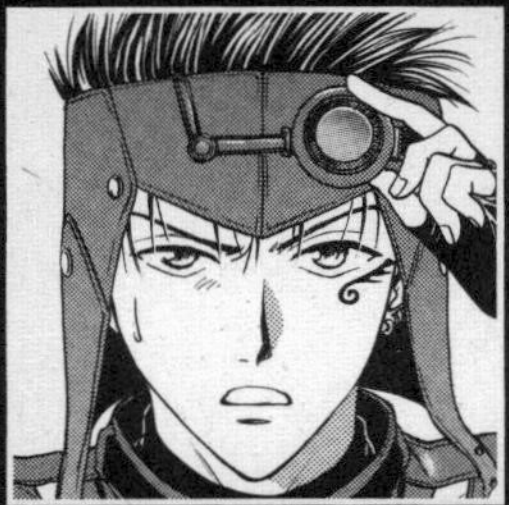

GAKU NAMIKIRI

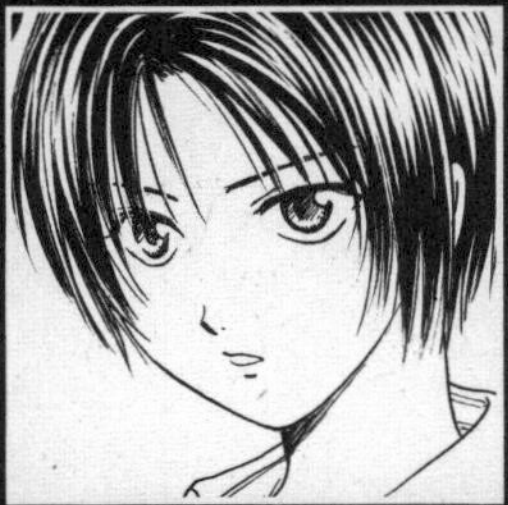

SATORI MIYABE

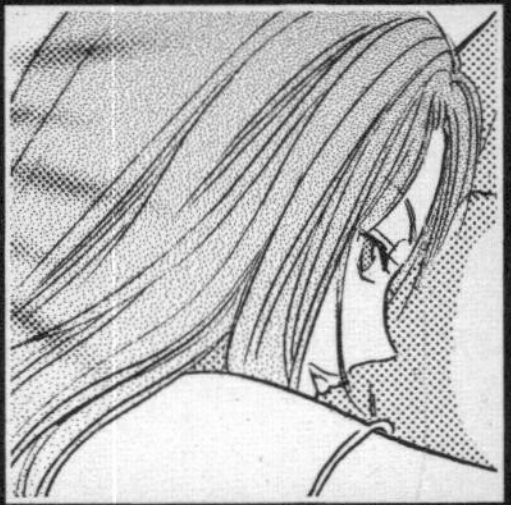

GUEST (HIDEMI)

STORY

DEPRESSED BY REJECTION, RIIKO BOUGHT THE IDEAL BOYFRIEND FIGURE FROM A STRANGELY DRESSED SALESMAN NAMED GAKU. ONCE ACTIVATED BY RIIKO'S KISS, NIGHT LOOKED COMPLETELY HUMAN! NOW NIGHT, JEALOUS OF RIIKO'S FEELINGS FOR SOSHI, DECIDES TO LEARN MORE ABOUT WOMEN BY TAKING A JOB AT A MALE ESCORT CLUB. BUT WHEN A CUSTOMER NAMED HIDEMI KISSES HIM, SHE UNDOES NIGHT'S SETTINGS AND BECOMES THE NEW OBJECT OF HIS DEVOTION! AND IF HIDEMI AND NIGHT MAKE LOVE, RIIKO WILL LOSE NIGHT FOREVER!

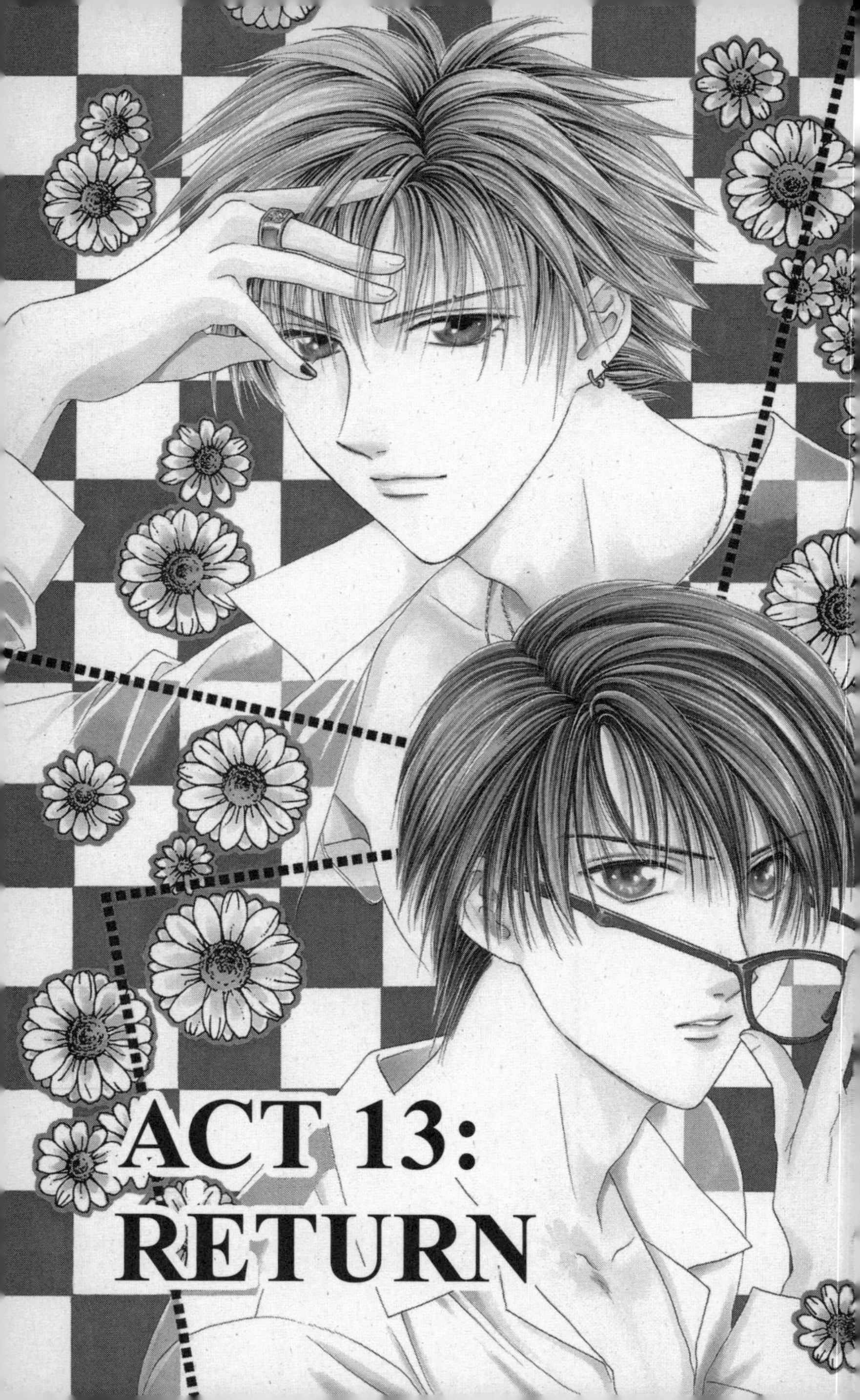
ACT 13:
RETURN

Absolute Boyfriend

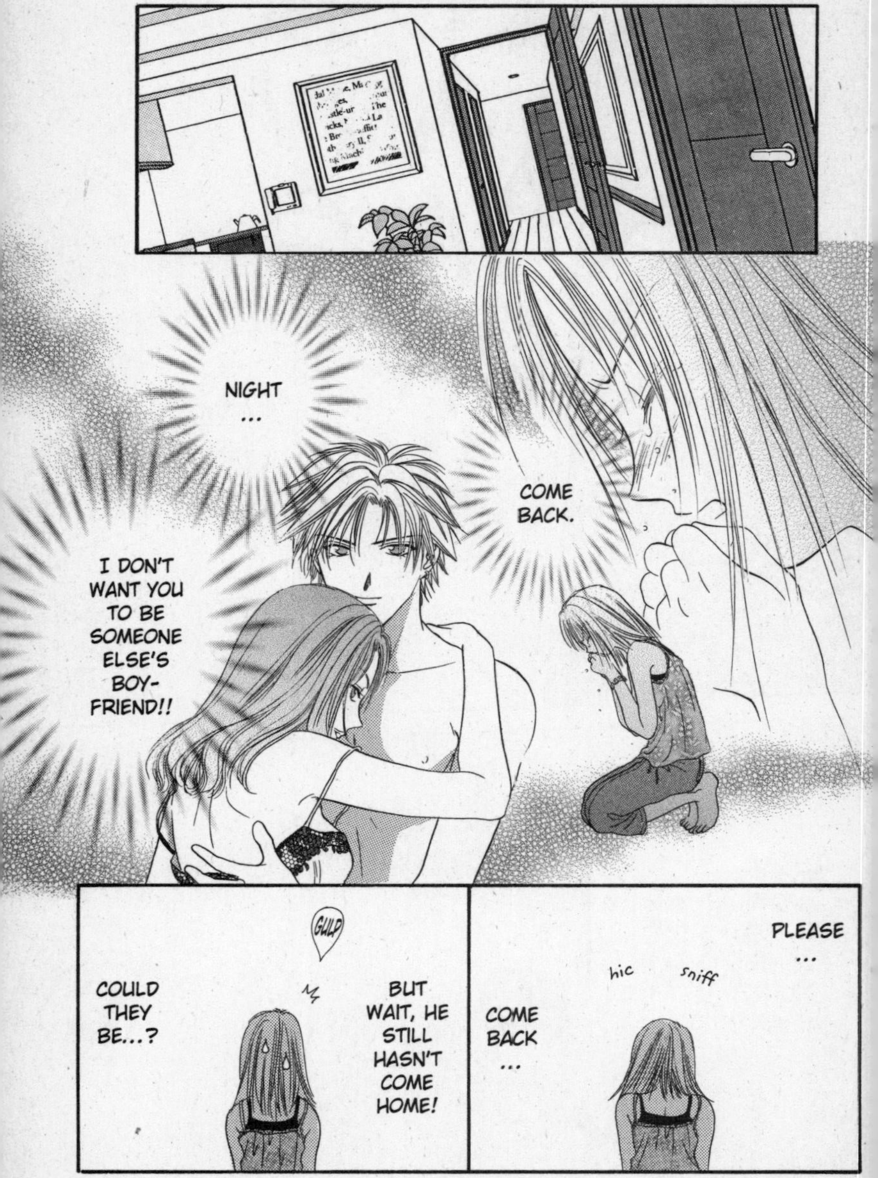
COME BACK.
NIGHT ...
I DON'T WANT YOU TO BE SOMEONE ELSE'S BOY-FRIEND!!
PLEASE ...
sniff
hic
COME BACK ...
GULP
BUT WAIT, HE STILL HASN'T COME HOME!
COULD THEY BE...?

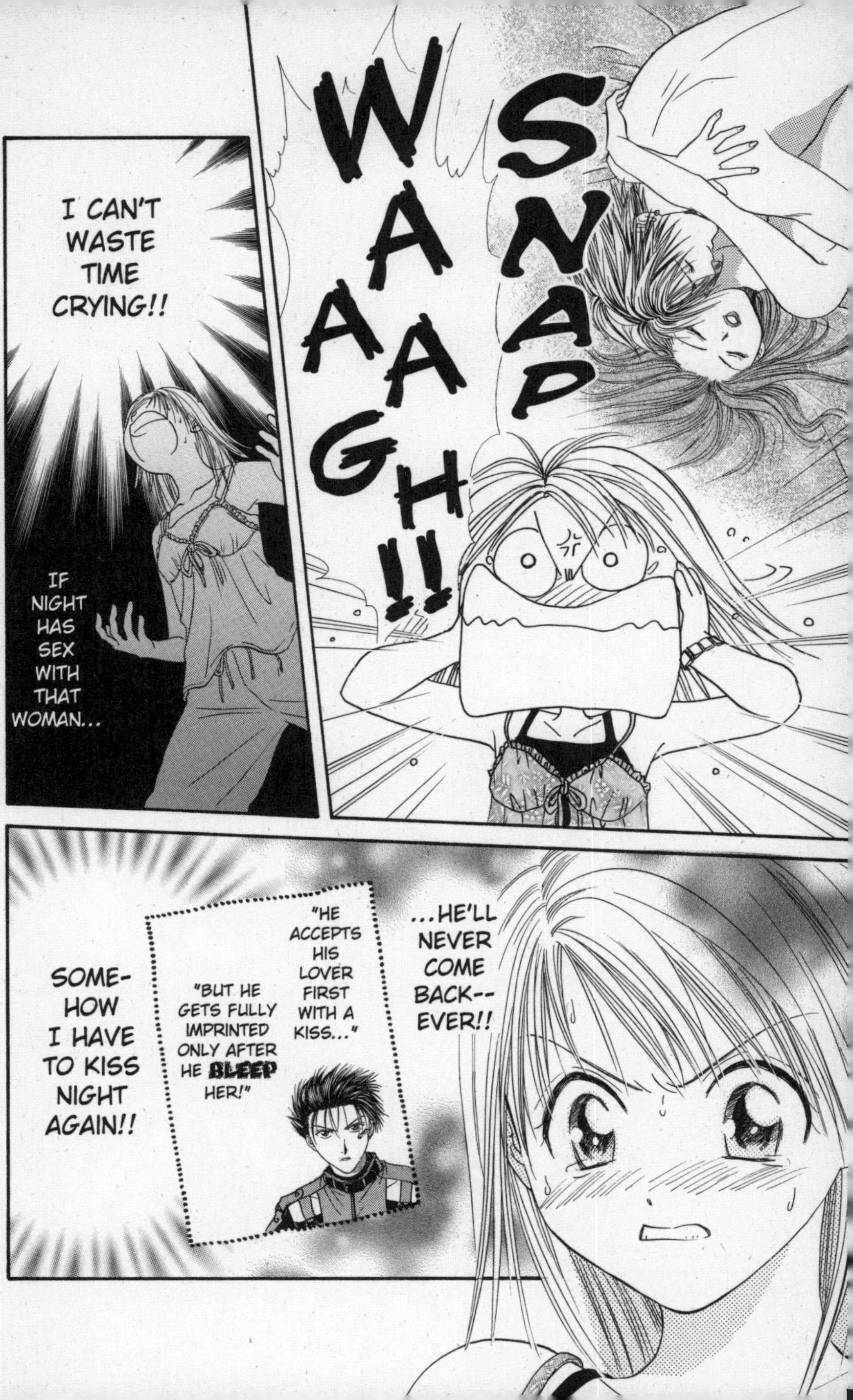
SNAP
WAAAGH!!
I CAN'T WASTE TIME CRYING!!
IF NIGHT HAS SEX WITH THAT WOMAN...
...HE'LL NEVER COME BACK--EVER!!
"HE ACCEPTS HIS LOVER FIRST WITH A KISS..."
"BUT HE GETS FULLY IMPRINTED ONLY AFTER HE BLEEP HER!"
SOME-HOW I HAVE TO KISS NIGHT AGAIN!!

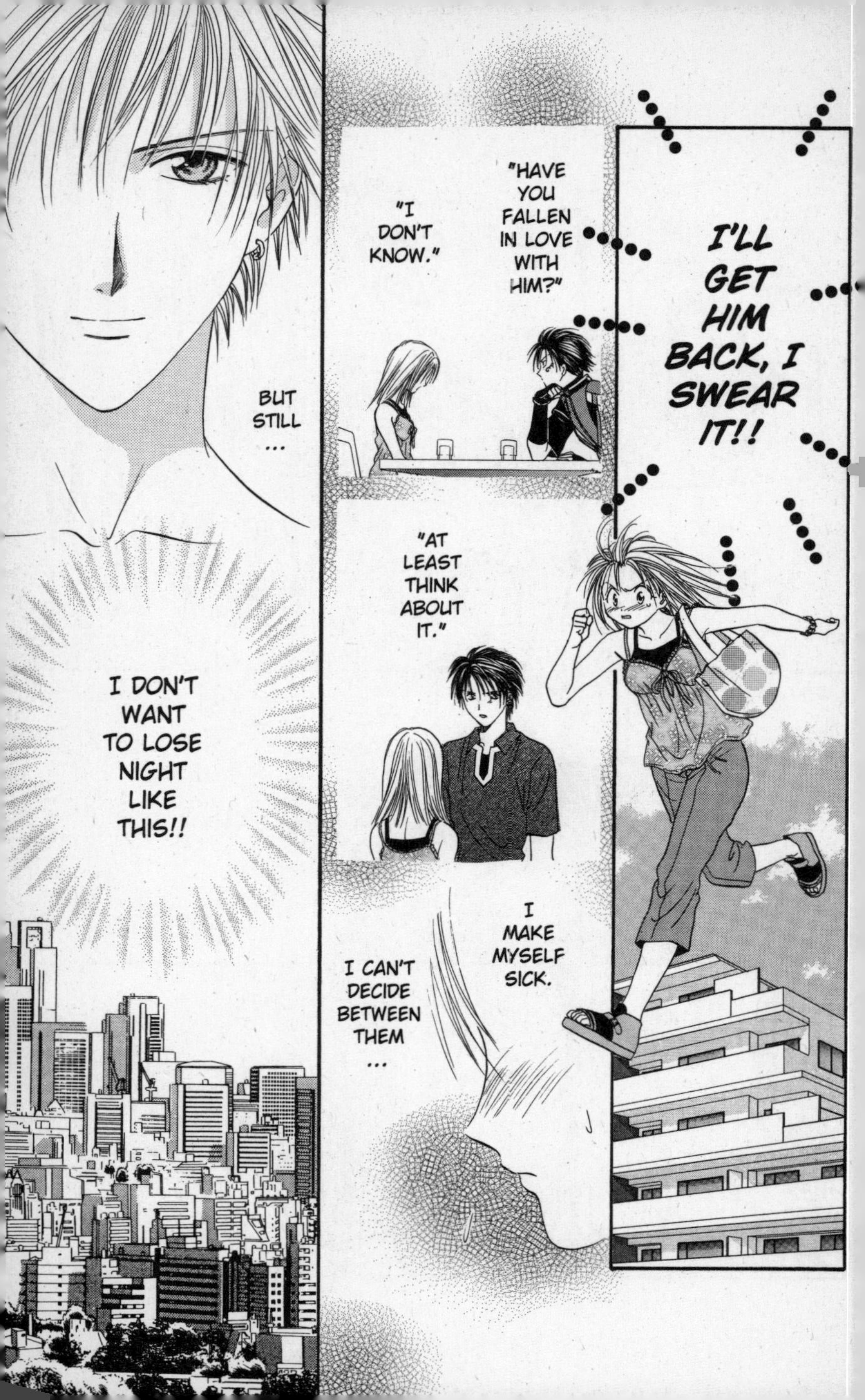
I'LL GET HIM BACK, I SWEAR IT!!
"HAVE YOU FALLEN IN LOVE WITH HIM?"
"I DON'T KNOW."
"AT LEAST THINK ABOUT IT."
I MAKE MYSELF SICK.
I CAN'T DECIDE BETWEEN THEM ...
BUT STILL ...
I DON'T WANT TO LOSE NIGHT LIKE THIS!!

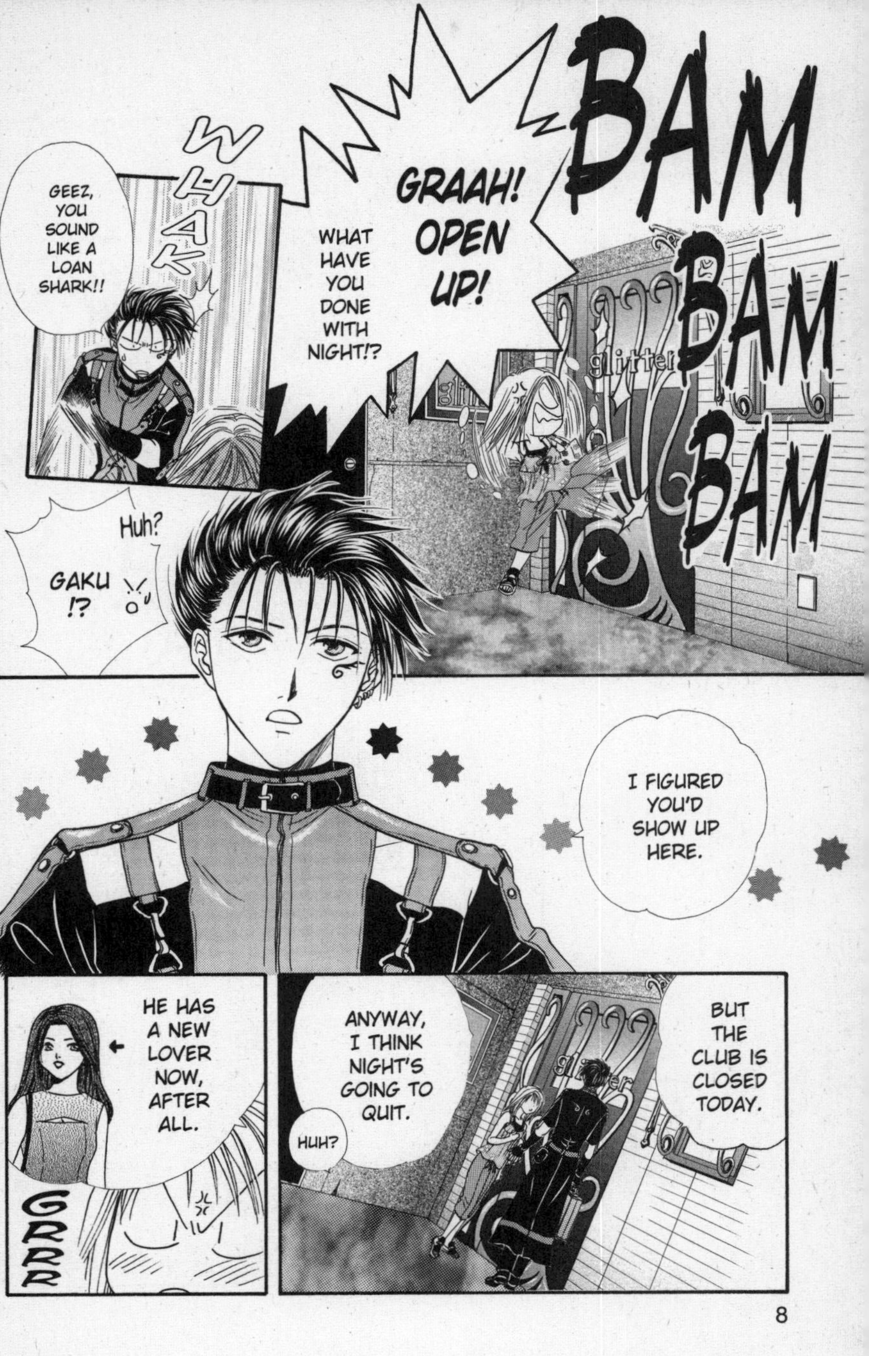
BAM
BAM
BAM
BAM
GRAAH! OPEN UP!
WHAT HAVE YOU DONE WITH NIGHT!?
glitter
WHAK
GEEZ, YOU SOUND LIKE A LOAN SHARK!!
Huh?
GAKU !?
I FIGURED YOU'D SHOW UP HERE.
BUT THE CLUB IS CLOSED TODAY.
ANYWAY, I THINK NIGHT'S GOING TO QUIT.
HUH?
HE HAS A NEW LOVER NOW, AFTER ALL.
GRRR

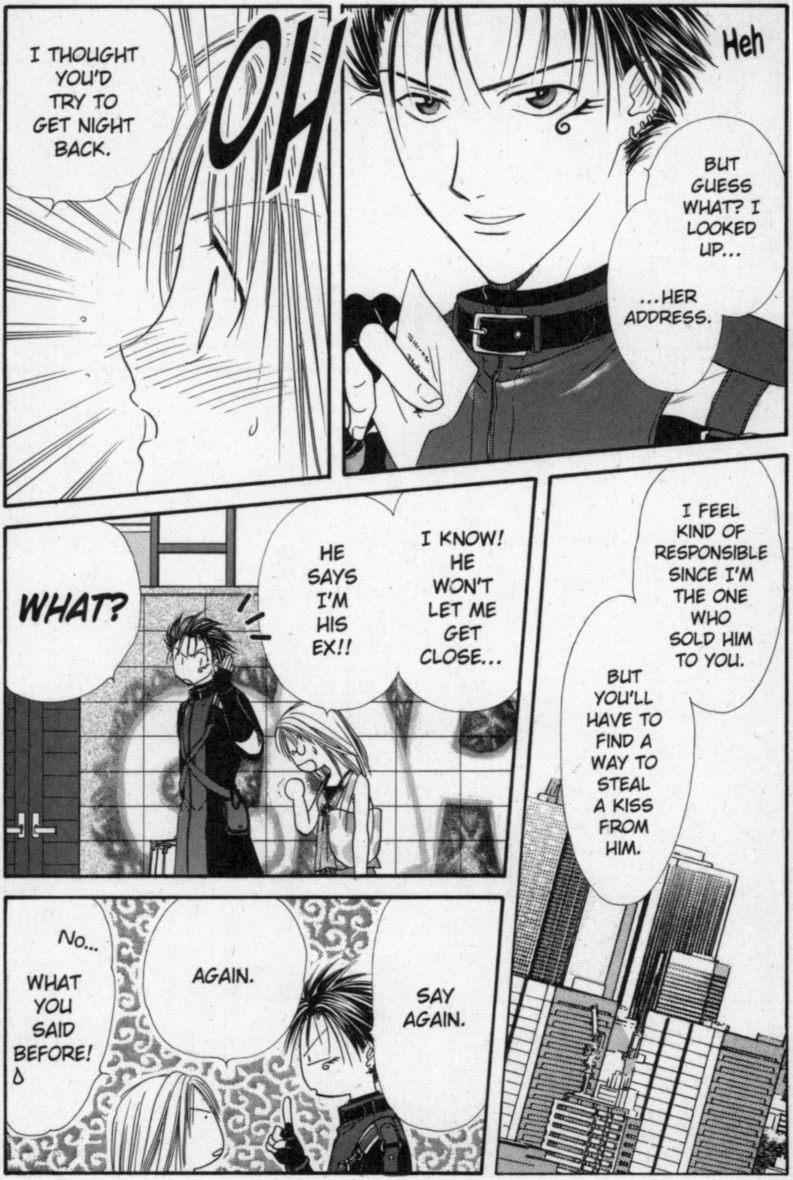
Heh
BUT GUESS WHAT? I LOOKED UP...
...HER ADDRESS.
OH
I THOUGHT YOU'D TRY TO GET NIGHT BACK.
I FEEL KIND OF RESPONSIBLE SINCE I'M THE ONE WHO SOLD HIM TO YOU.
BUT YOU'LL HAVE TO FIND A WAY TO STEAL A KISS FROM HIM.
I KNOW! HE WON'T LET ME GET CLOSE...
HE SAYS I'M HIS EX!!
WHAT?
SAY AGAIN.
AGAIN.
No... WHAT YOU SAID BEFORE!

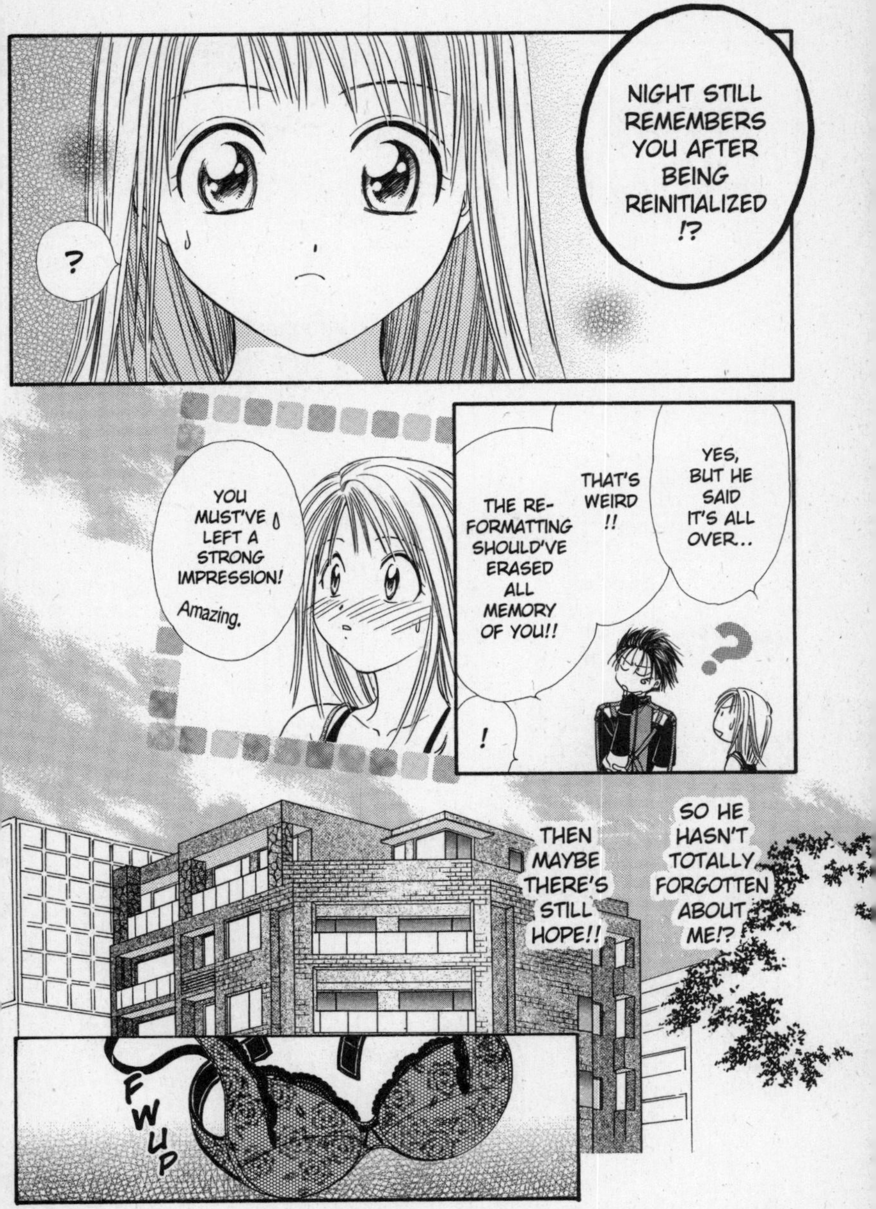
NIGHT STILL REMEMBERS YOU AFTER BEING REINITIALIZED !?
?
YES, BUT HE SAID IT'S ALL OVER...
THAT'S WEIRD !!
THE RE-FORMATTING SHOULD'VE ERASED ALL MEMORY OF YOU!!
!
YOU MUST'VE LEFT A STRONG IMPRESSION!
Amazing.
SO HE HASN'T TOTALLY FORGOTTEN ABOUT ME!?
THEN MAYBE THERE'S STILL HOPE!!
FWUP

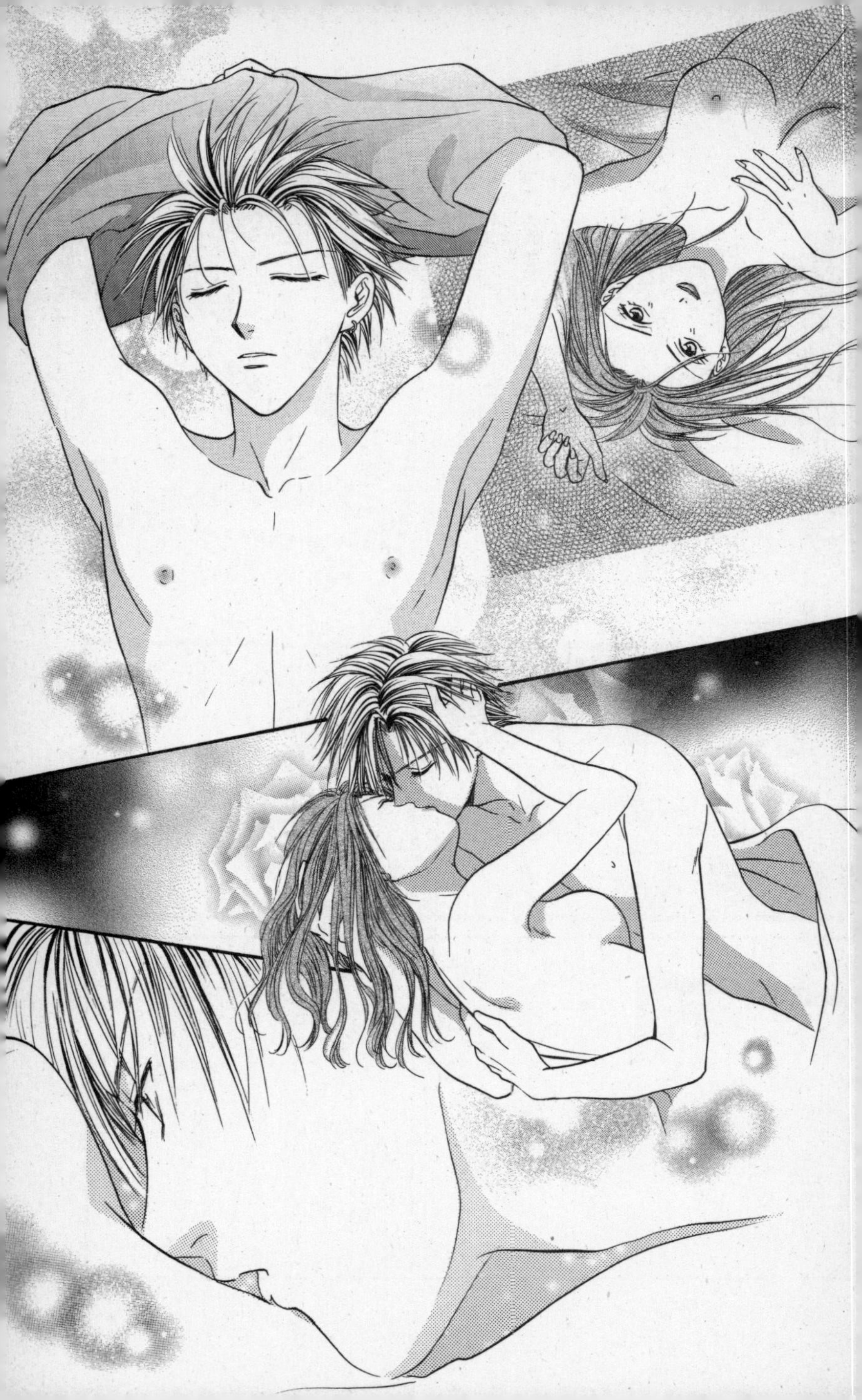

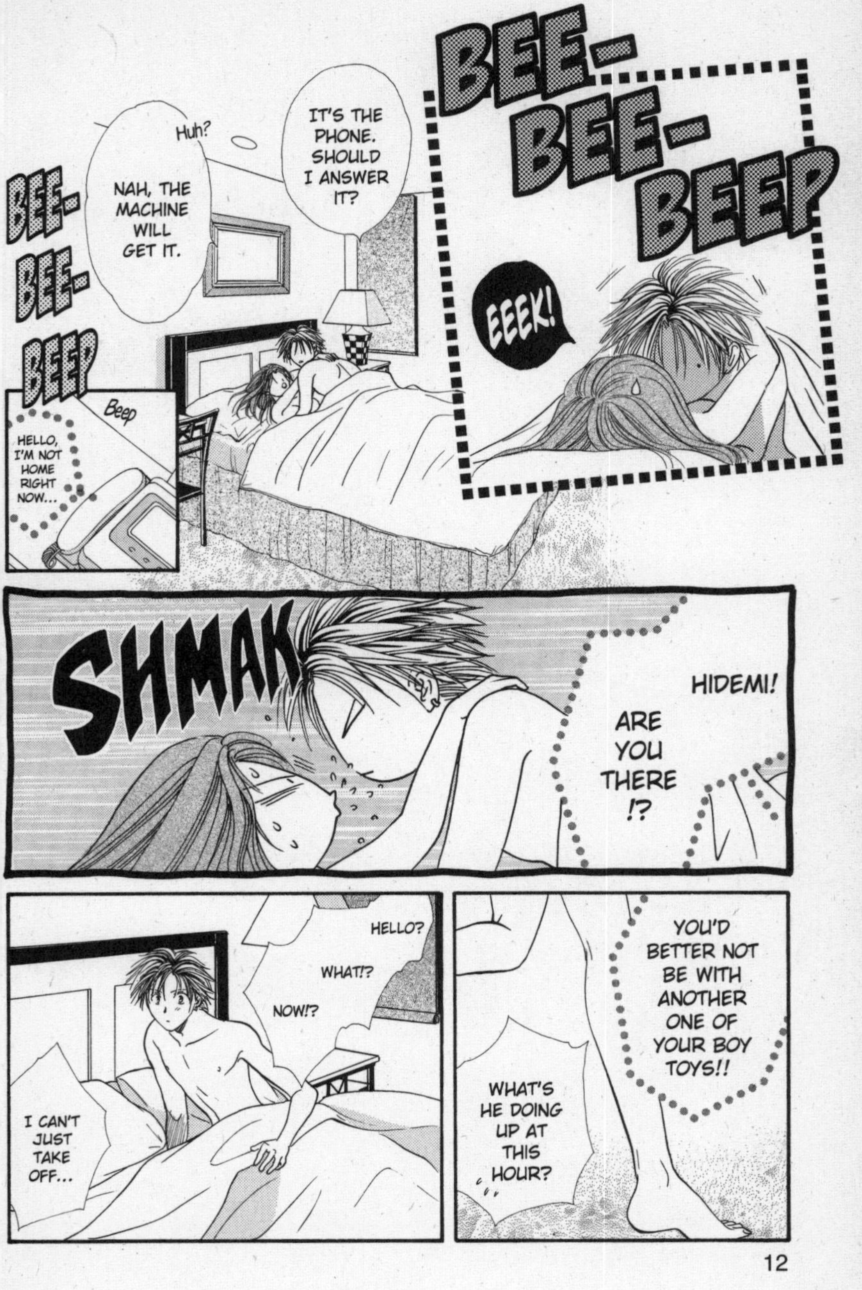
BEE-BEE-BEEP
EEEK!
IT'S THE PHONE. SHOULD I ANSWER IT?
Huh?
NAH, THE MACHINE WILL GET IT.
BEE-BEE-BEEP
Beep
HELLO, I'M NOT HOME RIGHT NOW...
HIDEMI!
ARE YOU THERE!?
SHMAK
YOU'D BETTER NOT BE WITH ANOTHER ONE OF YOUR BOY TOYS!!
WHAT'S HE DOING UP AT THIS HOUR?
HELLO?
WHAT!?
NOW!?
I CAN'T JUST TAKE OFF...

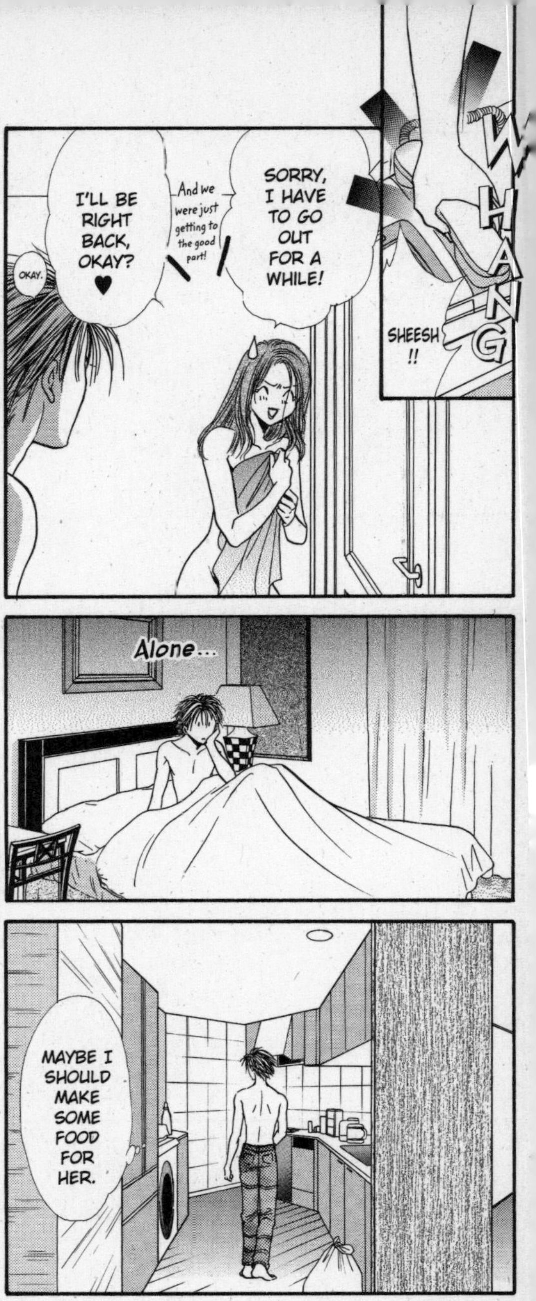
WHANG
SHEESH!!
SORRY, I HAVE TO GO OUT FOR A WHILE!
And we were just getting to the good part!
I'LL BE RIGHT BACK, OKAY? ♥
OKAY.
Alone...
MAYBE I SHOULD MAKE SOME FOOD FOR HER.

Hello, is everyone working hard!? I'm working too hard, and I'm so tired!! I wish I could stop writing, but I just started on this.

It's springtime. Every year, I miss out on seeing the cherry blossoms, but there are real cherry blossoms in my room right now (March '04)! My editors always send me a bouquet of flowers for my birthday on March 5, and there were cherry blossoms in it this year! Maybe it's because I kept going on and on about them. Maybe some of you will understand. (It's nothing, really.) This pen is hard to write with, so I'm getting a new one!

Got another one... ← **Uh-oh, the tip is mashed!** ← And this one's too thick! But back to the cherry blossoms. I'm having a picnic in my studio. I even have some cherry-scented incense. But I really want to go out. I'm planning to go see the cherry blossoms in Kyoto this year!! I wonder if I'll actually make it with my schedule!? I hope by the time this book comes out, it'll all be a pleasant memory. The blooming season will be almost over by late April! Oh, whatever. Anything cherry blossom-related puts me in a good mood--even a coffee-table book. So what if I'm being weird? It's spring!

Oh, thanks for all the birthday presents, everyone. And the chocolates for Valentine's Day. Those things really cheer me up when I'm exhausted! No really, a hundred times more than usual. Thank goodness for the kindness of strangers.

Now I **really** sound weird...

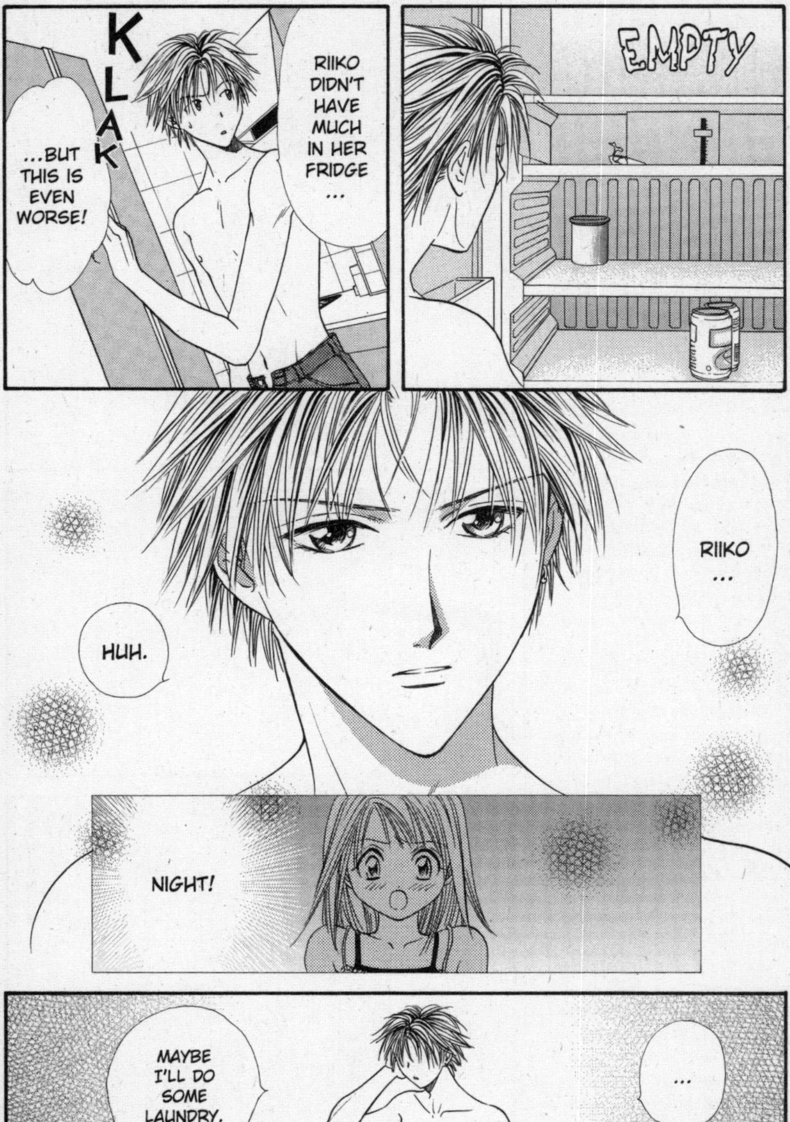
EMPTY
RIIKO DIDN'T HAVE MUCH IN HER FRIDGE ...
KLAK
...BUT THIS IS EVEN WORSE!
RIIKO ...
HUH.
NIGHT!
...
MAYBE I'LL DO SOME LAUNDRY.

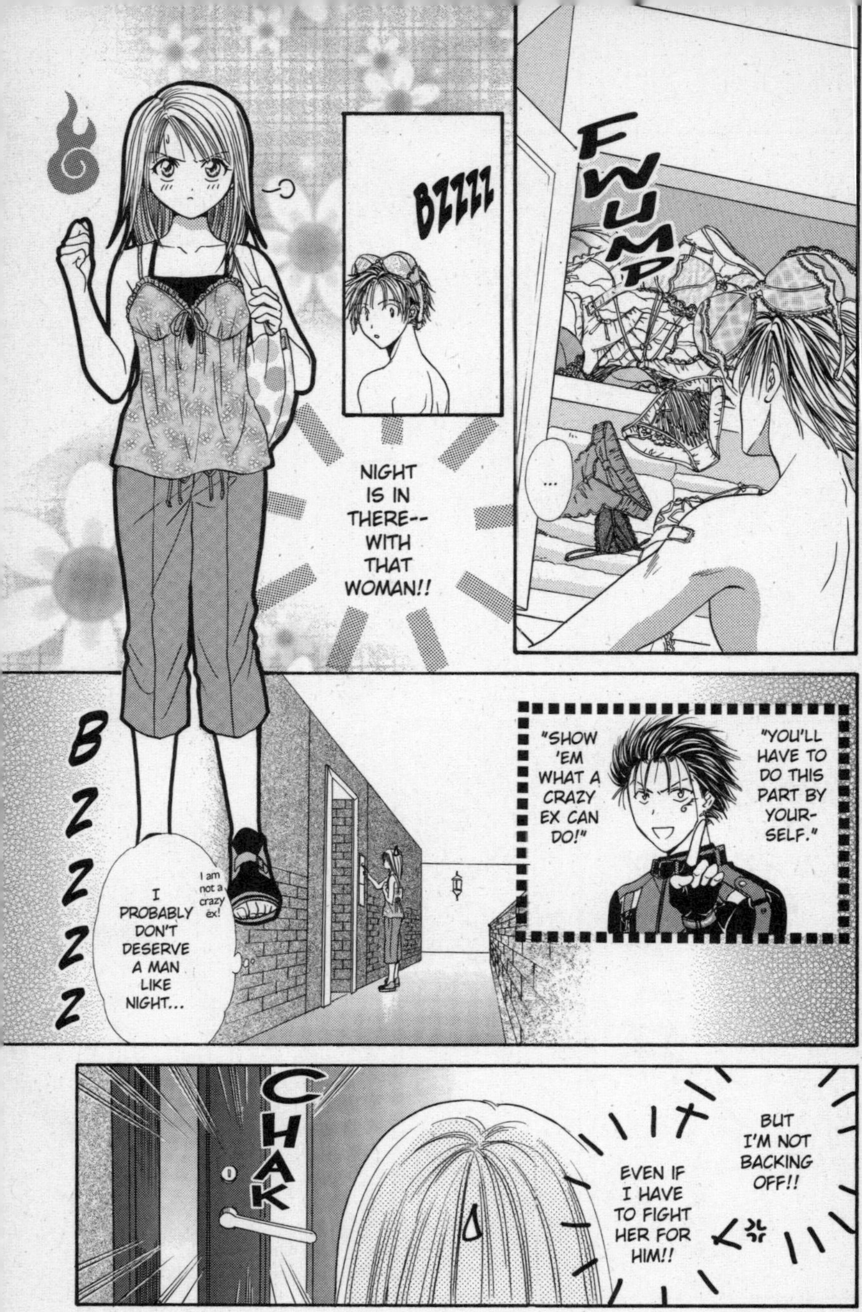
FWUMP
...
BZZZZ
NIGHT IS IN THERE-- WITH THAT WOMAN!!
"YOU'LL HAVE TO DO THIS PART BY YOURSELF."
"SHOW 'EM WHAT A CRAZY EX CAN DO!"
BZZZZZ
I PROBABLY DON'T DESERVE A MAN LIKE NIGHT...
I am not a crazy ex!
BUT I'M NOT BACKING OFF!!
EVEN IF I HAVE TO FIGHT HER FOR HIM!!
CHAK

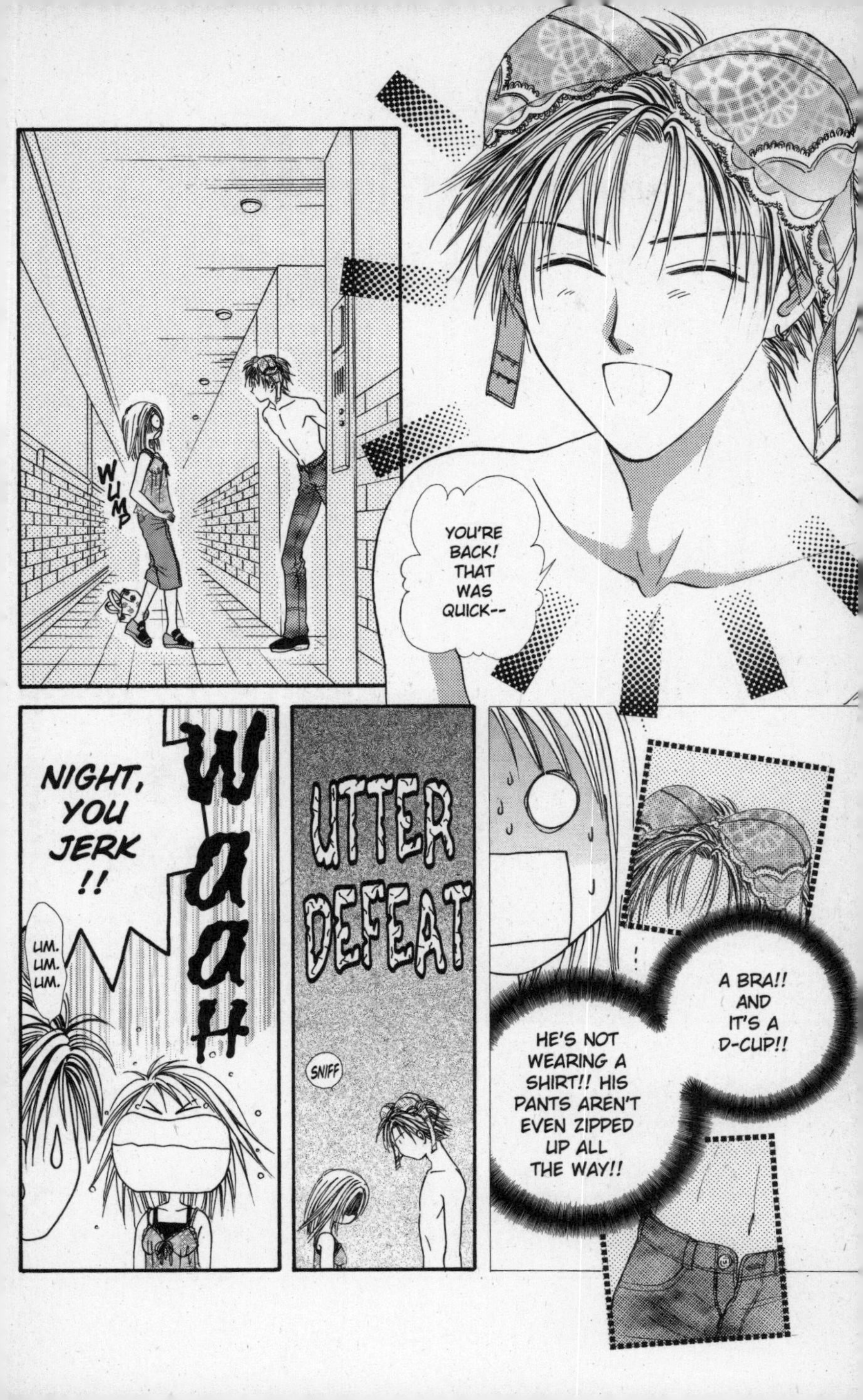
YOU'RE BACK! THAT WAS QUICK--
WUMP
!
A BRA!! AND IT'S A D-CUP!!
HE'S NOT WEARING A SHIRT!! HIS PANTS AREN'T EVEN ZIPPED UP ALL THE WAY!!
UTTER DEFEAT
SNIFF
WAAH
NIGHT, YOU JERK!!
UM. UM. UM.

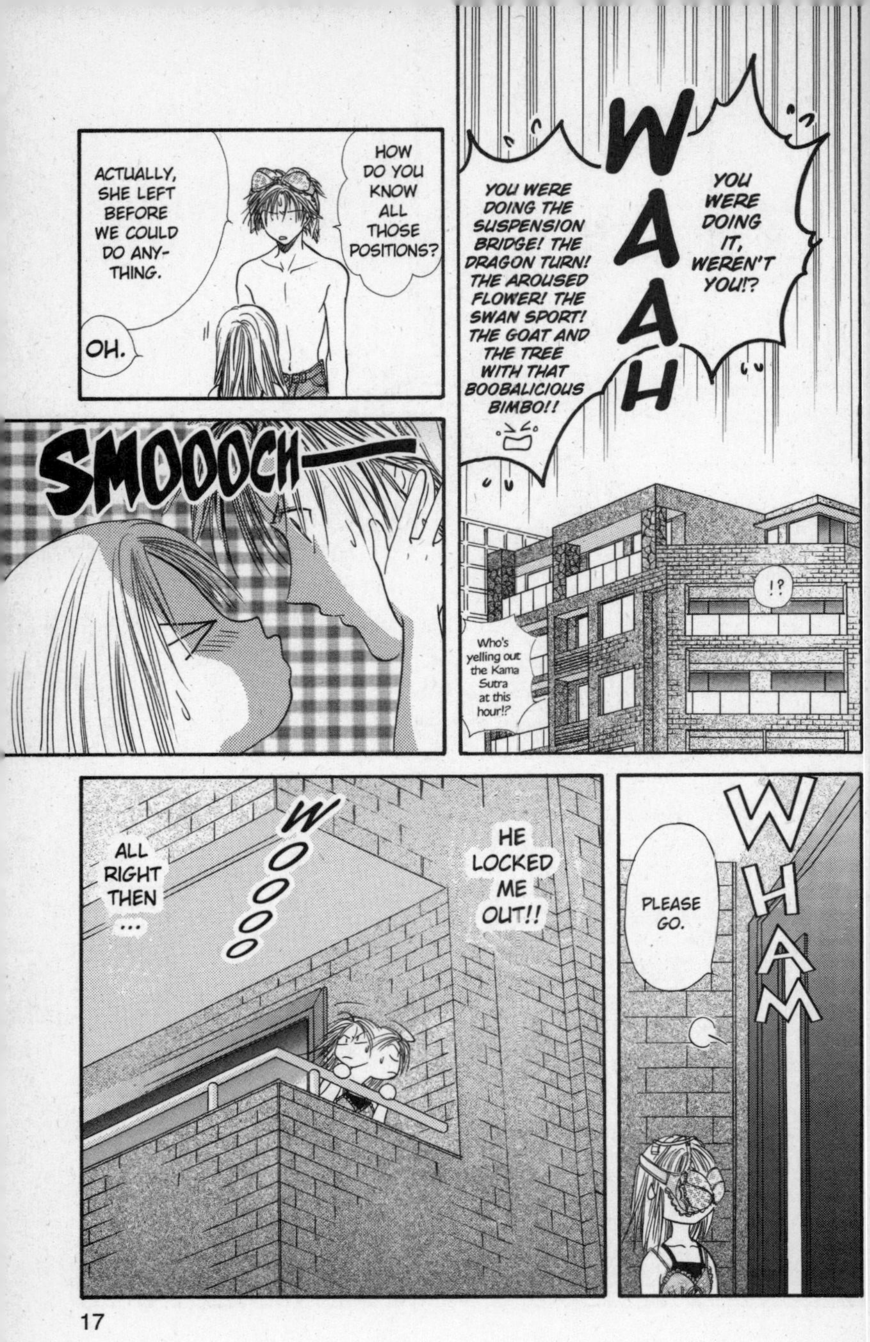

WAAH
YOU WERE DOING IT, WEREN'T YOU!?
YOU WERE DOING THE SUSPENSION BRIDGE! THE DRAGON TURN! THE AROUSED FLOWER! THE SWAN SPORT! THE GOAT AND THE TREE WITH THAT BOOBALICIOUS BIMBO!!
!?
Who's yelling out the Kama Sutra at this hour!?
HOW DO YOU KNOW ALL THOSE POSITIONS?
ACTUALLY, SHE LEFT BEFORE WE COULD DO ANY-THING.
OH.
SMOOOCH—
WHAM
PLEASE GO.
HE LOCKED ME OUT!!
WOOOOO
ALL RIGHT THEN ...

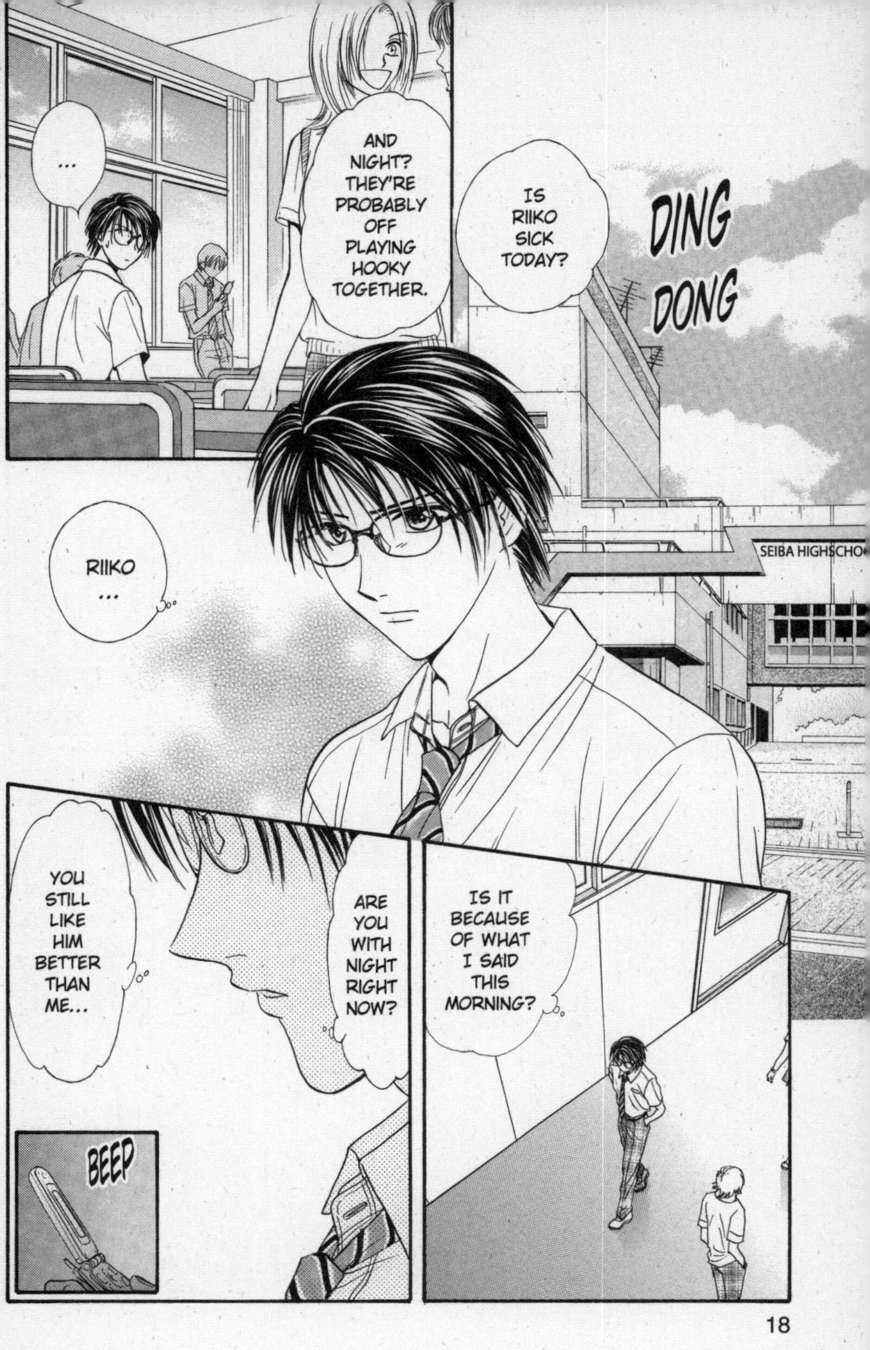

DING DONG
SEIBA HIGHSCHO
IS RIIKO SICK TODAY?
AND NIGHT? THEY'RE PROBABLY OFF PLAYING HOOKY TOGETHER.
...
RIIKO ...
IS IT BECAUSE OF WHAT I SAID THIS MORNING?
ARE YOU WITH NIGHT RIGHT NOW?
YOU STILL LIKE HIM BETTER THAN ME...
BEEP

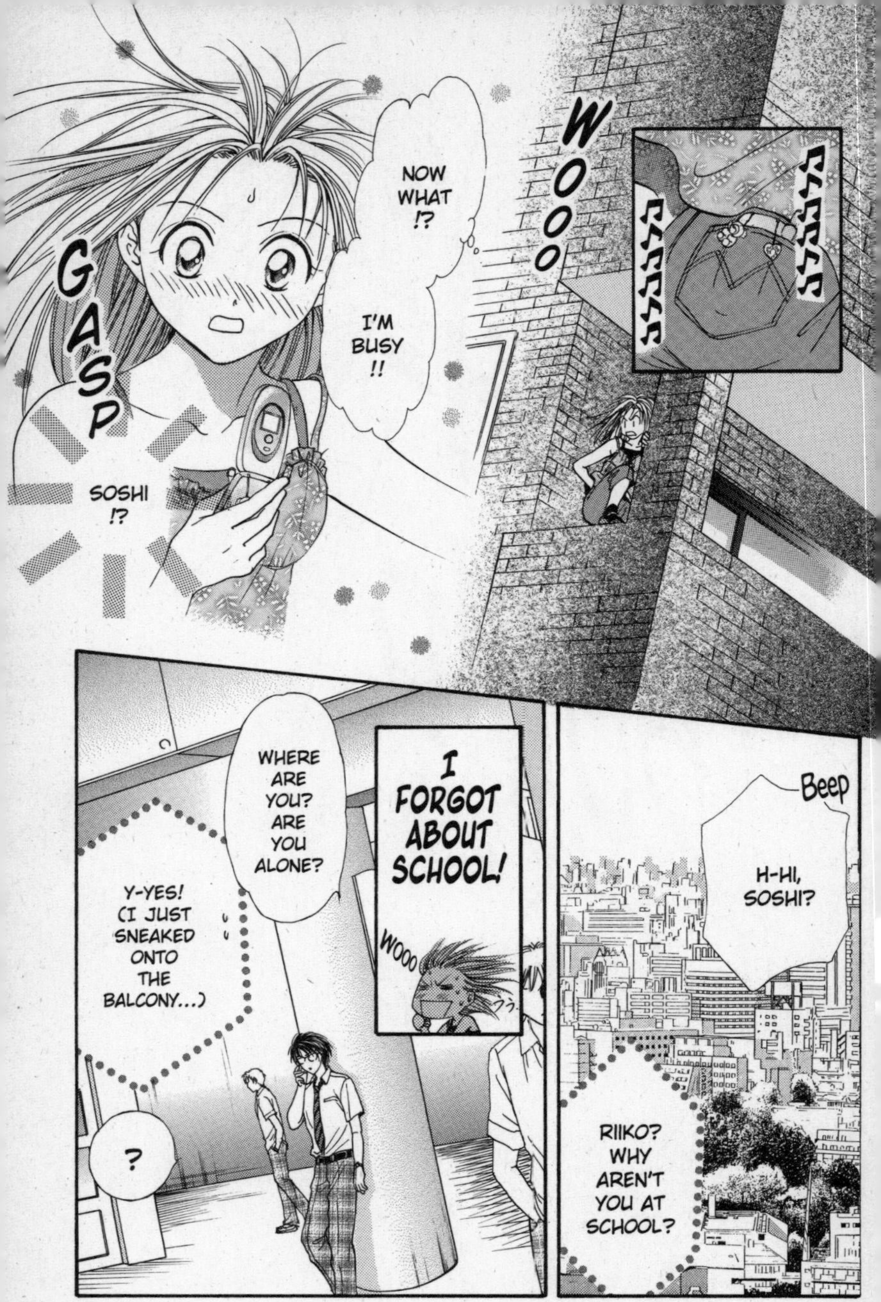
WOOO
NOW WHAT !?
I'M BUSY !!
GASP
SOSHI !?
Beep
H-HI, SOSHI?
RIIKO? WHY AREN'T YOU AT SCHOOL?
I FORGOT ABOUT SCHOOL!
WOOO
WHERE ARE YOU? ARE YOU ALONE?
Y-YES! (I JUST SNEAKED ONTO THE BALCONY...)
?

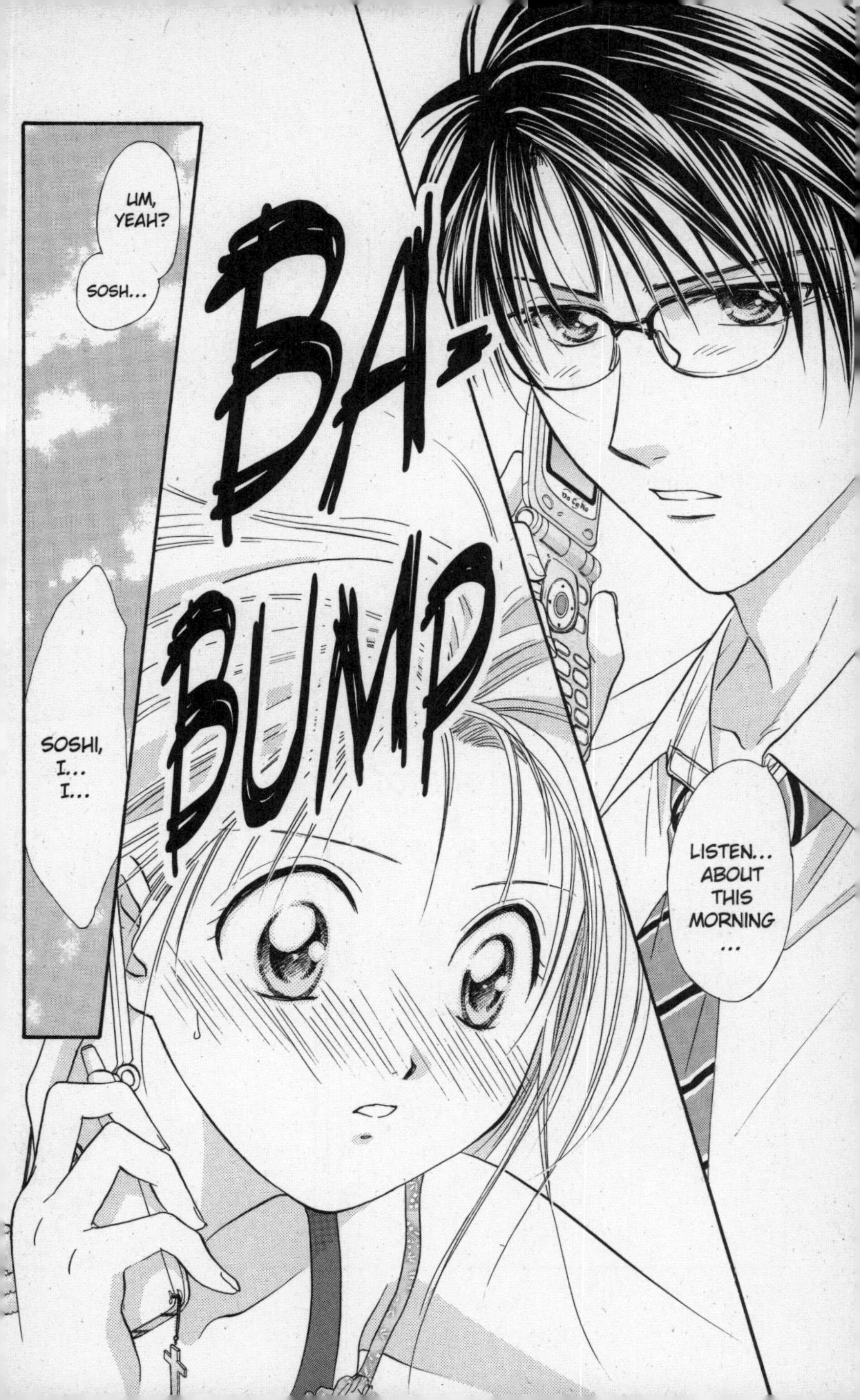
LISTEN... ABOUT THIS MORNING ...
BA-BUMP
UM, YEAH?
SOSH...
SOSHI, I... I...

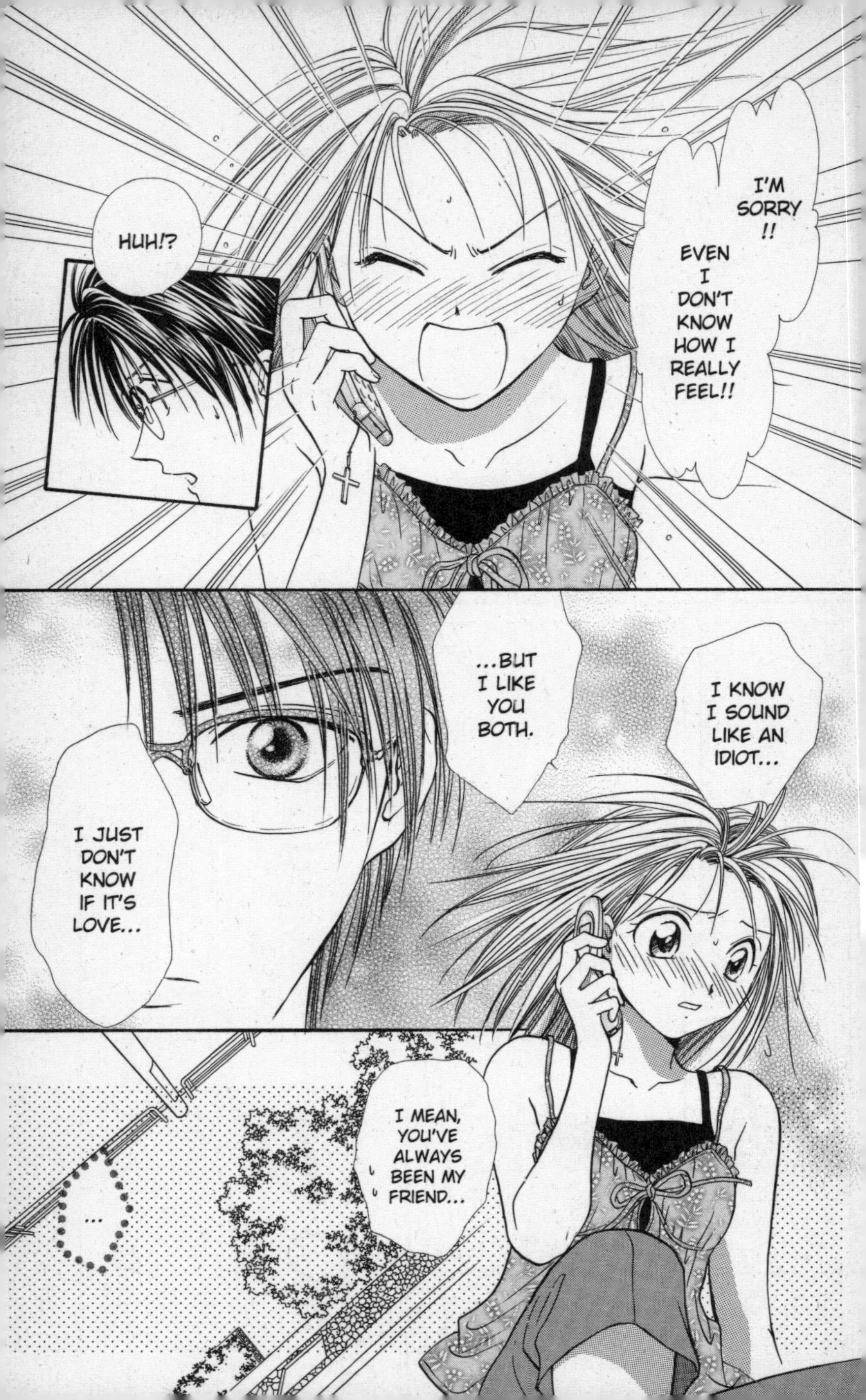
I'M SORRY!!
EVEN I DON'T KNOW HOW I REALLY FEEL!!
HUH!?
I KNOW I SOUND LIKE AN IDIOT...
...BUT I LIKE YOU BOTH.
I JUST DON'T KNOW IF IT'S LOVE...
I MEAN, YOU'VE ALWAYS BEEN MY FRIEND...
...

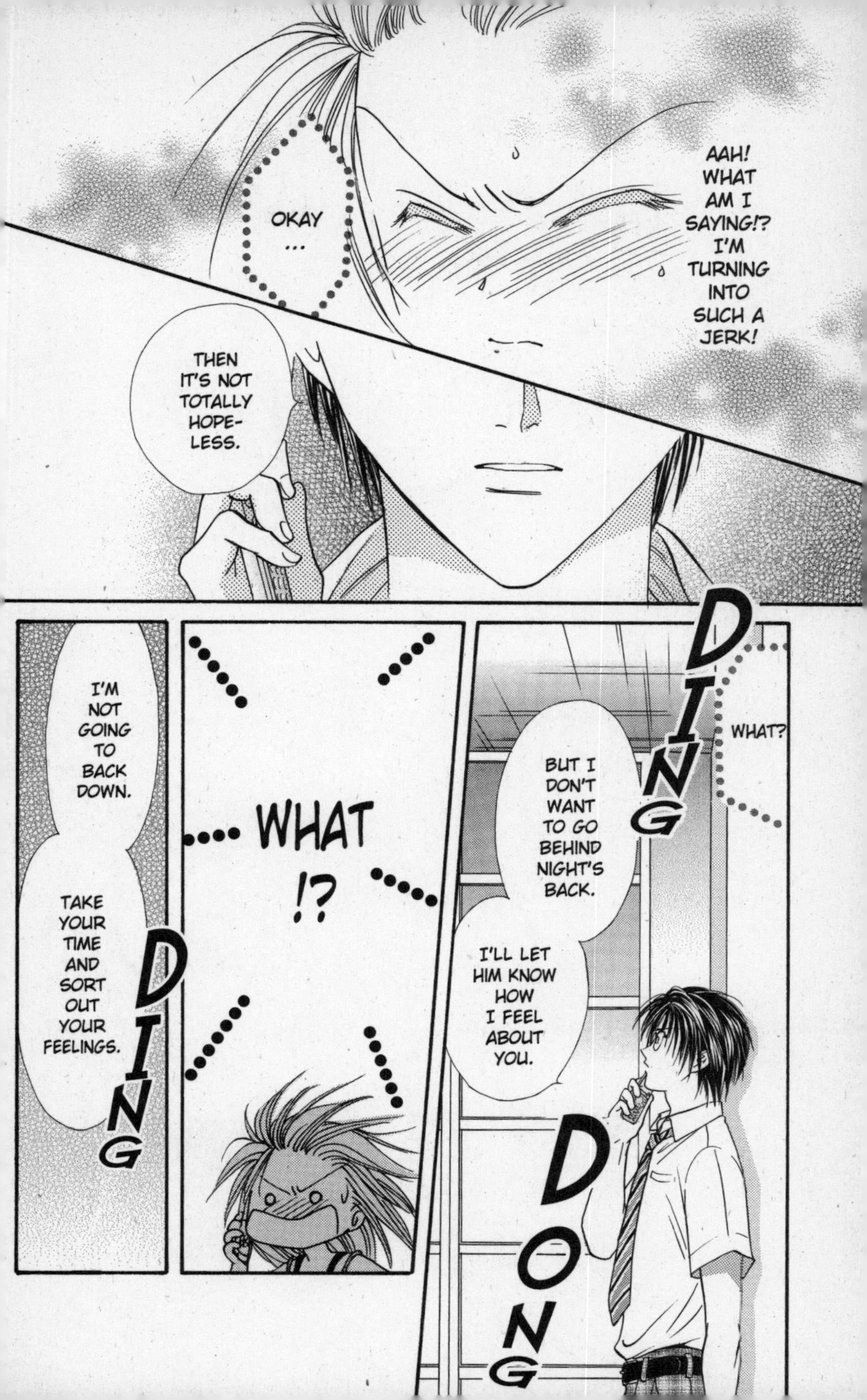
AAH! WHAT AM I SAYING!? I'M TURNING INTO SUCH A JERK!
OKAY...
THEN IT'S NOT TOTALLY HOPE-LESS.
WHAT?
DING
BUT I DON'T WANT TO GO BEHIND NIGHT'S BACK.
I'LL LET HIM KNOW HOW I FEEL ABOUT YOU.
DONG
...WHAT!?
I'M NOT GOING TO BACK DOWN.
DING
TAKE YOUR TIME AND SORT OUT YOUR FEELINGS.

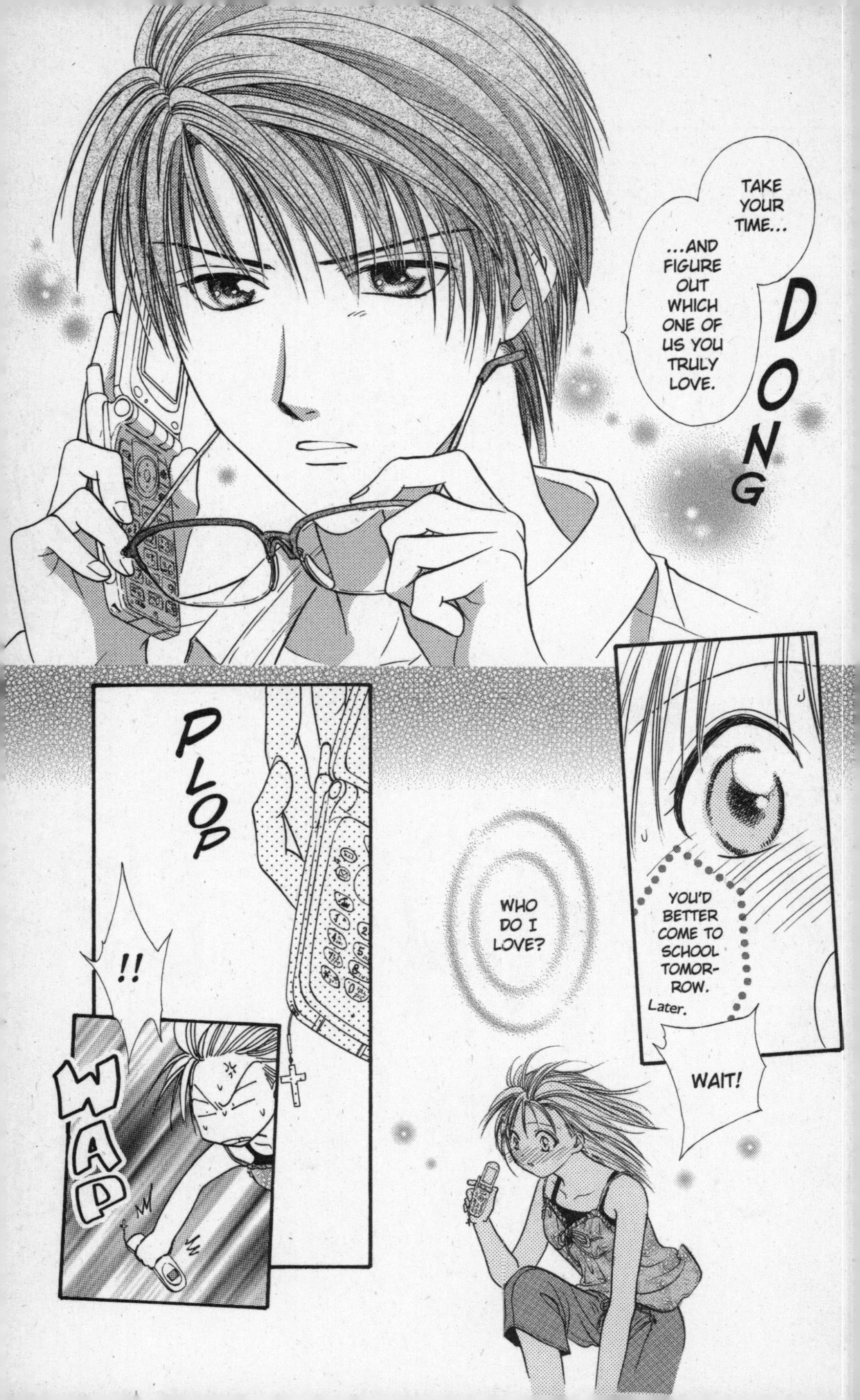
TAKE YOUR TIME...
...AND FIGURE OUT WHICH ONE OF US YOU TRULY LOVE.
DONG
YOU'D BETTER COME TO SCHOOL TOMORROW.
Later.
WHO DO I LOVE?
WAIT!
PLOP
!!
WAP

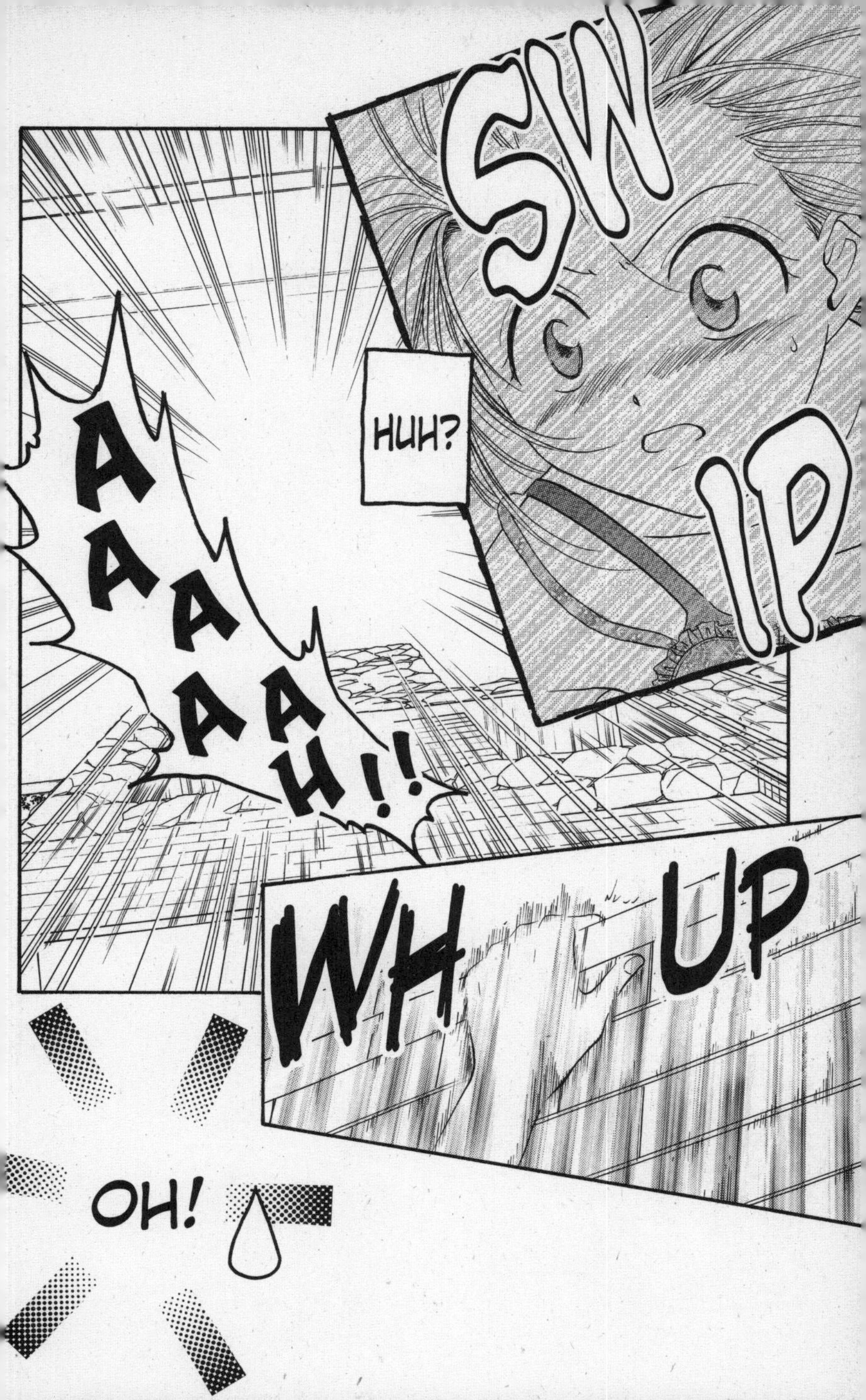
SWIP
HUH?
AAAAAH!!
WHUP
OH!

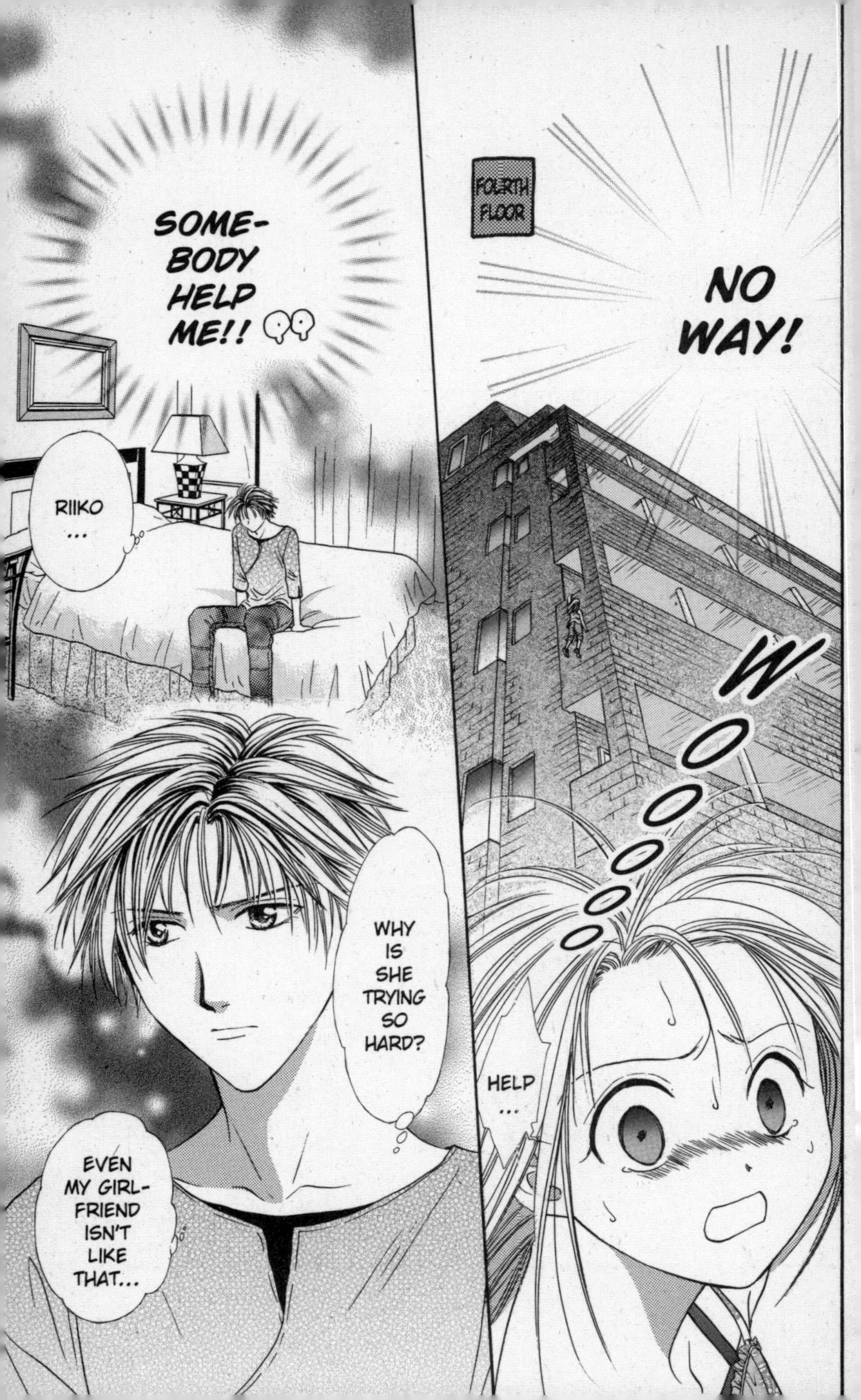
FOURTH FLOOR
NO WAY!
WOOOOOOO
HELP ...
SOME-BODY HELP ME!!
RIIKO ...
WHY IS SHE TRYING SO HARD?
EVEN MY GIRL-FRIEND ISN'T LIKE THAT...

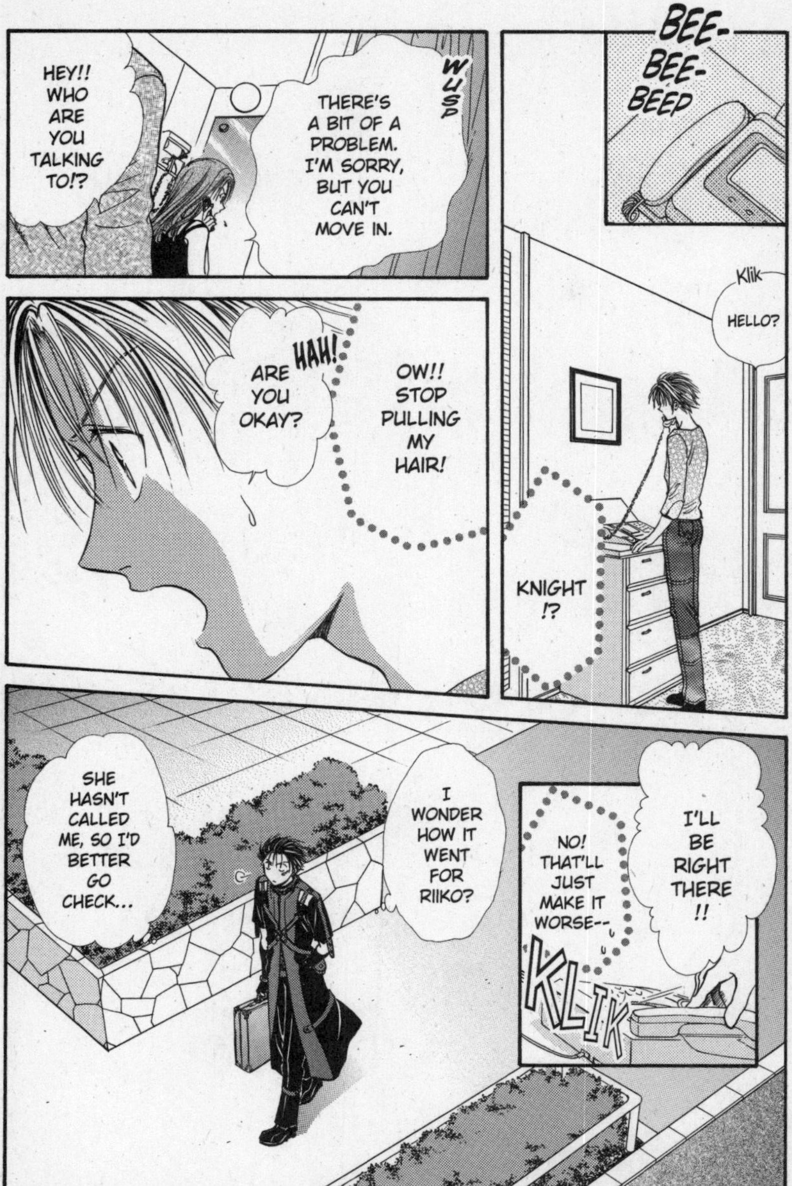
BEE-BEE-BEEP
Klik
HELLO?
KNIGHT!?
WUSP
THERE'S A BIT OF A PROBLEM. I'M SORRY, BUT YOU CAN'T MOVE IN.
HEY!! WHO ARE YOU TALKING TO!?
OW!! STOP PULLING MY HAIR!
HAH!
ARE YOU OKAY?
I'LL BE RIGHT THERE!!
NO! THAT'LL JUST MAKE IT WORSE--
KLIK
I WONDER HOW IT WENT FOR RIIKO?
SHE HASN'T CALLED ME, SO I'D BETTER GO CHECK...

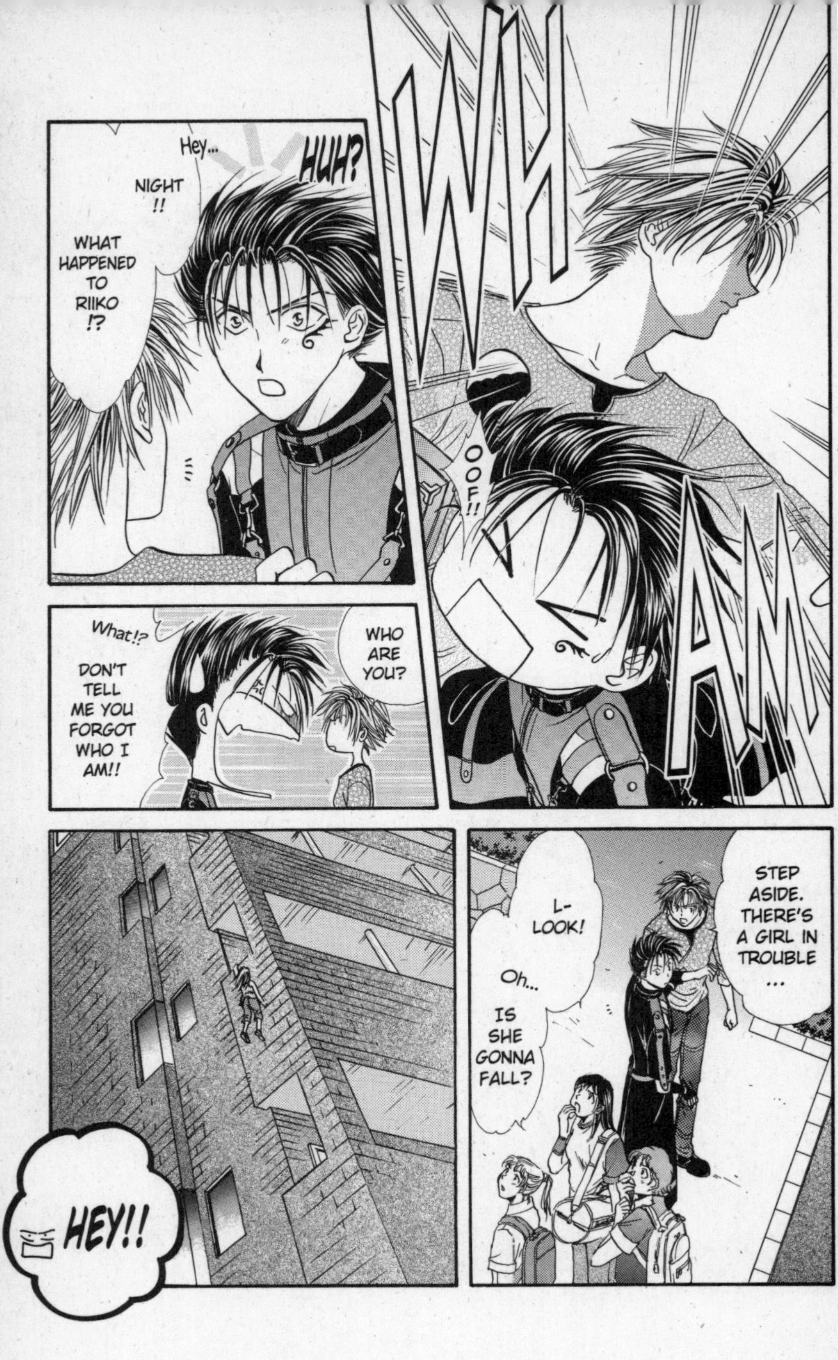
WHAM
OOF!!
HUH?
Hey...
NIGHT!!
WHAT HAPPENED TO RIIKO!?
WHO ARE YOU?
What!?
DON'T TELL ME YOU FORGOT WHO I AM!!
STEP ASIDE. THERE'S A GIRL IN TROUBLE...
L-LOOK!
Oh...
IS SHE GONNA FALL?
HEY!!

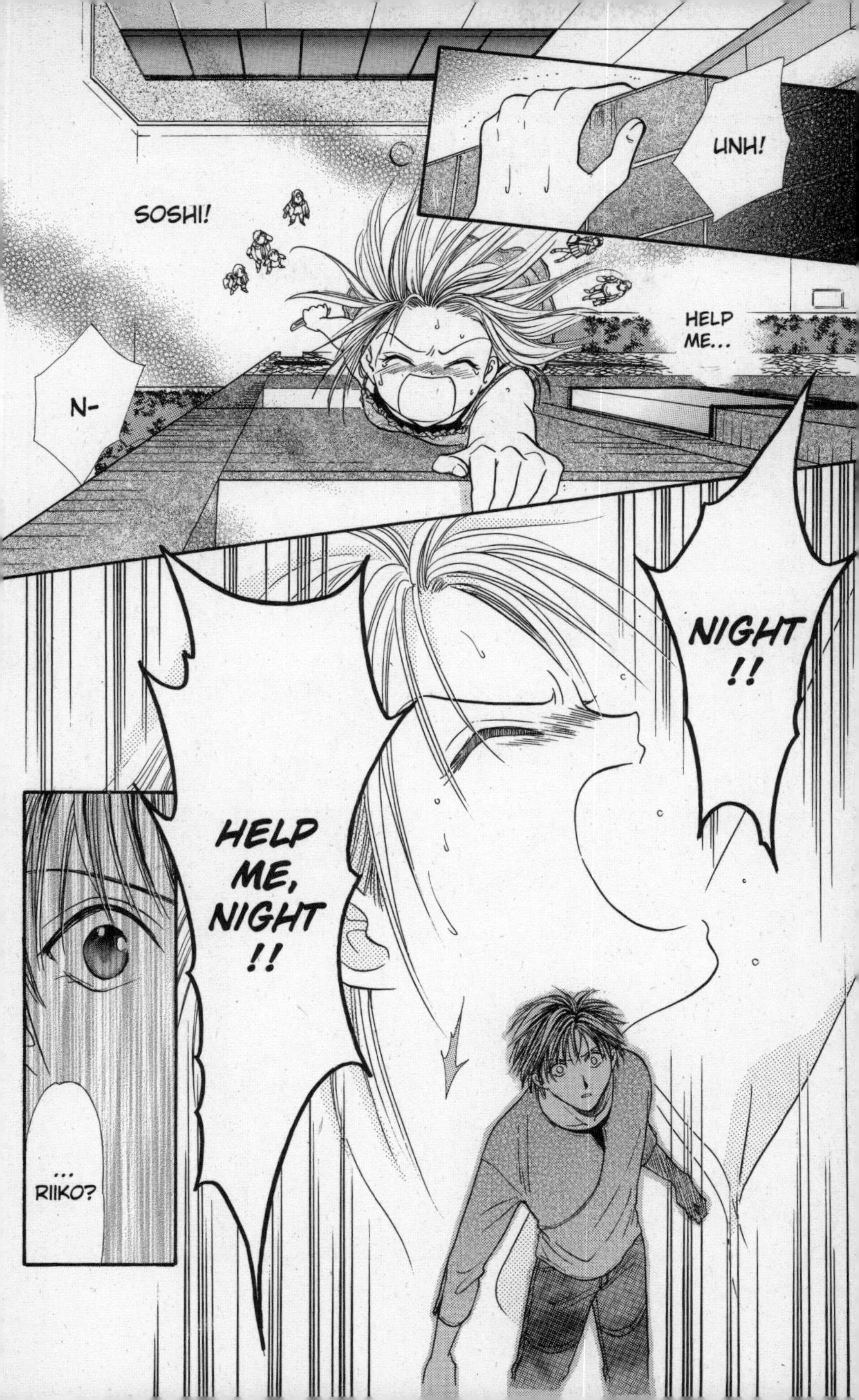
UNH!
HELP ME...
SOSHI!
N-
NIGHT !!
HELP ME, NIGHT !!
... RIIKO?

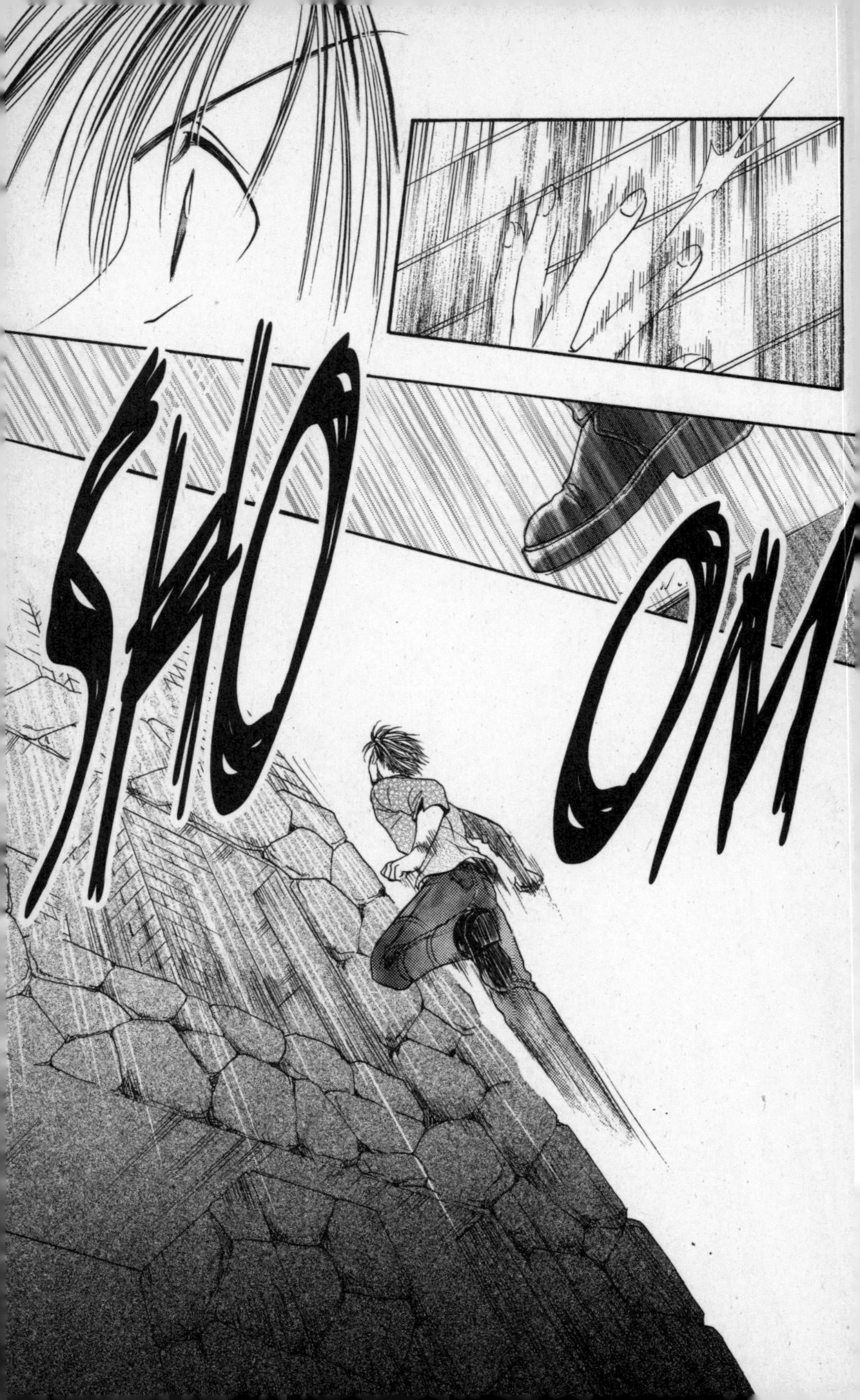
SHOOM

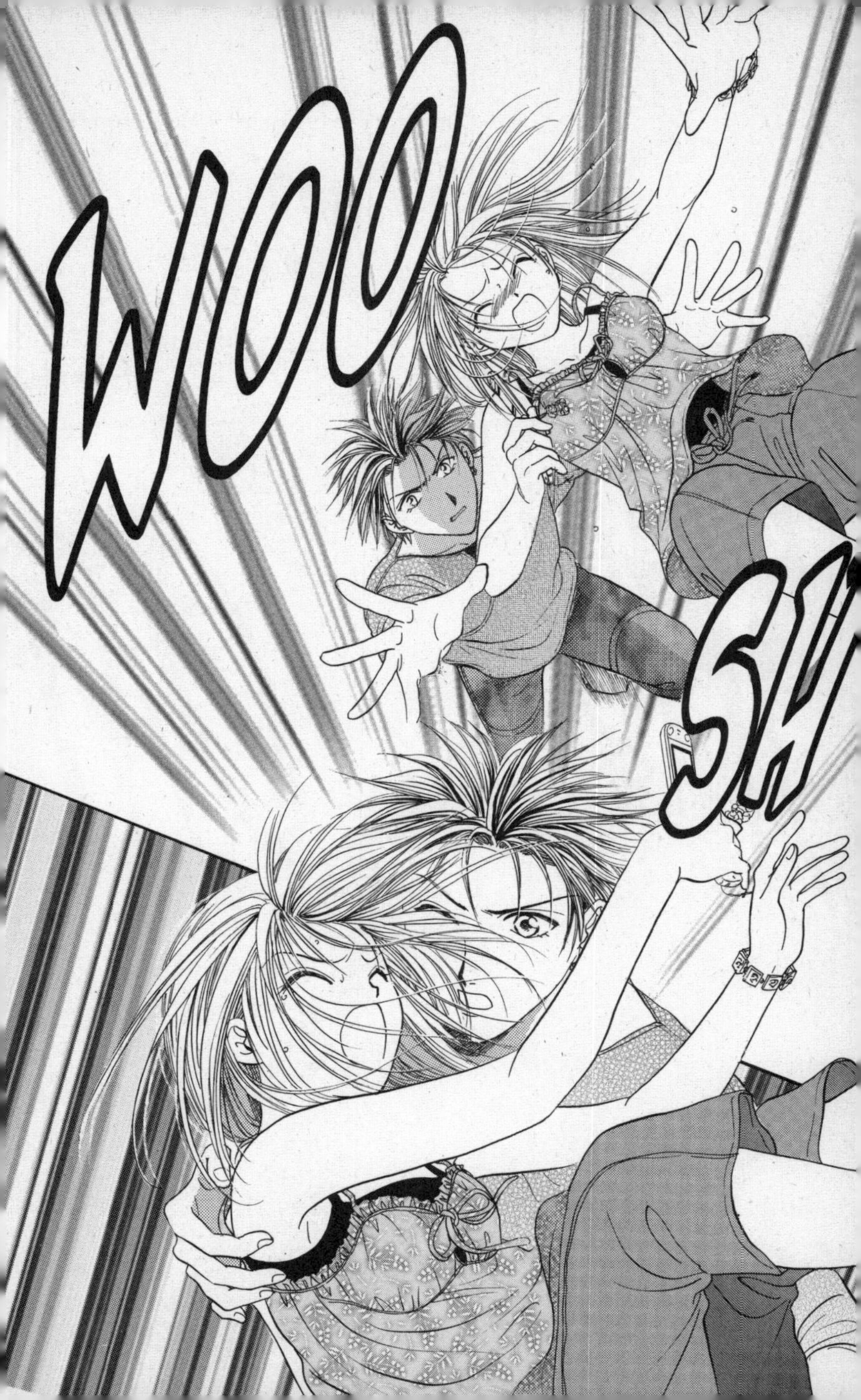
WOOSH

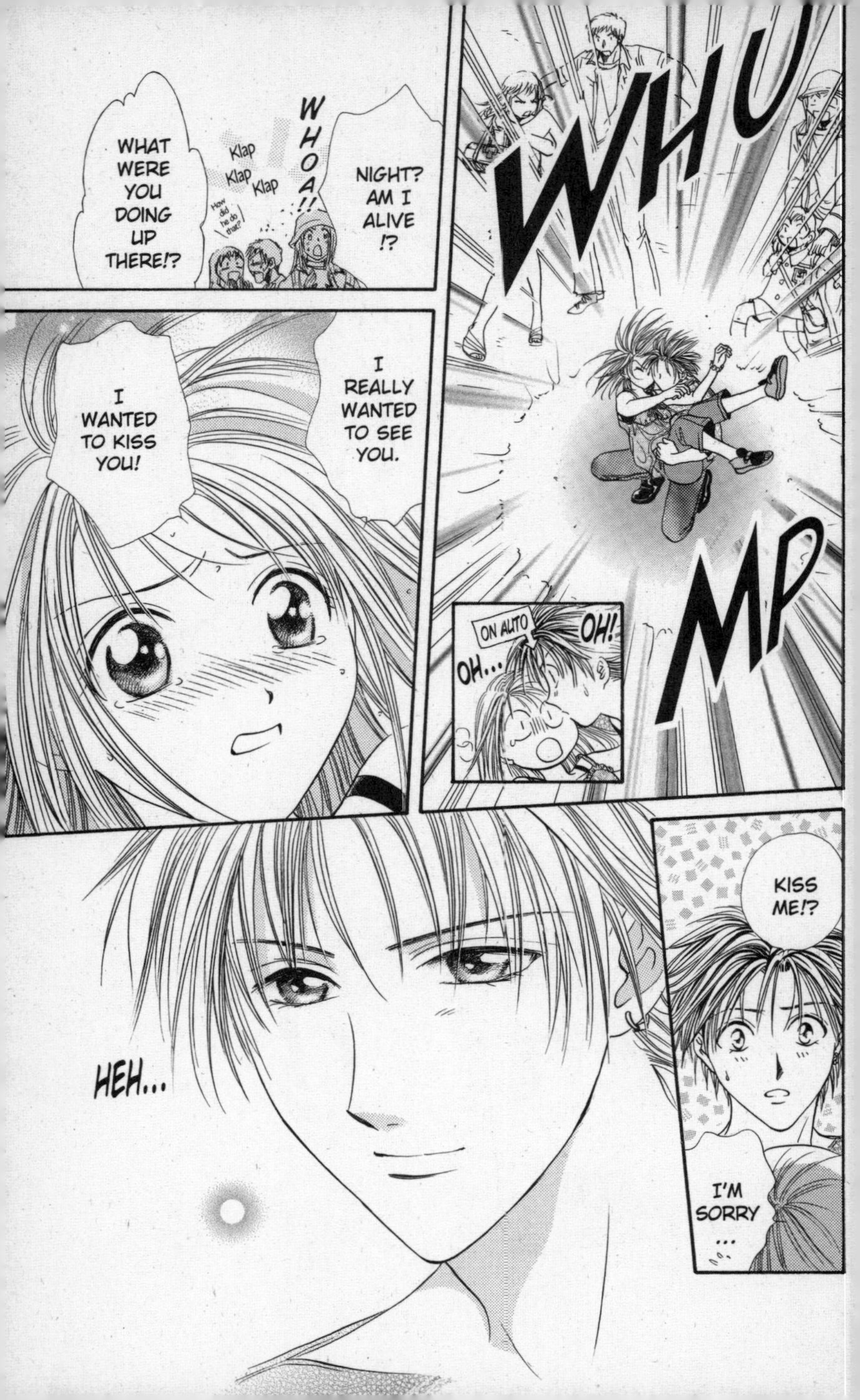
WHUMP
OH!
ON AUTO
OH...
NIGHT? AM I ALIVE!?
WHOA!!
Klap Klap Klap
How did he do that?
WHAT WERE YOU DOING UP THERE!?
I REALLY WANTED TO SEE YOU.
I WANTED TO KISS YOU!
KISS ME!?
I'M SORRY...
HEH...

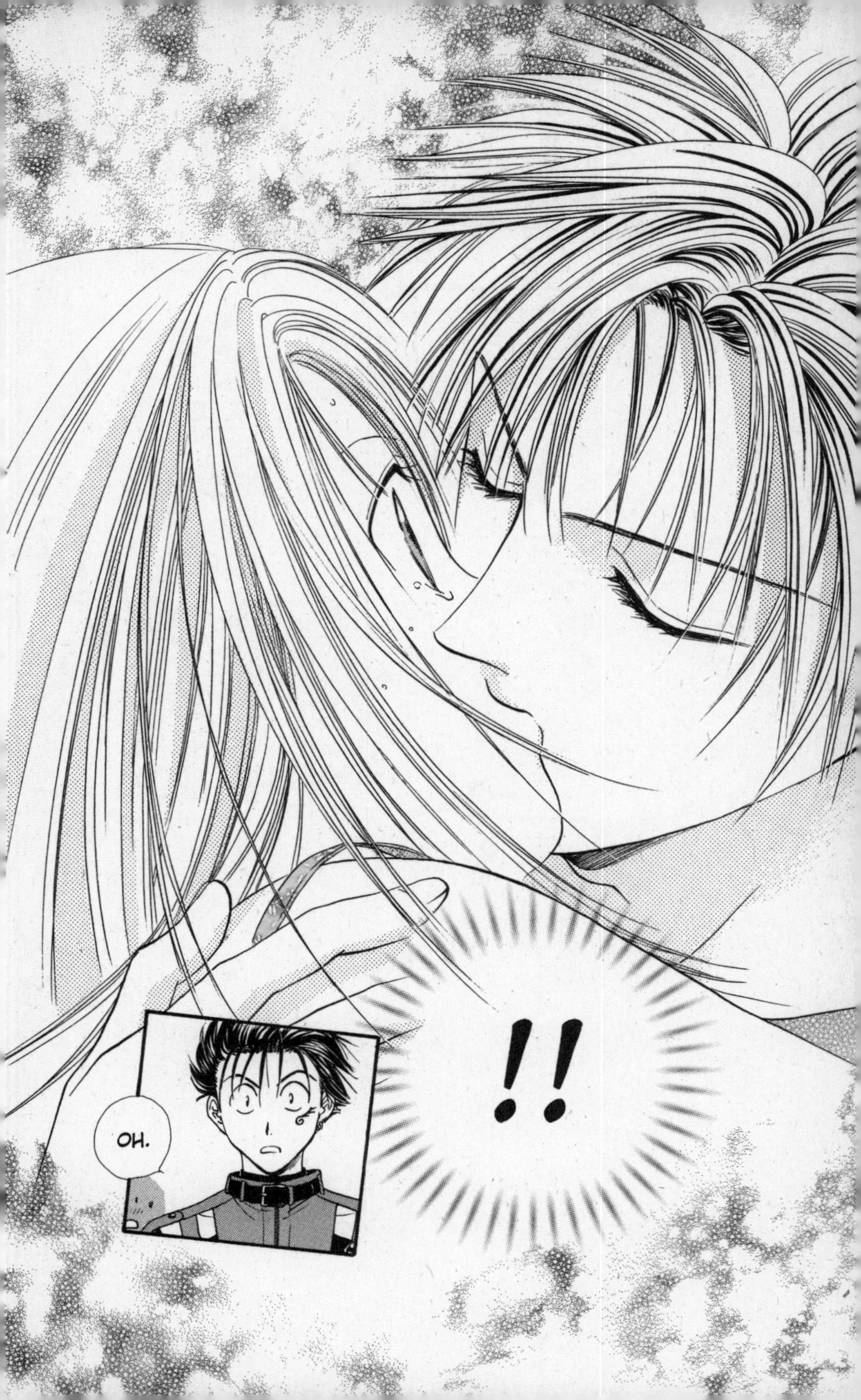
!!
OH.

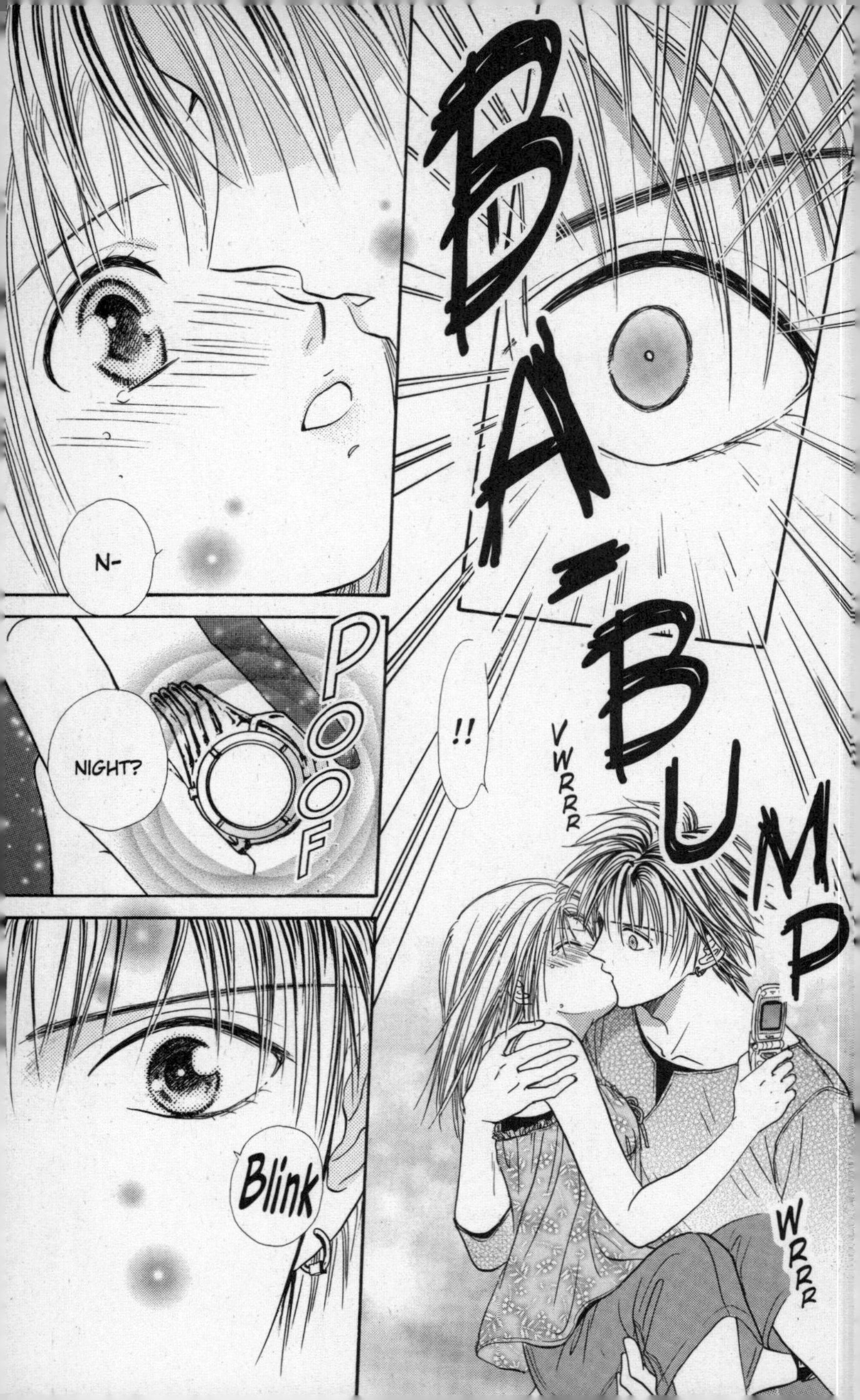
BA-BUMP
!!
VWRRR
WRRR
N-
NIGHT?
POOF
Blink

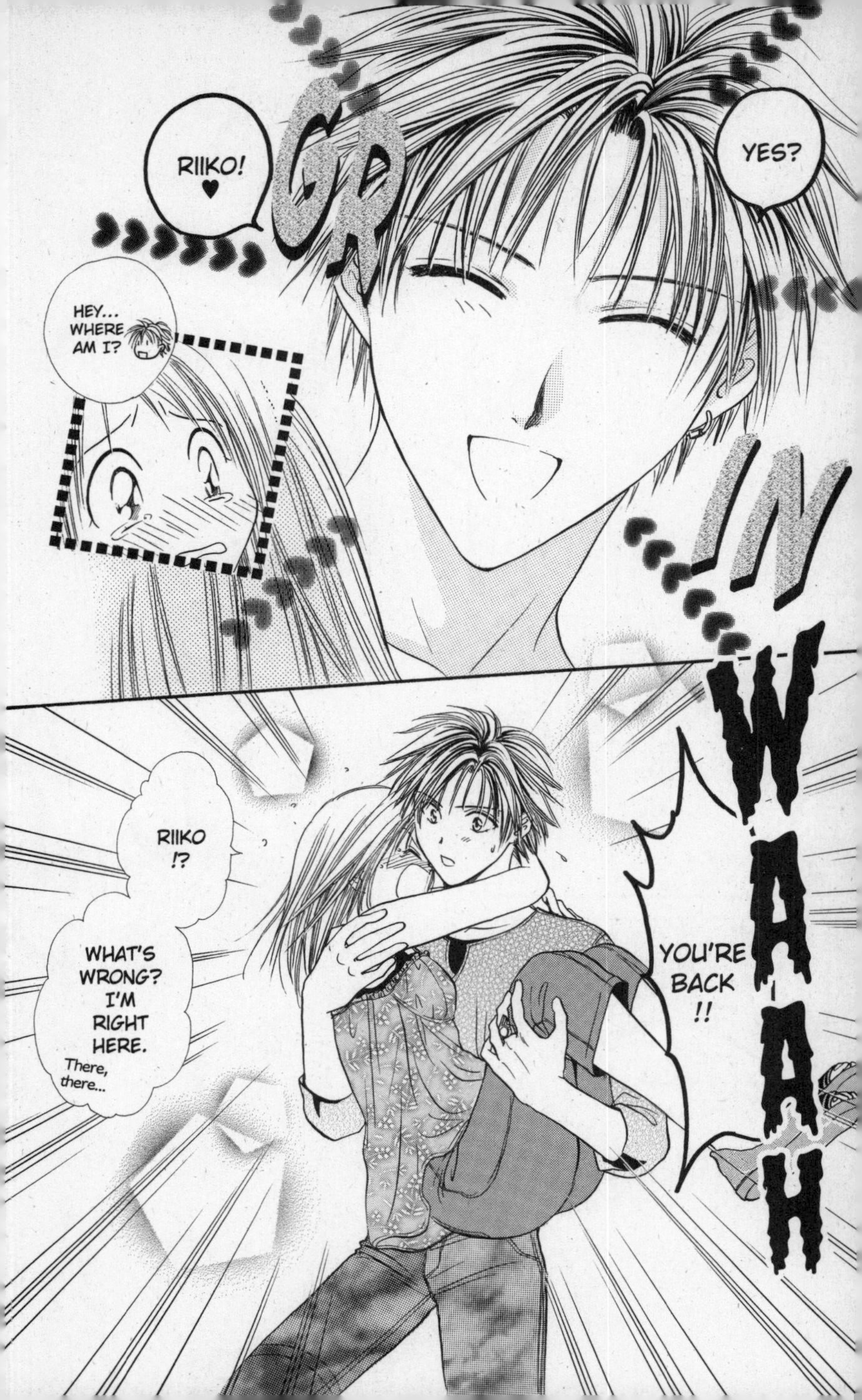
YES?
GR
RIIKO! ♥
HEY... WHERE AM I?
IN
WAAAH
YOU'RE BACK !!
RIIKO !?
WHAT'S WRONG? I'M RIGHT HERE.
There, there...

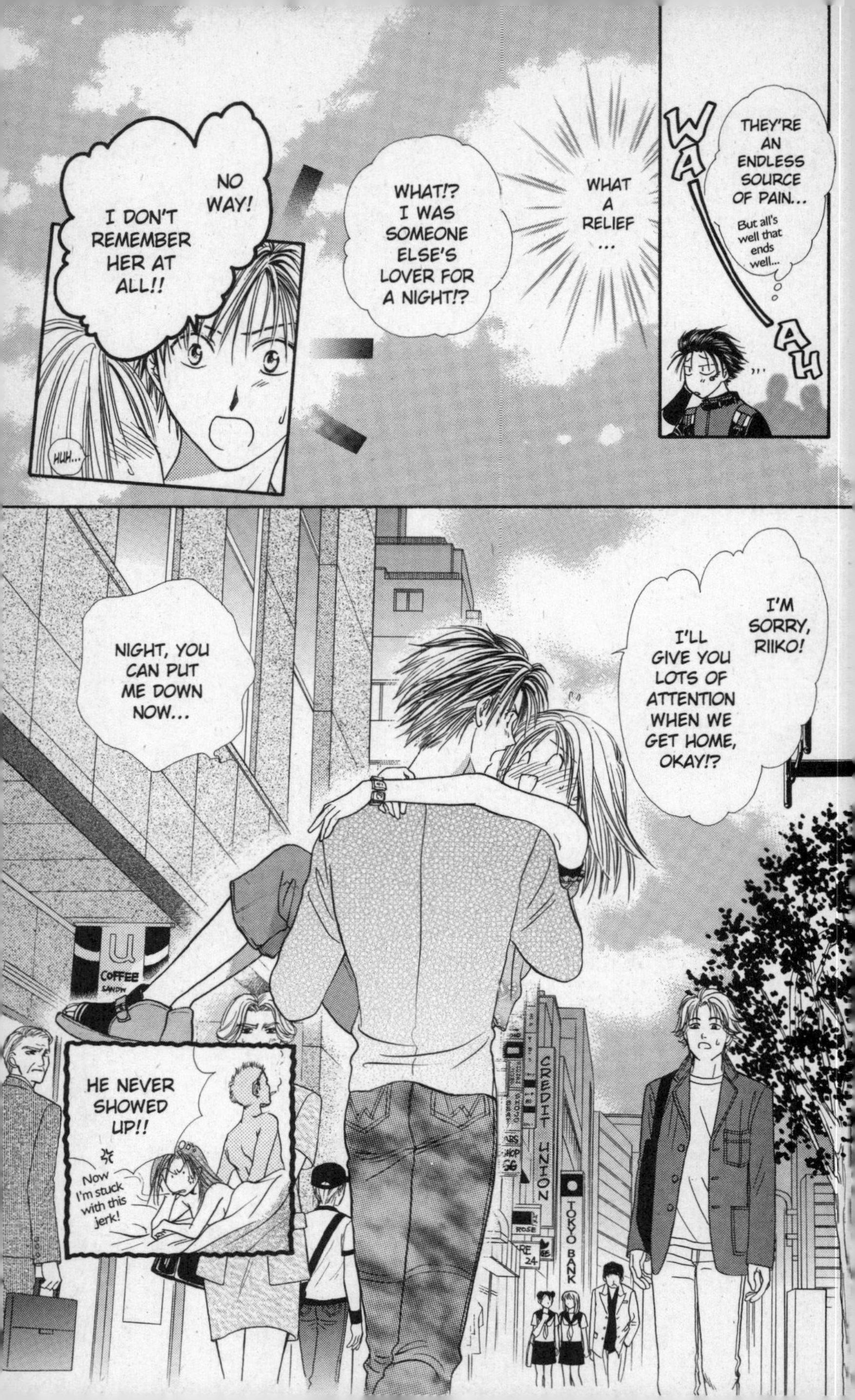
WA-AH
THEY'RE AN ENDLESS SOURCE OF PAIN...
But all's well that ends well...
WHAT A RELIEF...
WHAT!? I WAS SOMEONE ELSE'S LOVER FOR A NIGHT!?
NO WAY!
I DON'T REMEMBER HER AT ALL!!
HUH...
I'M SORRY, RIIKO!
I'LL GIVE YOU LOTS OF ATTENTION WHEN WE GET HOME, OKAY!?
NIGHT, YOU CAN PUT ME DOWN NOW...
CREDIT UNION
TOKYO BANK
COFFEE
HE NEVER SHOWED UP!!
Now I'm stuck with this jerk!

Absolute Boyfriend

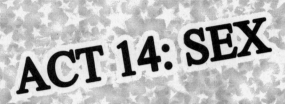

ACT 14: SEX

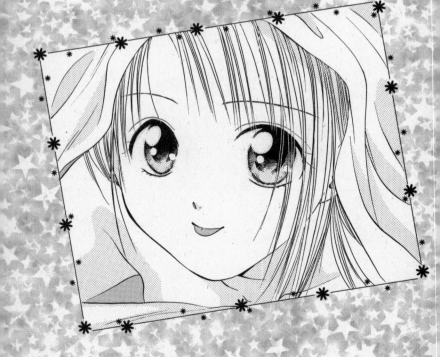

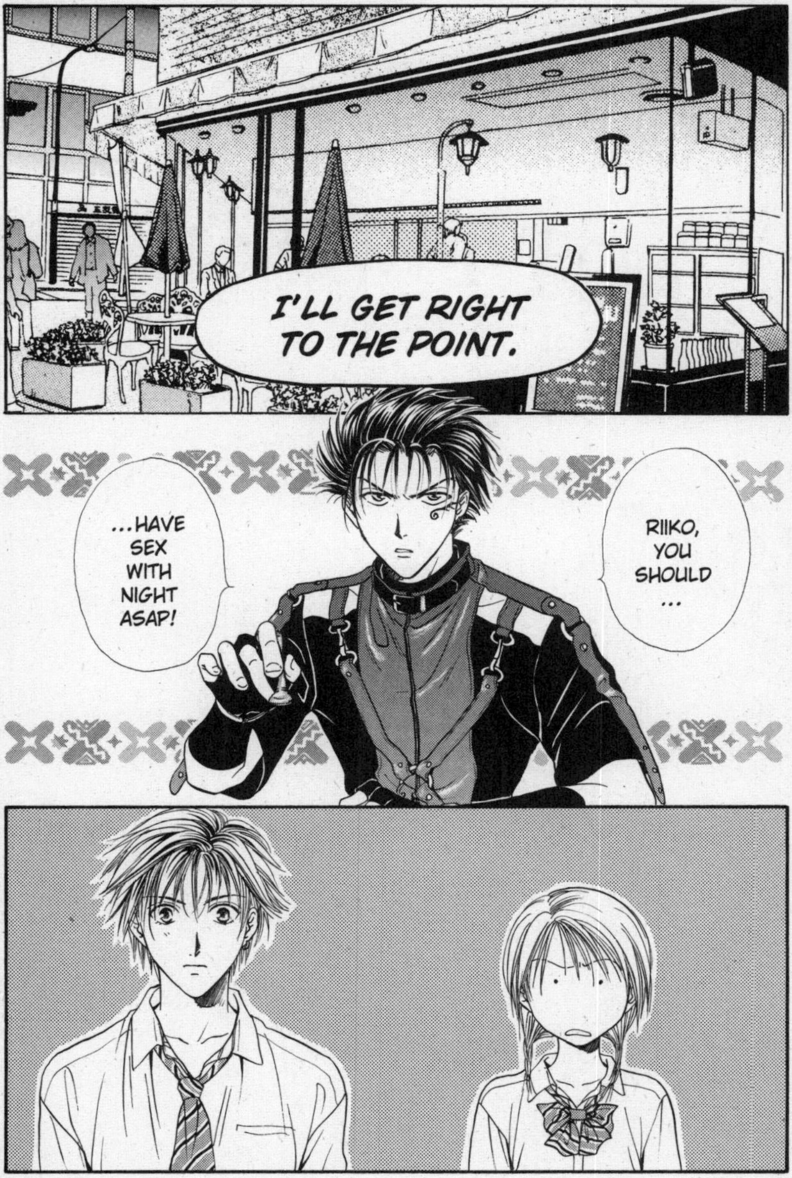
I'LL GET RIGHT TO THE POINT.
RIIKO, YOU SHOULD ...
...HAVE SEX WITH NIGHT ASAP!

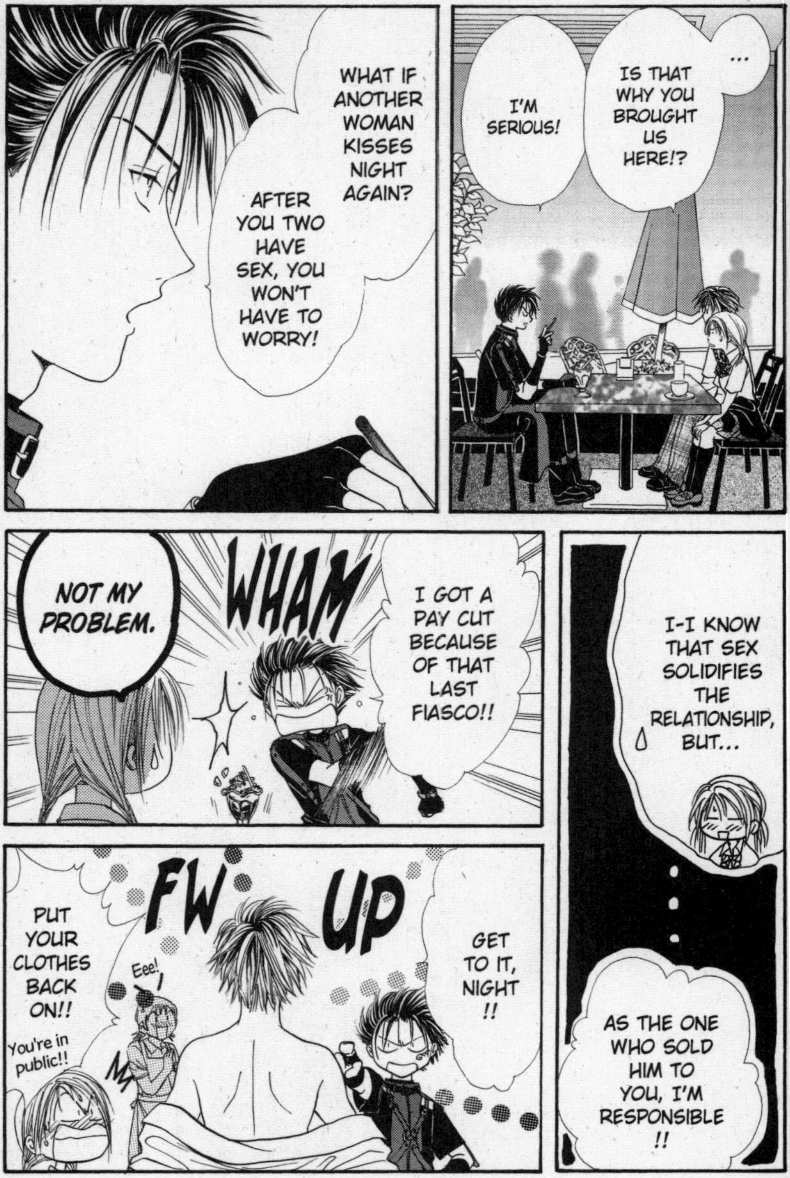
...
IS THAT WHY YOU BROUGHT US HERE!?
I'M SERIOUS!
WHAT IF ANOTHER WOMAN KISSES NIGHT AGAIN?
AFTER YOU TWO HAVE SEX, YOU WON'T HAVE TO WORRY!
I-I KNOW THAT SEX SOLIDIFIES THE RELATIONSHIP, BUT...
AS THE ONE WHO SOLD HIM TO YOU, I'M RESPONSIBLE!!
I GOT A PAY CUT BECAUSE OF THAT LAST FIASCO!!
WHAM
NOT MY PROBLEM.
GET TO IT, NIGHT!!
FW UP
PUT YOUR CLOTHES BACK ON!!
Eee!
You're in public!!

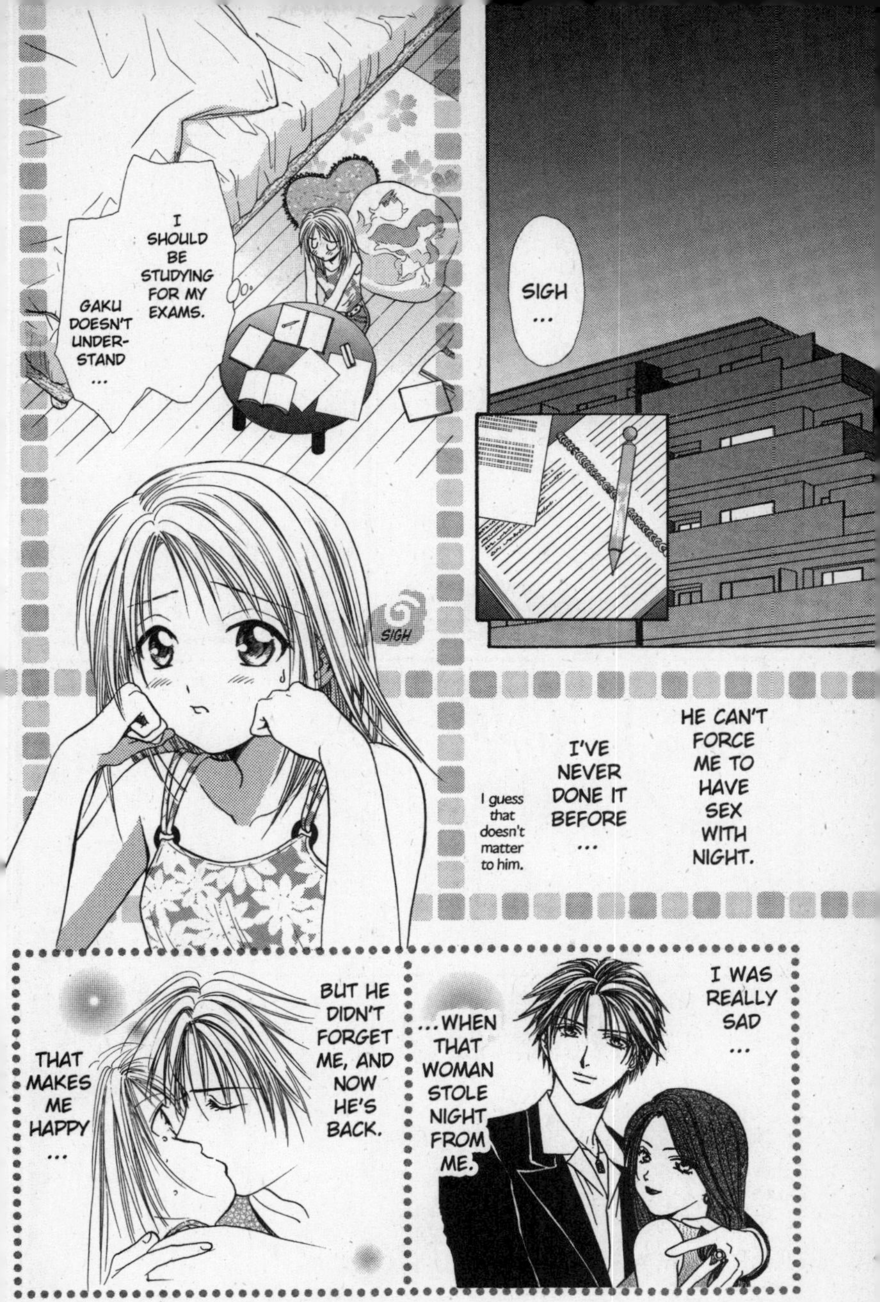
SIGH
...
I SHOULD BE STUDYING FOR MY EXAMS.
GAKU DOESN'T UNDER-STAND
...
HE CAN'T FORCE ME TO HAVE SEX WITH NIGHT.
I'VE NEVER DONE IT BEFORE
...
I guess that doesn't matter to him.
SIGH
I WAS REALLY SAD
...
...WHEN THAT WOMAN STOLE NIGHT FROM ME.
BUT HE DIDN'T FORGET ME, AND NOW HE'S BACK.
THAT MAKES ME HAPPY
...

SO, AM I IN LOVE...
...WITH NIGHT?
KNOCK KNOCK
RIIKO?
GASP
YES !?
HOW'S THE STUDYING GOING? MAKING PROGRESS?
He doesn't need to study.
UM... NOT MUCH... (I WASN'T EVEN THINKING ABOUT STUDYING!)
Heh heh...

I went to an autograph session in Taiwan on January 28, and the people there were as passionate as always!! It was first-come, first-serve, so some people actually started lining up on the night of the 25th...in the rain!! Wow!! One of them sent me a detailed report about the experience. Can you believe that!? Five girls, spending the night in the cold!! I was moved to tears. Thank you. The first girl came dressed as Riiko (in the outfit from the title page in the first volume) and was carrying a stuffed rabbit (Nyozeka from *Alice 19th*)!! There were two others dressed as Frey, also from *Alice 19th* (smile). One of them gave me a sash like the one Alice wore on the cover of volume 1, and it was so well made. The Frey costume was amazing. I wish I could show you. And the girl in it was so excited to meet me that she started crying, and that made me tear up. It made me feel so good! A lot of people gave me presents--I've been using all the necklaces and cell phone straps since I got back, and I have all the mugs and things on display. Oh yeah, there were a lot of male readers too. I was surprised at the part of the line that was all guys (smile). One of them even came to see me off at the airport. The people at Chang Hong Publishing, who publish *Absolute Boyfriend* in Taiwan, were very nice to me. (Better than I deserve.) Thank you so much. (Actually, will this part get translated?) Anyway, Taiwanese food is so good!! Too good!! And I only went to Taipei--I can't even imagine how good it must be in Tainan!! I'd love to go there again!

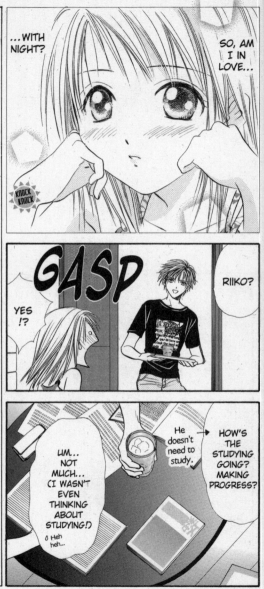

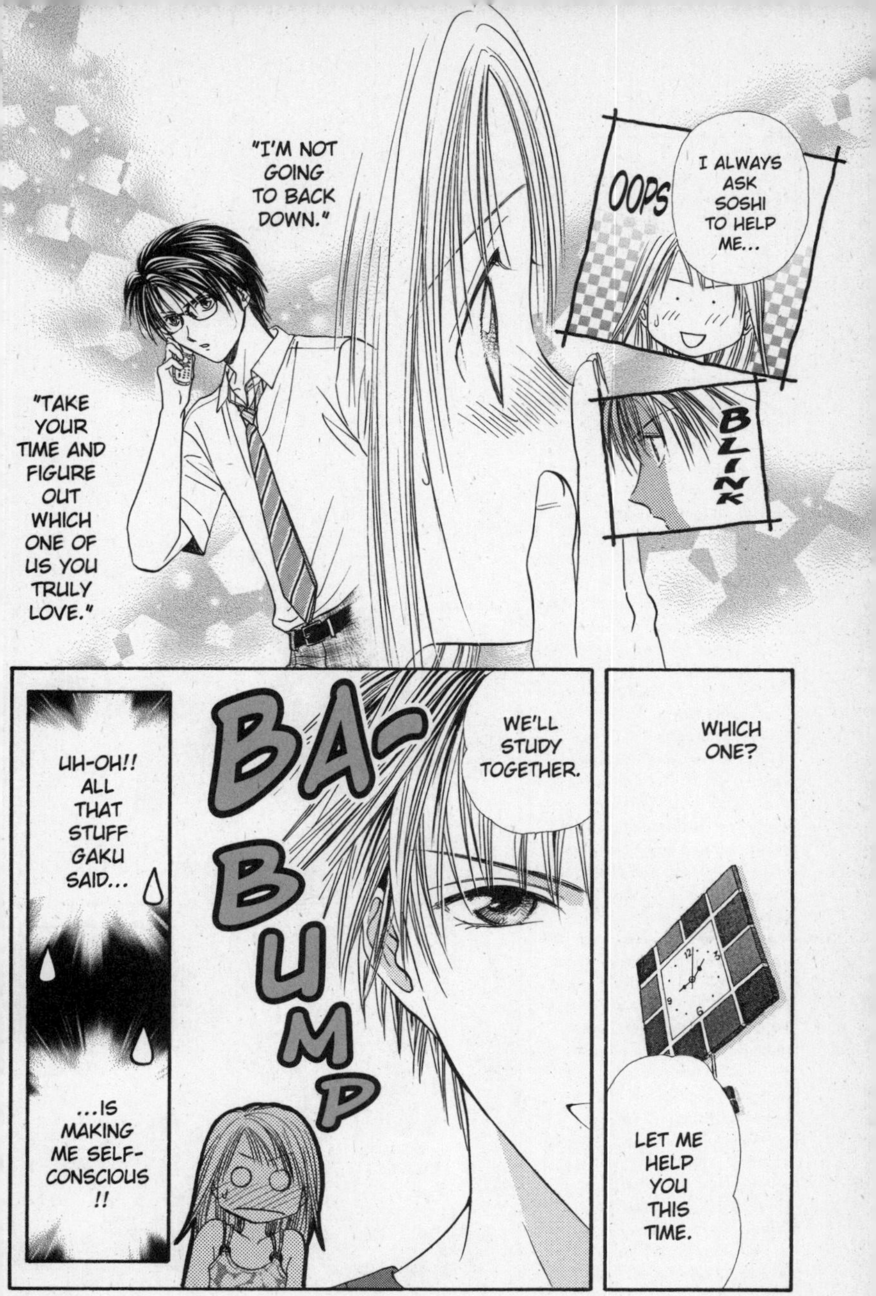
I ALWAYS ASK SOSHI TO HELP ME...
OOPS
BLINK
"I'M NOT GOING TO BACK DOWN."
"TAKE YOUR TIME AND FIGURE OUT WHICH ONE OF US YOU TRULY LOVE."
WHICH ONE?
LET ME HELP YOU THIS TIME.
WE'LL STUDY TOGETHER.
BA-BUMP
UH-OH!! ALL THAT STUFF GAKU SAID...
...IS MAKING ME SELF-CONSCIOUS!!

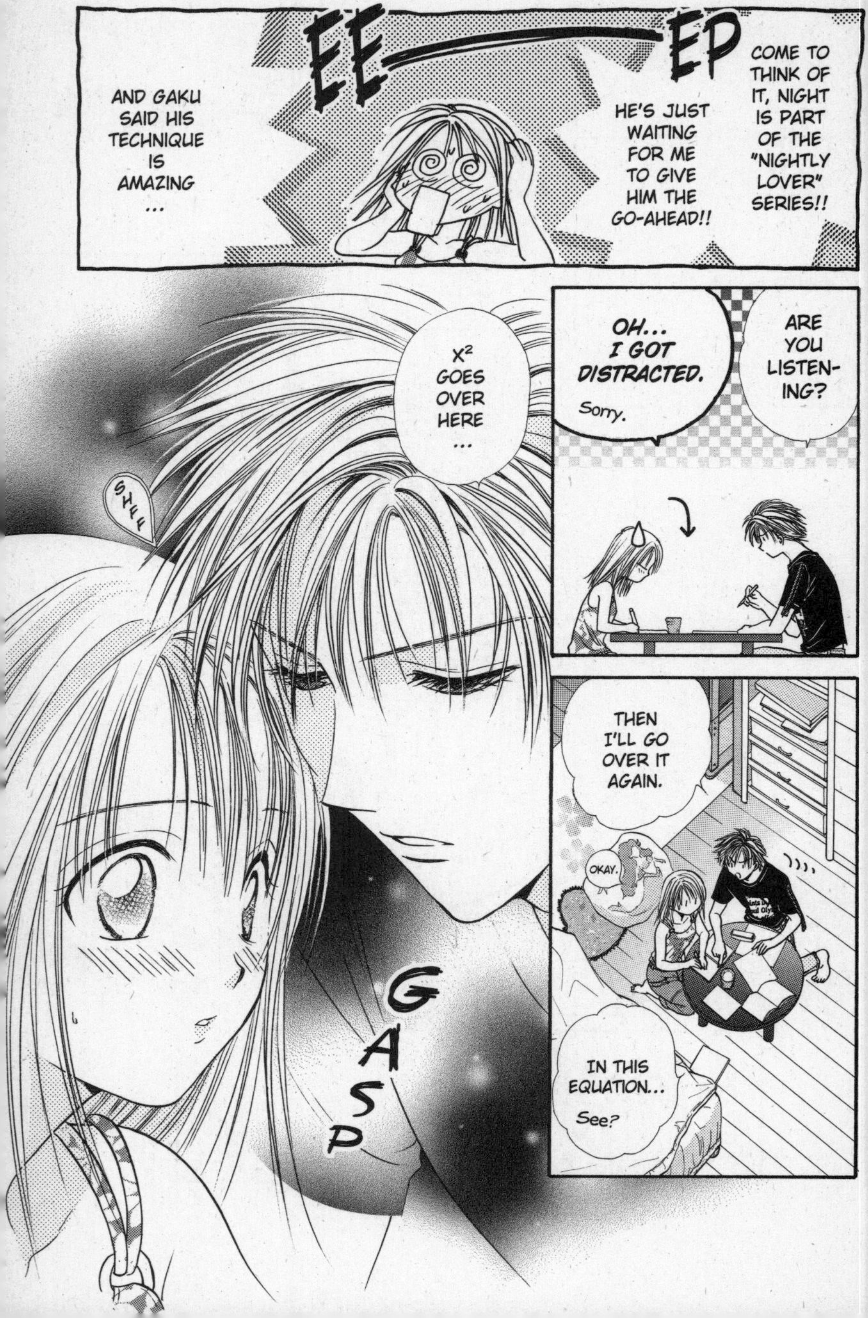

COME TO THINK OF IT, NIGHT IS PART OF THE "NIGHTLY LOVER" SERIES!!
EE——EP
HE'S JUST WAITING FOR ME TO GIVE HIM THE GO-AHEAD!!
AND GAKU SAID HIS TECHNIQUE IS AMAZING ...
ARE YOU LISTEN-ING?
OH... I GOT DISTRACTED.
Sorry.
THEN I'LL GO OVER IT AGAIN.
OKAY.
IN THIS EQUATION...
See?
X² GOES OVER HERE ...
SHFF
GASP

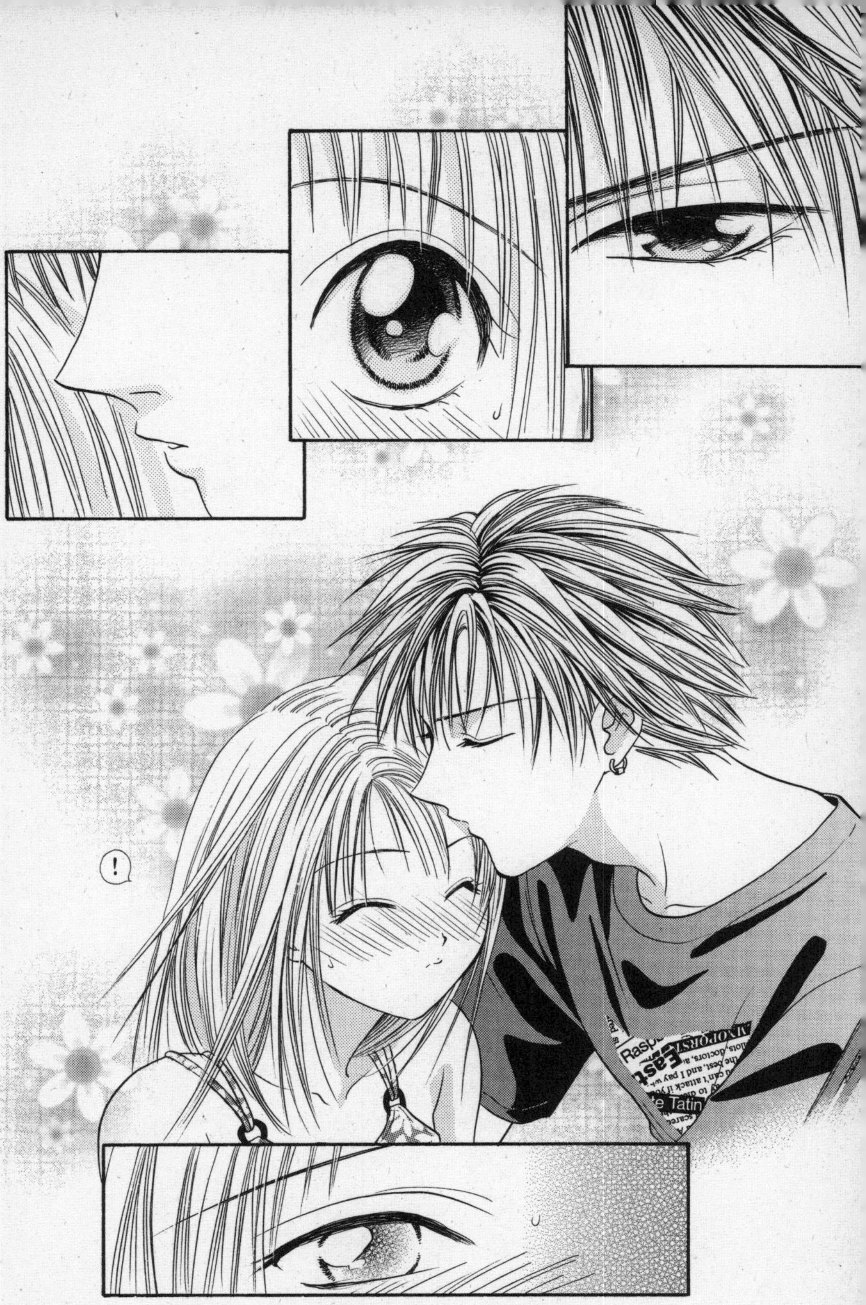
!

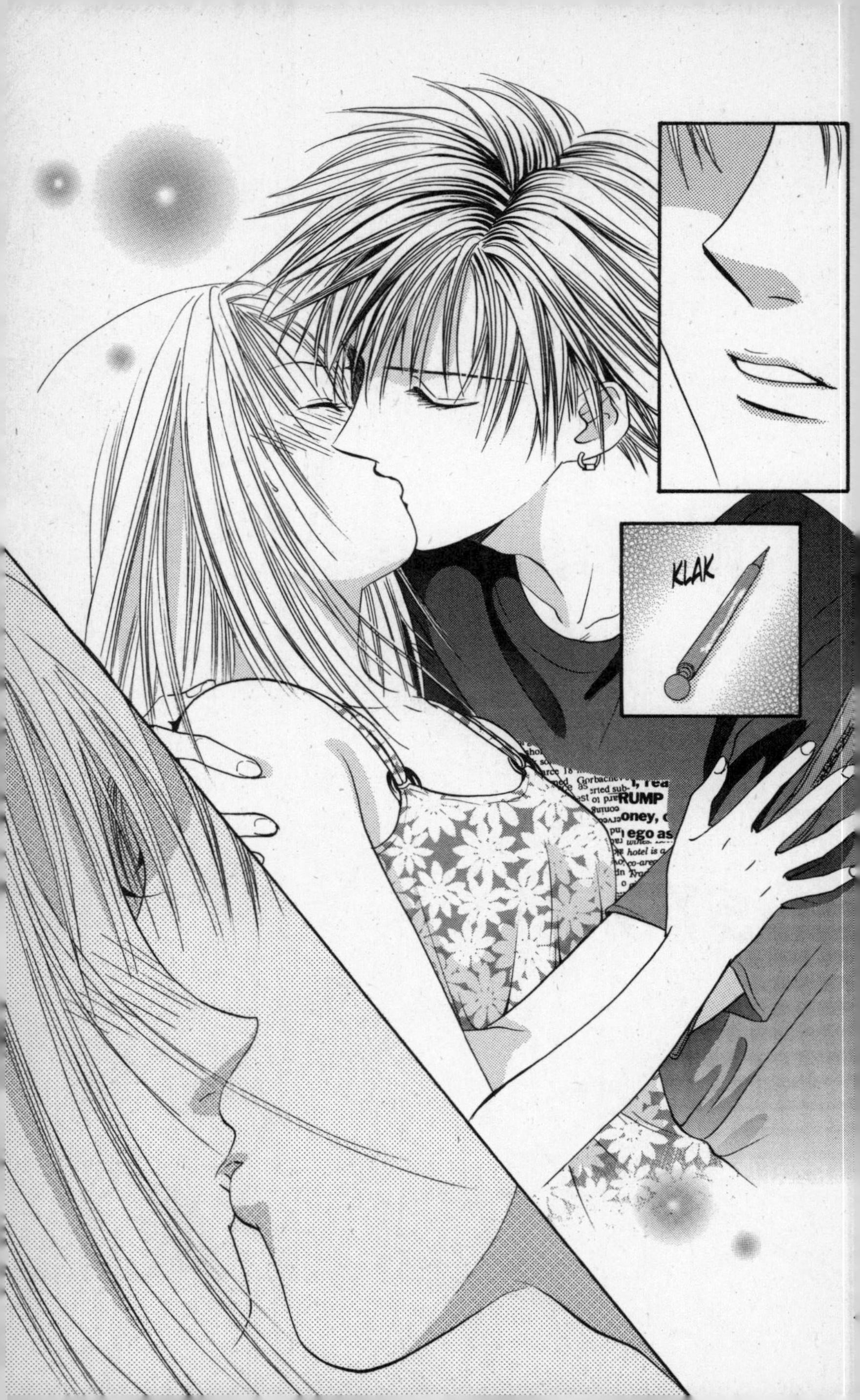
KLAK

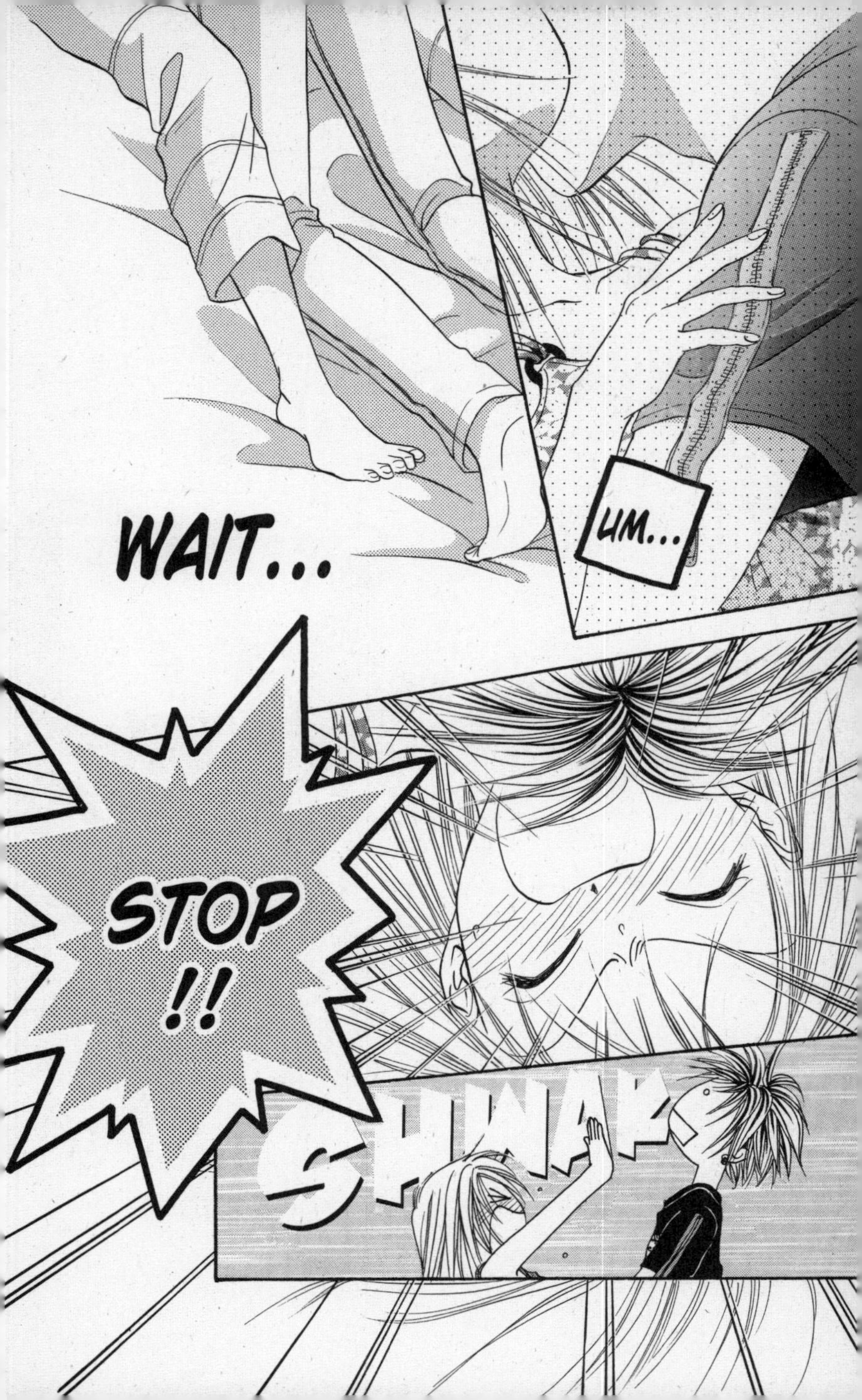
UM...
WAIT...
STOP!!
SHWAK

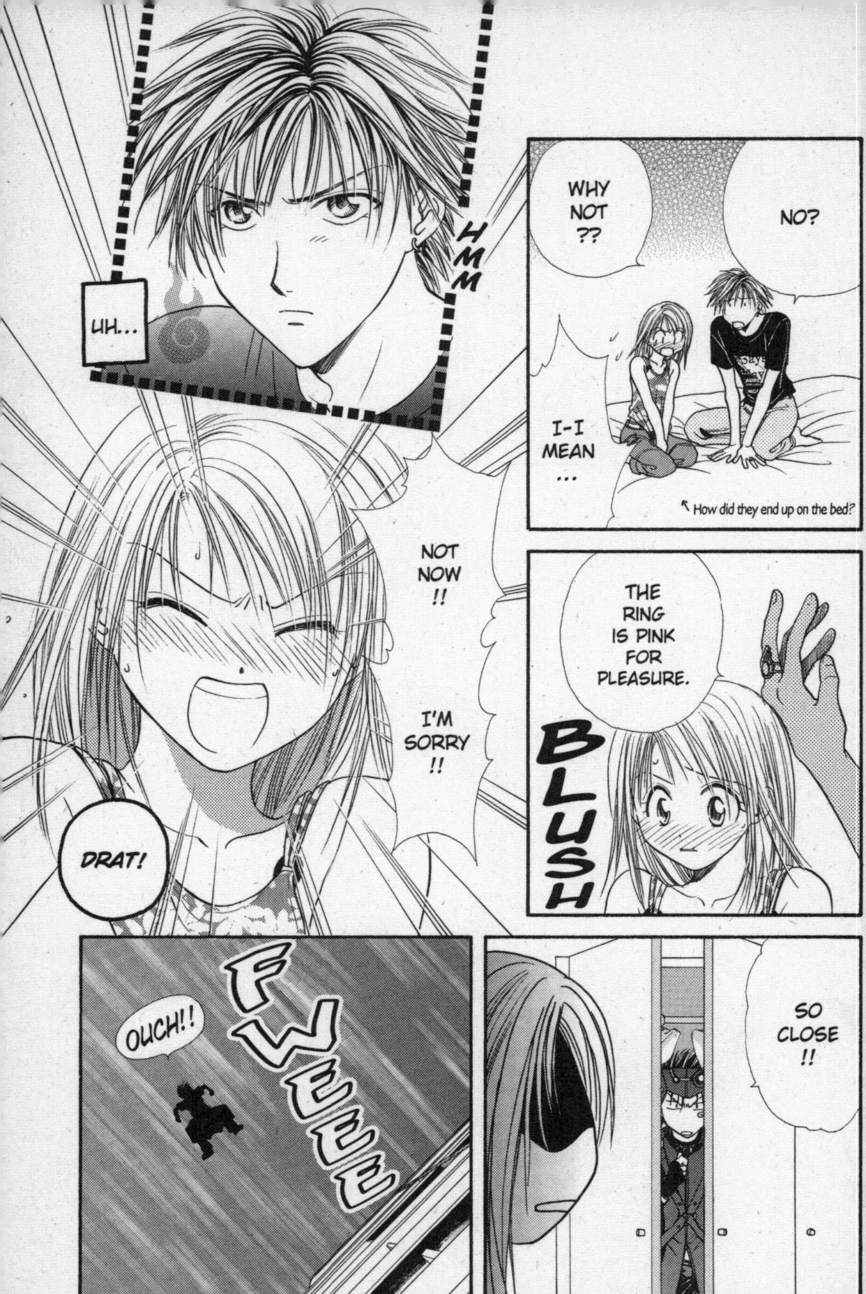
NO?
WHY NOT ??
I-I MEAN ...
↖ How did they end up on the bed?
HMMM
UH...
THE RING IS PINK FOR PLEASURE.
BLUSH
NOT NOW !!
I'M SORRY !!
DRAT!
SO CLOSE !!
FWEEE
OUCH!!

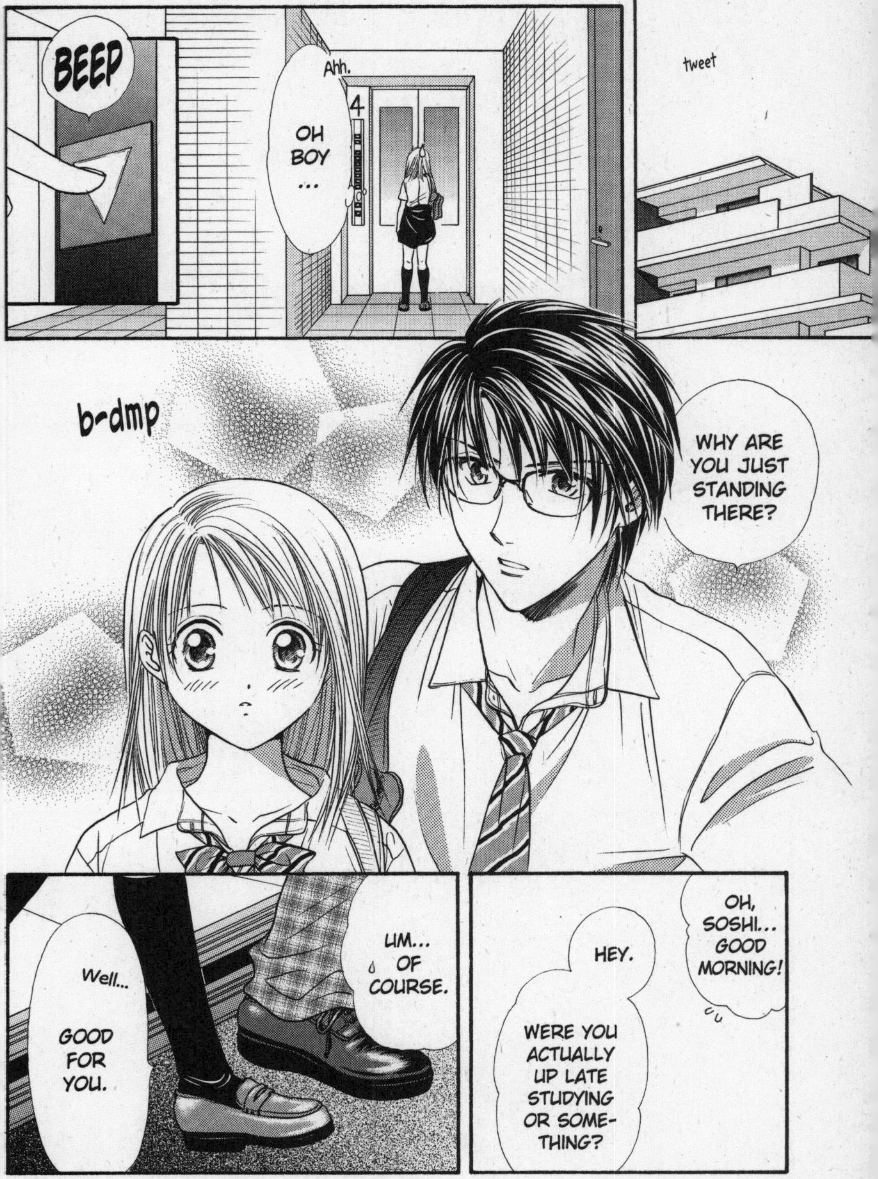
tweet
Ahh.
OH BOY ...
BEEP
WHY ARE YOU JUST STANDING THERE?
b-dmp
OH, SOSHI... GOOD MORNING!
HEY.
WERE YOU ACTUALLY UP LATE STUDYING OR SOME-THING?
UM... OF COURSE.
Well... GOOD FOR YOU.

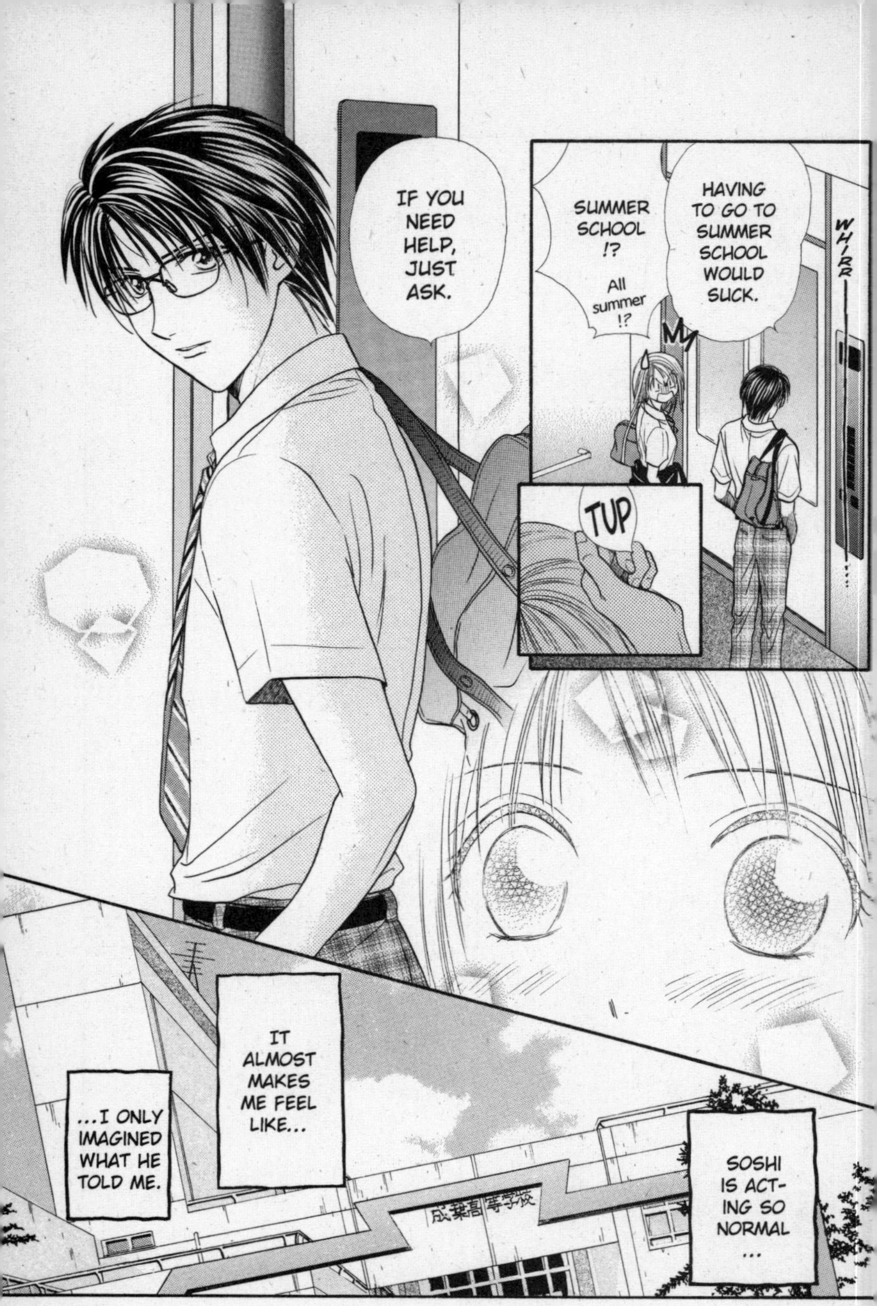
WHIRR
HAVING TO GO TO SUMMER SCHOOL WOULD SUCK.
SUMMER SCHOOL !? All summer !?
TUP
IF YOU NEED HELP, JUST ASK.
SOSHI IS ACTING SO NORMAL ...
IT ALMOST MAKES ME FEEL LIKE...
...I ONLY IMAGINED WHAT HE TOLD ME.

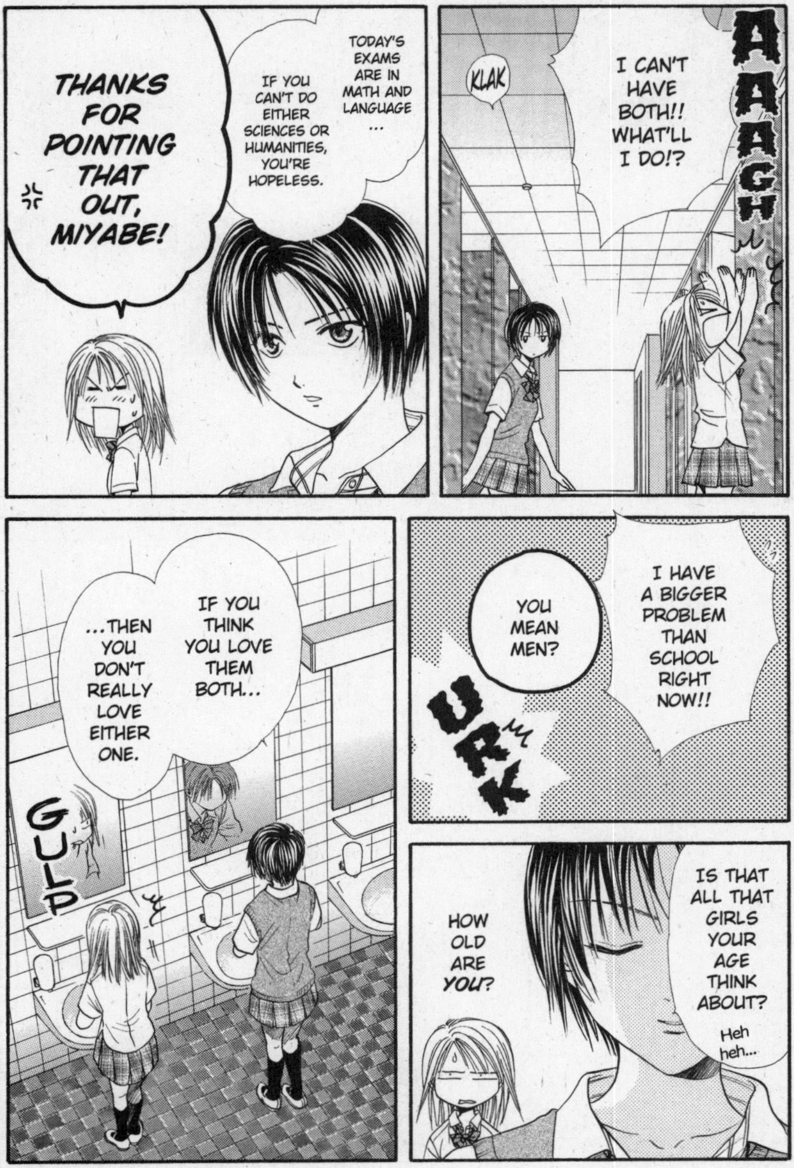
AAAGH
I CAN'T HAVE BOTH!! WHAT'LL I DO!?
KLAK
TODAY'S EXAMS ARE IN MATH AND LANGUAGE ...
IF YOU CAN'T DO EITHER SCIENCES OR HUMANITIES, YOU'RE HOPELESS.
THANKS FOR POINTING THAT OUT, MIYABE!
I HAVE A BIGGER PROBLEM THAN SCHOOL RIGHT NOW!!
YOU MEAN MEN?
URK
IF YOU THINK YOU LOVE THEM BOTH...
...THEN YOU DON'T REALLY LOVE EITHER ONE.
GULP
IS THAT ALL THAT GIRLS YOUR AGE THINK ABOUT?
Heh heh...
HOW OLD ARE YOU?

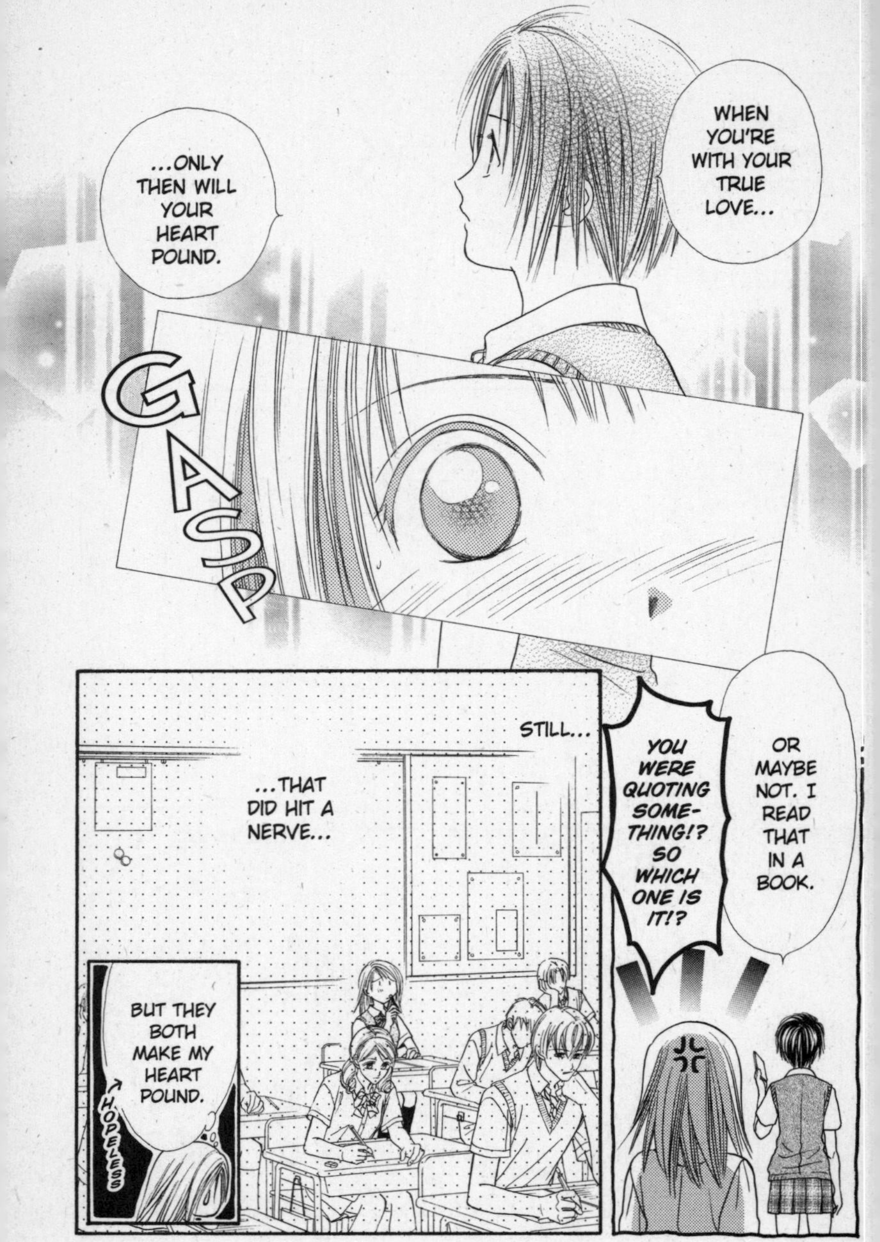
WHEN YOU'RE WITH YOUR TRUE LOVE...
...ONLY THEN WILL YOUR HEART POUND.
GASP
OR MAYBE NOT. I READ THAT IN A BOOK.
YOU WERE QUOTING SOMETHING!? SO WHICH ONE IS IT!?
STILL...
...THAT DID HIT A NERVE...
BUT THEY BOTH MAKE MY HEART POUND.
HOPELESS

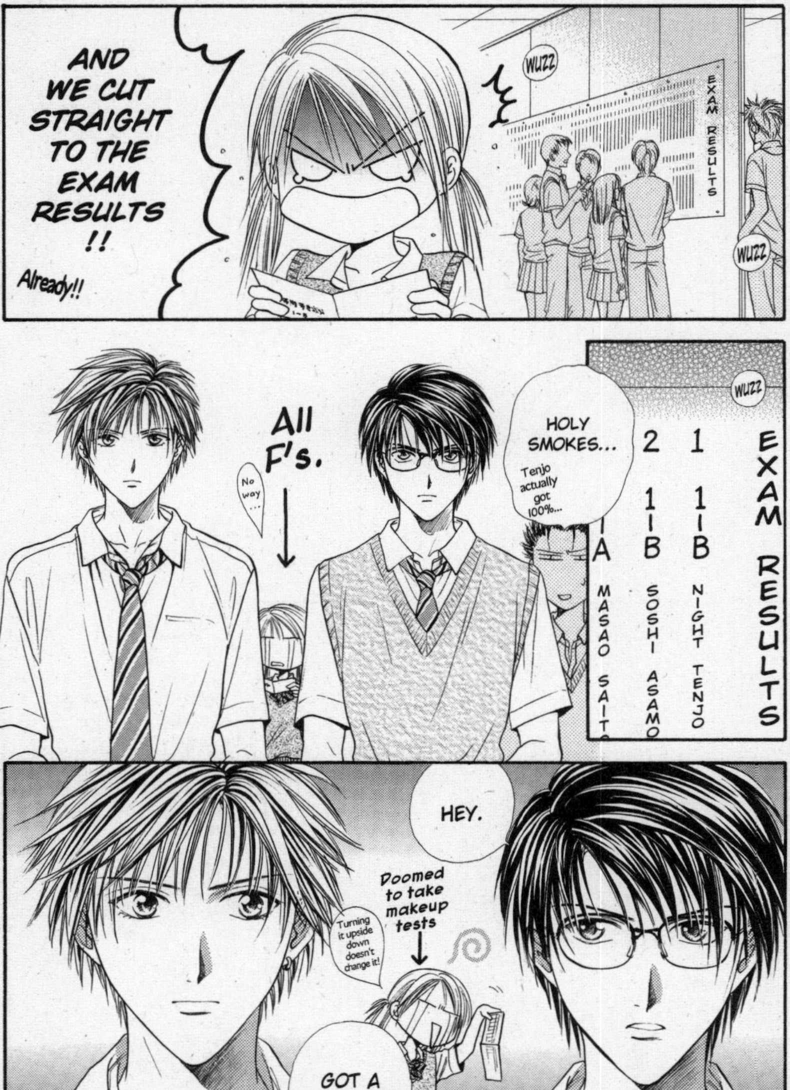
AND WE CUT STRAIGHT TO THE EXAM RESULTS!!
Already!!
WUZZ
EXAM RESULTS
WUZZ
EXAM RESULTS
1 1B NIGHT TENJO
2 1B SOSHI ASAMO
1A MASAO SAIT
WUZZ
HOLY SMOKES...
Tenjo actually got 100%...
All F's.
No way...
HEY.
Doomed to take makeup tests
Turning it upside down doesn't change it!
GOT A MINUTE?

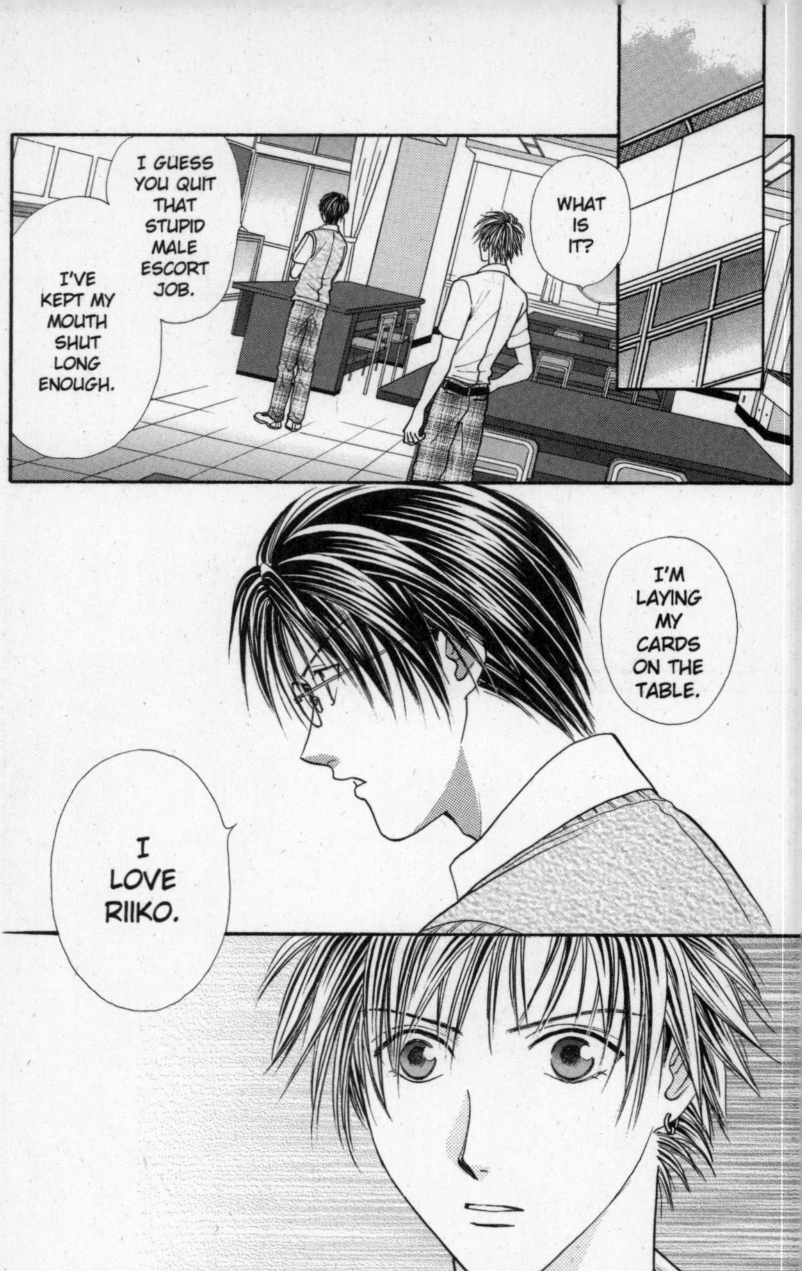
WHAT IS IT?
I GUESS YOU QUIT THAT STUPID MALE ESCORT JOB.
I'VE KEPT MY MOUTH SHUT LONG ENOUGH.
I'M LAYING MY CARDS ON THE TABLE.
I LOVE RIIKO.

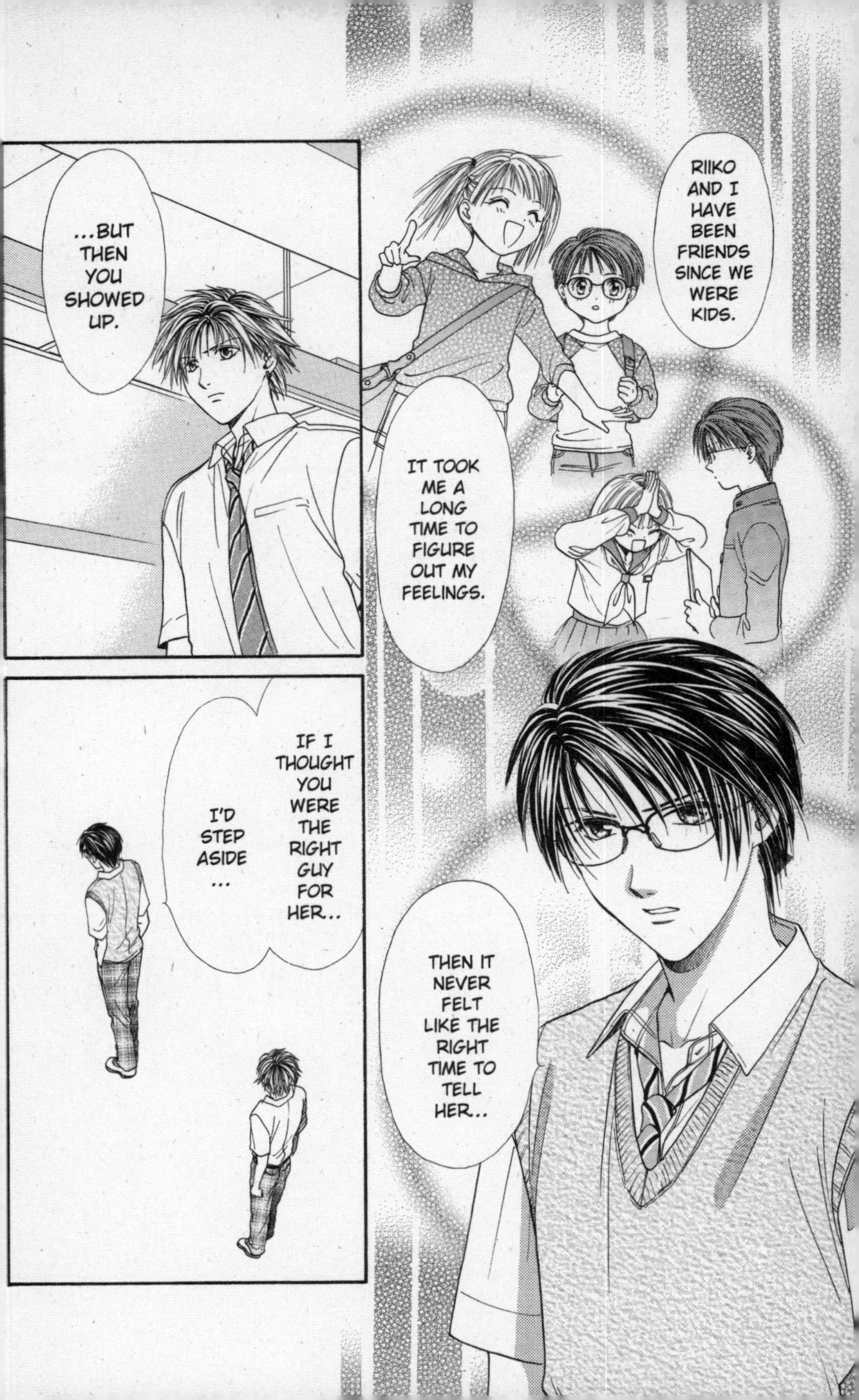
RIIKO AND I HAVE BEEN FRIENDS SINCE WE WERE KIDS.
IT TOOK ME A LONG TIME TO FIGURE OUT MY FEELINGS.
THEN IT NEVER FELT LIKE THE RIGHT TIME TO TELL HER...
...BUT THEN YOU SHOWED UP.
IF I THOUGHT YOU WERE THE RIGHT GUY FOR HER...
I'D STEP ASIDE ...

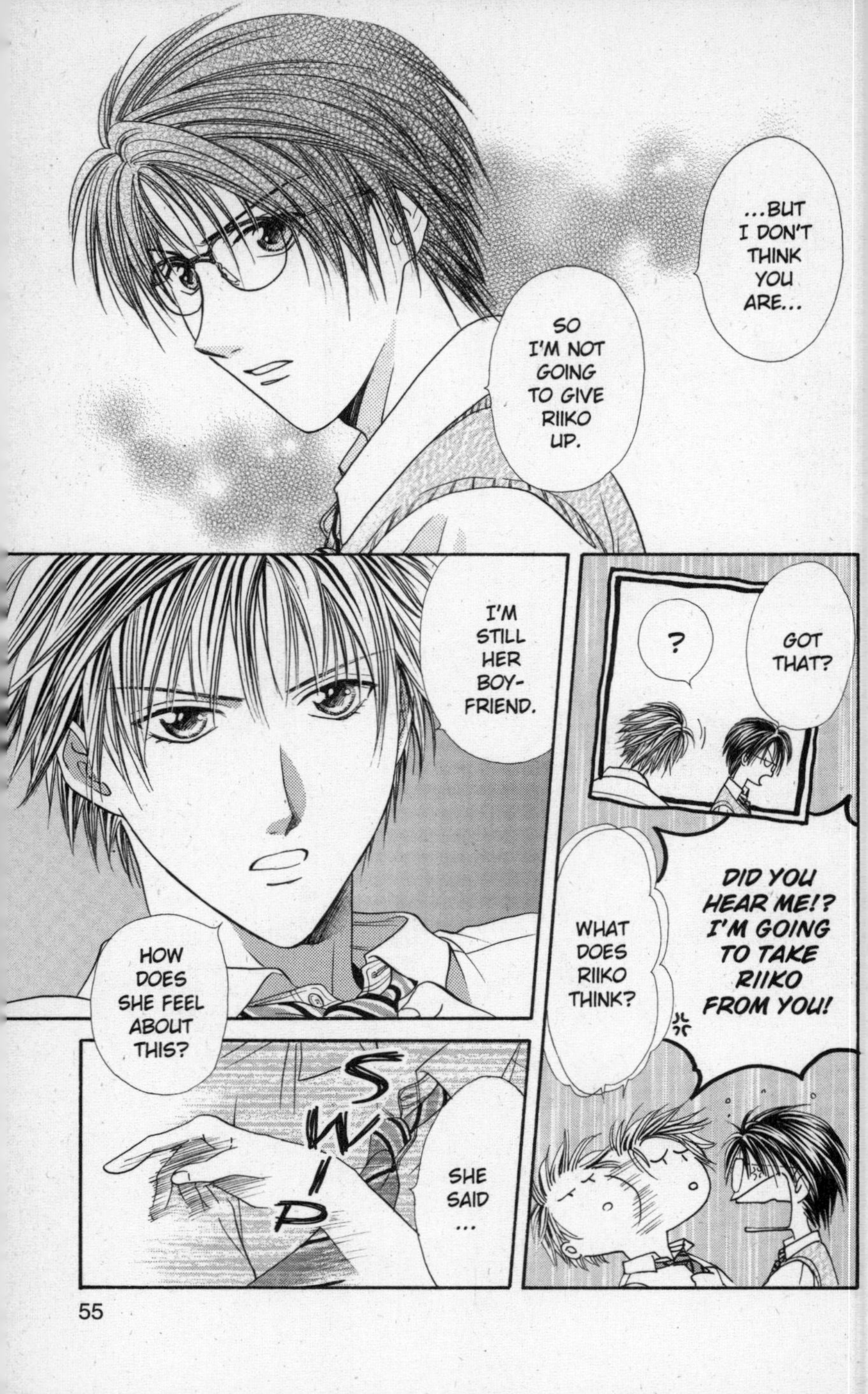
...BUT I DON'T THINK YOU ARE...
SO I'M NOT GOING TO GIVE RIIKO UP.
GOT THAT?
?
DID YOU HEAR ME!? I'M GOING TO TAKE RIIKO FROM YOU!
WHAT DOES RIIKO THINK?
I'M STILL HER BOY-FRIEND.
HOW DOES SHE FEEL ABOUT THIS?
SWIP
SHE SAID ...

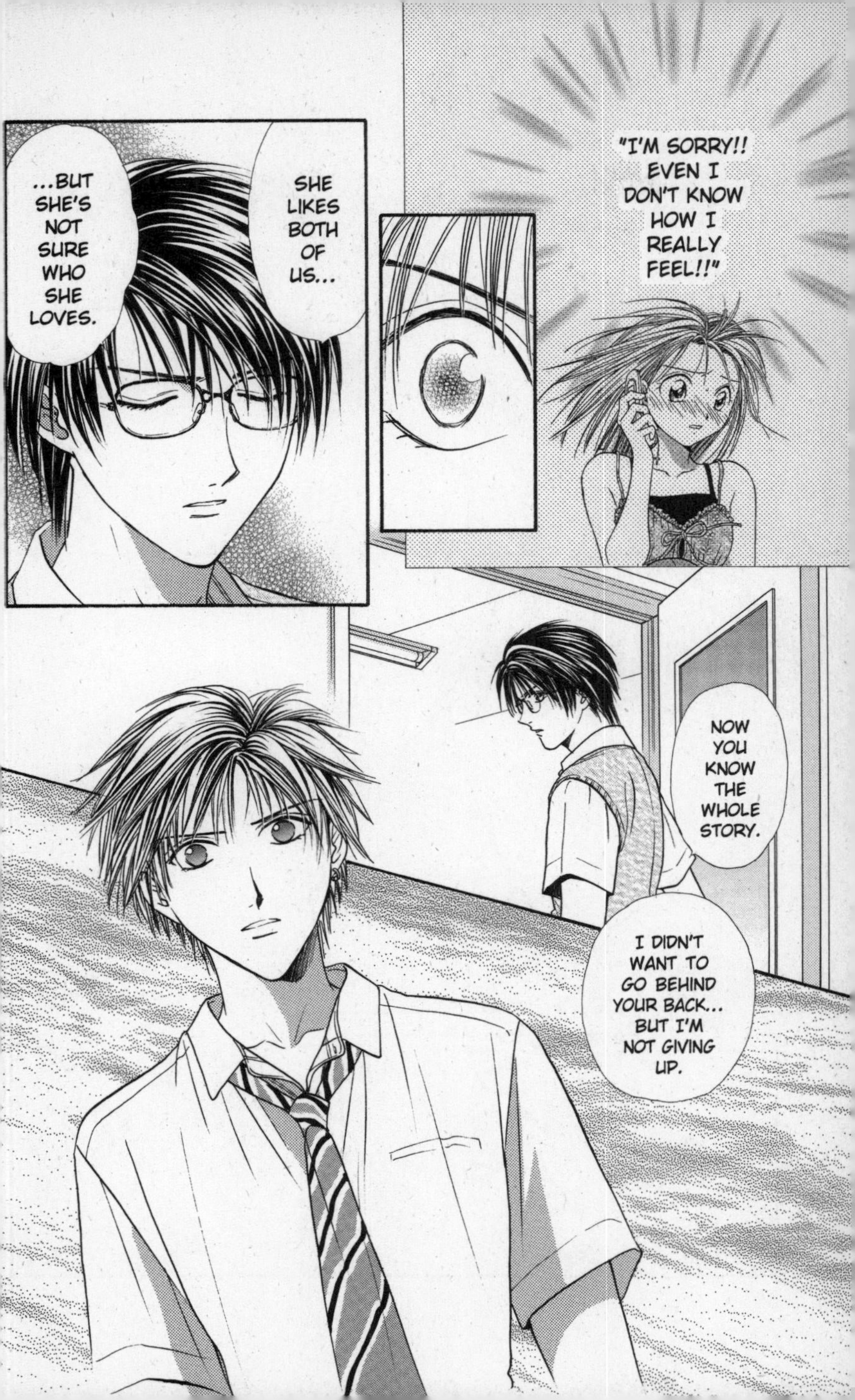
"I'M SORRY!! EVEN I DON'T KNOW HOW I REALLY FEEL!!"
SHE LIKES BOTH OF US...
...BUT SHE'S NOT SURE WHO SHE LOVES.
NOW YOU KNOW THE WHOLE STORY.
I DIDN'T WANT TO GO BEHIND YOUR BACK... BUT I'M NOT GIVING UP.

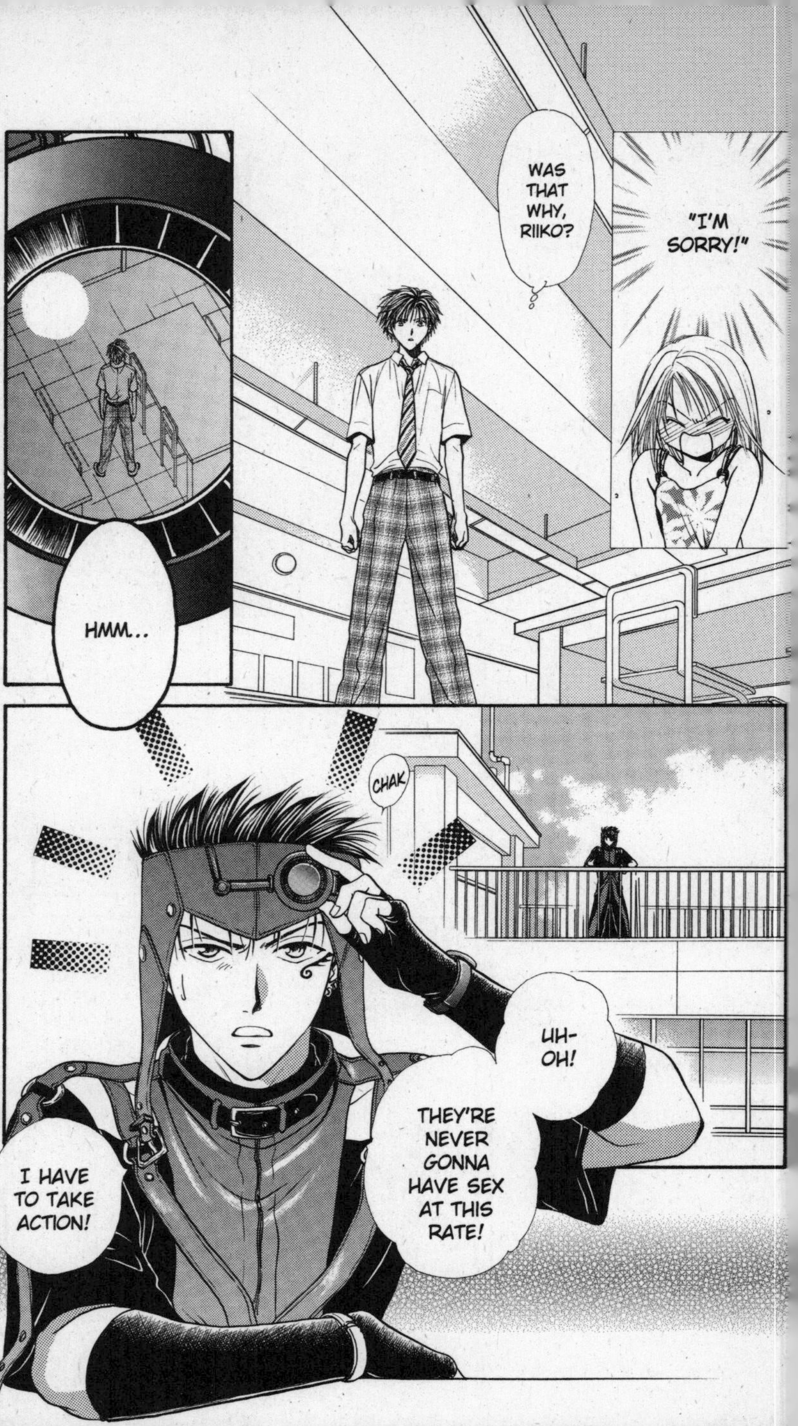
"I'M SORRY!"
WAS THAT WHY, RIIKO?
HMM...
CHAK
UH-OH!
THEY'RE NEVER GONNA HAVE SEX AT THIS RATE!
I HAVE TO TAKE ACTION!

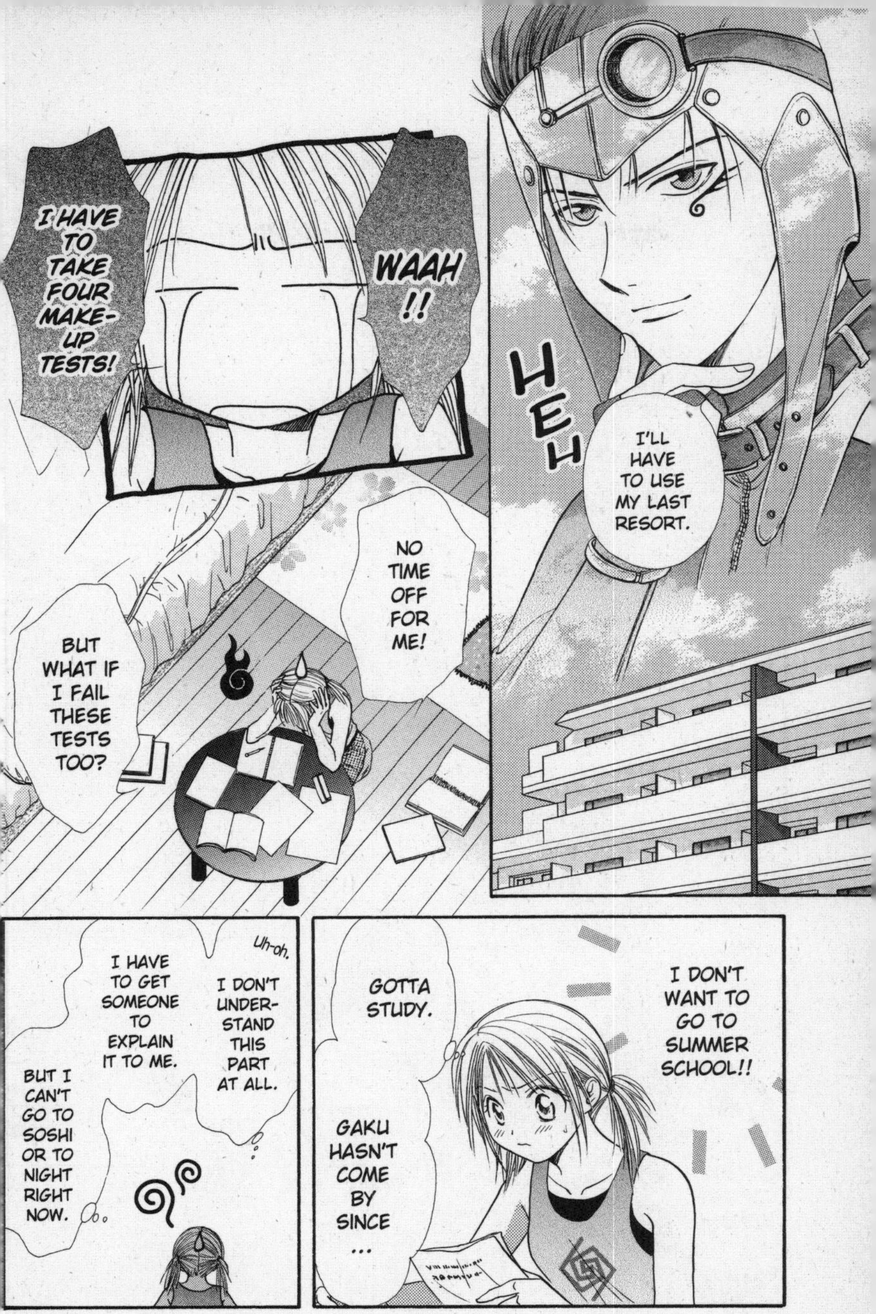
HEH
I'LL HAVE TO USE MY LAST RESORT.
WAAH!!
I HAVE TO TAKE FOUR MAKE-UP TESTS!
NO TIME OFF FOR ME!
BUT WHAT IF I FAIL THESE TESTS TOO?
I DON'T WANT TO GO TO SUMMER SCHOOL!!
GOTTA STUDY.
GAKU HASN'T COME BY SINCE...
Uh-oh.
I DON'T UNDER-STAND THIS PART AT ALL.
I HAVE TO GET SOMEONE TO EXPLAIN IT TO ME.
BUT I CAN'T GO TO SOSHI OR TO NIGHT RIGHT NOW.

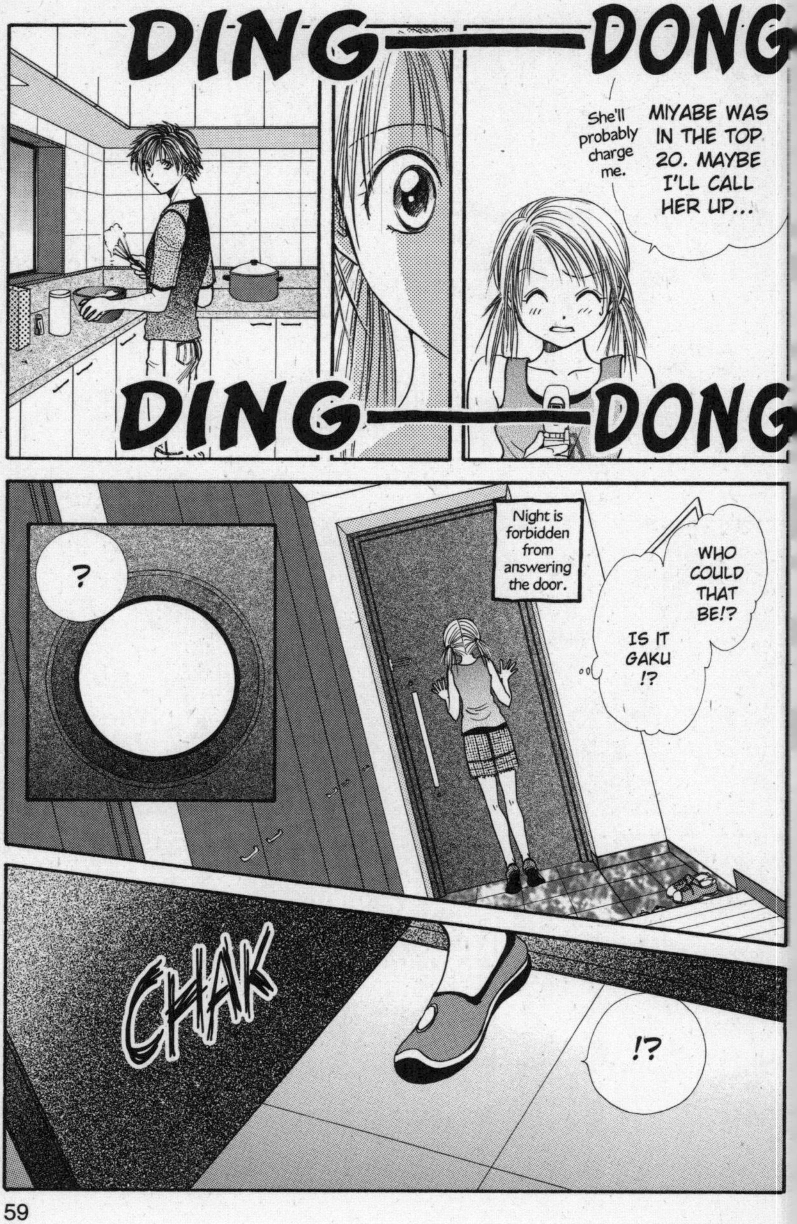
DING——DONG
MIYABE WAS IN THE TOP 20. MAYBE I'LL CALL HER UP...
She'll probably charge me.
DING——DONG
WHO COULD THAT BE!?
IS IT GAKU !?
Night is forbidden from answering the door.
?
!?
CHAK

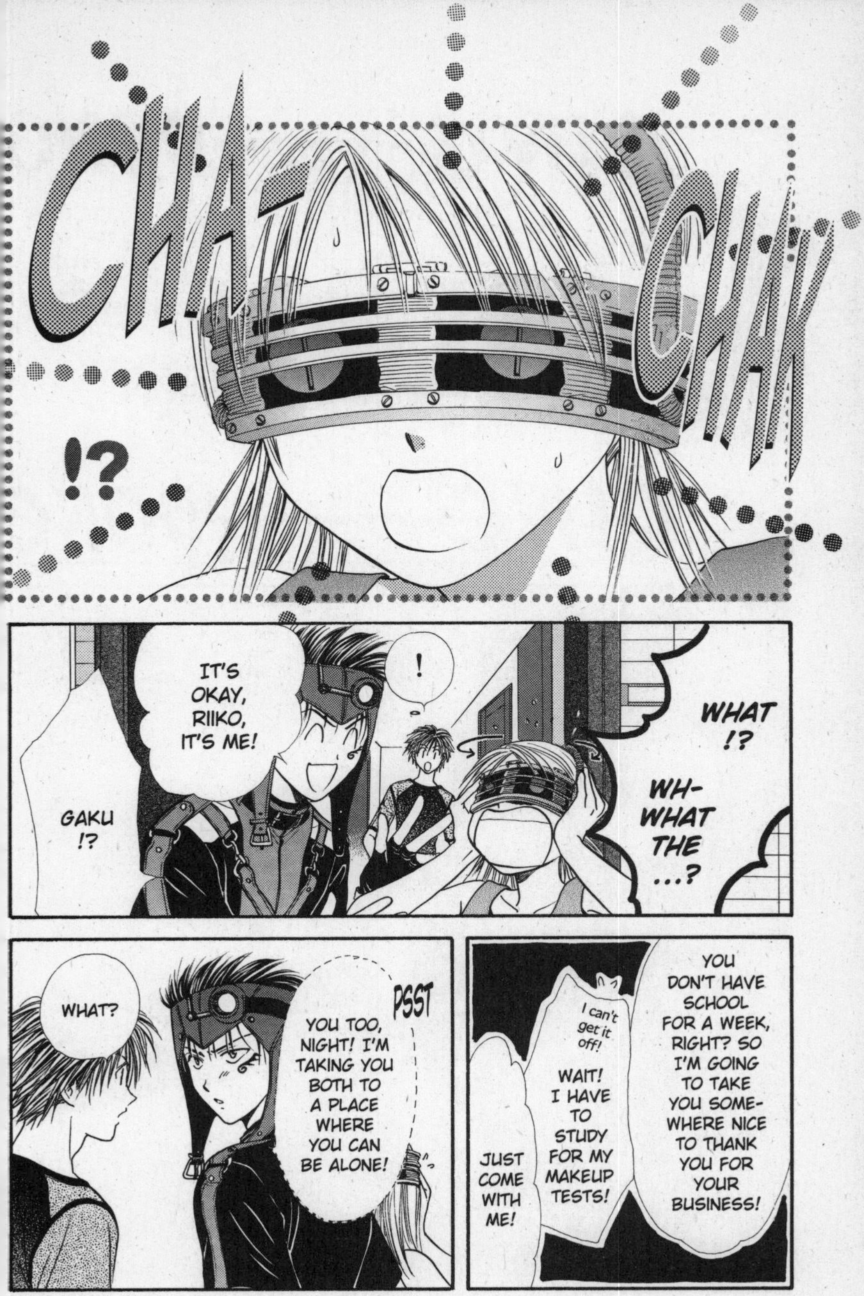
CHA-CHAK
!?
WHAT!?
WH-WHAT THE...?
!
IT'S OKAY, RIIKO, IT'S ME!
GAKU!?
YOU DON'T HAVE SCHOOL FOR A WEEK, RIGHT? SO I'M GOING TO TAKE YOU SOMEWHERE NICE TO THANK YOU FOR YOUR BUSINESS!
WAIT! I HAVE TO STUDY FOR MY MAKEUP TESTS!
I can't get it off!
JUST COME WITH ME!
PSST
YOU TOO, NIGHT! I'M TAKING YOU BOTH TO A PLACE WHERE YOU CAN BE ALONE!
WHAT?

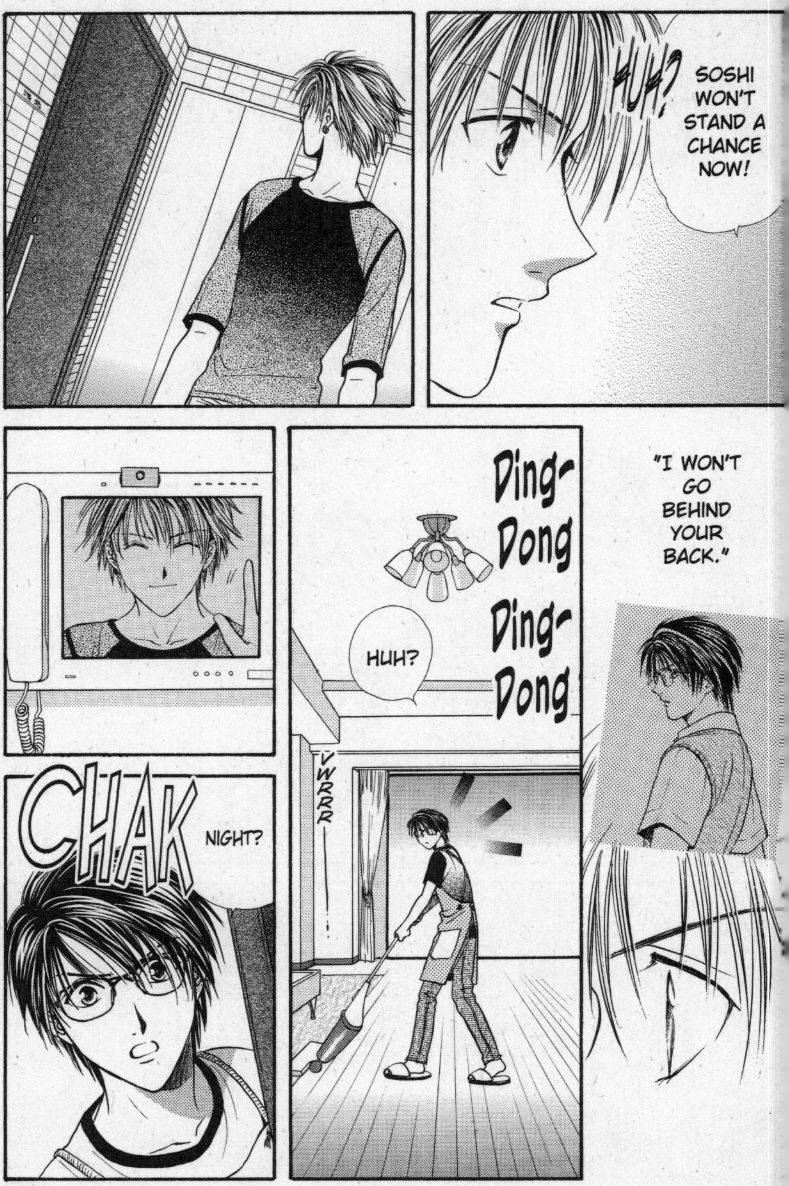
HUH?
SOSHI WON'T STAND A CHANCE NOW!
"I WON'T GO BEHIND YOUR BACK."
Ding-Dong Ding-Dong
HUH?
VWRRR
CHAK
NIGHT?

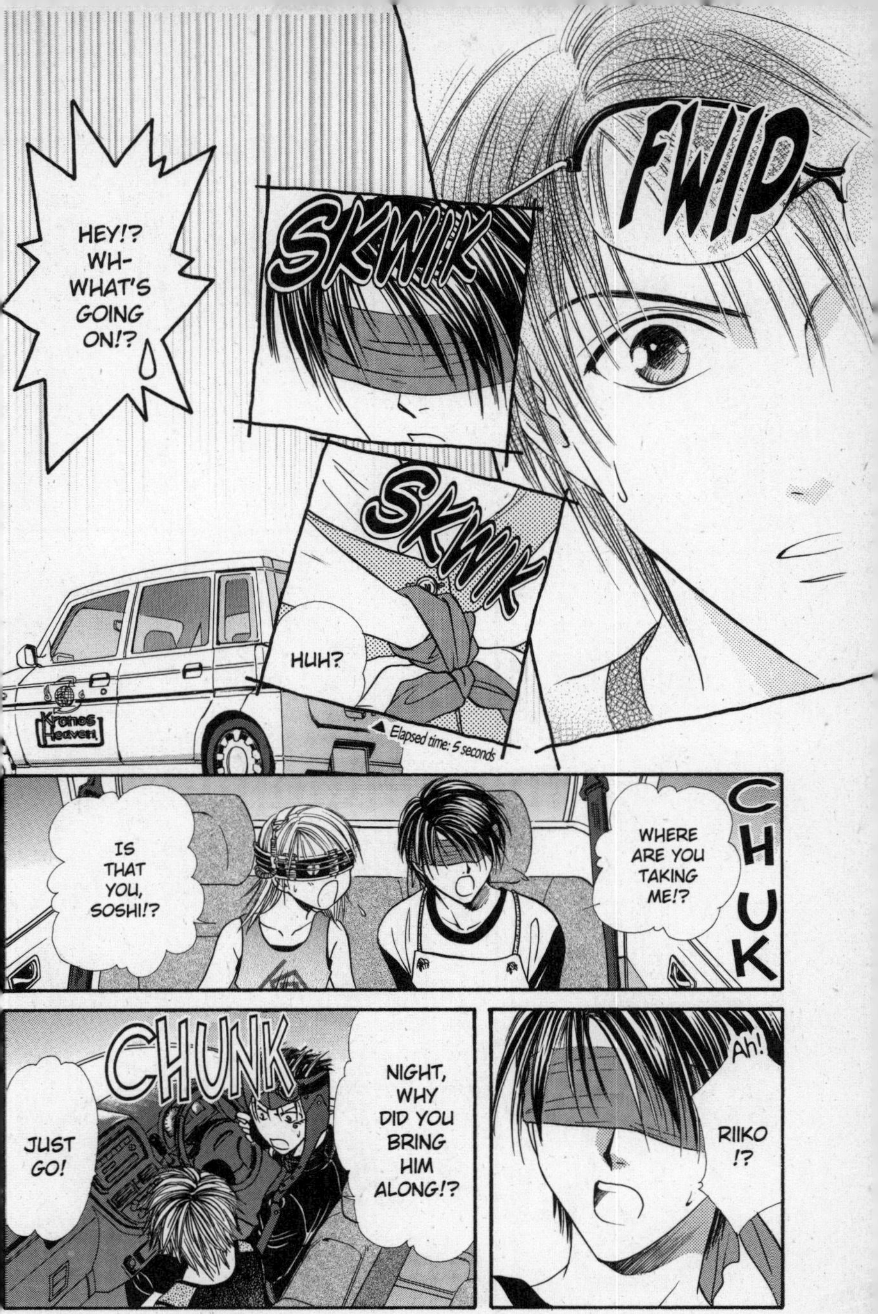
FWIP
SKWIK
HEY!? WH- WHAT'S GOING ON!?
SKWIK
HUH?
▲ Elapsed time: 5 seconds
CHUK
WHERE ARE YOU TAKING ME!?
IS THAT YOU, SOSHI!?
Ah!
RIIKO !?
NIGHT, WHY DID YOU BRING HIM ALONG!?
CHUNK
JUST GO!

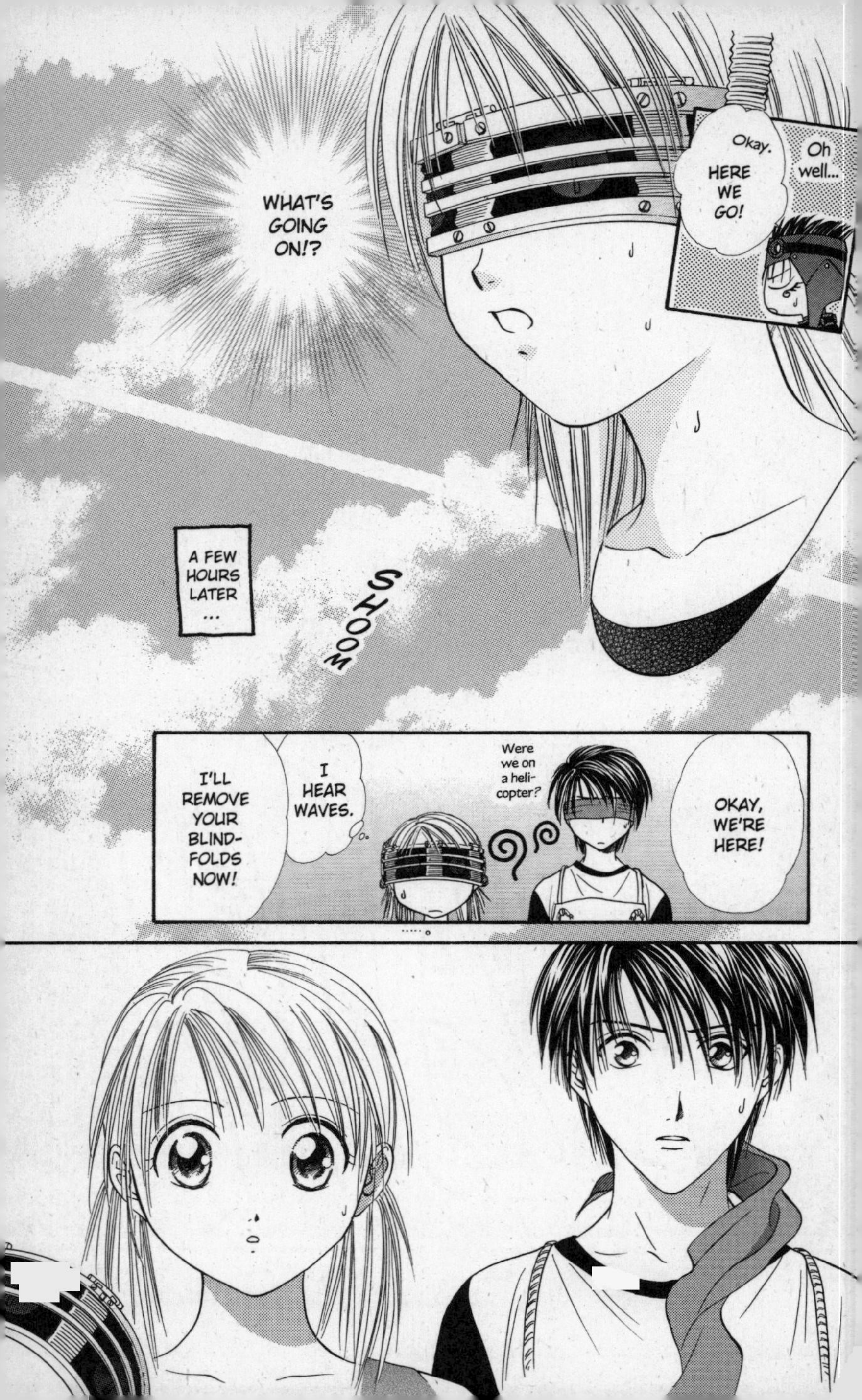
Oh well...
Okay. HERE WE GO!
WHAT'S GOING ON!?
SHOOOM
A FEW HOURS LATER ...
OKAY, WE'RE HERE!
Were we on a heli-copter?
I HEAR WAVES.
I'LL REMOVE YOUR BLIND-FOLDS NOW!
.....

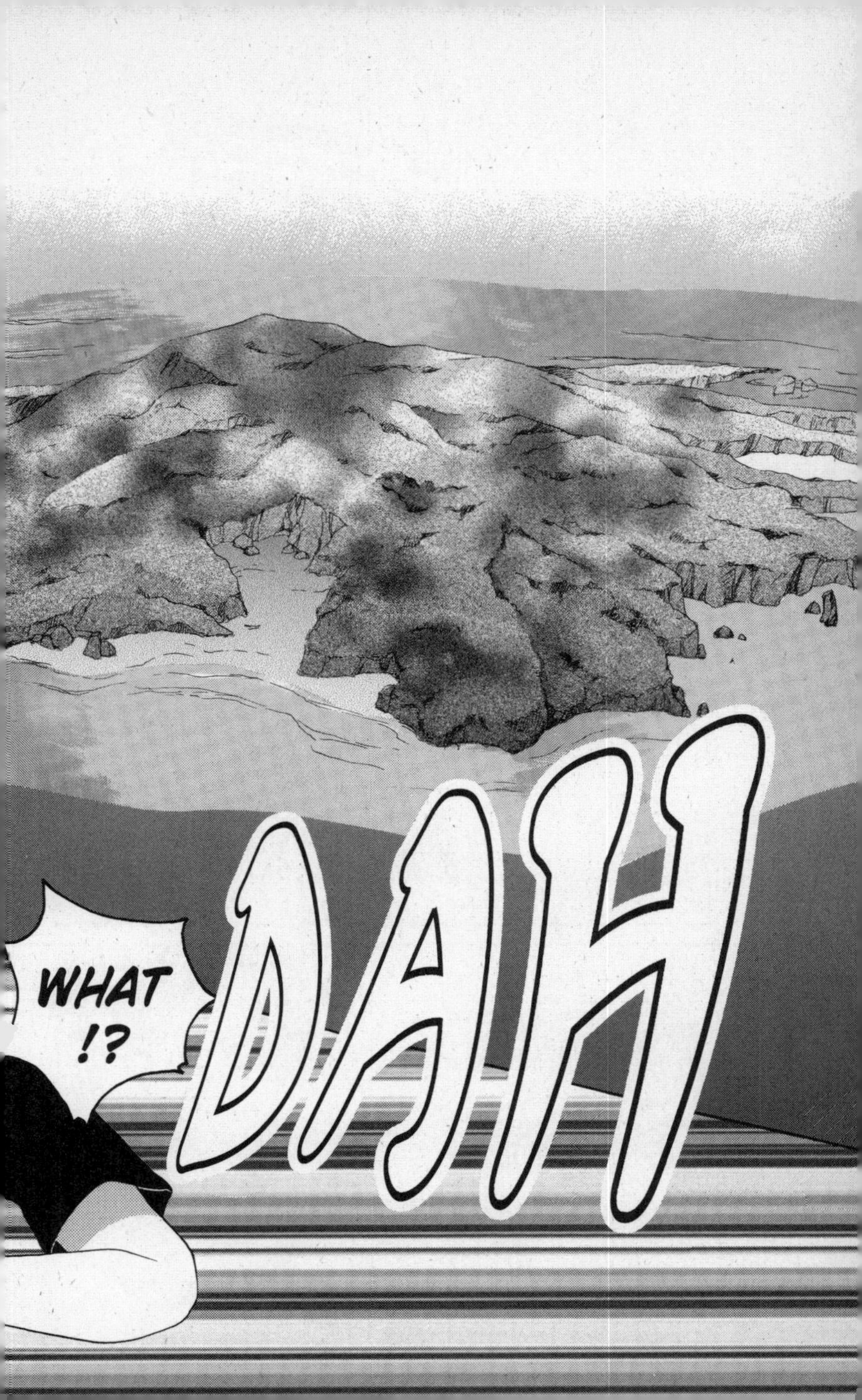
DAH
WHAT !?

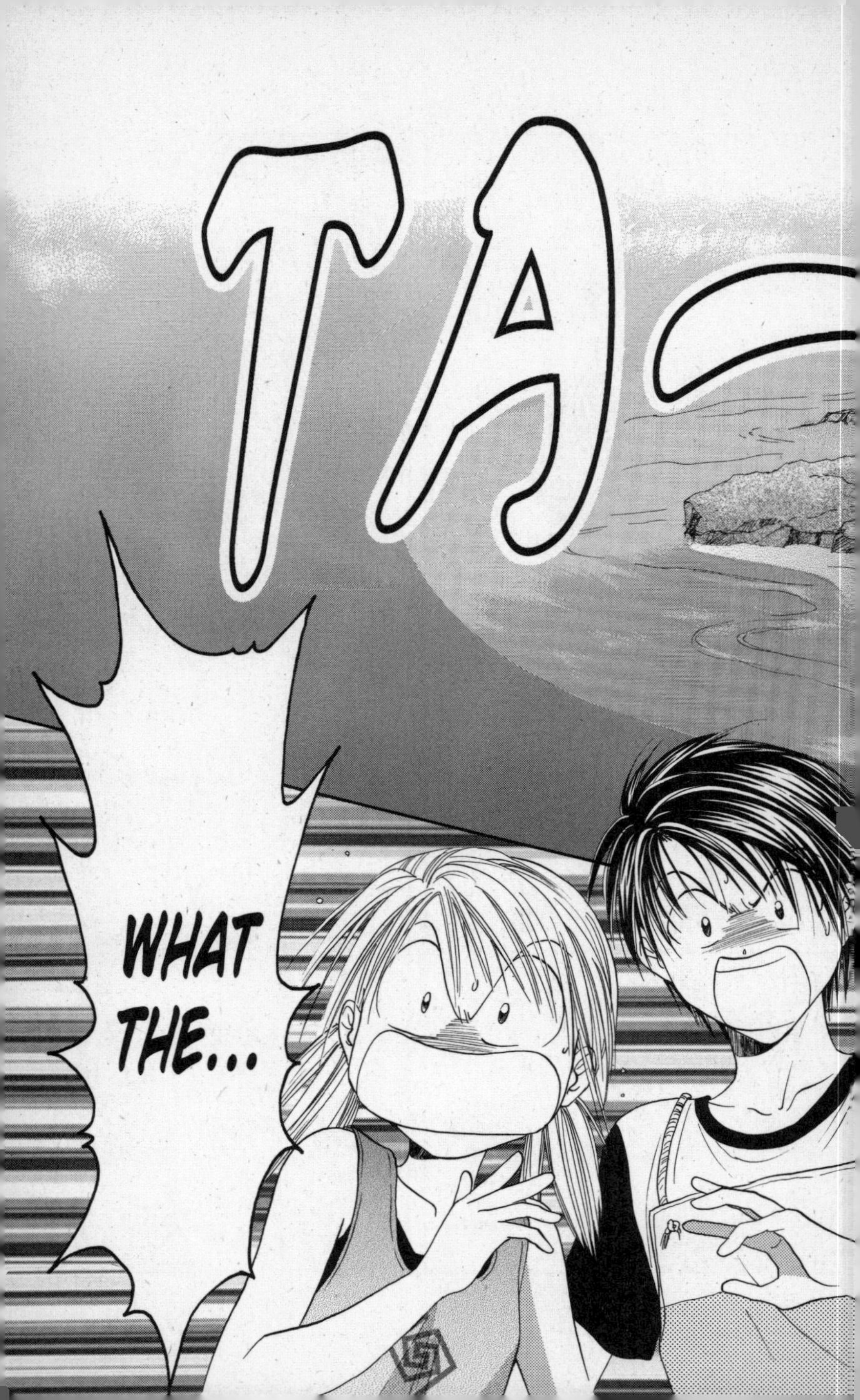
TA-
WHAT THE...

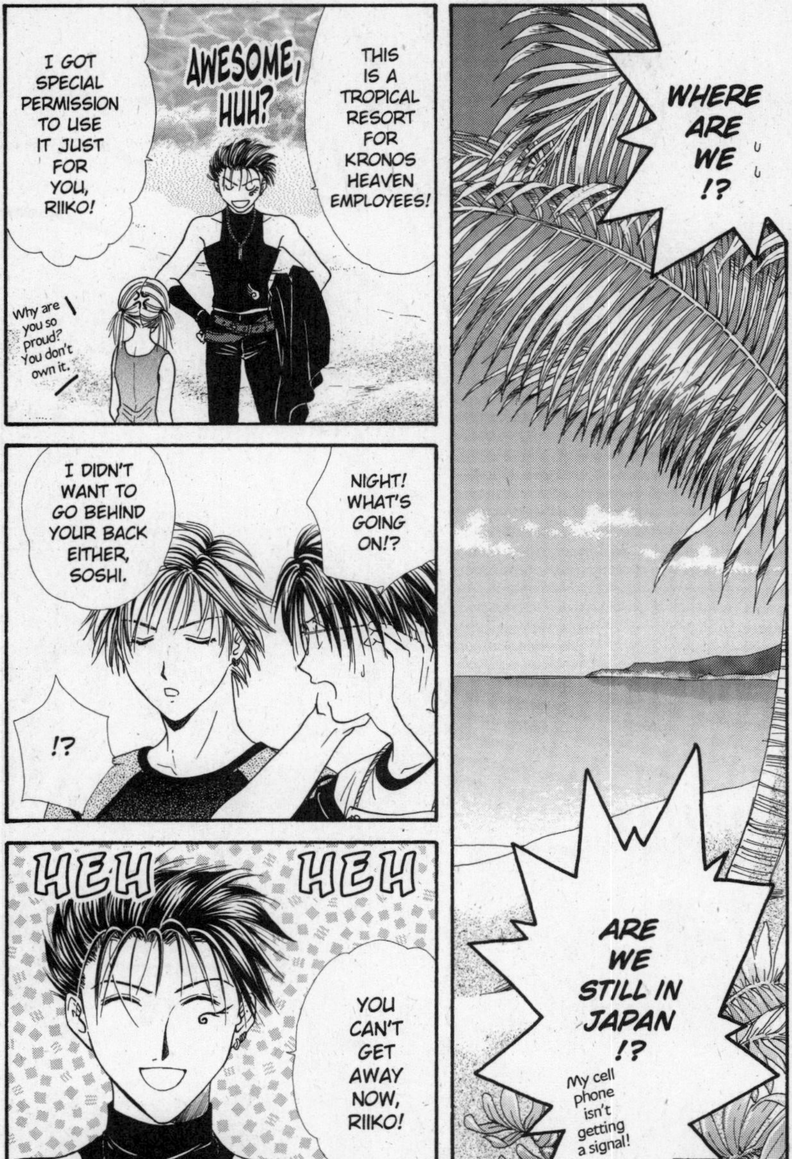
WHERE ARE WE !?
ARE WE STILL IN JAPAN !?
My cell phone isn't getting a signal!
THIS IS A TROPICAL RESORT FOR KRONOS HEAVEN EMPLOYEES!
AWESOME, HUH?
I GOT SPECIAL PERMISSION TO USE IT JUST FOR YOU, RIIKO!
Why are you so proud? You don't own it.
NIGHT! WHAT'S GOING ON!?
I DIDN'T WANT TO GO BEHIND YOUR BACK EITHER, SOSHI.
!?
HEH HEH
YOU CAN'T GET AWAY NOW, RIIKO!

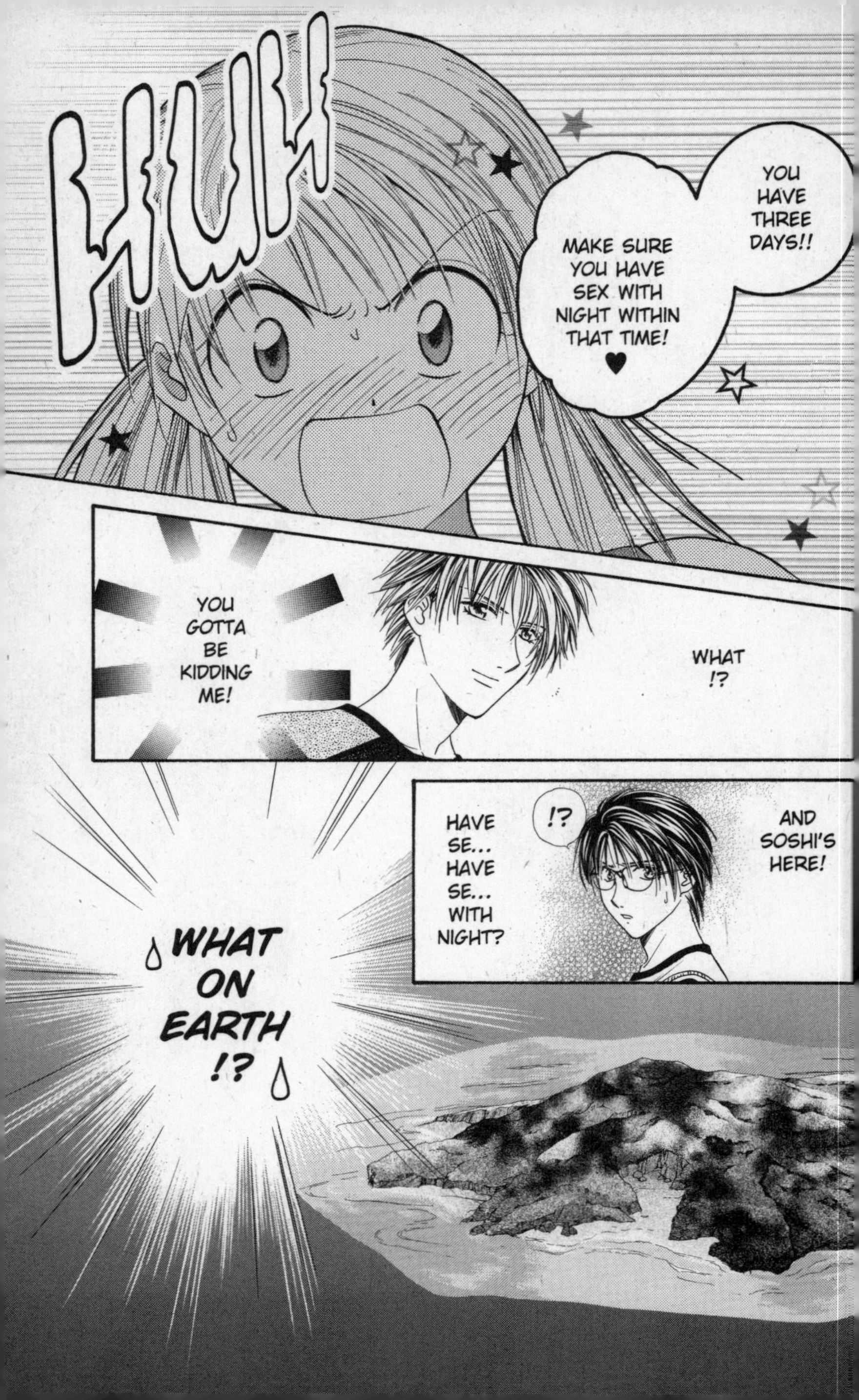
YOU HAVE THREE DAYS!!
MAKE SURE YOU HAVE SEX WITH NIGHT WITHIN THAT TIME! ♥
WHAT !?
YOU GOTTA BE KIDDING ME!
AND SOSHI'S HERE!
!?
HAVE SE... HAVE SE... WITH NIGHT?
WHAT ON EARTH !?

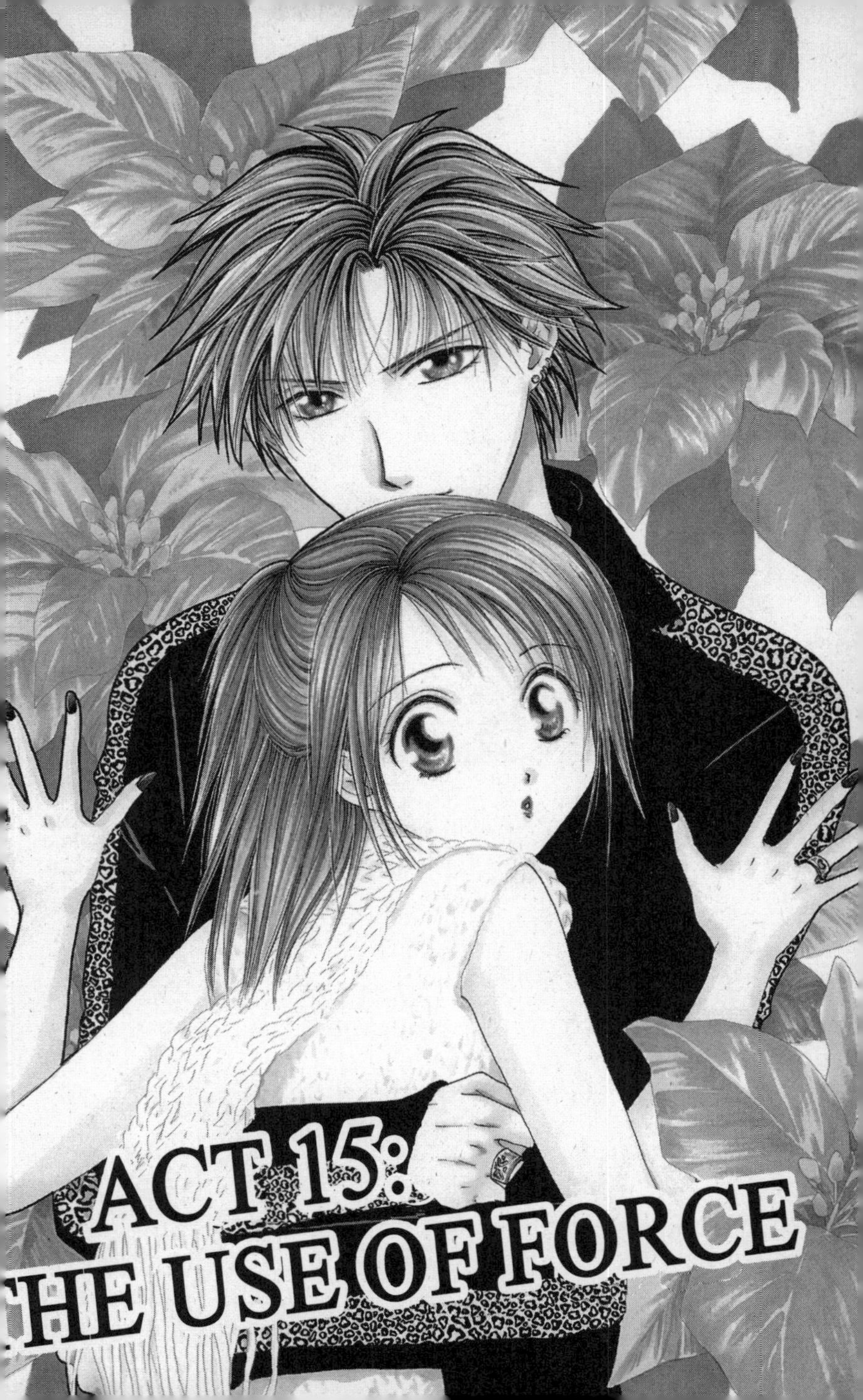
ACT 15:
THE USE OF FORCE

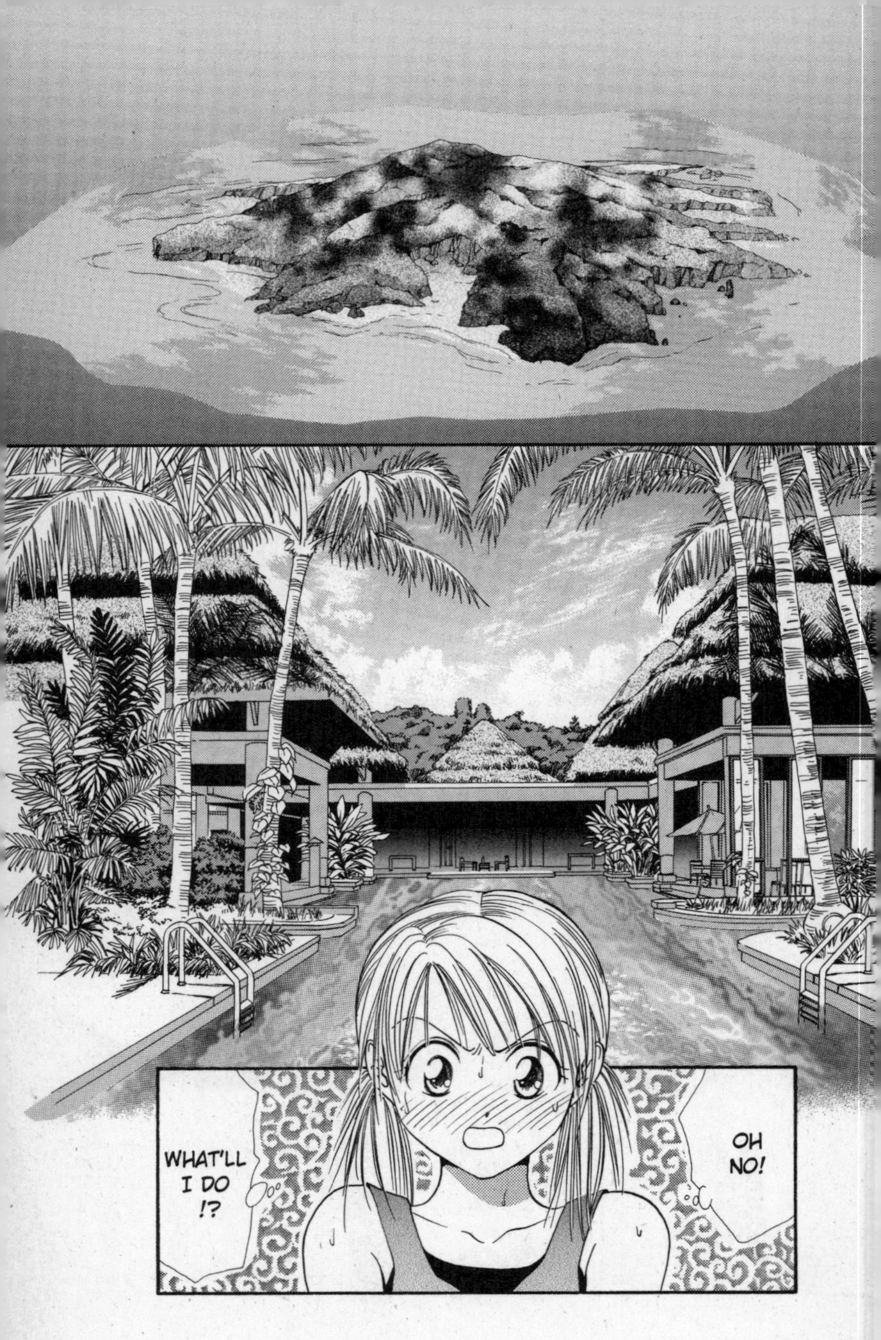
OH NO!
WHAT'LL I DO !?

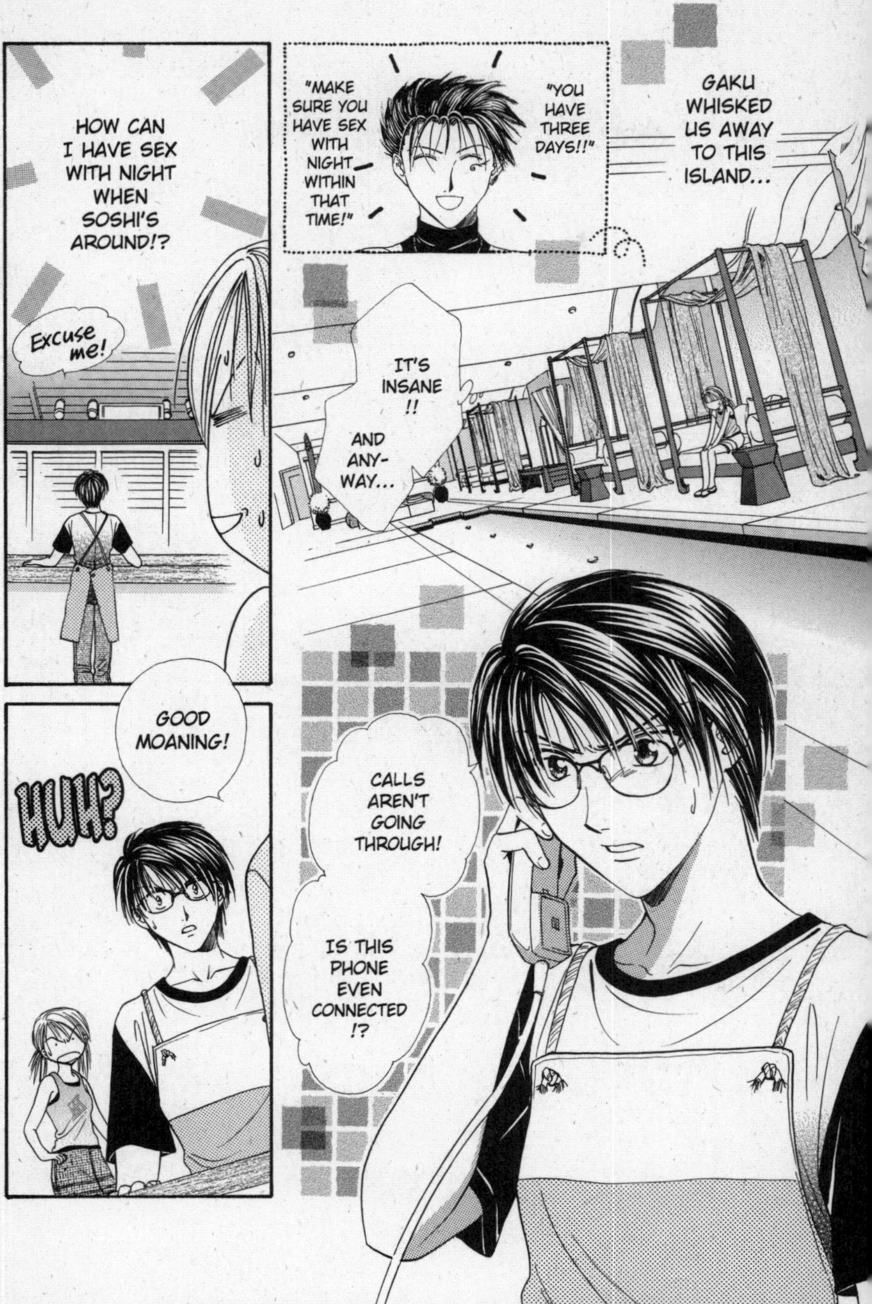
GAKU WHISKED US AWAY TO THIS ISLAND...
"YOU HAVE THREE DAYS!!"
"MAKE SURE YOU HAVE SEX WITH NIGHT WITHIN THAT TIME!"
IT'S INSANE!!
AND ANYWAY...
HOW CAN I HAVE SEX WITH NIGHT WHEN SOSHI'S AROUND!?
Excuse me!
CALLS AREN'T GOING THROUGH!
IS THIS PHONE EVEN CONNECTED!?
GOOD MOANING!
HUH?

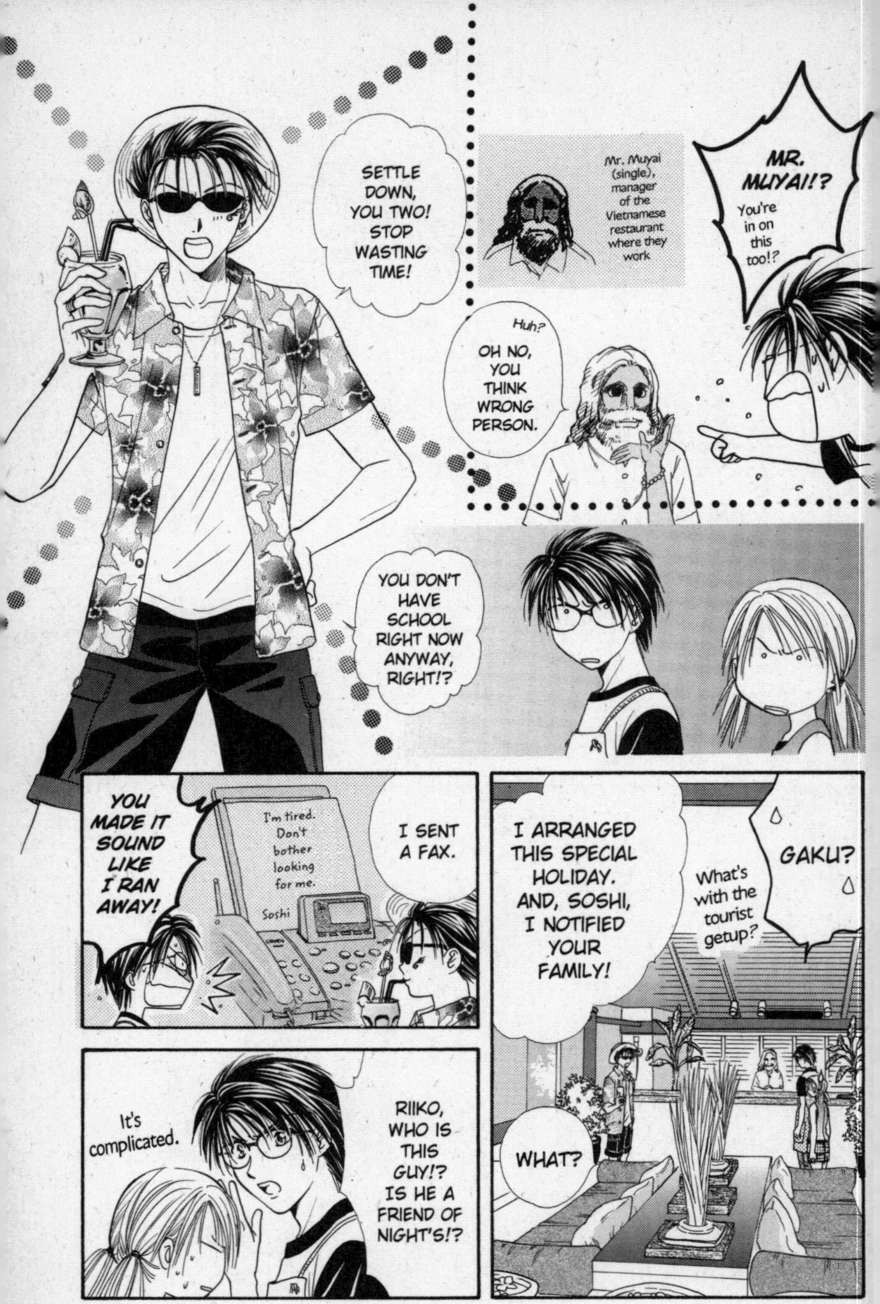
MR. MUYAI!?
You're in on this too!?
Mr. Muyai (single), manager of the Vietnamese restaurant where they work
Huh?
OH NO, YOU THINK WRONG PERSON.
SETTLE DOWN, YOU TWO! STOP WASTING TIME!
YOU DON'T HAVE SCHOOL RIGHT NOW ANYWAY, RIGHT!?
GAKU?
What's with the tourist getup?
I ARRANGED THIS SPECIAL HOLIDAY. AND, SOSHI, I NOTIFIED YOUR FAMILY!
WHAT?
I SENT A FAX.
I'm tired. Don't bother looking for me.
Soshi
YOU MADE IT SOUND LIKE I RAN AWAY!
RIIKO, WHO IS THIS GUY!? IS HE A FRIEND OF NIGHT'S!?
It's complicated.

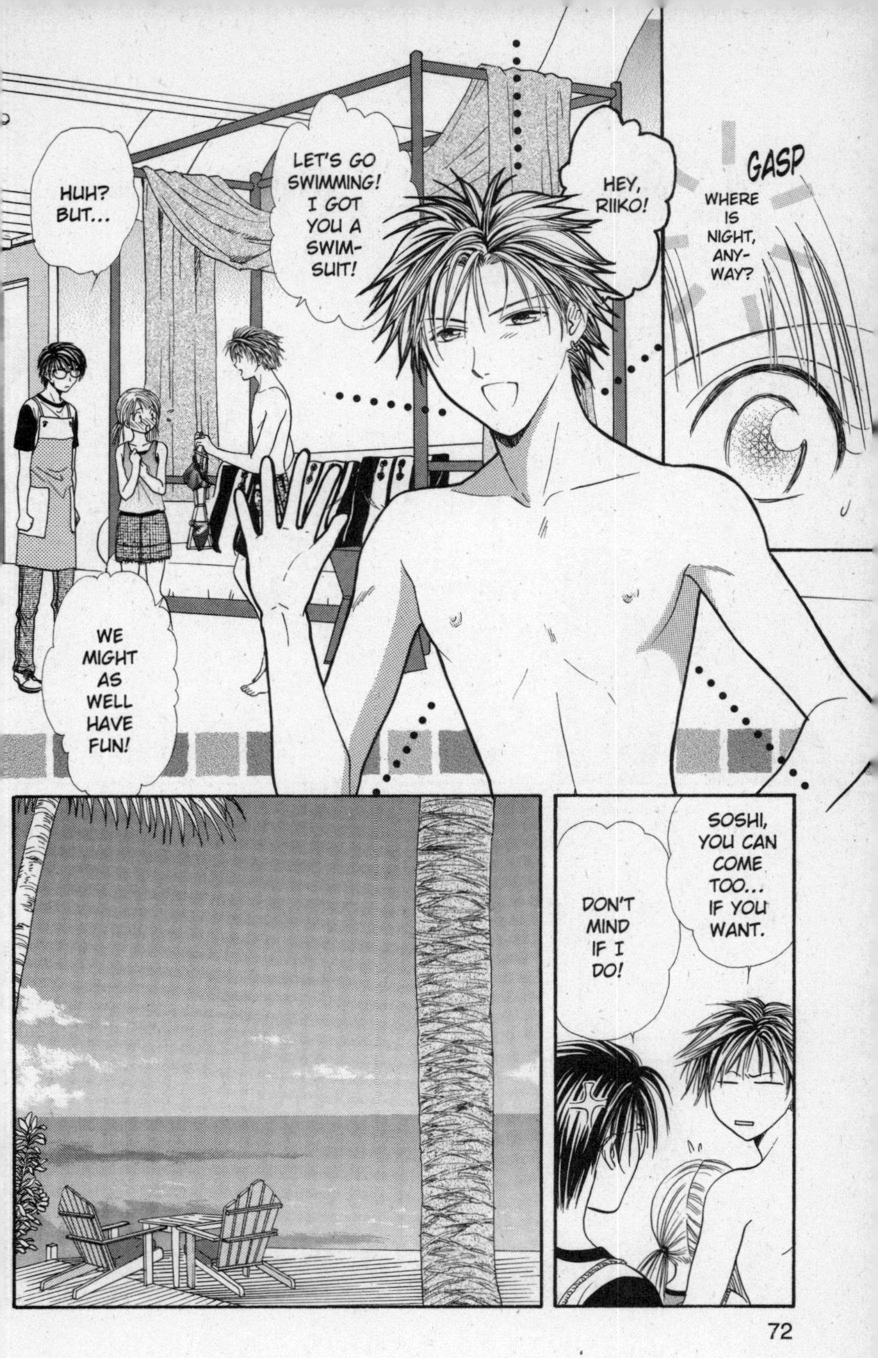
GASP
WHERE IS NIGHT, ANYWAY?
HEY, RIIKO!
LET'S GO SWIMMING! I GOT YOU A SWIMSUIT!
HUH? BUT...
WE MIGHT AS WELL HAVE FUN!
SOSHI, YOU CAN COME TOO... IF YOU WANT.
DON'T MIND IF I DO!

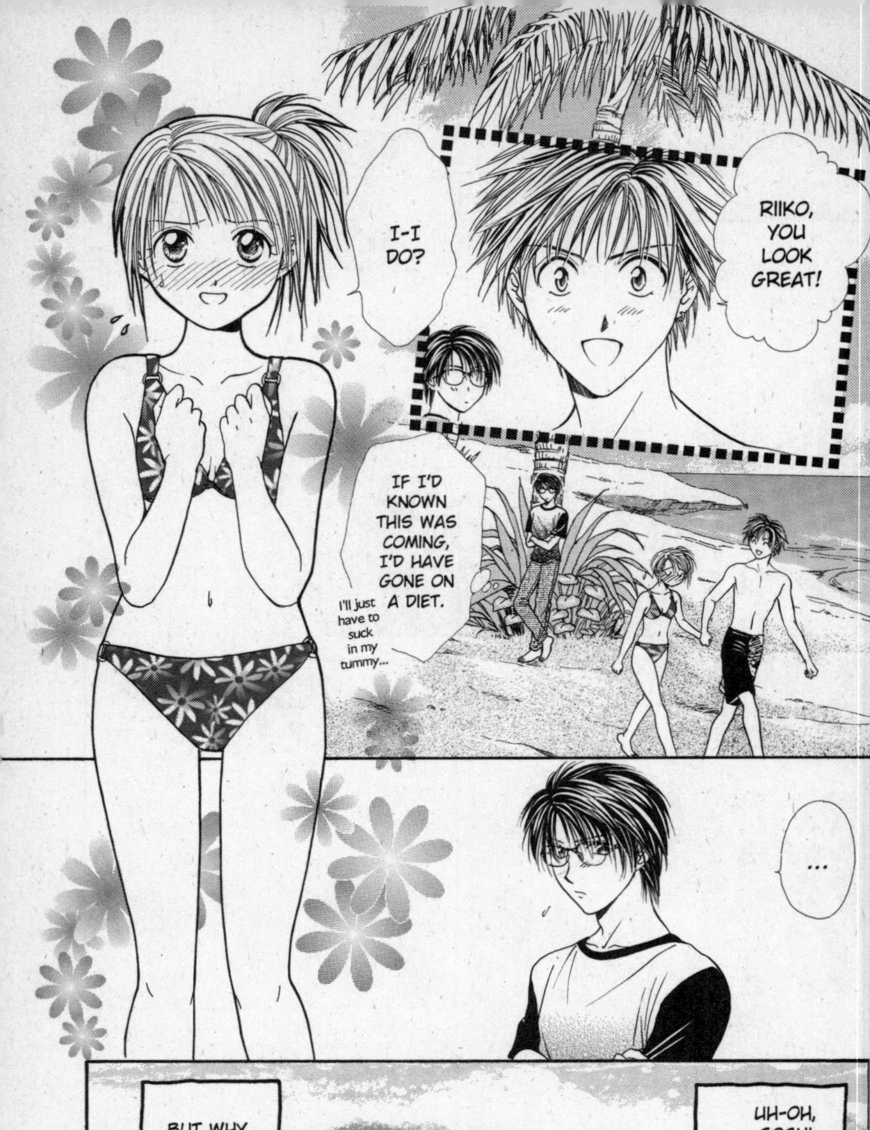
RIIKO, YOU LOOK GREAT!
I-I DO?
IF I'D KNOWN THIS WAS COMING, I'D HAVE GONE ON A DIET.
I'll just have to suck in my tummy...
...
UH-OH, SOSHI DOESN'T KNOW WHAT'S GOING ON.
Well, duh.
BUT WHY DID NIGHT BRING HIM ALONG ANYWAY?

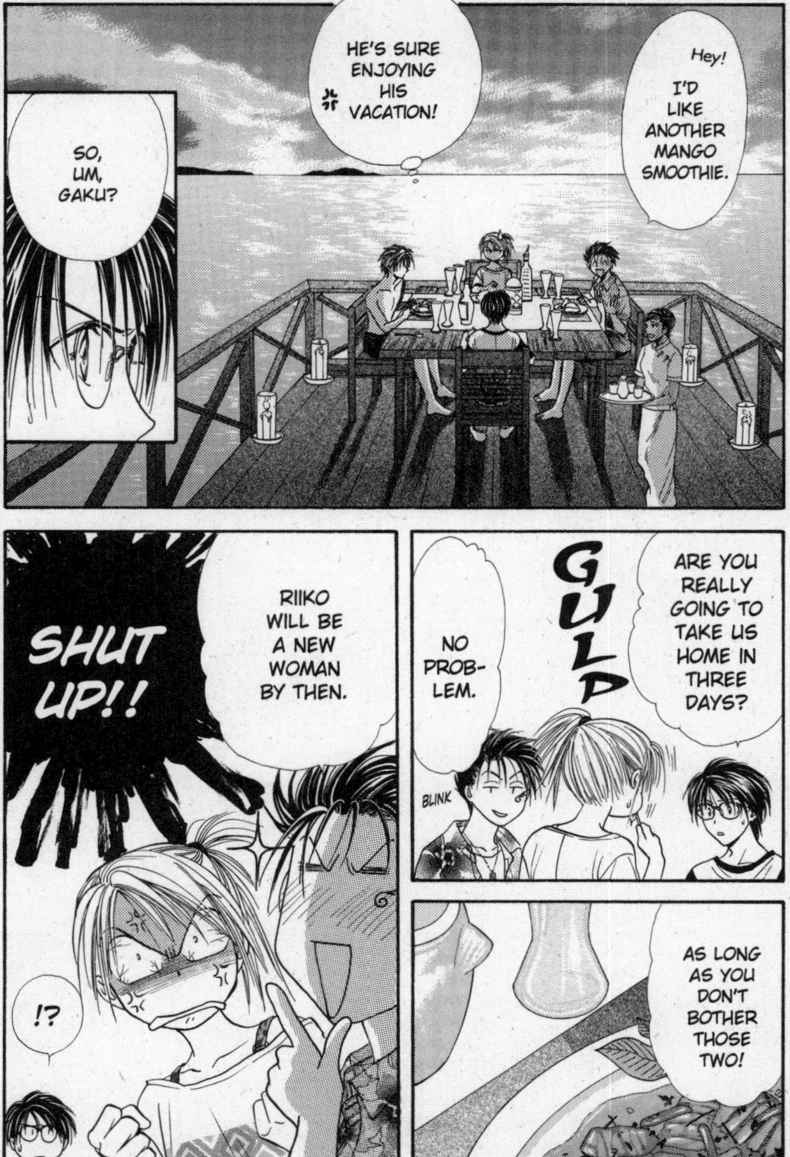
Hey! I'D LIKE ANOTHER MANGO SMOOTHIE.
HE'S SURE ENJOYING HIS VACATION!
SO, UM, GAKU?
ARE YOU REALLY GOING TO TAKE US HOME IN THREE DAYS?
GULP
NO PROB-LEM.
BLINK
AS LONG AS YOU DON'T BOTHER THOSE TWO!
RIIKO WILL BE A NEW WOMAN BY THEN.
SHUT UP!!
!?

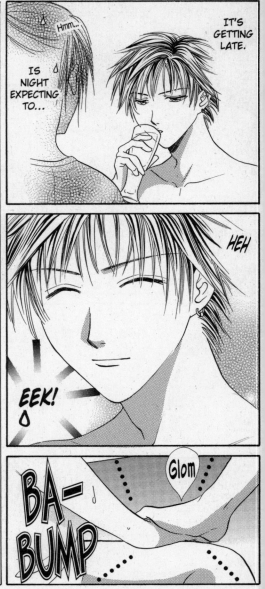

IT'S GETTING LATE.
Hmm...
IS NIGHT EXPECTING TO...
HEH
EEK!
Glom
BA-BUMP

Ahhh... I've been working so much that everyone is worried about me. Even my readers are expressing concern in their letters. Thank you so much, everyone, but I feel happy and productive! I'm a workaholic! (←That's not good!) It's already been three years since I got chronic fatigue syndrome. (That's even worse!) But it's not as bad as it sounds. Sometimes I get cold sweats and I throw up, and sometimes the stress even gives me a fever. But I'm fine!! I'm masochistic that way. Um... It's worse to imagine myself not wanting to draw manga at all. I don't care about the fatigue as long as I can do this. I still have so many things I want to do. If only I had one of those clone robots from Perman!! It would be great if there were five of me!! Dammit, let me draw! (No, they do--I'm not going to bite the hands that feed me.) Okay, I'm high on endogenous opiates. I should take a bath and relax. I'm really into bath salts and bubbles. And cherry blossoms. They say relaxation is the only way to cure autonomic imbalance. What a pain. But my endogenous opiates kick in and I get euphoric when I'm drawing stuff I like. Does that count as relaxing? I hate writing, so that gets a little stressful, but it's all right. I'm listening to the piano channel on cable. The piano's so nice. I'm just rambling, aren't I? I should take a nap and do this later, but there's no time. I'll keep writing. I'll keep scrawling. My brain is emitting alpha waves, so I'm going to go pet my dog now.

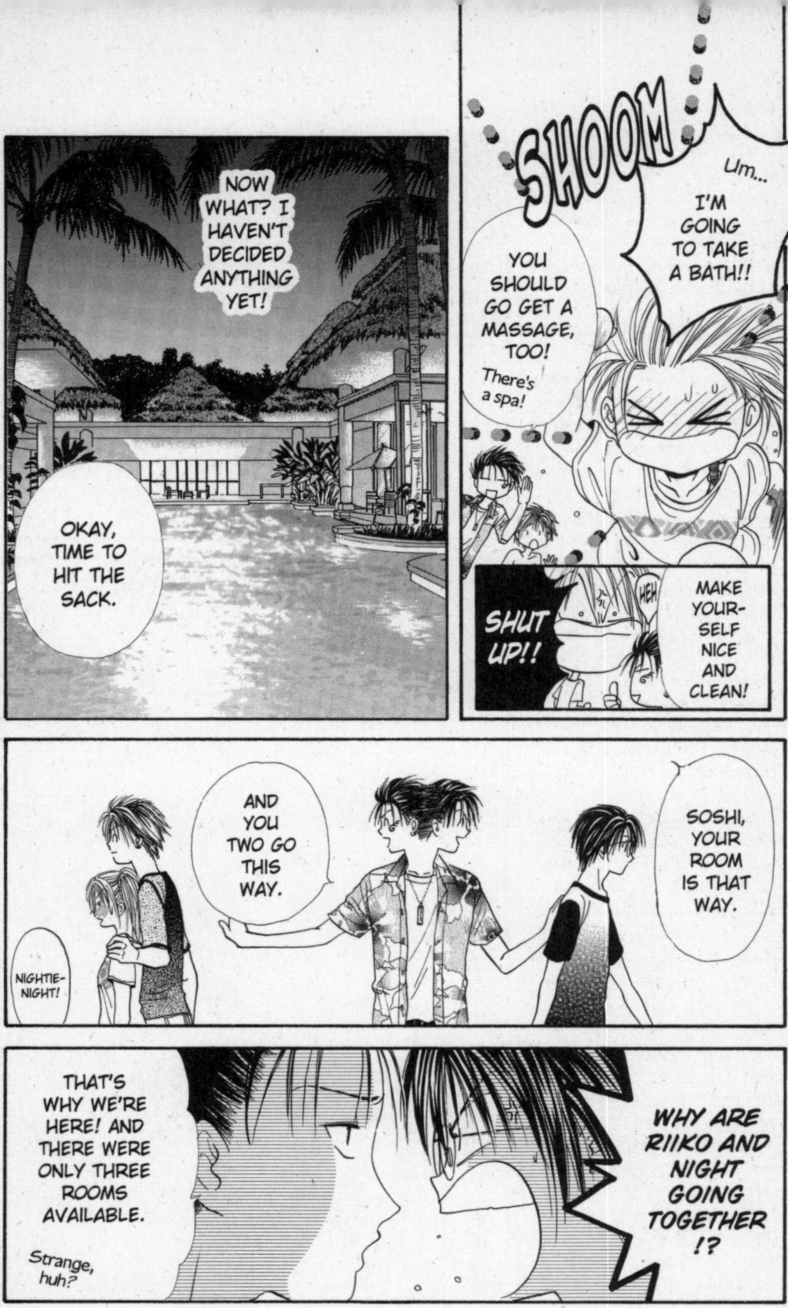
SHOOM
Um... I'M GOING TO TAKE A BATH!!
YOU SHOULD GO GET A MASSAGE, TOO!
There's a spa!
MAKE YOURSELF NICE AND CLEAN!
HEH
SHUT UP!!
NOW WHAT? I HAVEN'T DECIDED ANYTHING YET!
OKAY, TIME TO HIT THE SACK.
SOSHI, YOUR ROOM IS THAT WAY.
AND YOU TWO GO THIS WAY.
NIGHTIE-NIGHT!
WHY ARE RIIKO AND NIGHT GOING TOGETHER!?
THAT'S WHY WE'RE HERE! AND THERE WERE ONLY THREE ROOMS AVAILABLE.
Strange, huh?

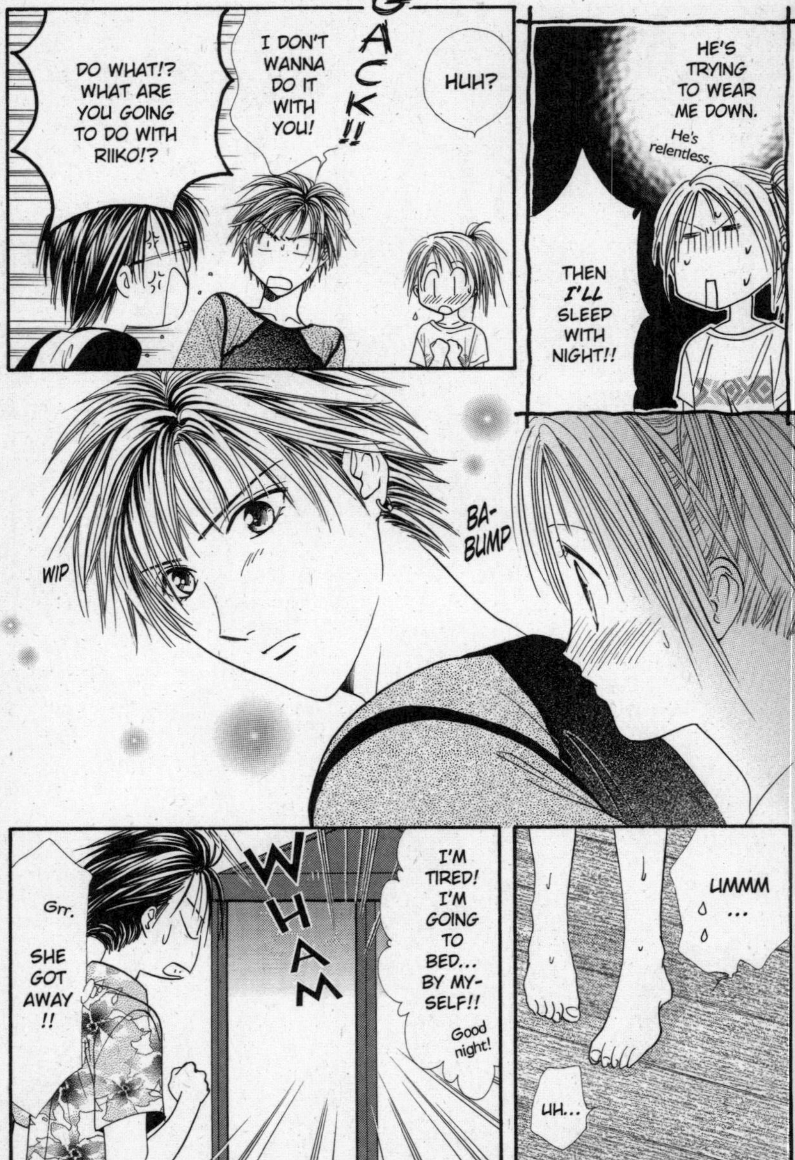
HE'S TRYING TO WEAR ME DOWN.
He's relentless.
THEN I'LL SLEEP WITH NIGHT!!
HUH?
GACK!!
I DON'T WANNA DO IT WITH YOU!
DO WHAT!? WHAT ARE YOU GOING TO DO WITH RIIKO!?
BA-BUMP
WIP
UMMM...
UH...
I'M TIRED! I'M GOING TO BED... BY MY-SELF!!
Good night!
WHAM
Grr.
SHE GOT AWAY!!

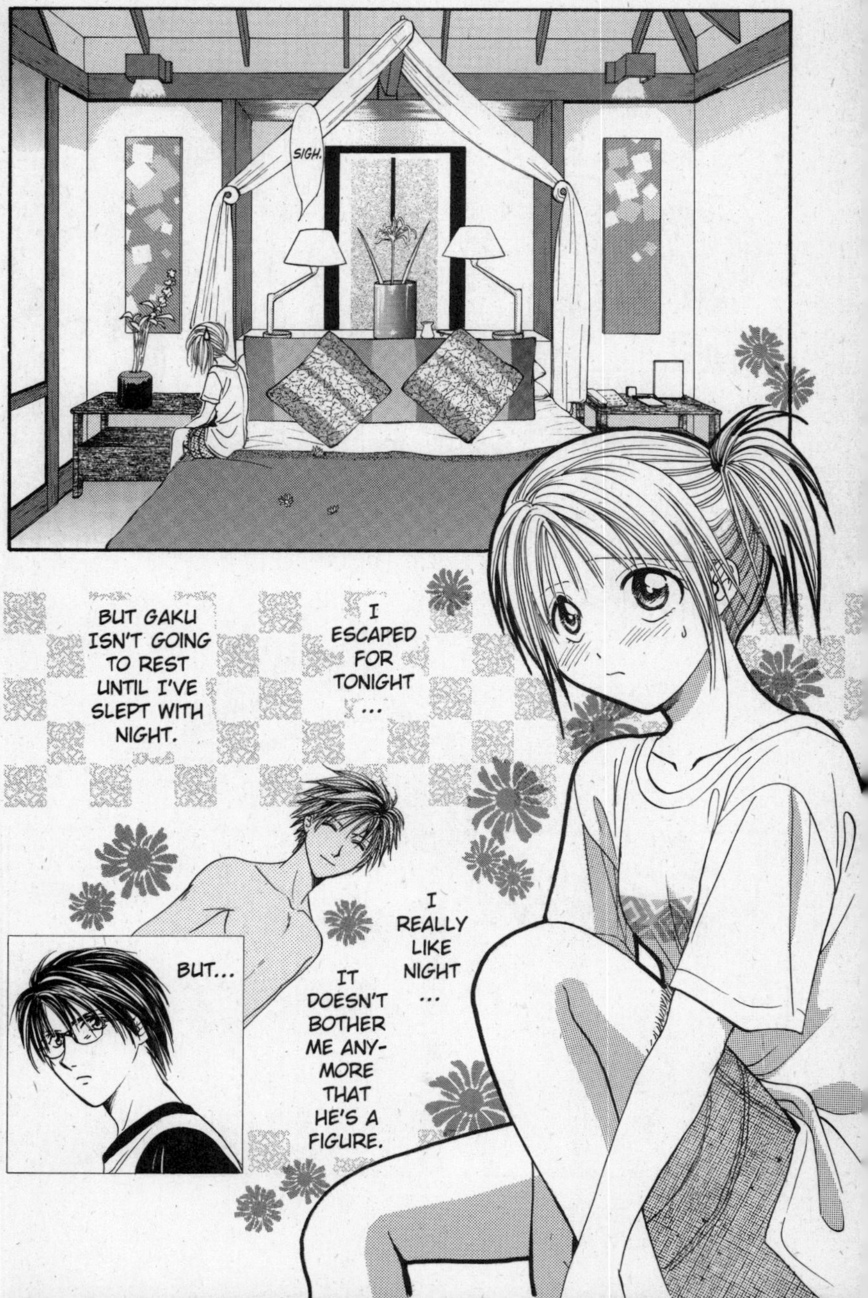
SIGH.
I ESCAPED FOR TONIGHT...
BUT GAKU ISN'T GOING TO REST UNTIL I'VE SLEPT WITH NIGHT.
I REALLY LIKE NIGHT...
IT DOESN'T BOTHER ME ANY-MORE THAT HE'S A FIGURE.
BUT...

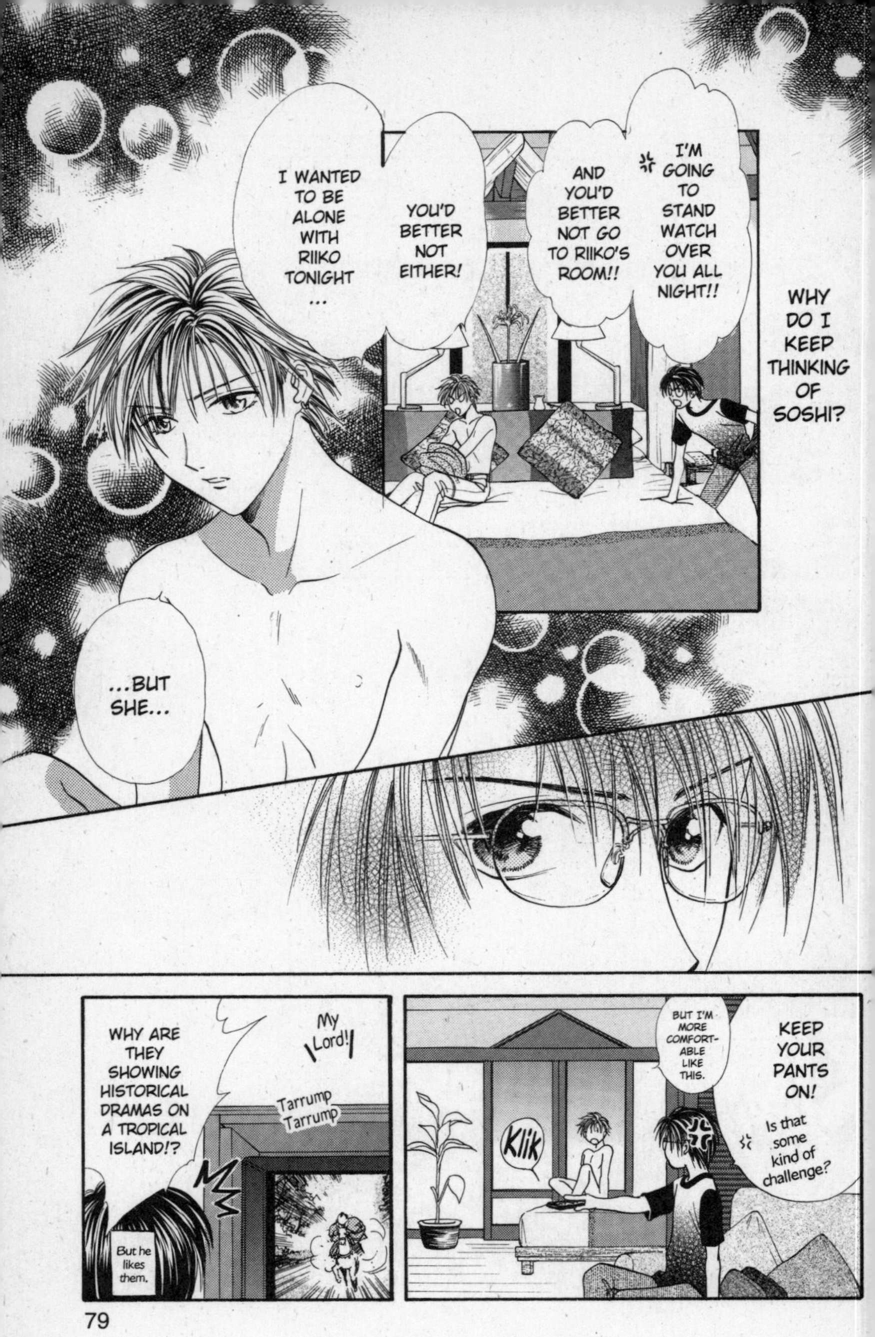
WHY DO I KEEP THINKING OF SOSHI?
I'M GOING TO STAND WATCH OVER YOU ALL NIGHT!!
AND YOU'D BETTER NOT GO TO RIIKO'S ROOM!!
YOU'D BETTER NOT EITHER!
I WANTED TO BE ALONE WITH RIIKO TONIGHT ...
...BUT SHE...
KEEP YOUR PANTS ON!
Is that some kind of challenge?
BUT I'M MORE COMFORTABLE LIKE THIS.
Klik
My Lord!
Tarrump Tarrump
WHY ARE THEY SHOWING HISTORICAL DRAMAS ON A TROPICAL ISLAND!?
MM
But he likes them.

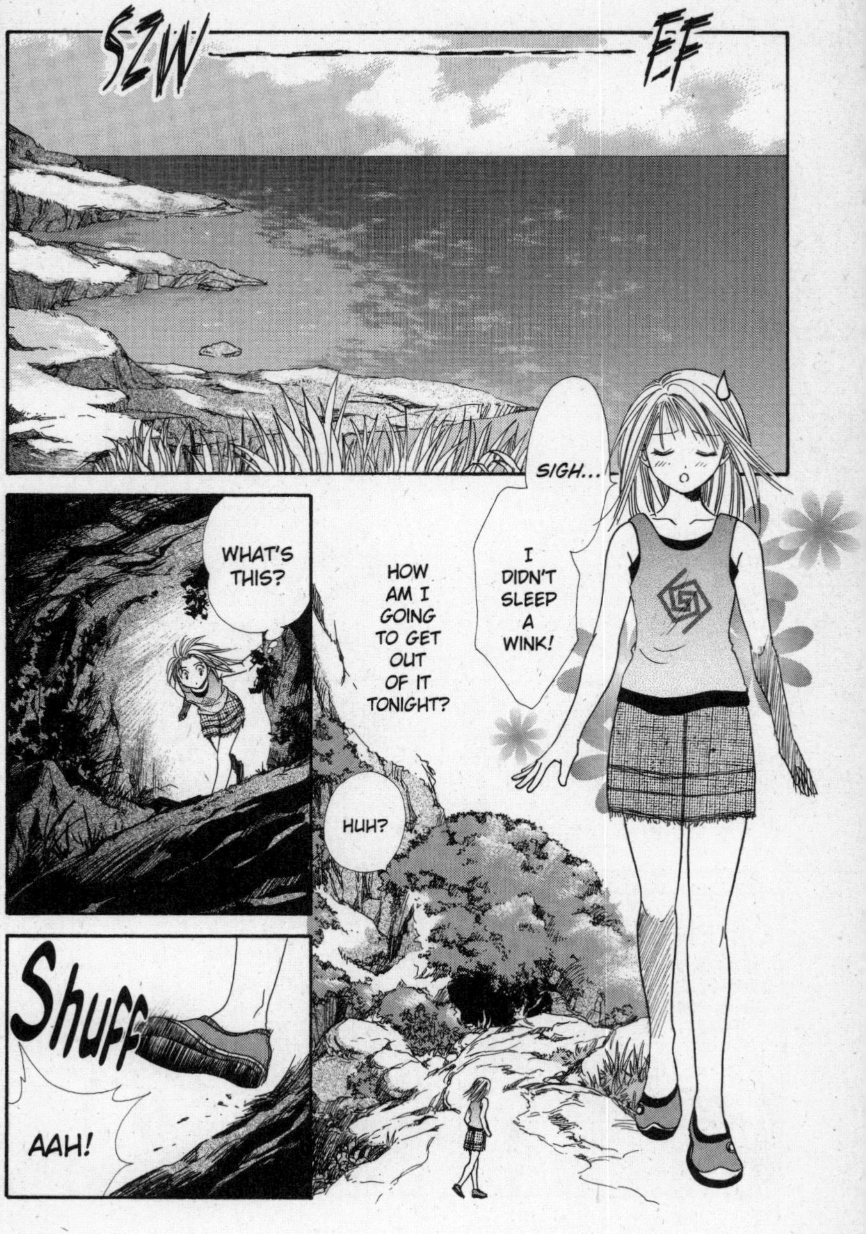

SZW—EF
SIGH...
I DIDN'T SLEEP A WINK!
HOW AM I GOING TO GET OUT OF IT TONIGHT?
HUH?
WHAT'S THIS?
Shuff
AAH!

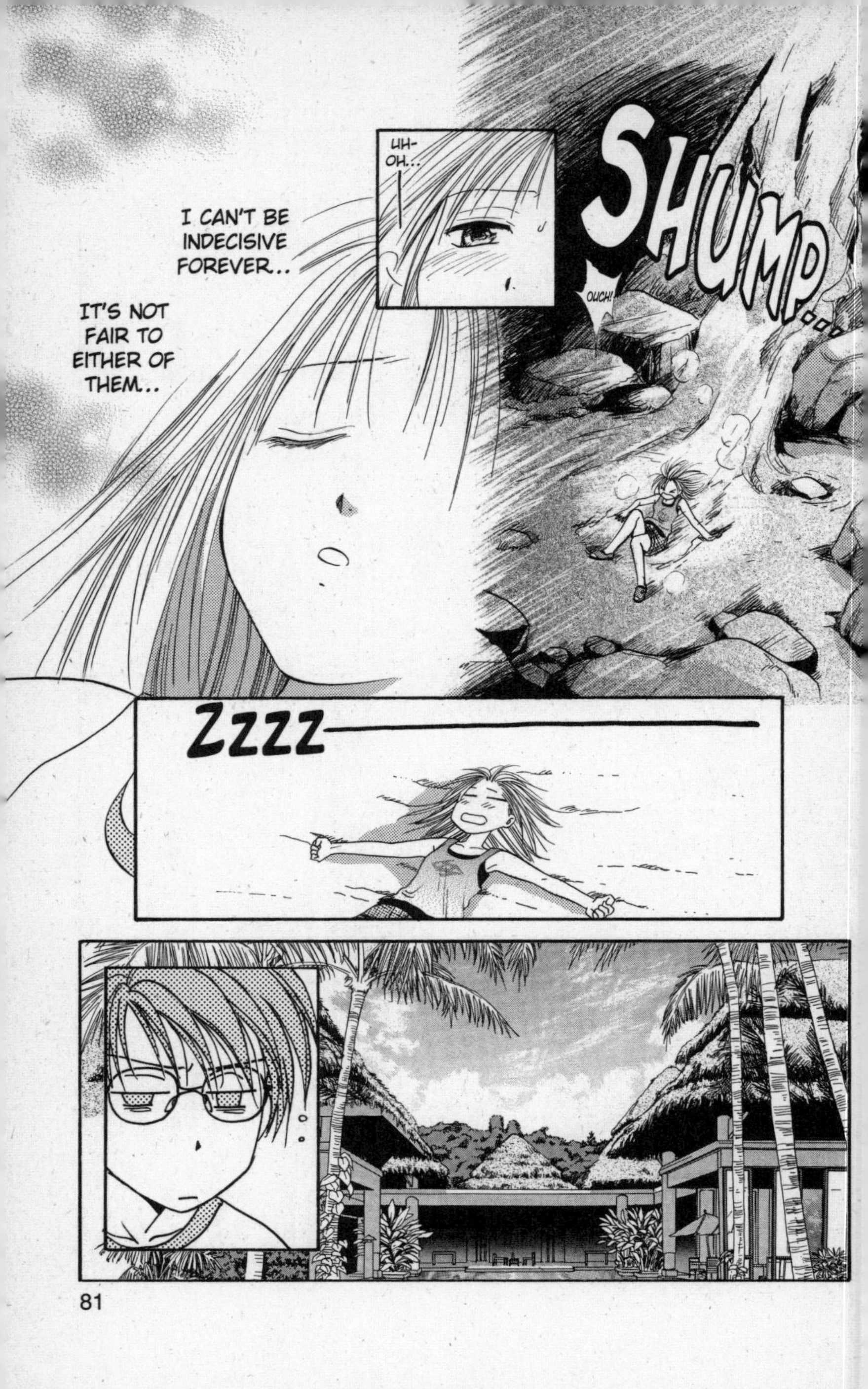
SHUMP...
OUCH!
UH-OH...
I CAN'T BE INDECISIVE FOREVER...
IT'S NOT FAIR TO EITHER OF THEM...
Zzzz

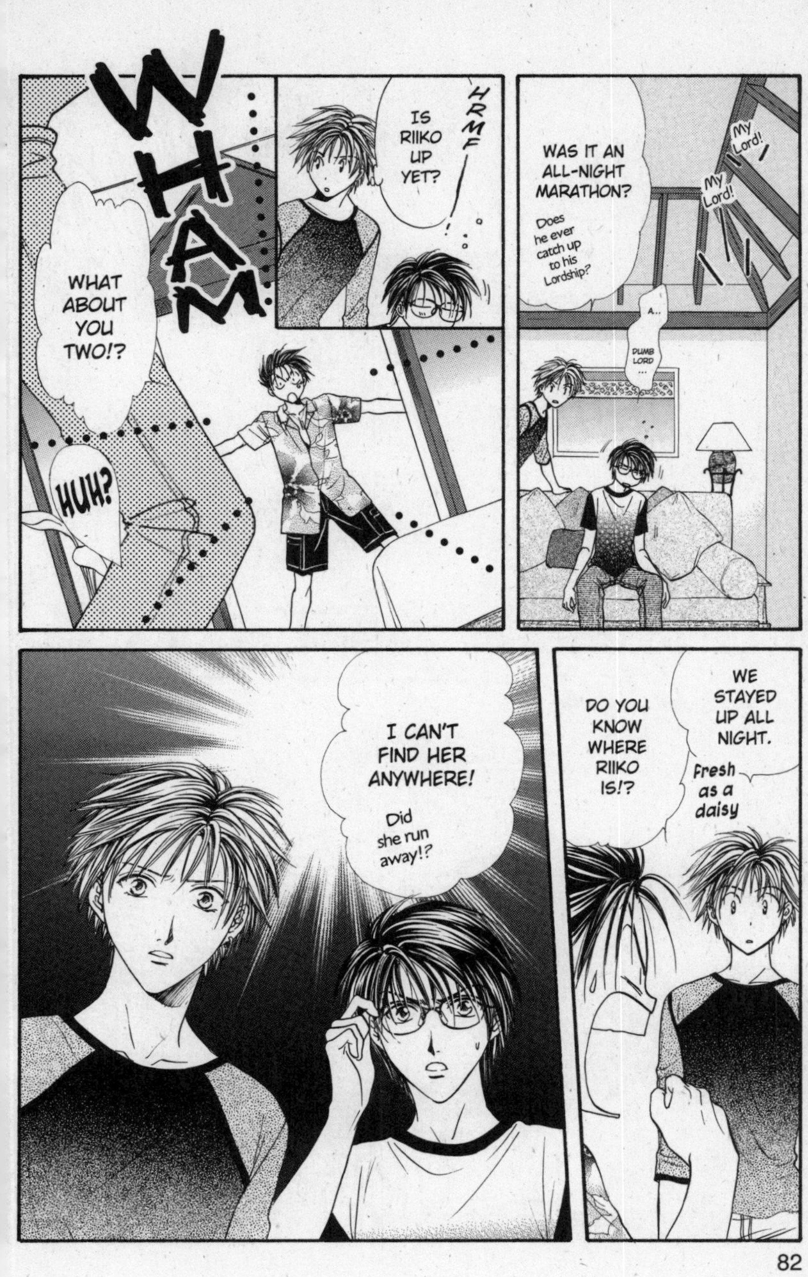

My Lord!
My Lord!
WAS IT AN ALL-NIGHT MARATHON?
Does he ever catch up to his Lordship?
A...
DUMB LORD...
HRMF
IS RIIKO UP YET?
WHAM
WHAT ABOUT YOU TWO!?
HUH?
WE STAYED UP ALL NIGHT.
Fresh as a daisy
DO YOU KNOW WHERE RIIKO IS!?
I CAN'T FIND HER ANYWHERE!
Did she run away!?

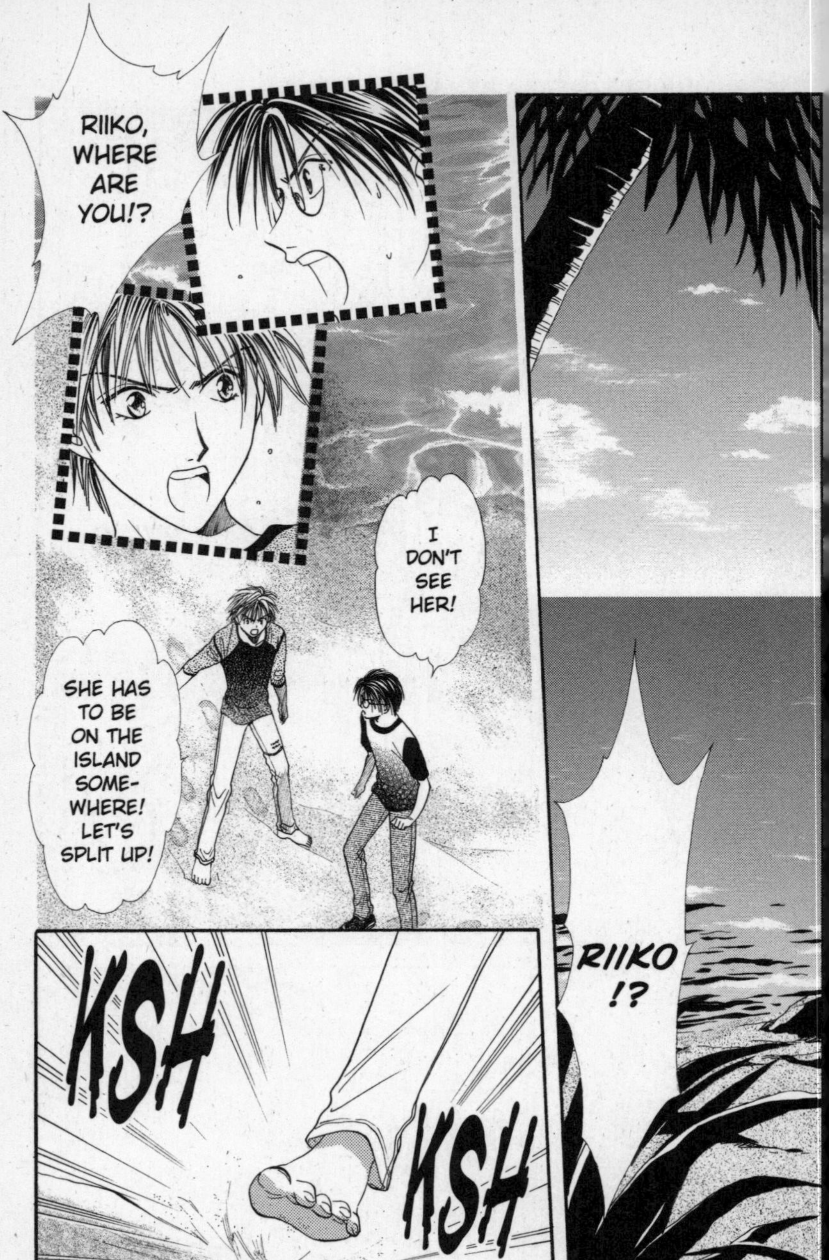
RIIKO !?
RIIKO, WHERE ARE YOU!?
I DON'T SEE HER!
SHE HAS TO BE ON THE ISLAND SOME-WHERE! LET'S SPLIT UP!
KSH
KSH

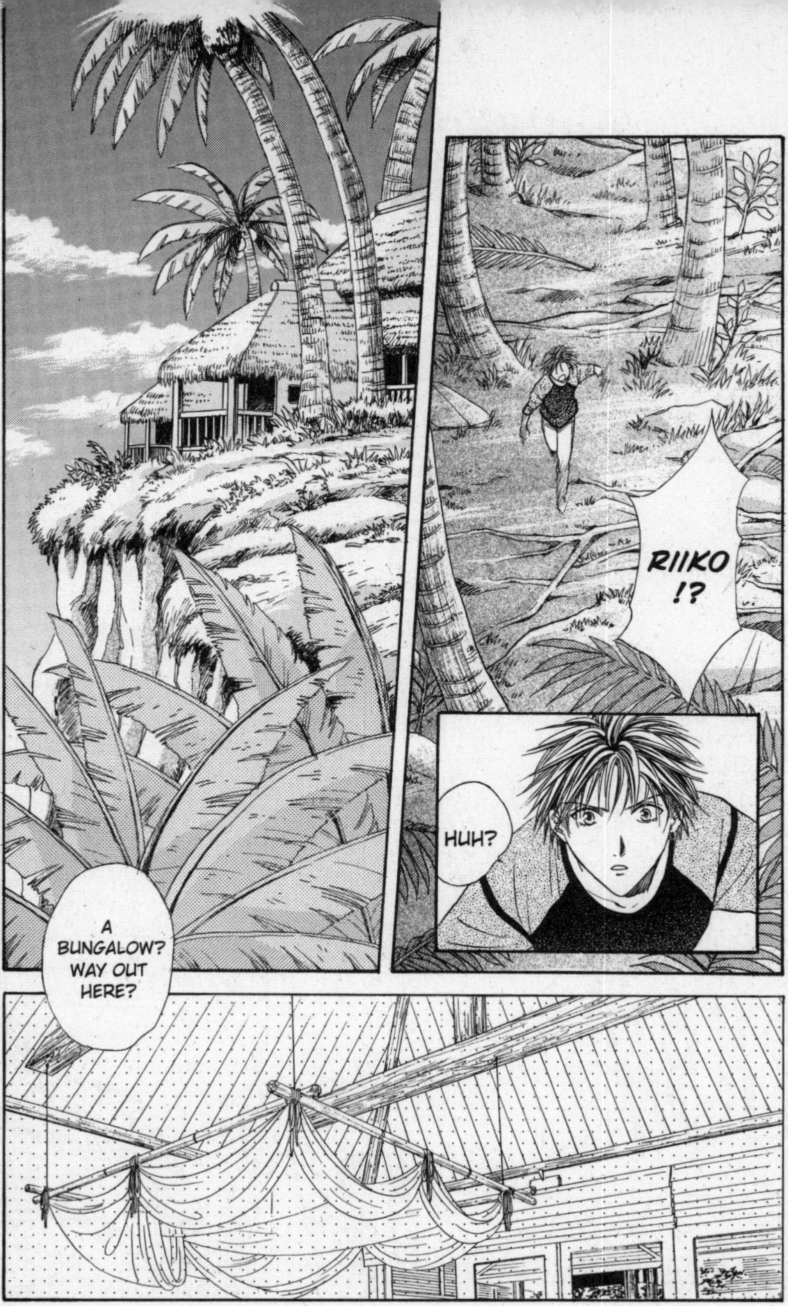
RIIKO !?
HUH?
A BUNGALOW? WAY OUT HERE?

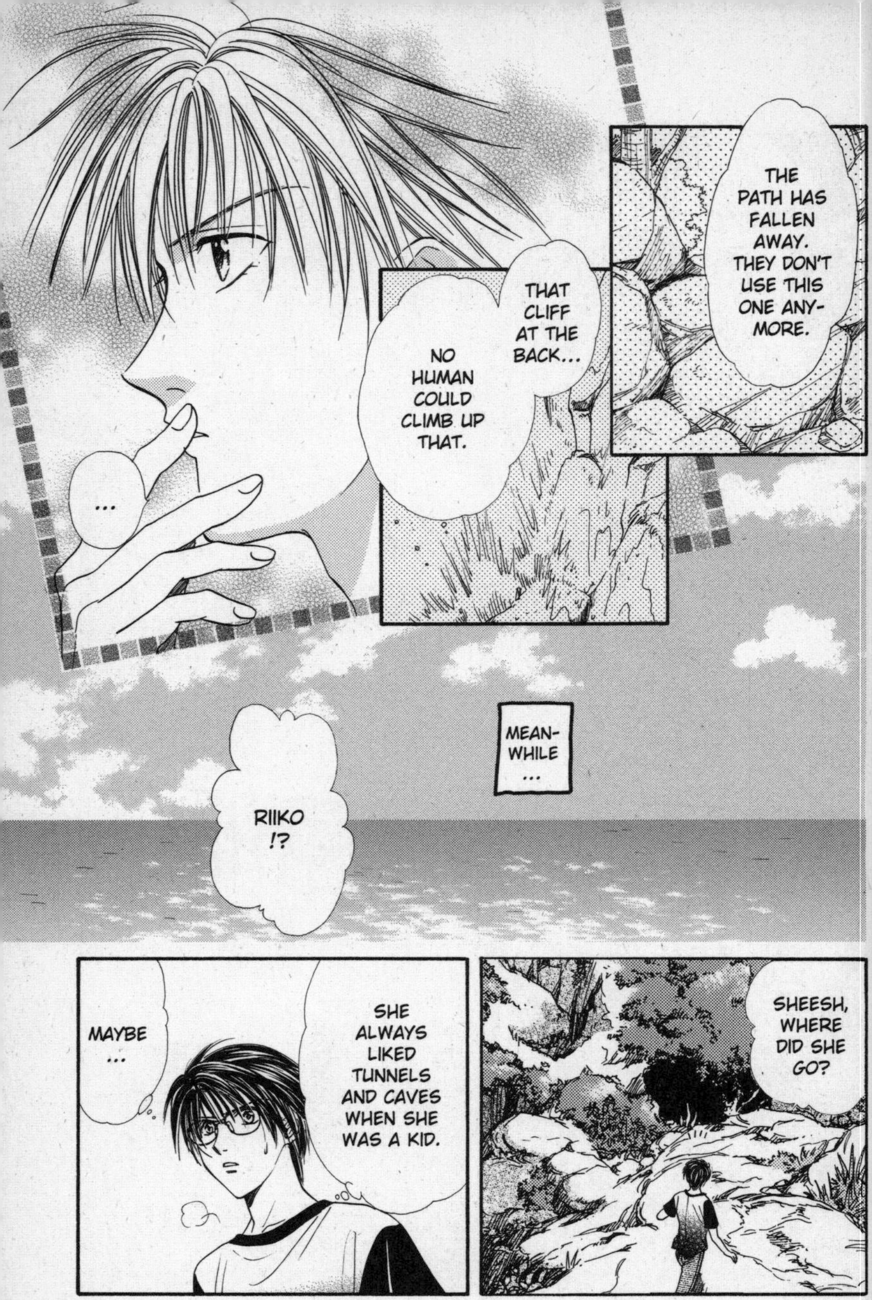
THE PATH HAS FALLEN AWAY. THEY DON'T USE THIS ONE ANY-MORE.
THAT CLIFF AT THE BACK...
NO HUMAN COULD CLIMB UP THAT.
...
MEAN-WHILE ...
RIIKO !?
SHEESH, WHERE DID SHE GO?
SHE ALWAYS LIKED TUNNELS AND CAVES WHEN SHE WAS A KID.
MAYBE ...

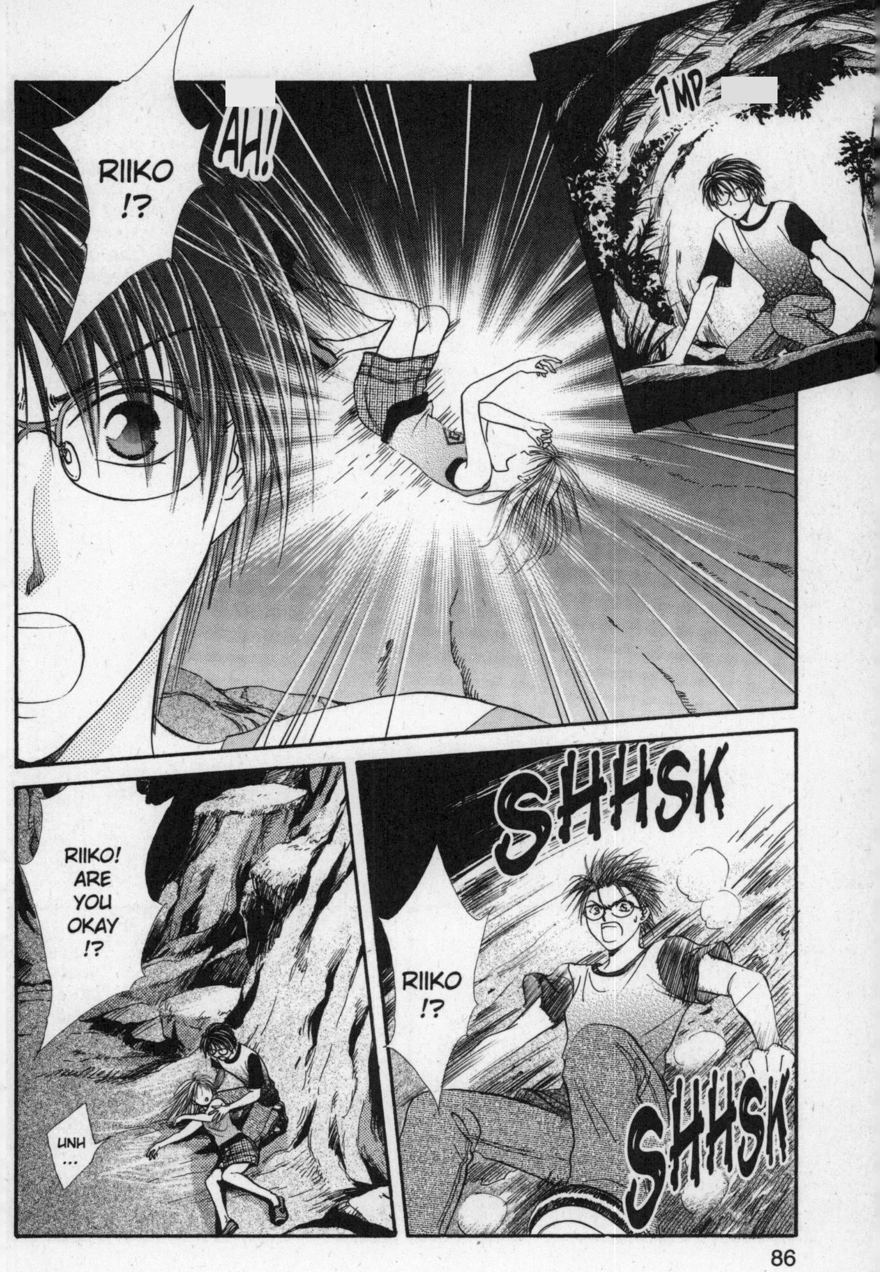
TMP
AH!
RIIKO !?
SHHSK
RIIKO !?
SHHSK
RIIKO! ARE YOU OKAY !?
UNH ...

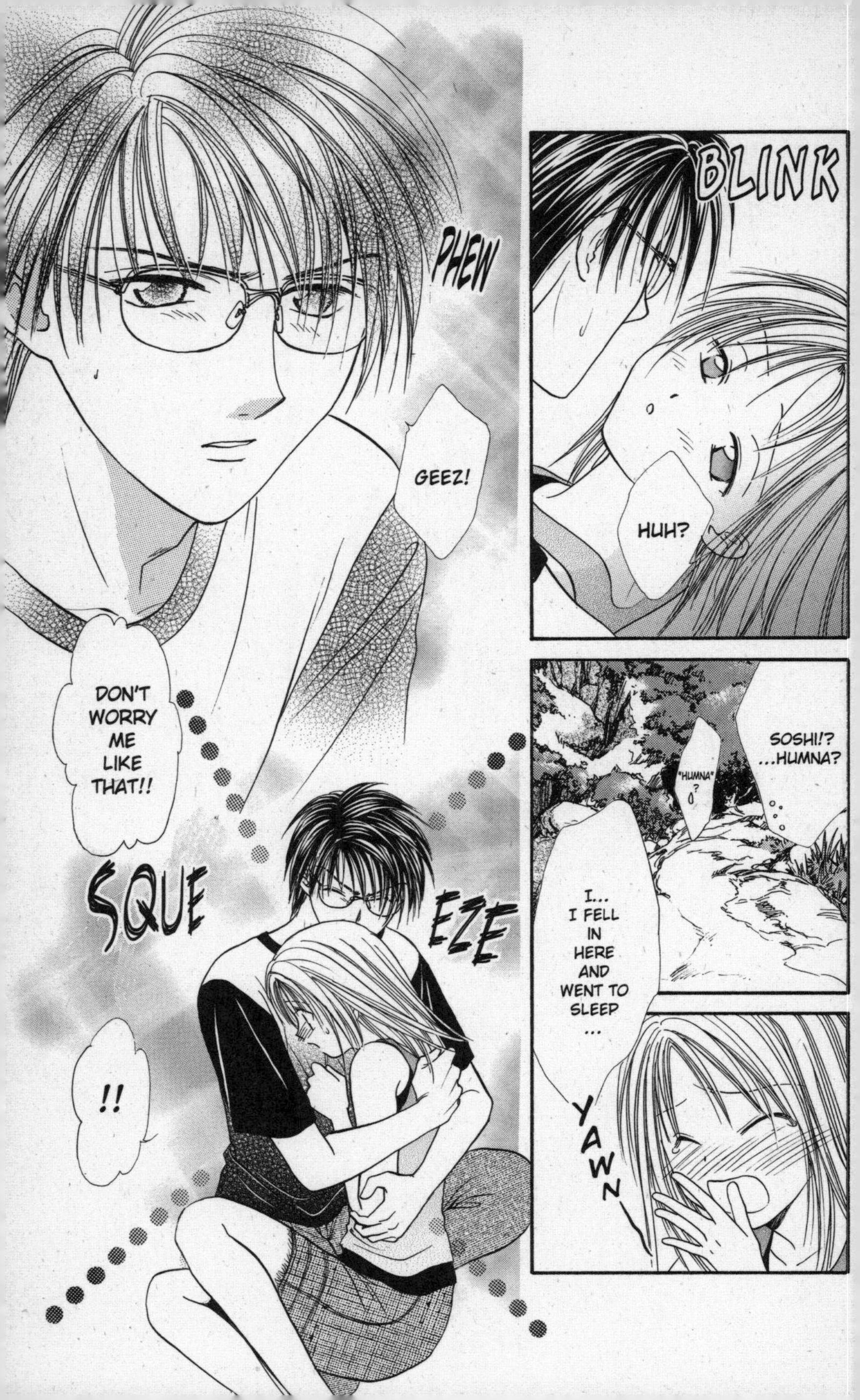
BLINK
HUH?
SOSHI!? ...HUMNA?
"HUMNA"?
I... I FELL IN HERE AND WENT TO SLEEP...
YAWN
PHEW
GEEZ!
DON'T WORRY ME LIKE THAT!!
SQUEEZE
!!

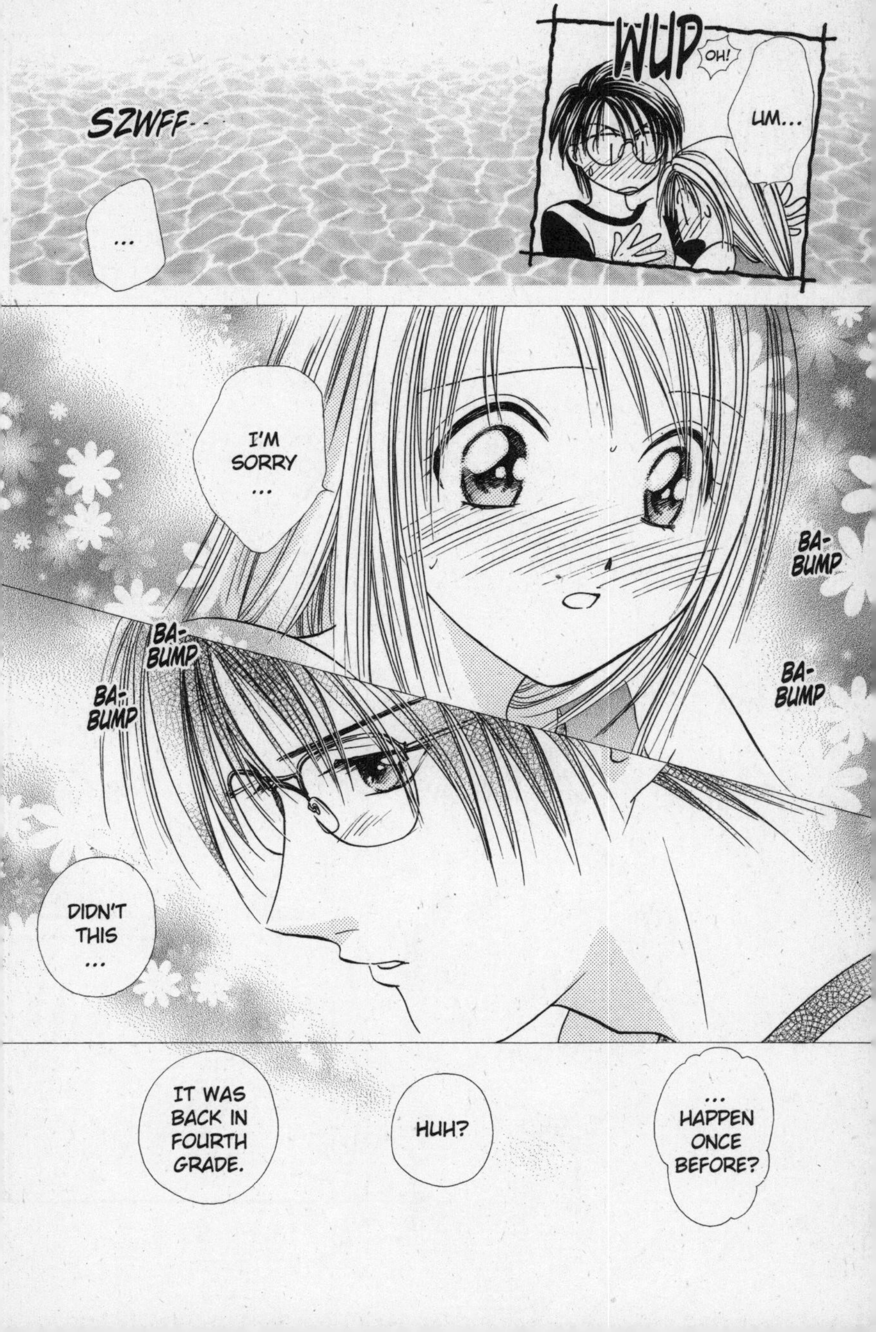
WUP
OH!
UM...
SZWFF...
...
I'M SORRY...
BA-BUMP
BA-BUMP
BA-BUMP
BA-BUMP
DIDN'T THIS...
...HAPPEN ONCE BEFORE?
HUH?
IT WAS BACK IN FOURTH GRADE.

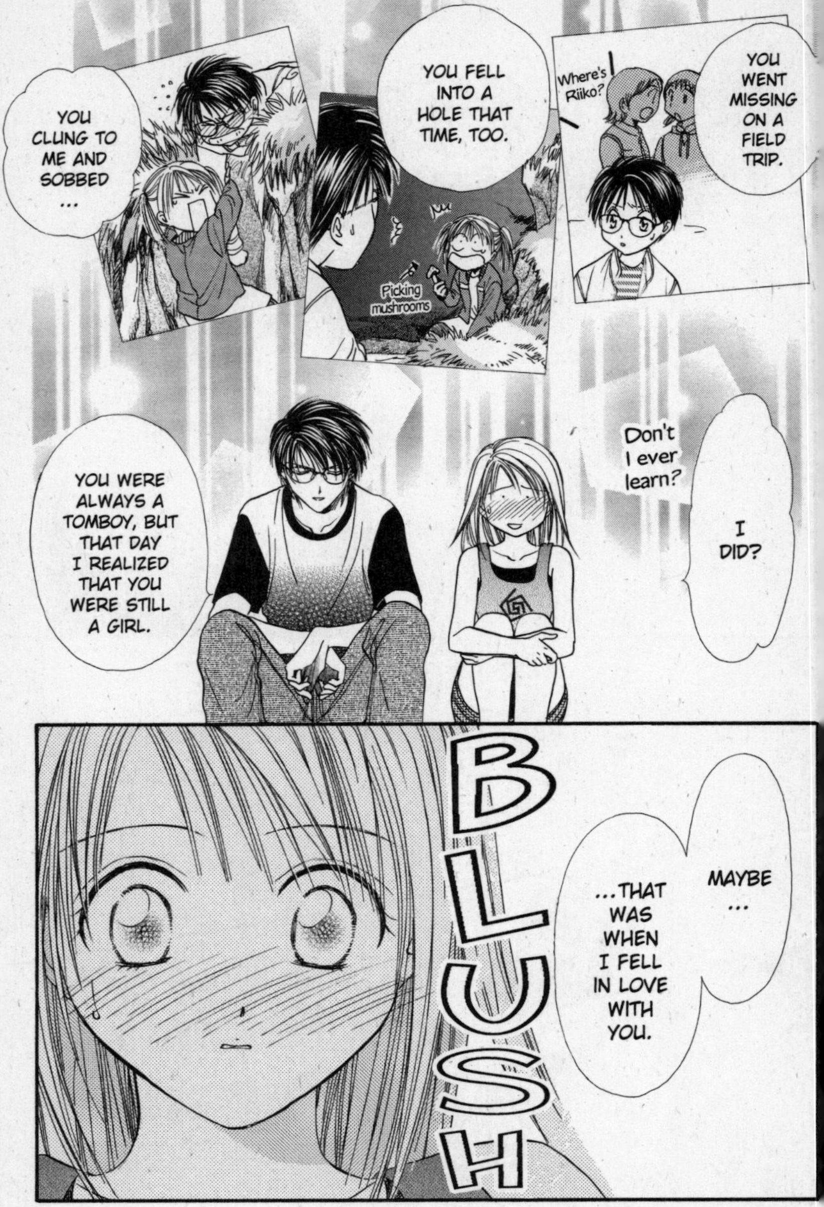
YOU WENT MISSING ON A FIELD TRIP.
Where's Riiko?
YOU FELL INTO A HOLE THAT TIME, TOO.
Picking mushrooms
YOU CLUNG TO ME AND SOBBED ...
I DID?
Don't I ever learn?
YOU WERE ALWAYS A TOMBOY, BUT THAT DAY I REALIZED THAT YOU WERE STILL A GIRL.
MAYBE ...
...THAT WAS WHEN I FELL IN LOVE WITH YOU.
BLUSH

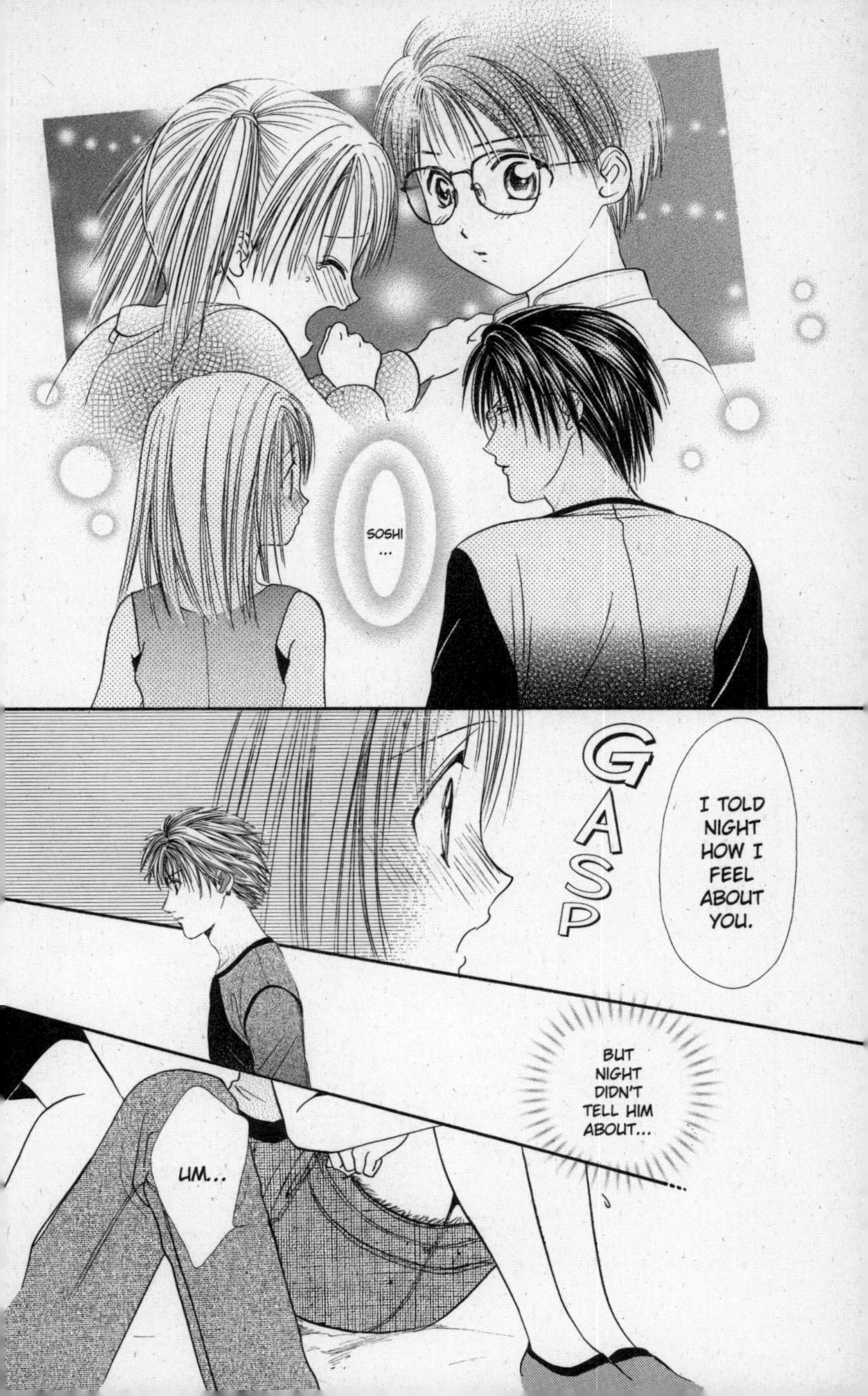
SOSHI ...
GASP
I TOLD NIGHT HOW I FEEL ABOUT YOU.
BUT NIGHT DIDN'T TELL HIM ABOUT...
UM...

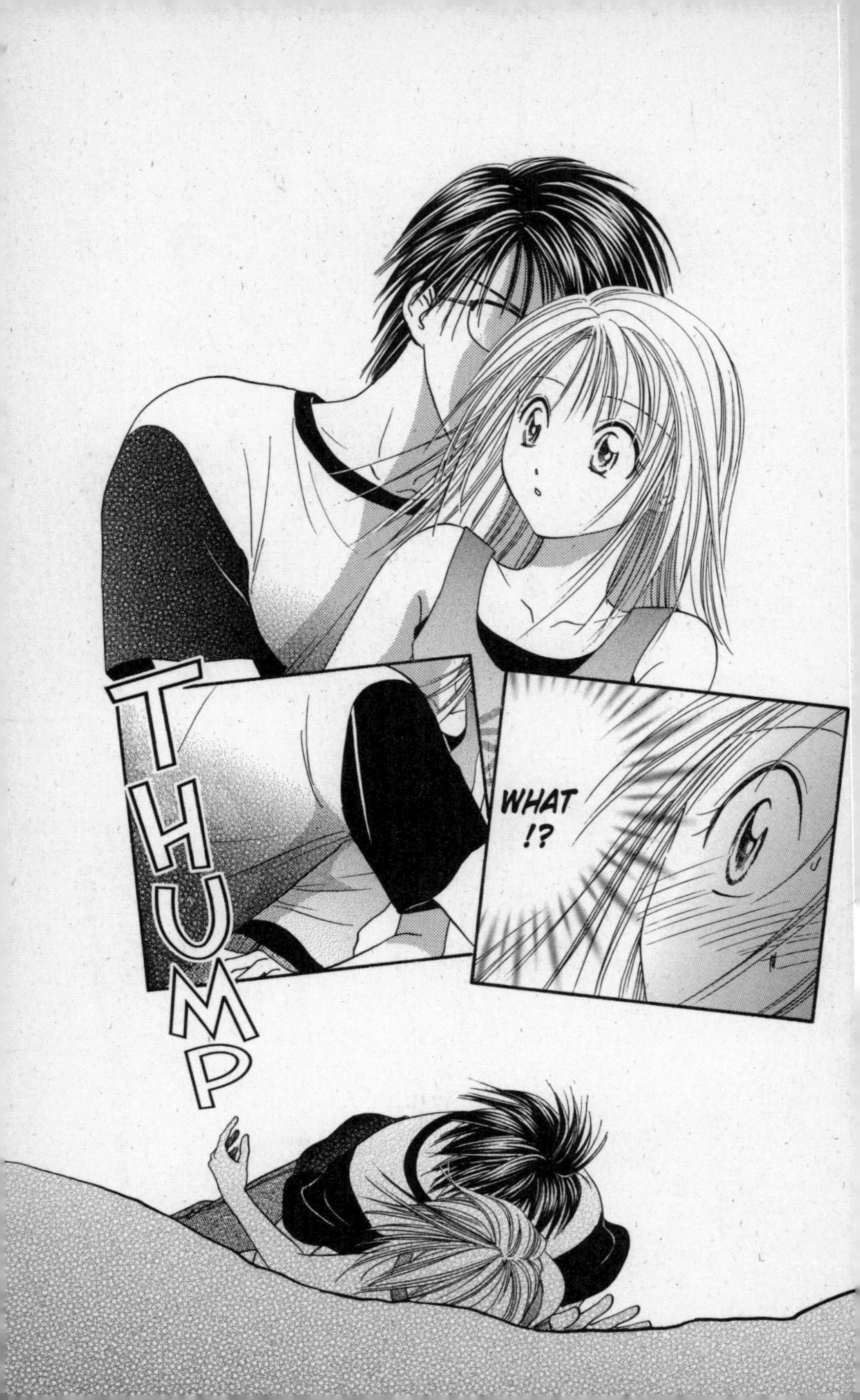
WHAT !?
THUMP

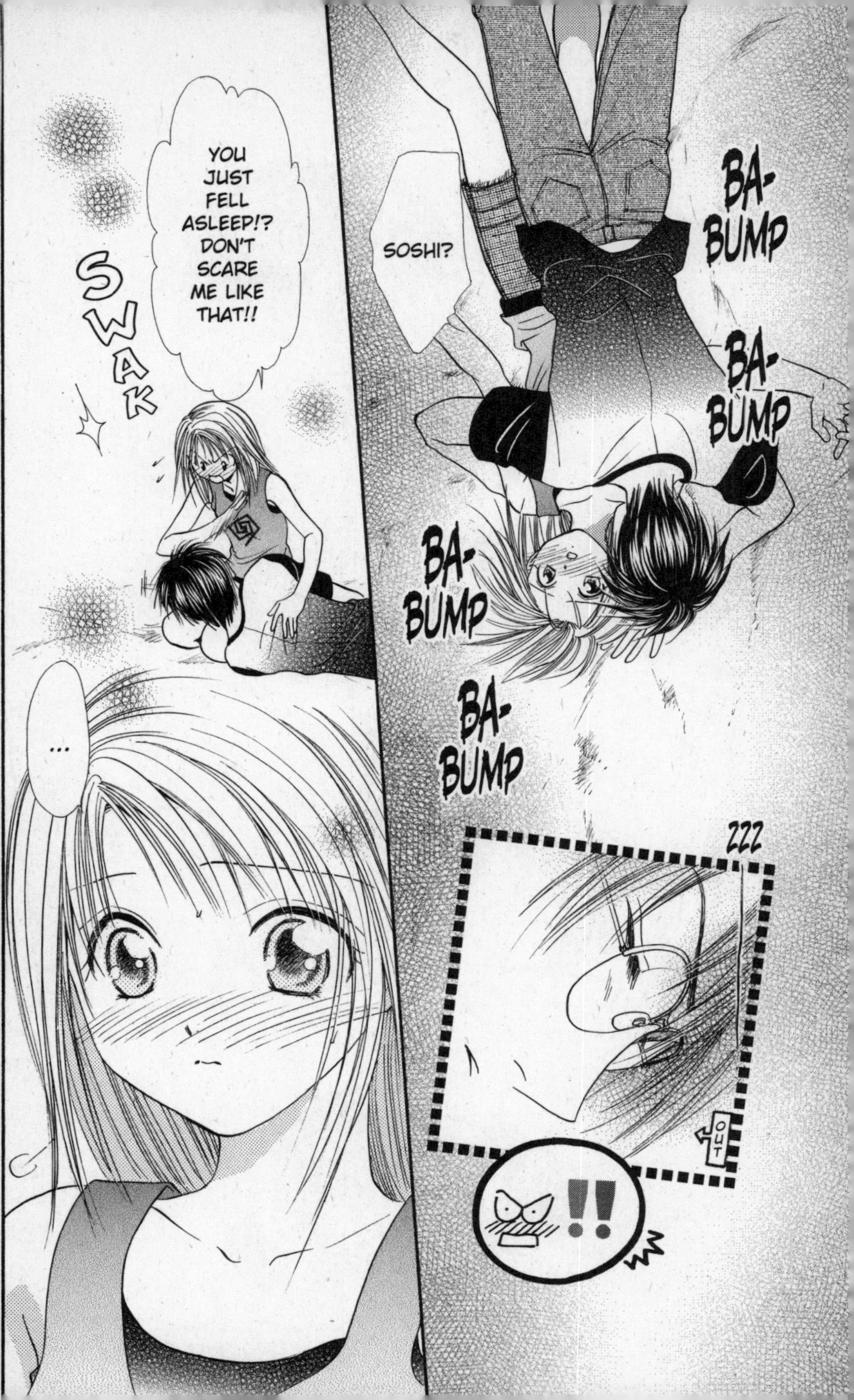
SOSHI?
BA-BUMP
BA-BUMP
BA-BUMP
BA-BUMP
222
OUT
!!
YOU JUST FELL ASLEEP!? DON'T SCARE ME LIKE THAT!!
SWAK
...

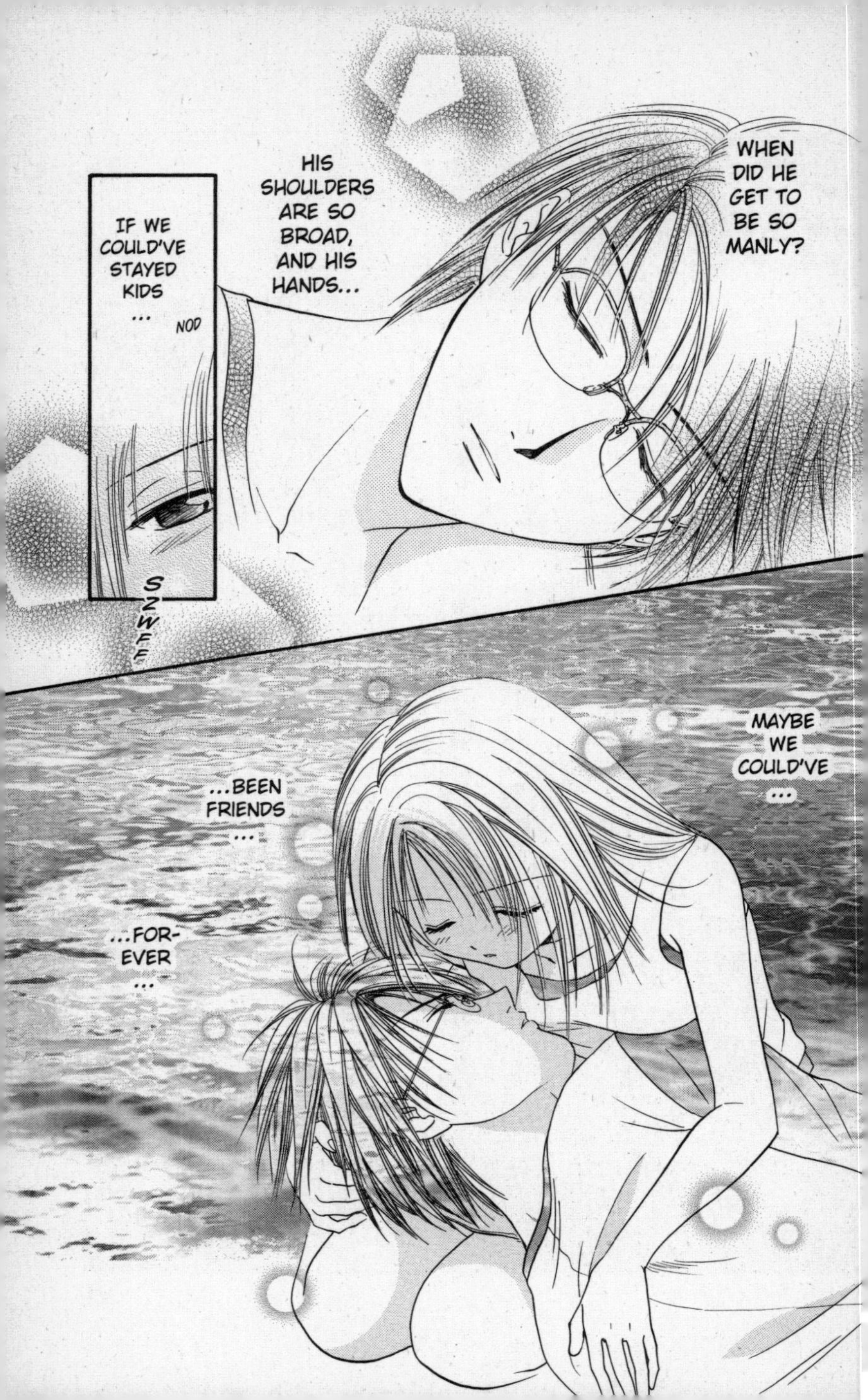
WHEN DID HE GET TO BE SO MANLY?
HIS SHOULDERS ARE SO BROAD, AND HIS HANDS...
IF WE COULD'VE STAYED KIDS ...
NOD
SZWFF
MAYBE WE COULD'VE ...
...BEEN FRIENDS ...
...FOR-EVER ...

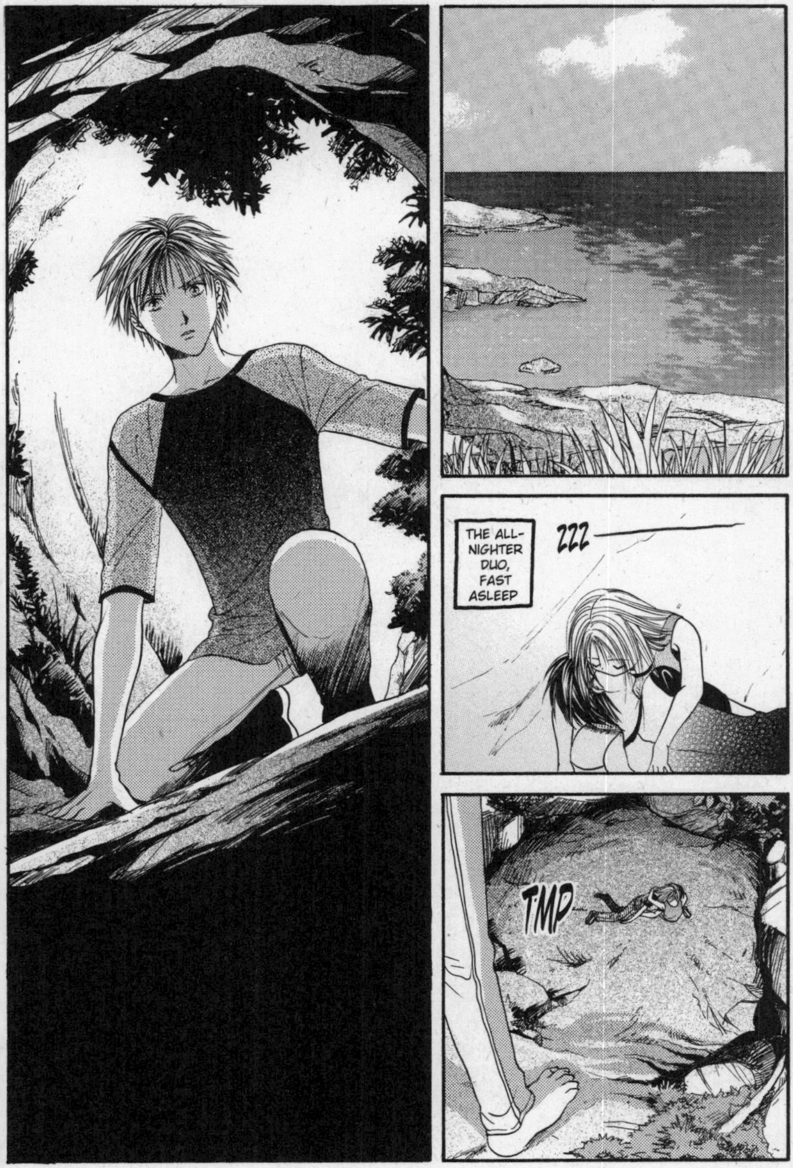
THE ALL-NIGHTER DUO, FAST ASLEEP
ZZZ
TMP

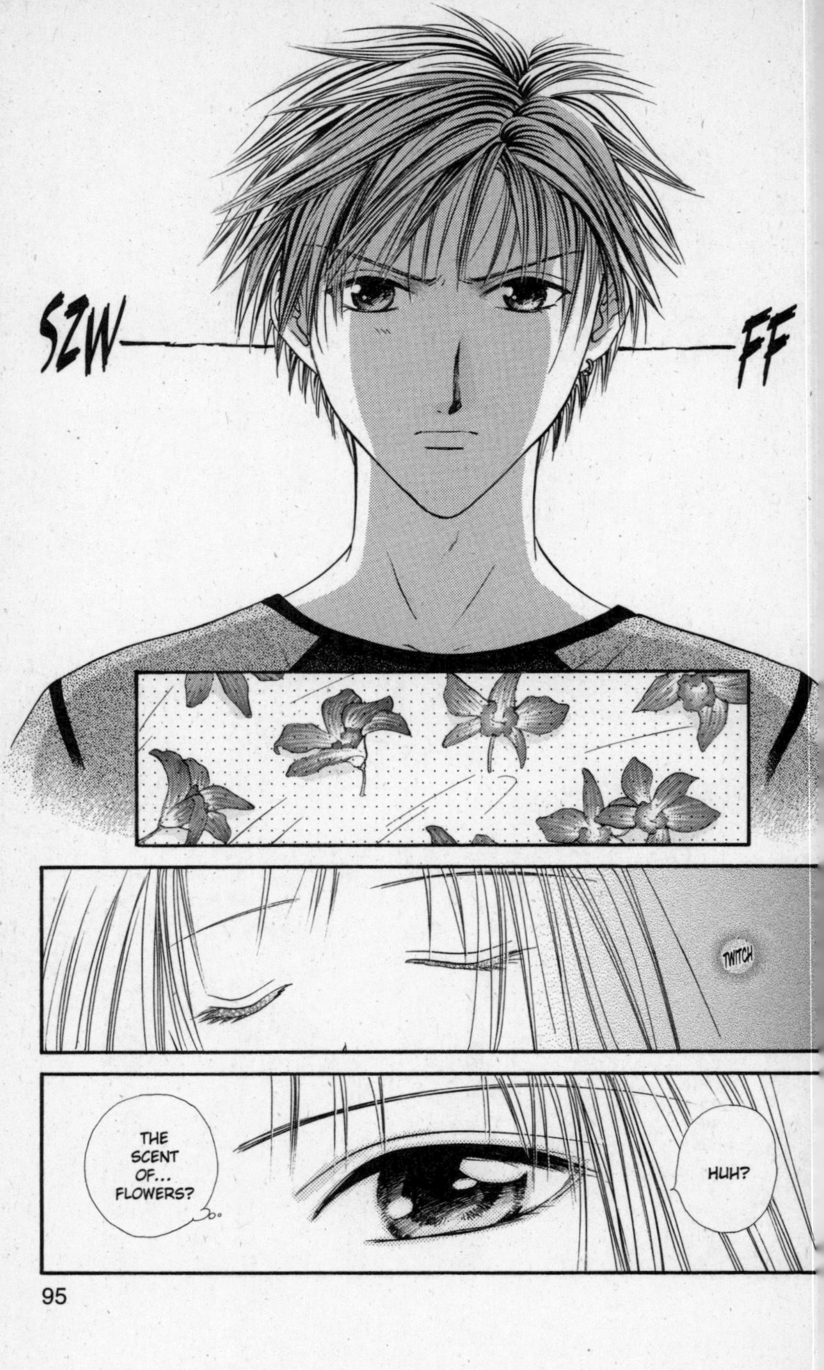
SZW——FF
TWITCH
HUH?
THE SCENT OF... FLOWERS?

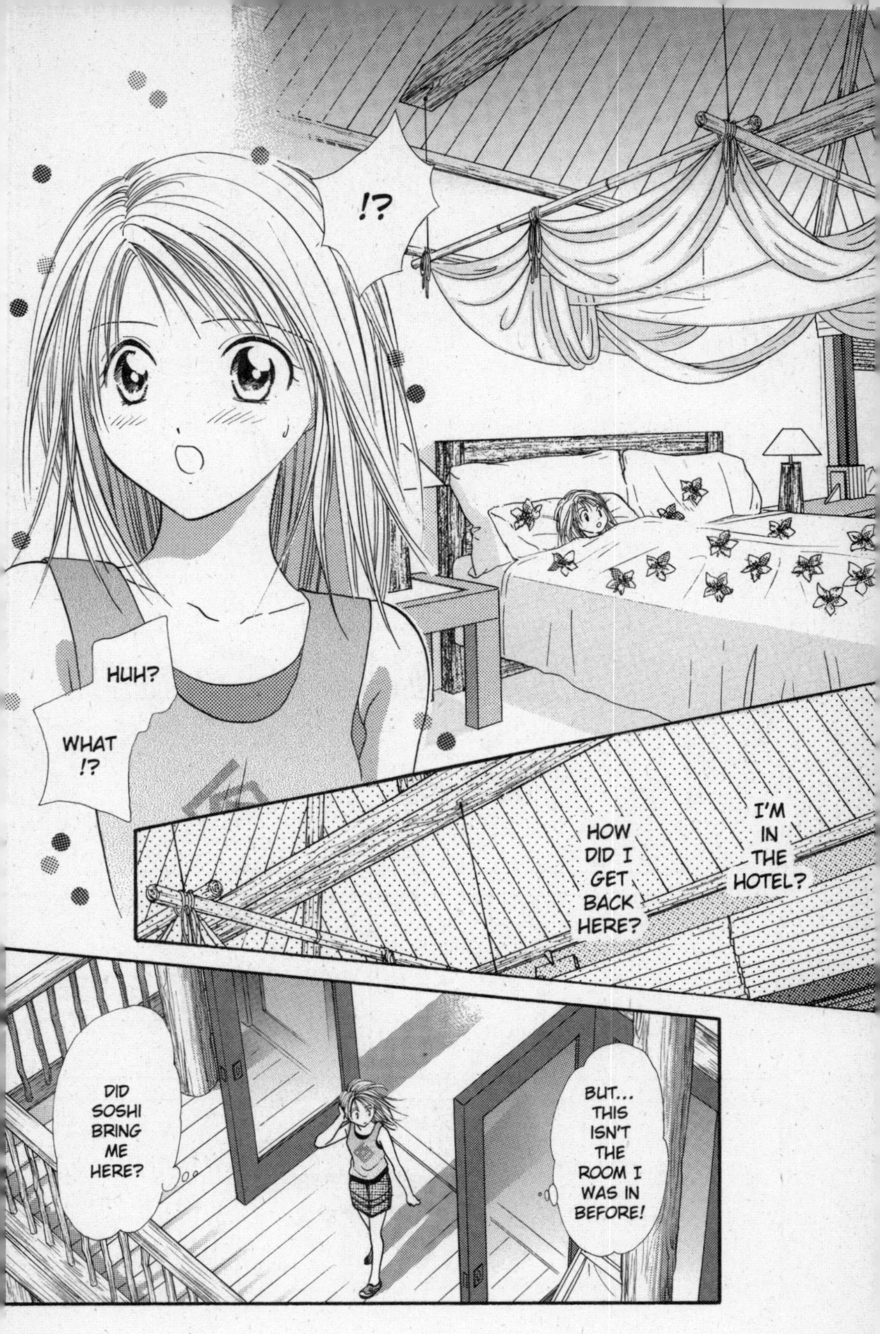
!?
HUH?
WHAT !?
I'M IN THE HOTEL?
HOW DID I GET BACK HERE?
BUT... THIS ISN'T THE ROOM I WAS IN BEFORE!
DID SOSHI BRING ME HERE?

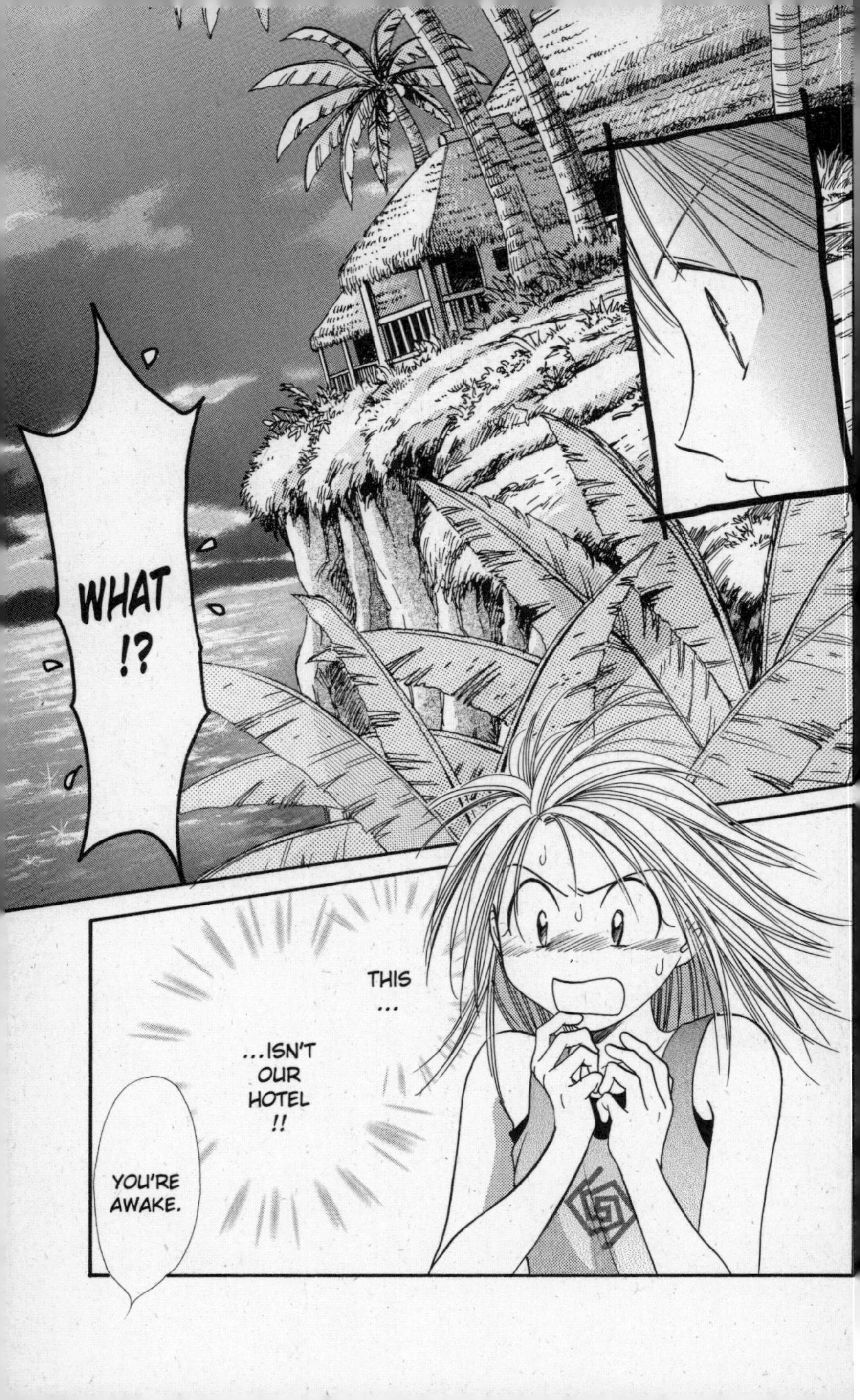
WHAT !?
THIS ...
...ISN'T OUR HOTEL !!
YOU'RE AWAKE.

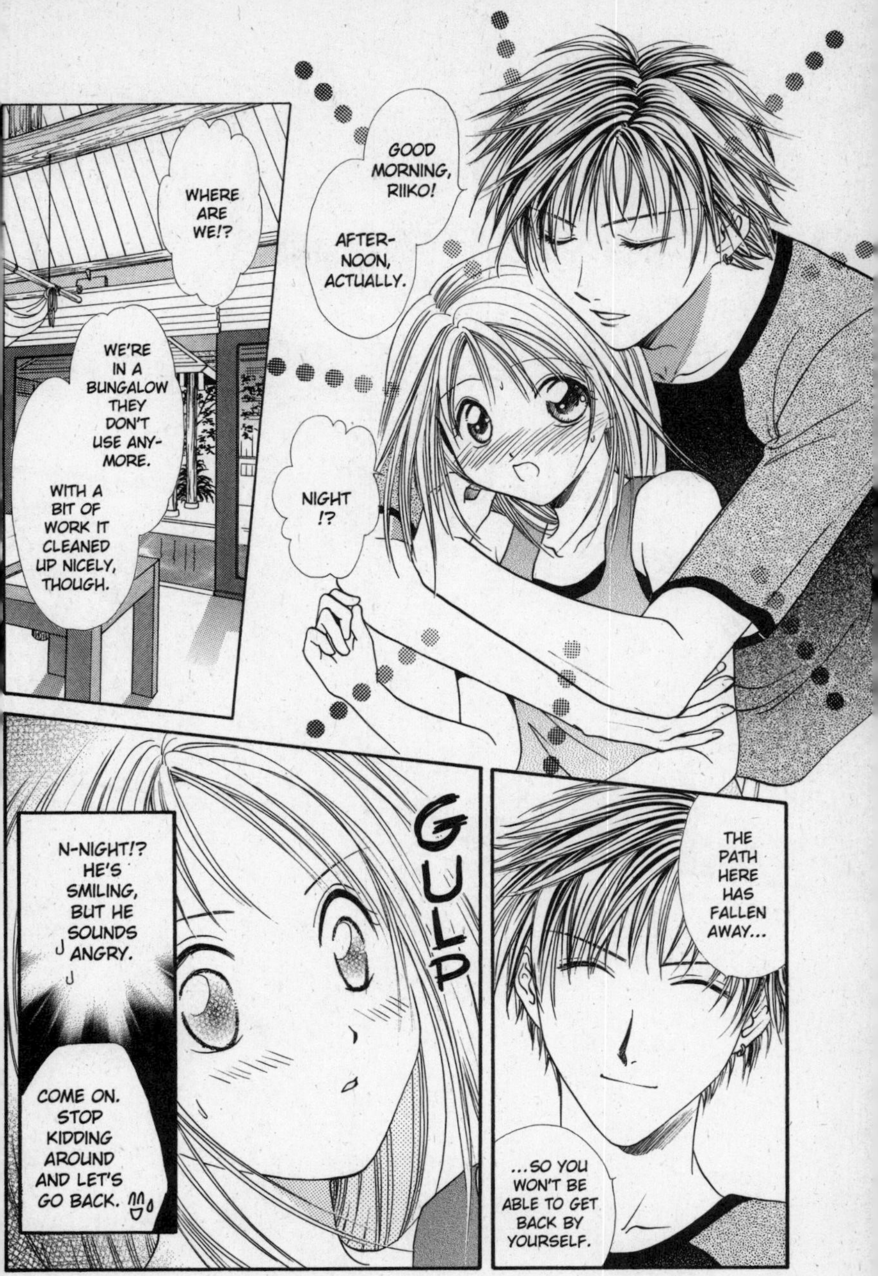
GOOD MORNING, RIIKO!
AFTER-NOON, ACTUALLY.
NIGHT !?
WHERE ARE WE!?
WE'RE IN A BUNGALOW THEY DON'T USE ANY-MORE.
WITH A BIT OF WORK IT CLEANED UP NICELY, THOUGH.
THE PATH HERE HAS FALLEN AWAY...
...SO YOU WON'T BE ABLE TO GET BACK BY YOURSELF.
GULP
N-NIGHT!? HE'S SMILING, BUT HE SOUNDS ANGRY.
COME ON. STOP KIDDING AROUND AND LET'S GO BACK.

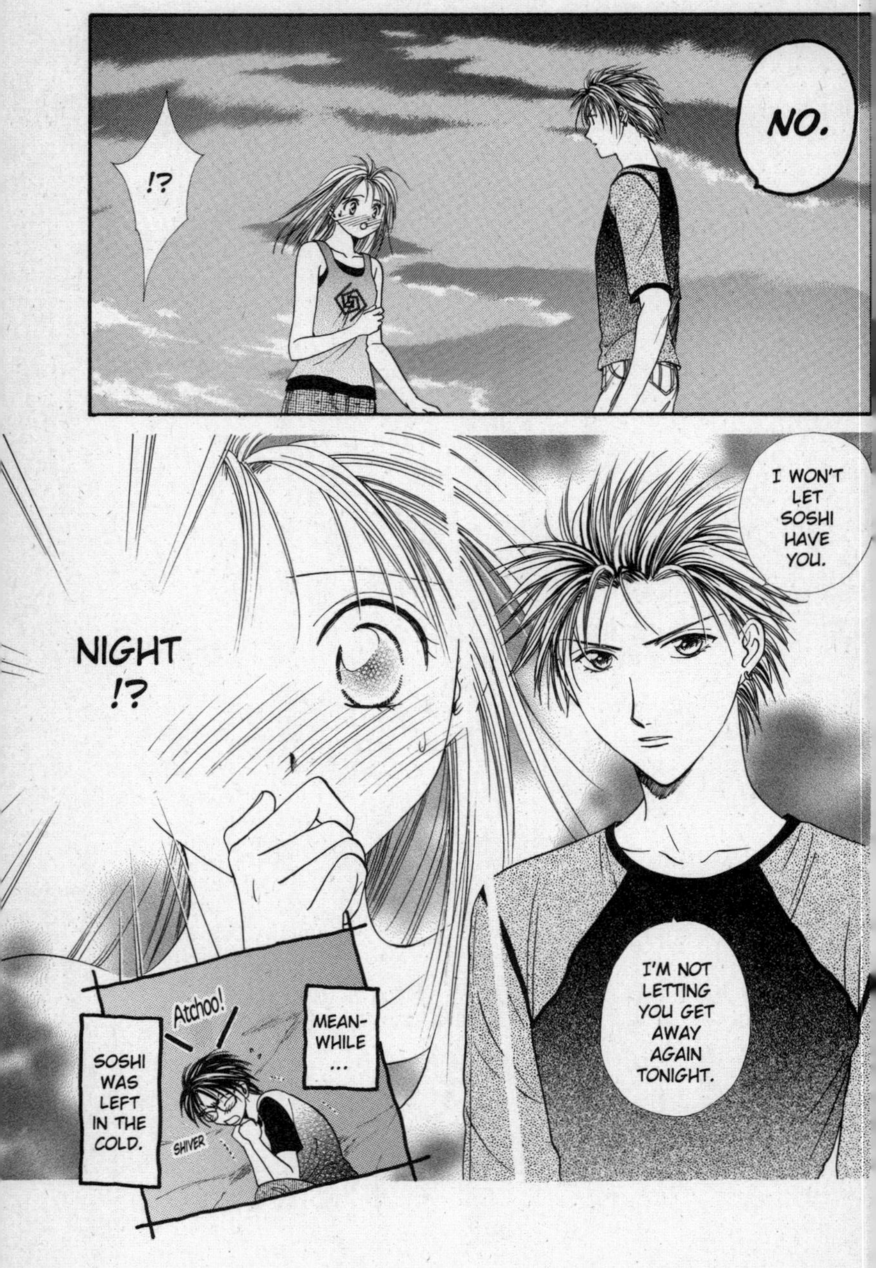
NO.
!?
I WON'T LET SOSHI HAVE YOU.
NIGHT !?
I'M NOT LETTING YOU GET AWAY AGAIN TONIGHT.
MEAN-WHILE ...
Atchoo!
SOSHI WAS LEFT IN THE COLD.
SHIVER

Absolute Boyfriend

Act 16: Stay with M

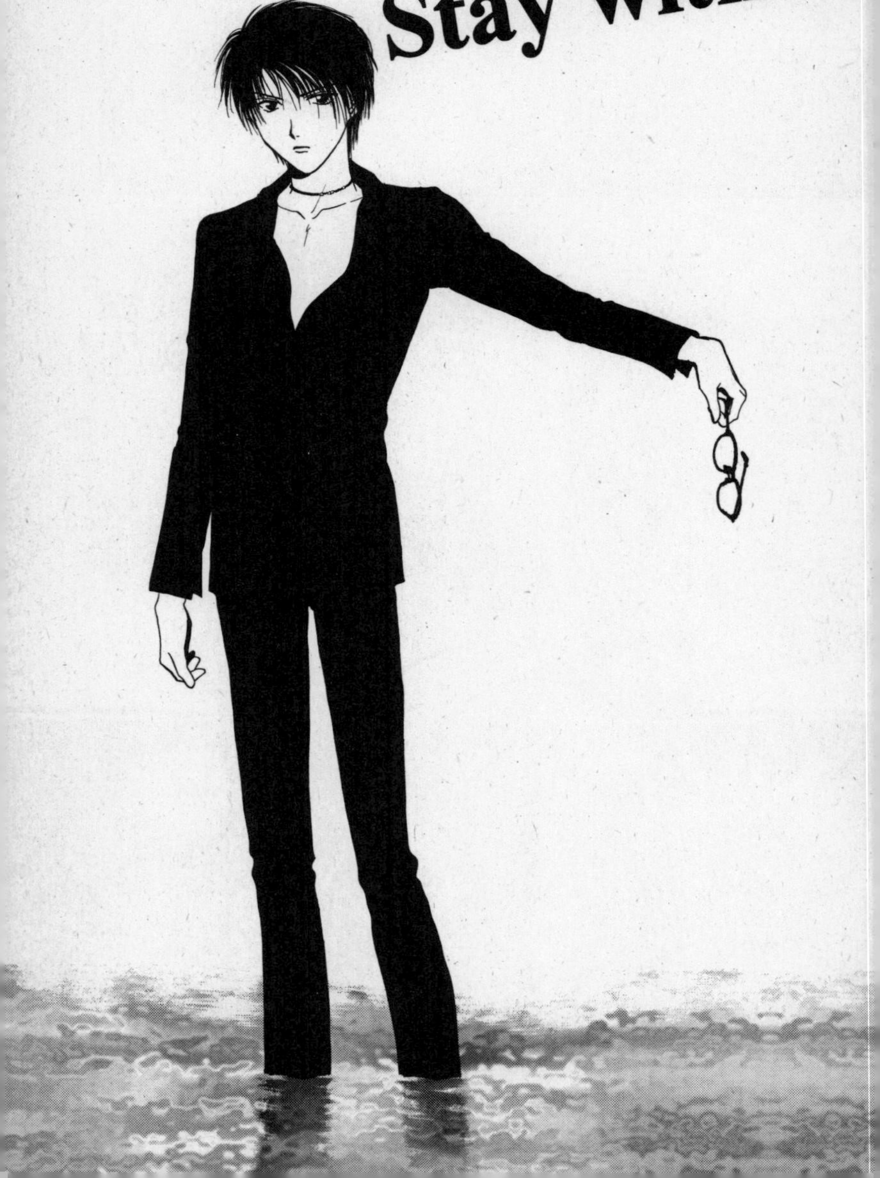

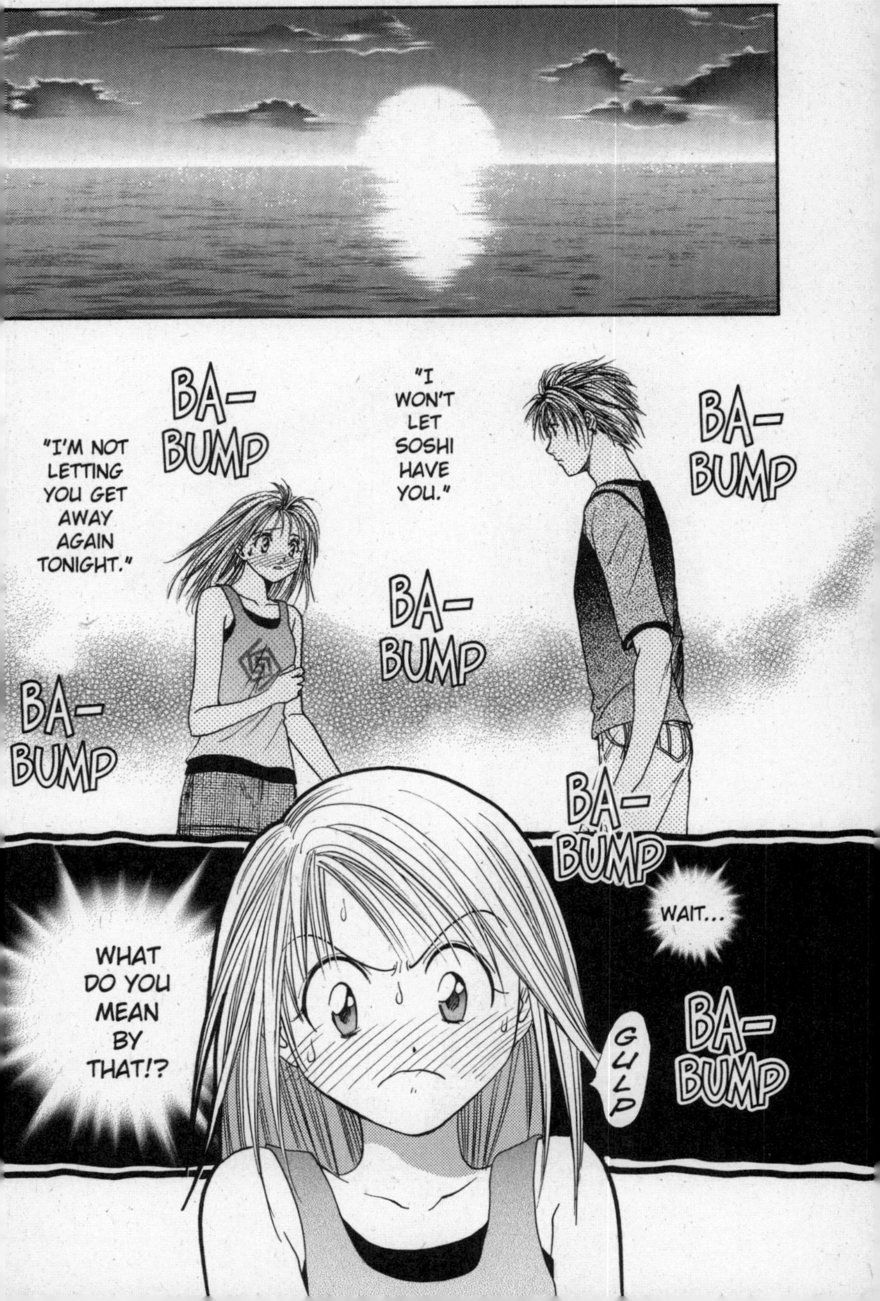
BA-BUMP
"I WON'T LET SOSHI HAVE YOU."
BA-BUMP
"I'M NOT LETTING YOU GET AWAY AGAIN TONIGHT."
BA-BUMP
BA-BUMP
BA-BUMP
WAIT...
BA-BUMP
GULP
WHAT DO YOU MEAN BY THAT!?

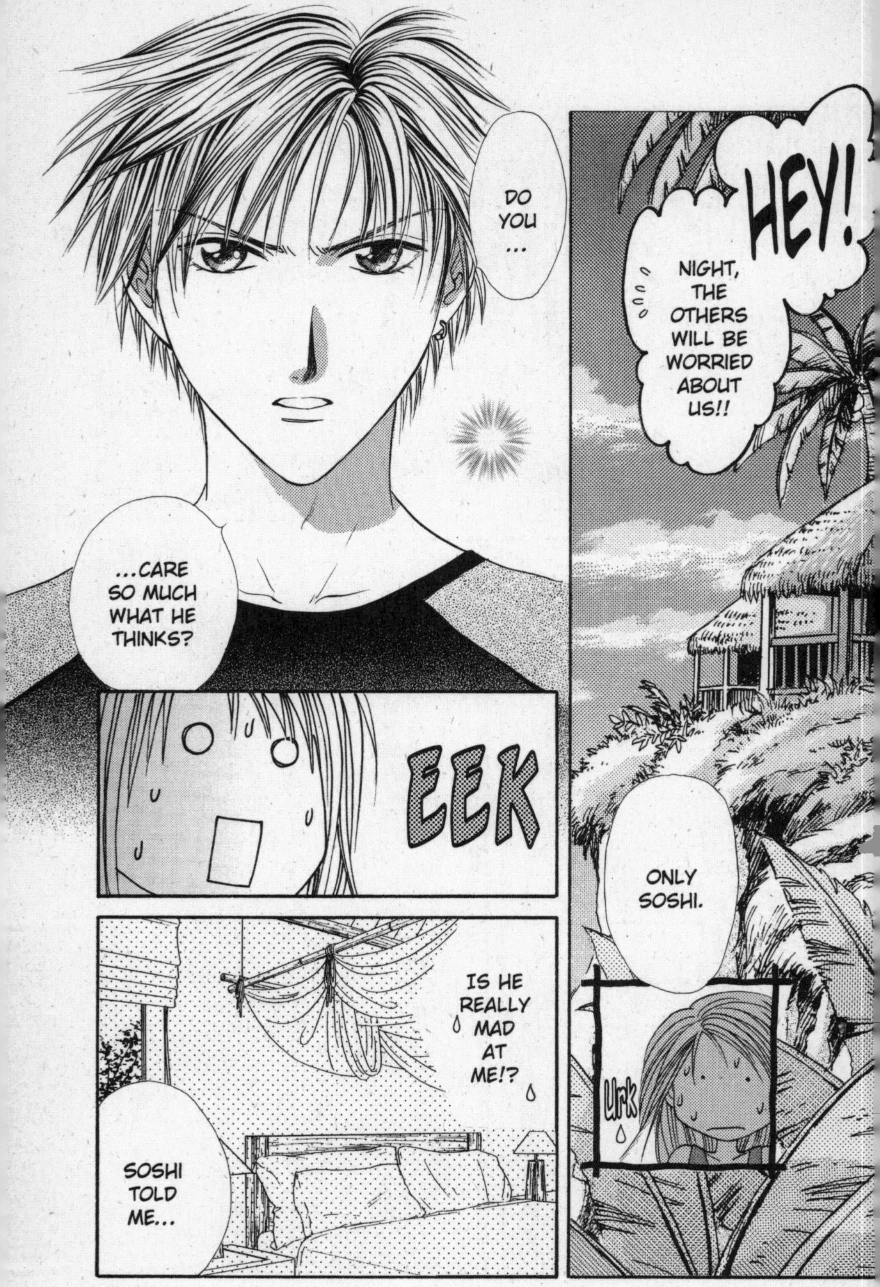
HEY!
NIGHT, THE OTHERS WILL BE WORRIED ABOUT US!!
ONLY SOSHI.
Urk
DO YOU ...
...CARE SO MUCH WHAT HE THINKS?
EEK
IS HE REALLY MAD AT ME!?
SOSHI TOLD ME...

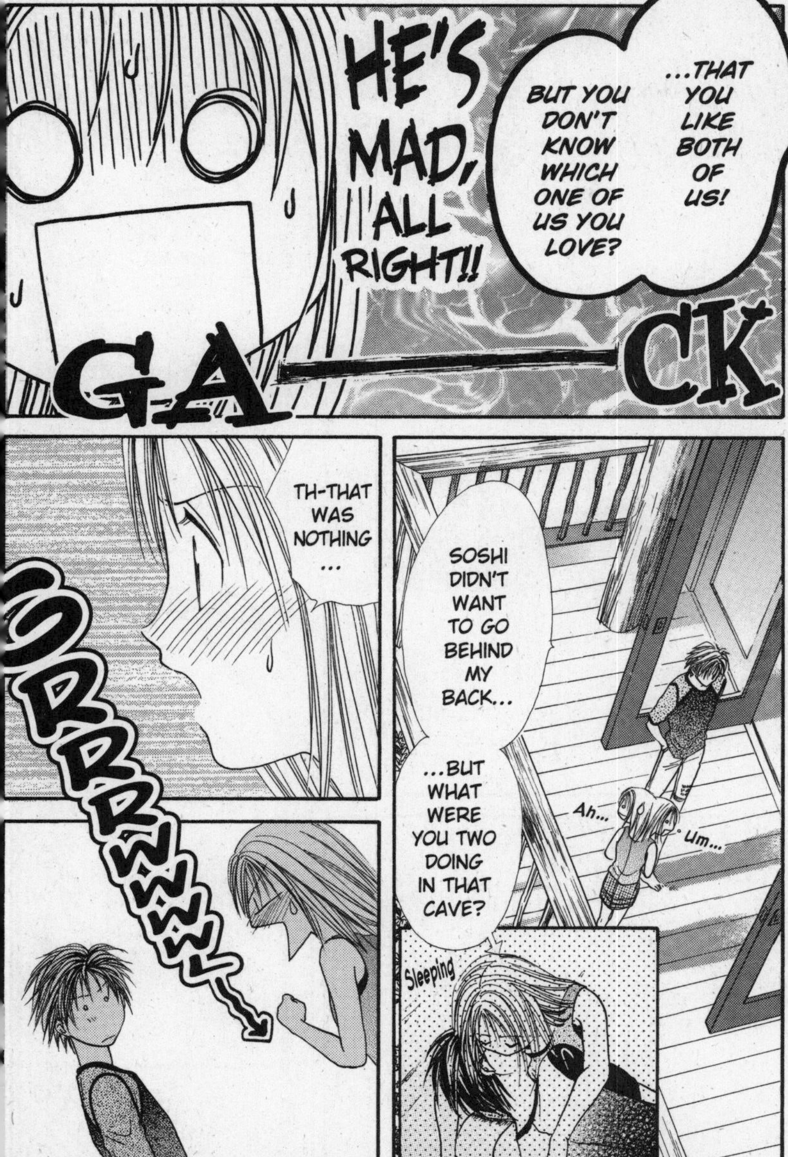

...THAT YOU LIKE BOTH OF US!
BUT YOU DON'T KNOW WHICH ONE OF US YOU LOVE?
HE'S MAD, ALL RIGHT!!
GA—CK
SOSHI DIDN'T WANT TO GO BEHIND MY BACK...
...BUT WHAT WERE YOU TWO DOING IN THAT CAVE?
Um...
Ah...
Sleeping
TH-THAT WAS NOTHING ...

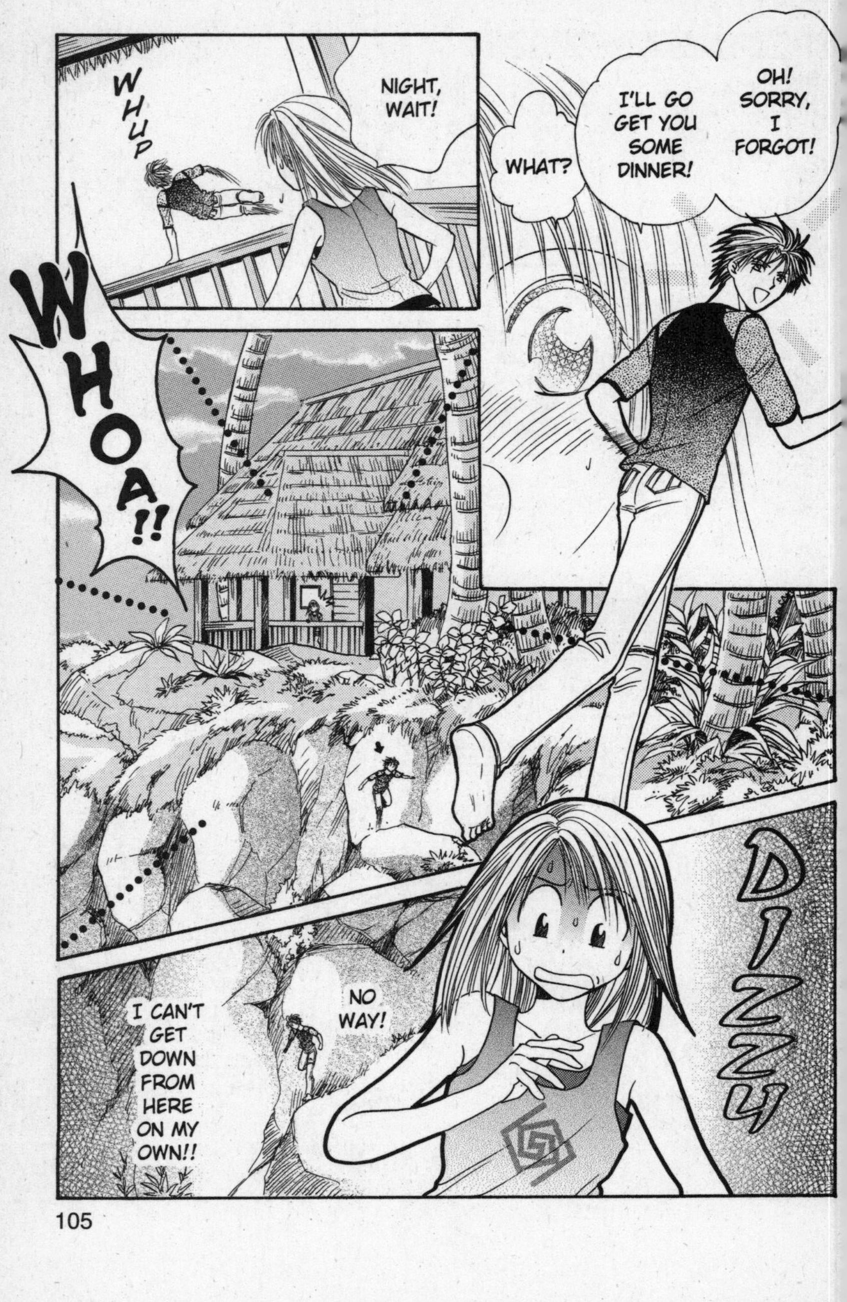
OH! SORRY, I FORGOT!
I'LL GO GET YOU SOME DINNER!
WHAT?
NIGHT, WAIT!
WHUP
WHOA!!
DIZZY
NO WAY!
I CAN'T GET DOWN FROM HERE ON MY OWN!!

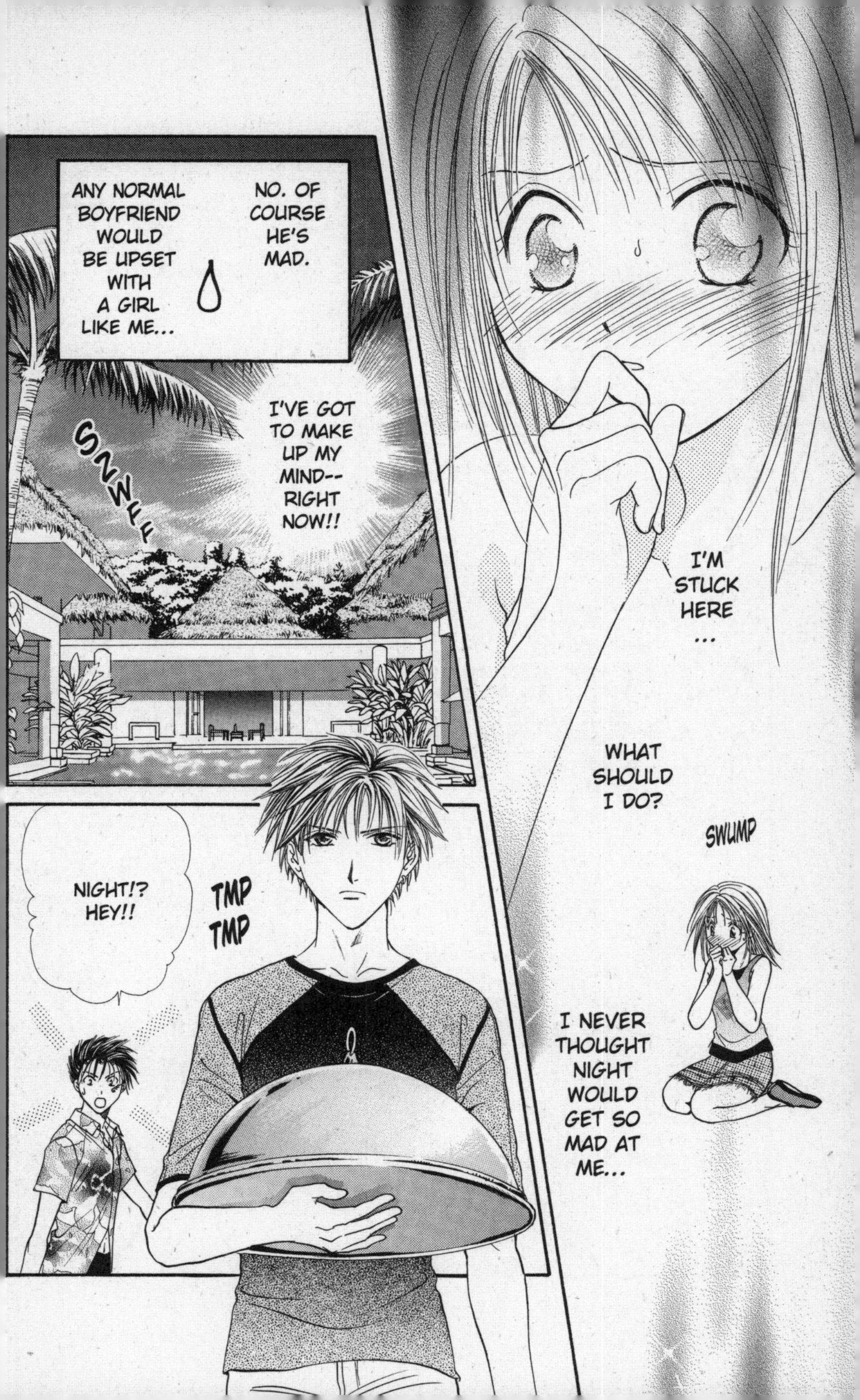

I'M STUCK HERE...
WHAT SHOULD I DO?
SWUMP
I NEVER THOUGHT NIGHT WOULD GET SO MAD AT ME...
NO. OF COURSE HE'S MAD.
ANY NORMAL BOYFRIEND WOULD BE UPSET WITH A GIRL LIKE ME...
I'VE GOT TO MAKE UP MY MIND--RIGHT NOW!!
SNWFF
TMP TMP
NIGHT!? HEY!!

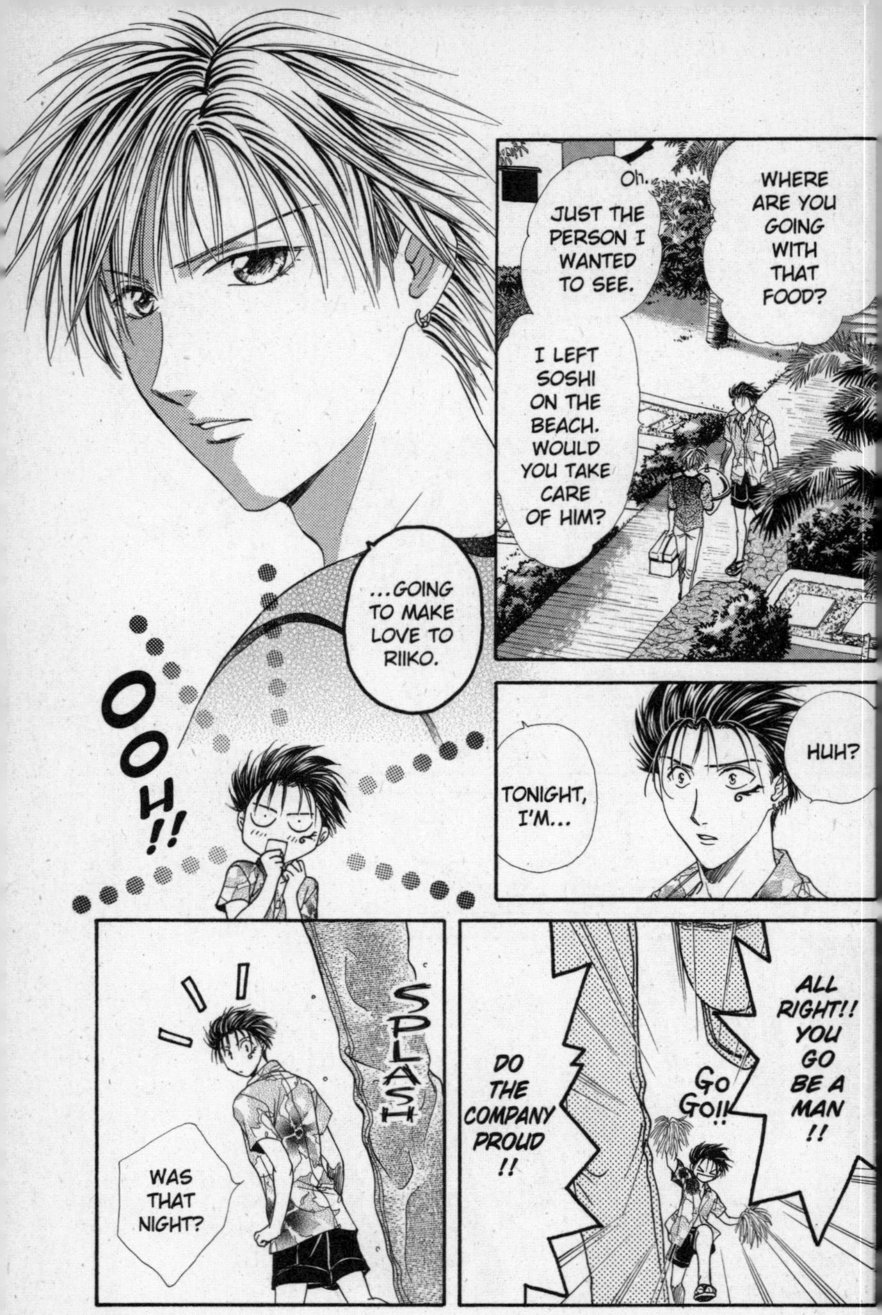
WHERE ARE YOU GOING WITH THAT FOOD?
Oh. JUST THE PERSON I WANTED TO SEE.
I LEFT SOSHI ON THE BEACH. WOULD YOU TAKE CARE OF HIM?
HUH?
TONIGHT, I'M...
...GOING TO MAKE LOVE TO RIIKO.
OOOH!!
ALL RIGHT!! YOU GO BE A MAN!!
GO GO!!
DO THE COMPANY PROUD!!
SPLASH
WAS THAT NIGHT?

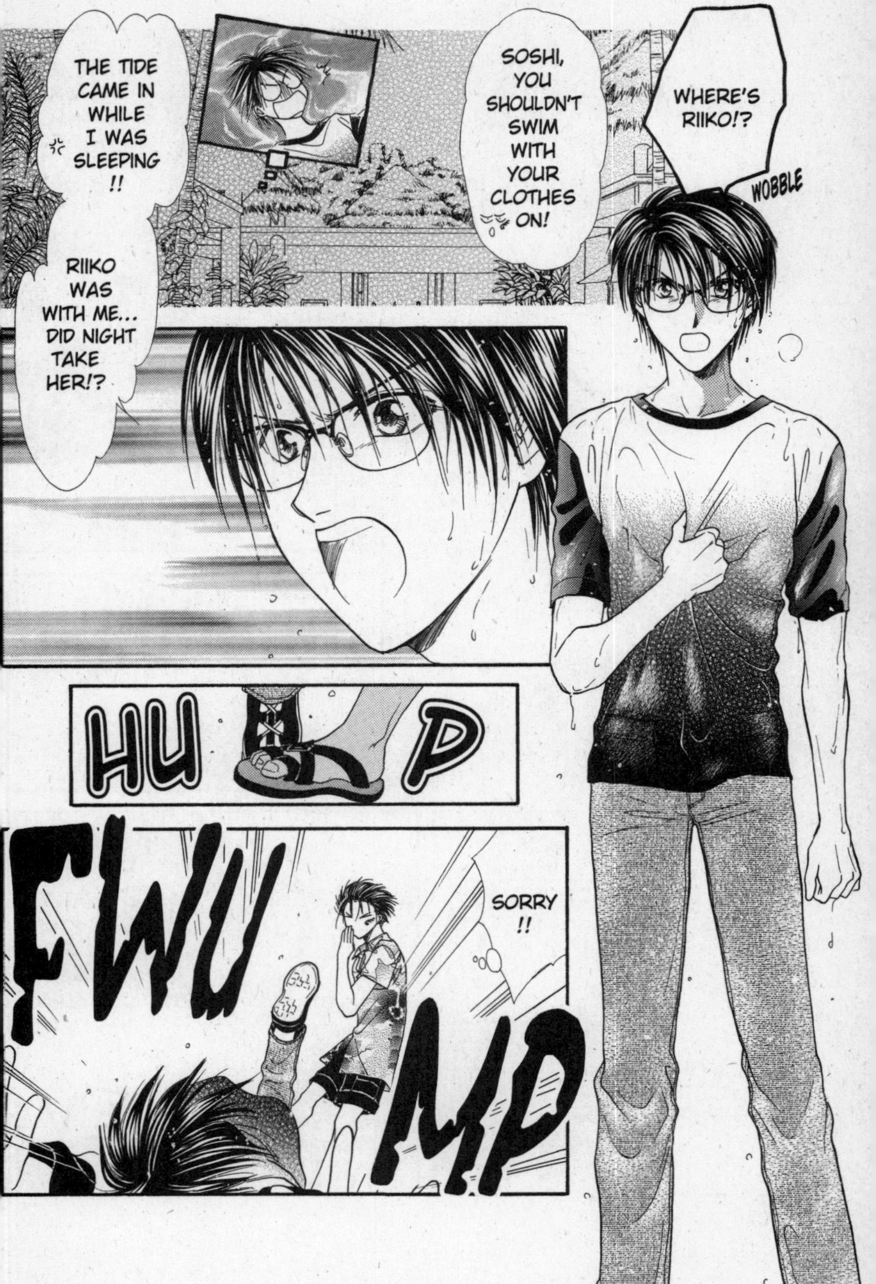
WHERE'S RIIKO!?
WOBBLE
SOSHI, YOU SHOULDN'T SWIM WITH YOUR CLOTHES ON!
THE TIDE CAME IN WHILE I WAS SLEEPING!!
RIIKO WAS WITH ME... DID NIGHT TAKE HER!?
HUP
FWUMP
SORRY!!

WHAT WAS THAT FOR?
WHUMP
HUH?
Uh-oh.
YOU HAVE A FEVER!!
RII...
...KO
...

Uh-oh! My arm is starting to hurt, so I'm going to put some ointment on it. Hmm, I can draw forever, but writing is hard. I think it has to do with the way I hold the pen. A writer friend of mine told me that my grip was good for drawing fast, but not for writing. It's so hard to write. But I've gotten so used to writing like this that I can't change. It's a very distinctive grip. I showed it to a bunch of artists and none of them could do it. The pinky is the axis. But this allows me to draw really fast. I haven't had any calluses in the 15 years that I've been doing this (a source of pride), and I only get tired after 60 pages or so. I wonder what it's like for other artists? Also, I have no pen pressure... I had a grip of only 25 back in high school. I'm so wimpy (15 in my left). My arm exists only to hold the pen (I hope). So I write really fast, too, probably as fast as I draw. I never noticed it myself, but other people have said that my hand moves really fast. This is fast? I think I've slowed down as I've gotten older. If I sleep for 7 or 8 hours a night and get started at 11 AM, it takes me a day and a half to do a 30-page draft. Is that fast? I used to be able to do it in one day. I want an arm that can go at the speed of light. And I'm not good at time management, so if I were more efficient, I'd be able to do even more work!! People tell me I'm fast, but there must be others who are even faster!! I can ink at the same speed, too. Sigh... But I'm just no good at writing. (I never have been.)

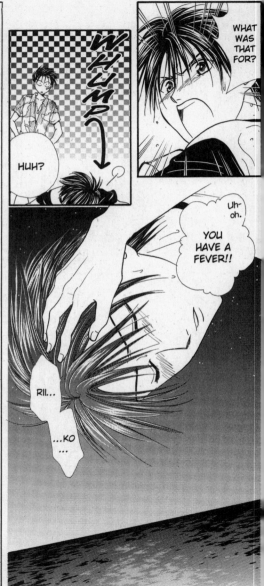

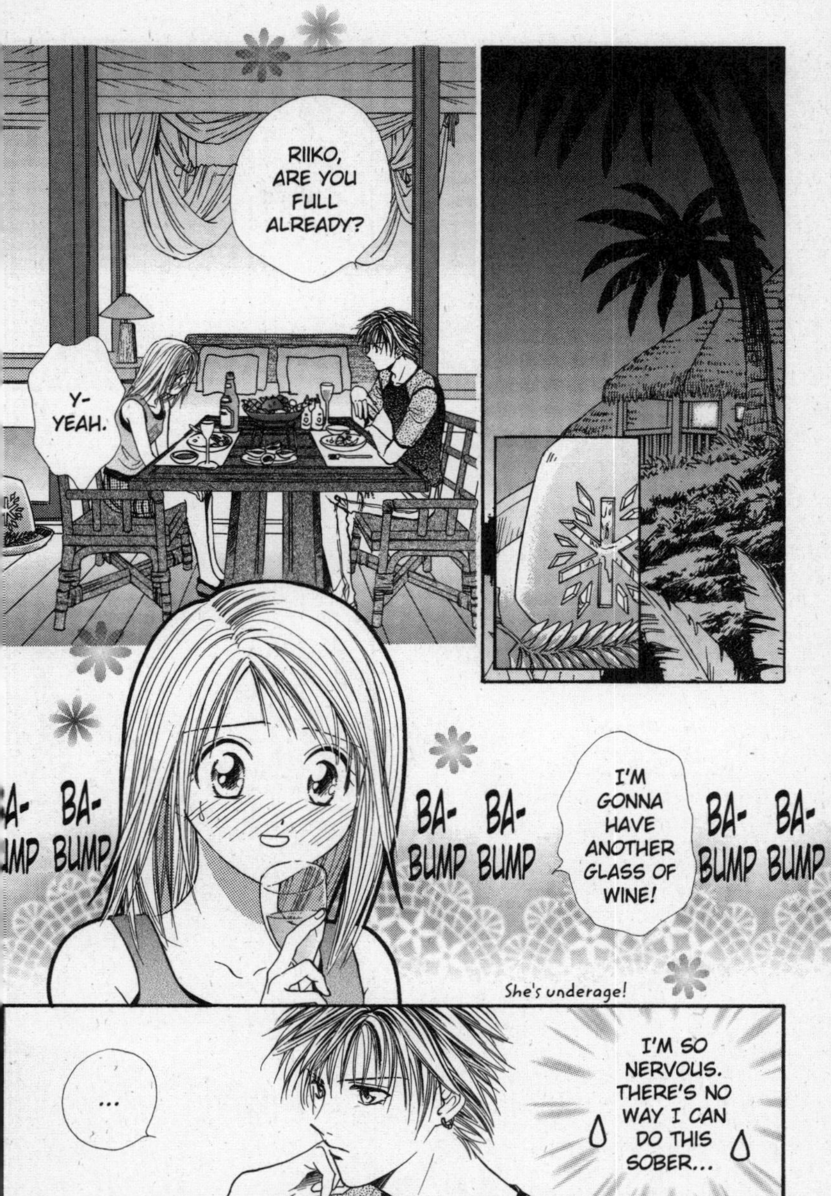
RIIKO, ARE YOU FULL ALREADY?
Y-YEAH.
BA-BUMP BA-BUMP
I'M GONNA HAVE ANOTHER GLASS OF WINE!
BA-BUMP BA-BUMP
BA-BUMP
She's underage!
I'M SO NERVOUS. THERE'S NO WAY I CAN DO THIS SOBER...
...

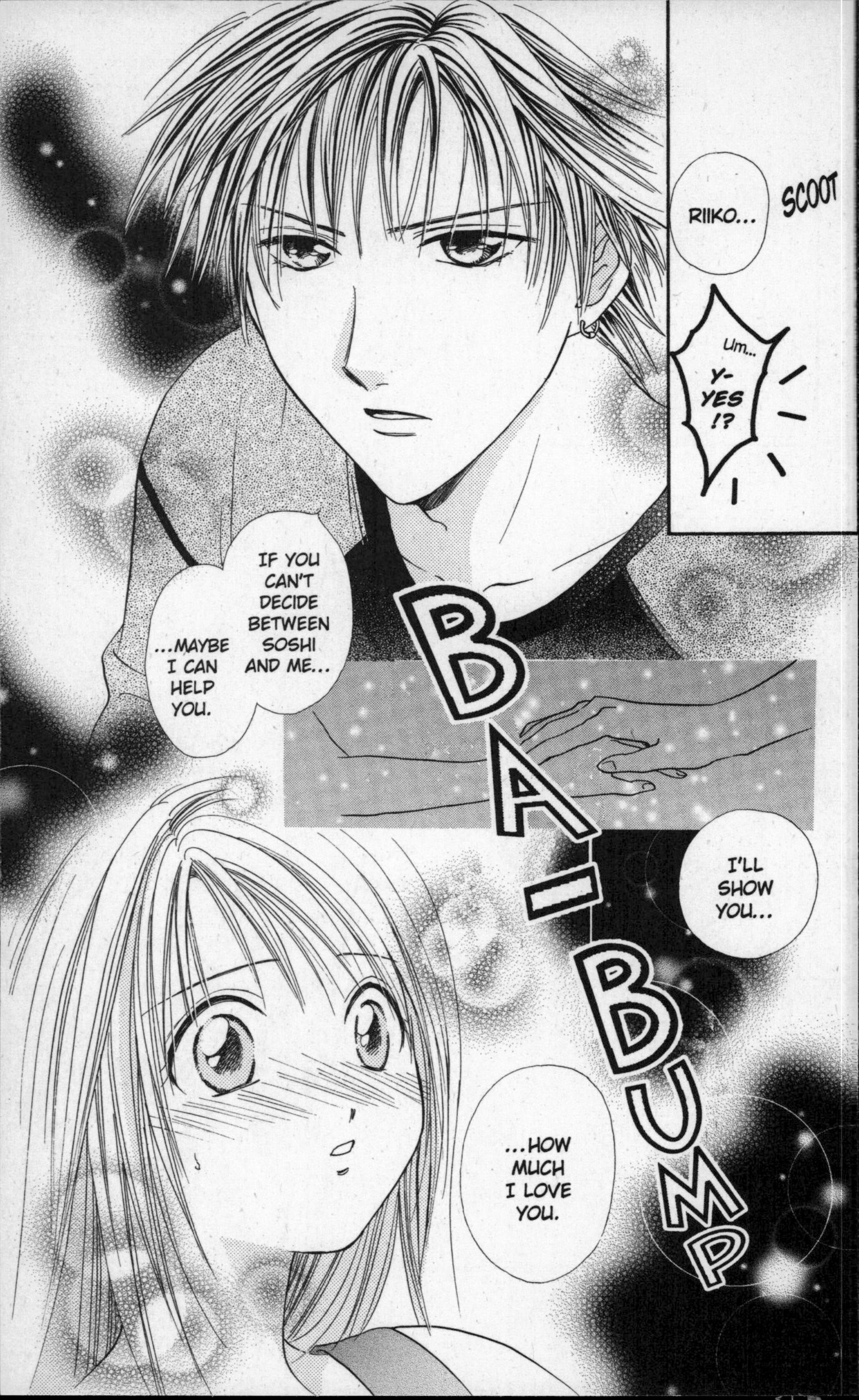
RIIKO...
SCOOT
Um... Y-YES!?
IF YOU CAN'T DECIDE BETWEEN SOSHI AND ME...
...MAYBE I CAN HELP YOU.
BA-BUMP
I'LL SHOW YOU...
...HOW MUCH I LOVE YOU.

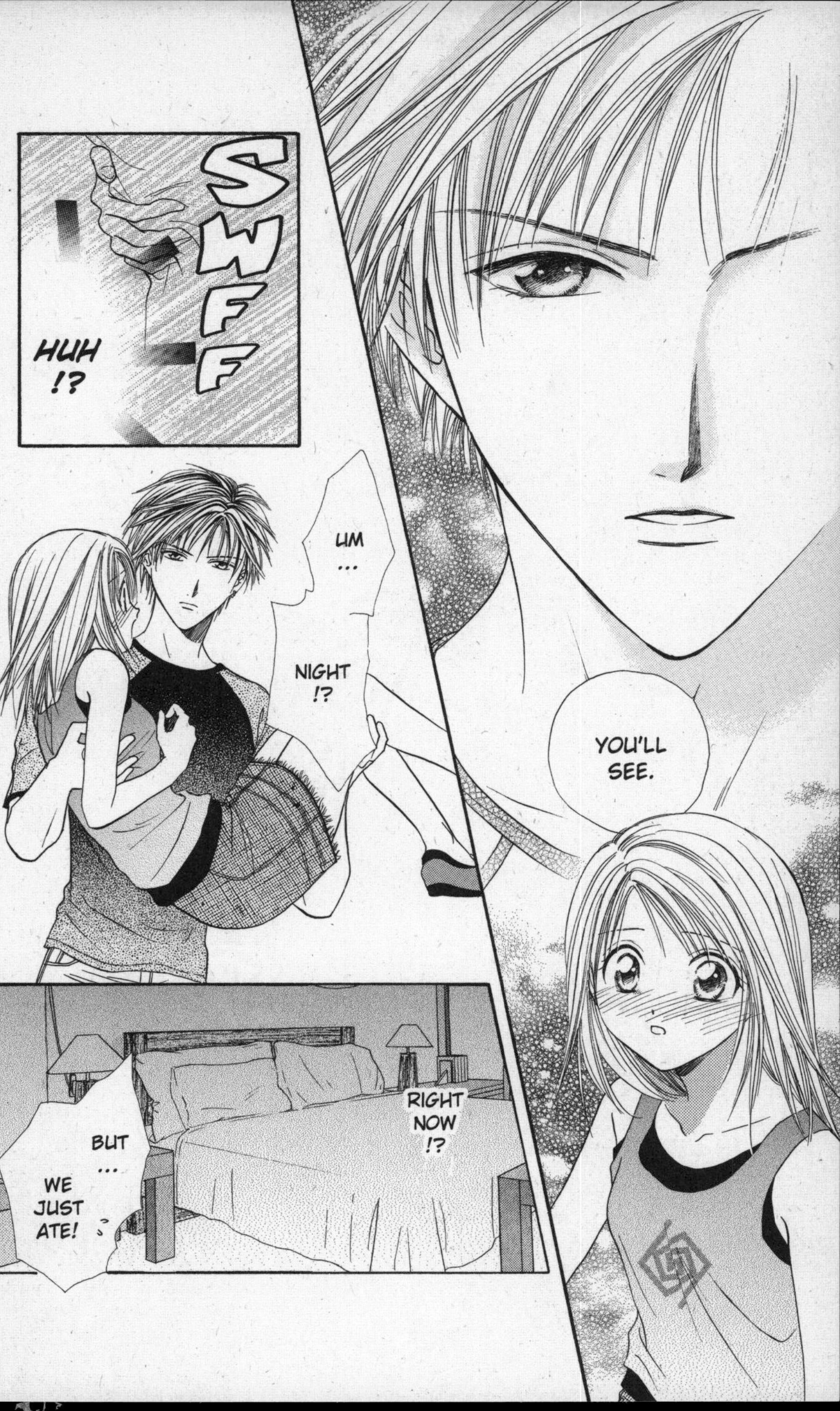
YOU'LL SEE.
SWFF
HUH !?
UM ...
NIGHT !?
RIGHT NOW !?
BUT ...
WE JUST ATE!

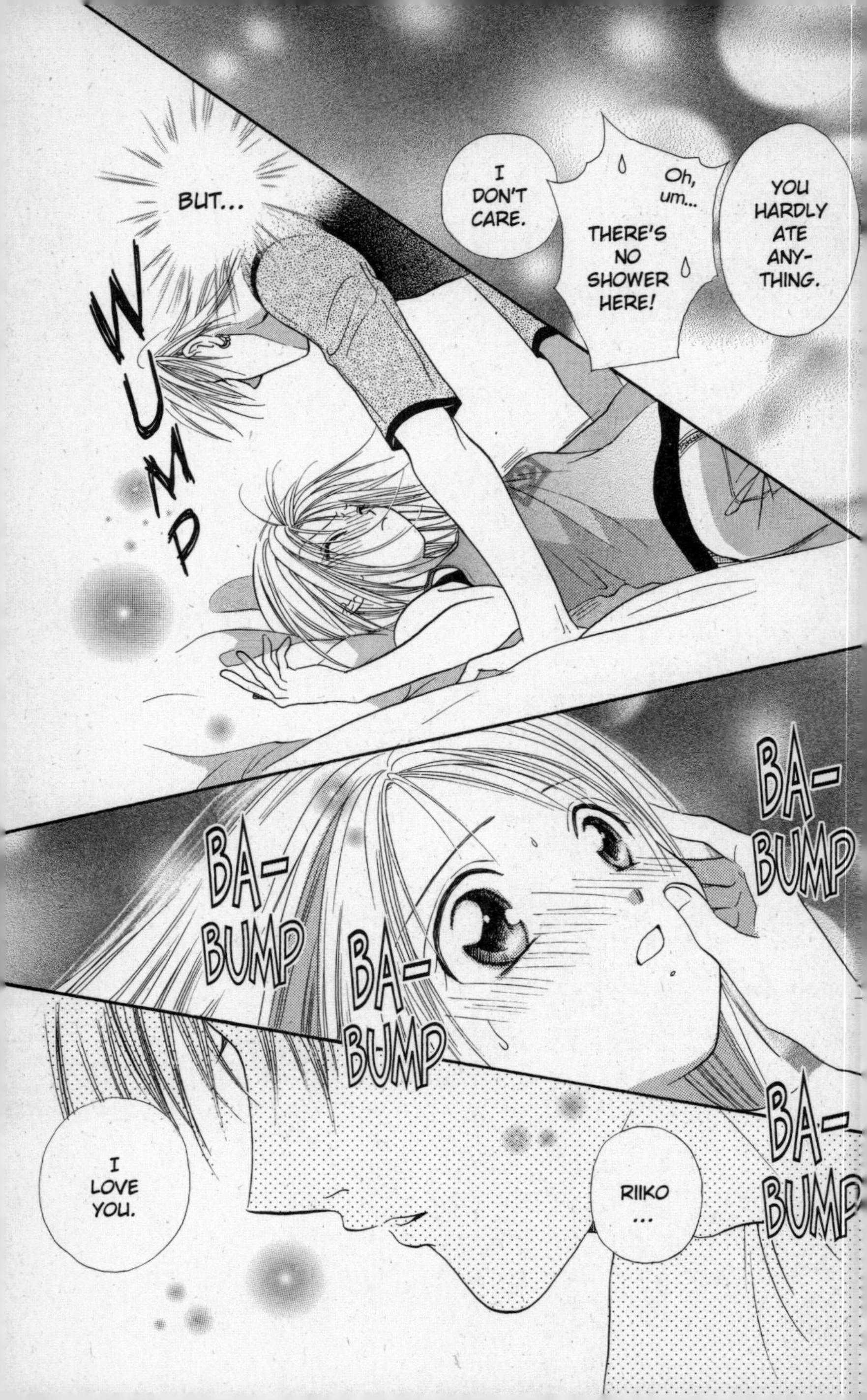

YOU HARDLY ATE ANY-THING.
Oh, um...
THERE'S NO SHOWER HERE!
I DON'T CARE.
BUT...
WUMP
BA-BUMP
BA-BUMP
BA-BUMP
BA-BUMP
RIIKO ...
I LOVE YOU.

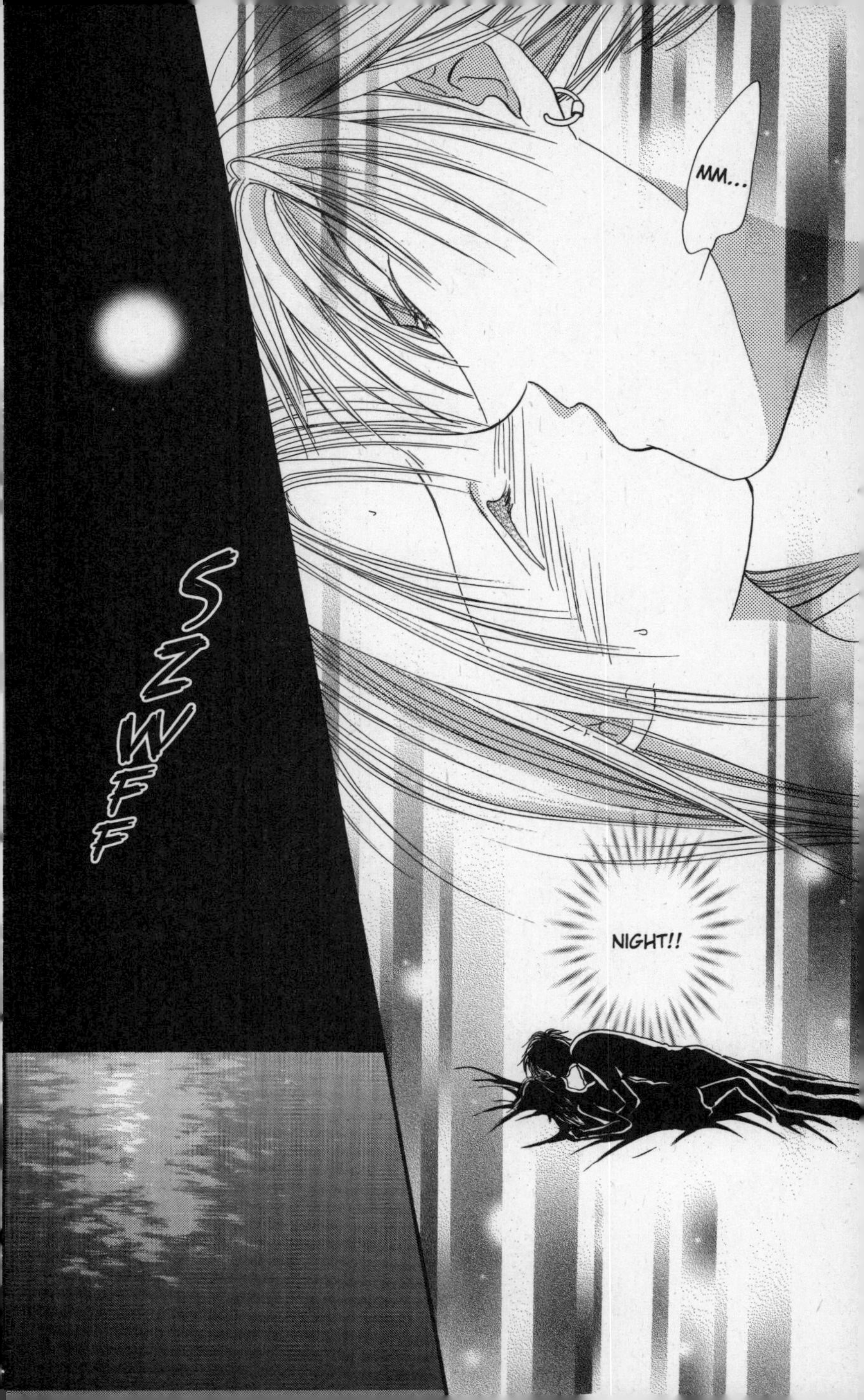
MM...
NIGHT!!
SZWFF

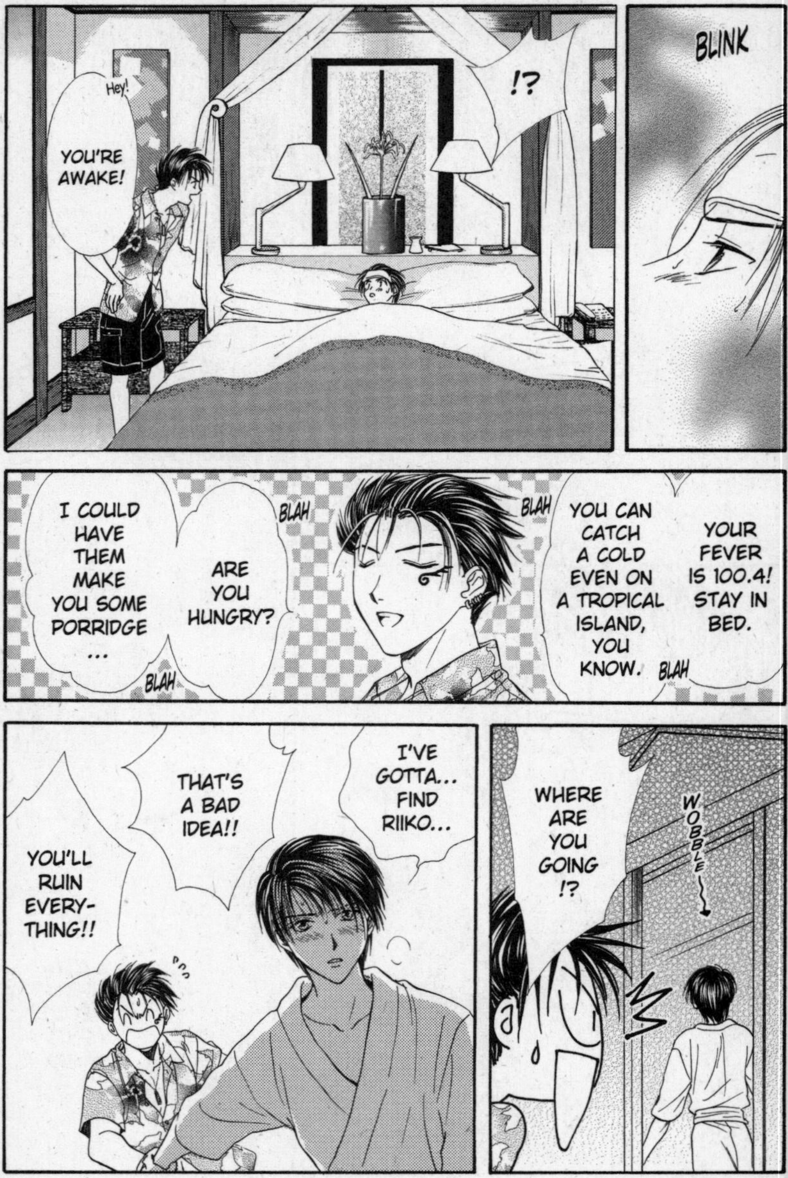
BLINK
!?
Hey!
YOU'RE AWAKE!
YOUR FEVER IS 100.4! STAY IN BED.
BLAH
YOU CAN CATCH A COLD EVEN ON A TROPICAL ISLAND, YOU KNOW.
BLAH
BLAH
ARE YOU HUNGRY?
I COULD HAVE THEM MAKE YOU SOME PORRIDGE...
BLAH
WOBBLE
WHERE ARE YOU GOING!?
I'VE GOTTA... FIND RIIKO...
THAT'S A BAD IDEA!!
YOU'LL RUIN EVERY-THING!!

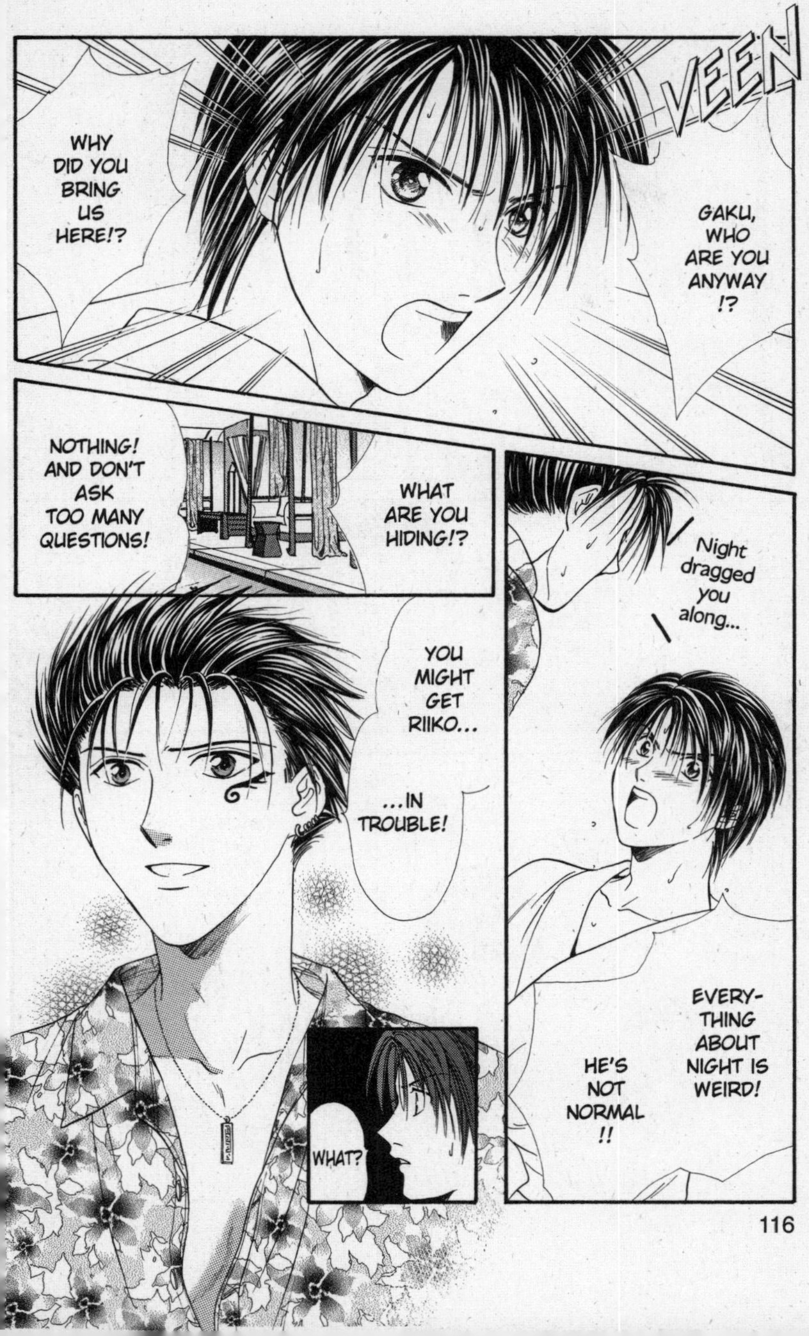
VEEN
GAKU, WHO ARE YOU ANYWAY!?
WHY DID YOU BRING US HERE!?
Night dragged you along...
EVERYTHING ABOUT NIGHT IS WEIRD!
HE'S NOT NORMAL!!
WHAT ARE YOU HIDING!?
NOTHING! AND DON'T ASK TOO MANY QUESTIONS!
YOU MIGHT GET RIIKO...
...IN TROUBLE!
WHAT?

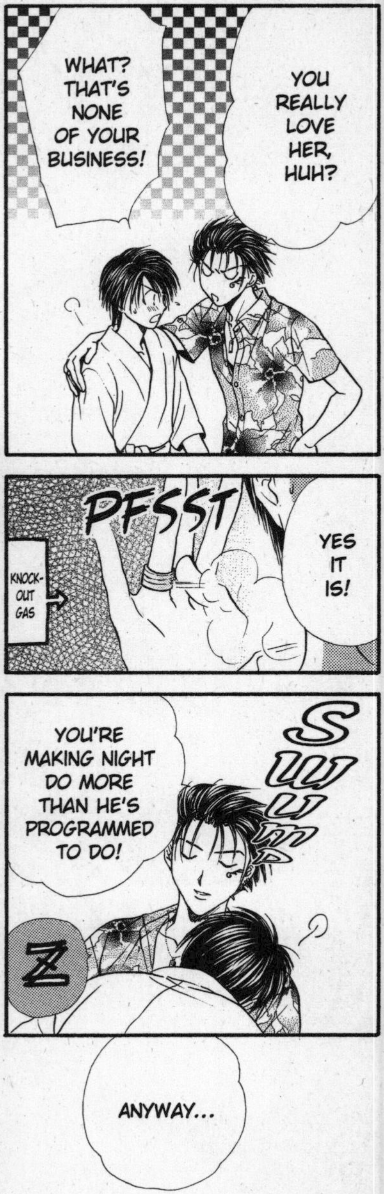
YOU REALLY LOVE HER, HUH?
WHAT? THAT'S NONE OF YOUR BUSINESS!
YES IT IS!
PFSSST
KNOCK-OUT GAS
SWUMP
YOU'RE MAKING NIGHT DO MORE THAN HE'S PROGRAMMED TO DO!
Z
ANYWAY...
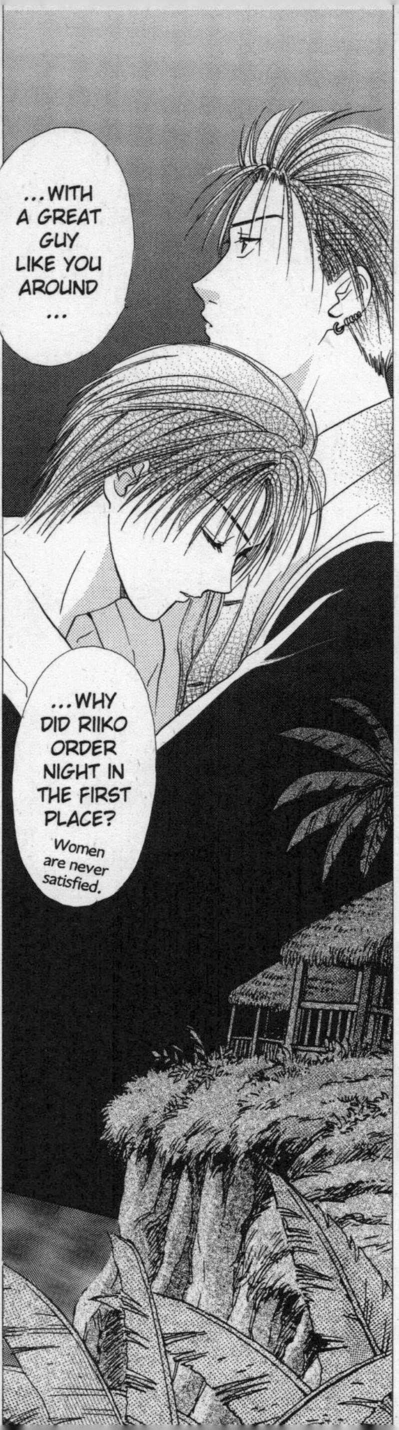
...WITH A GREAT GUY LIKE YOU AROUND ...
...WHY DID RIIKO ORDER NIGHT IN THE FIRST PLACE?
Women are never satisfied.

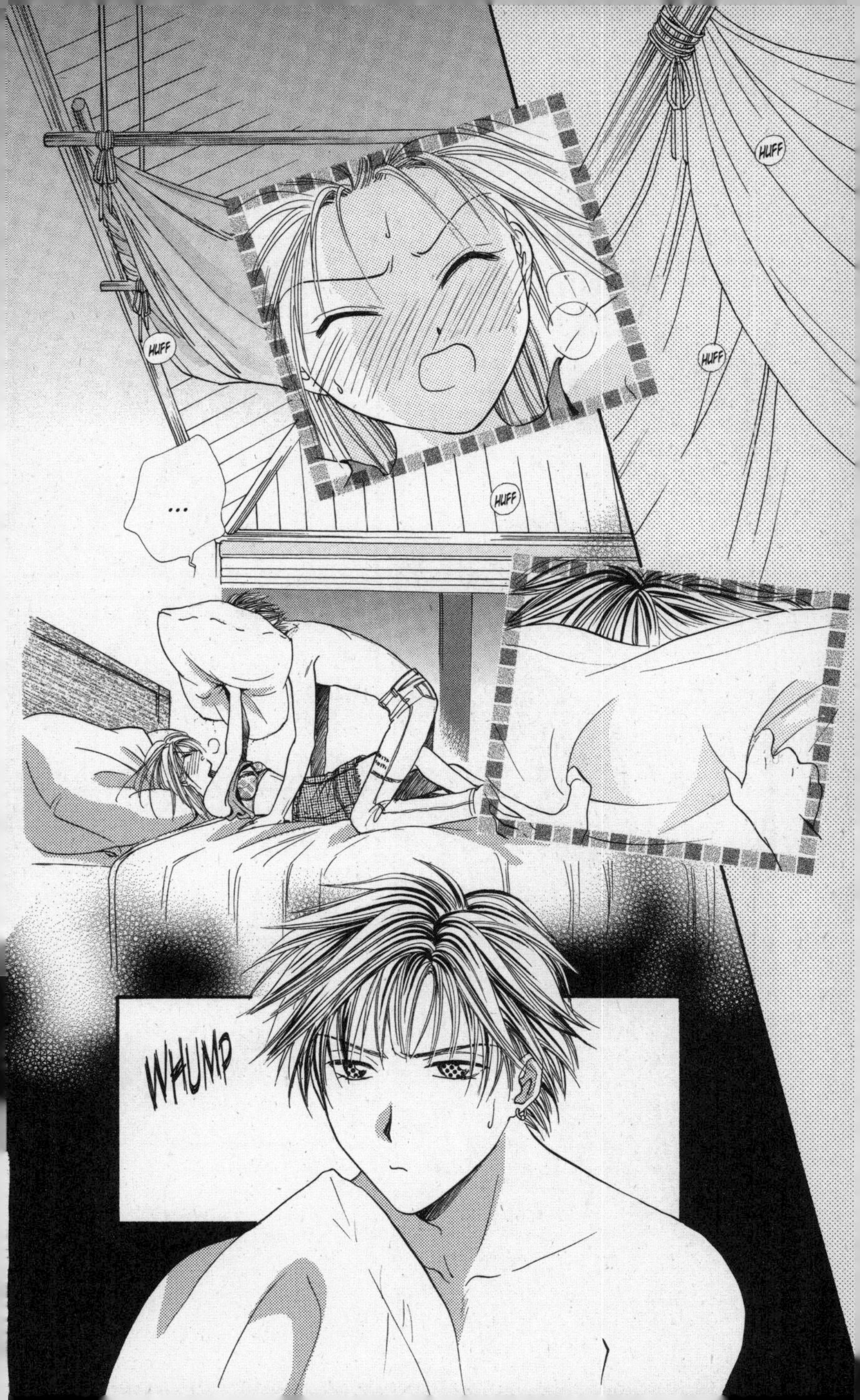
HUFF
HUFF
HUFF
HUFF
...
WHUMP

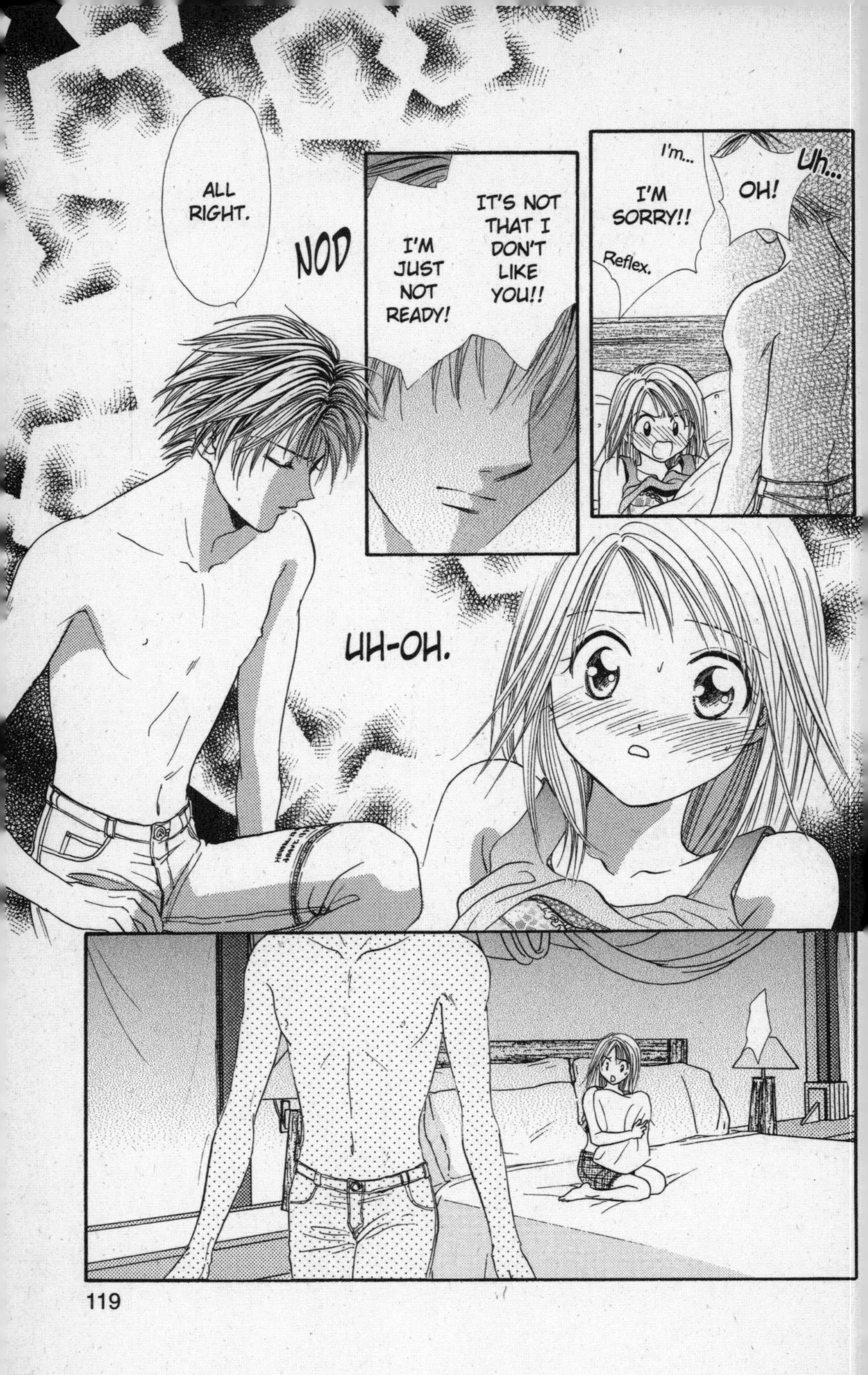
Uh...
OH!
I'm...
I'M SORRY!!
Reflex.
IT'S NOT THAT I DON'T LIKE YOU!!
I'M JUST NOT READY!
ALL RIGHT.
NOD
UH-OH.

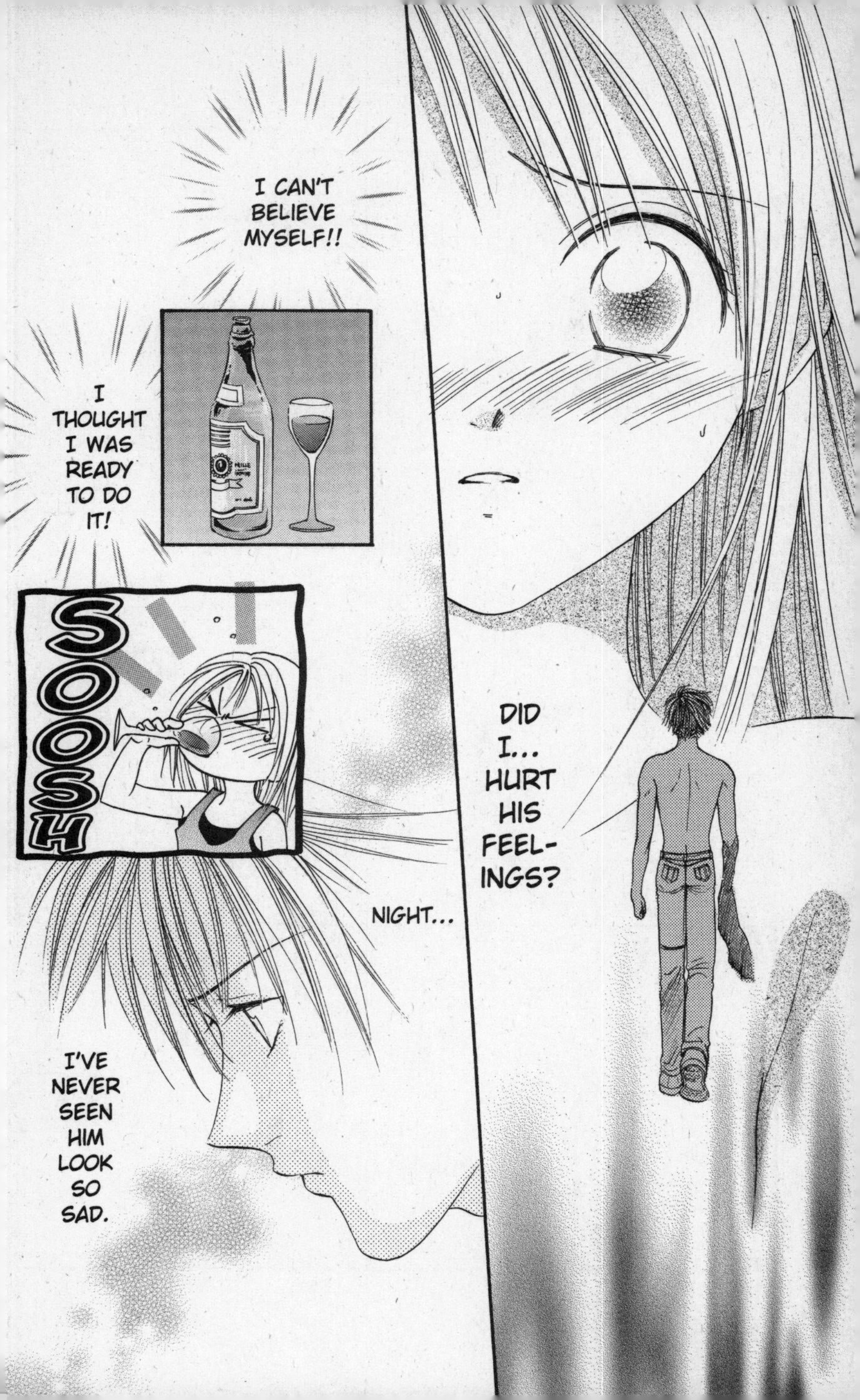

DID I... HURT HIS FEELINGS?
I CAN'T BELIEVE MYSELF!!
I THOUGHT I WAS READY TO DO IT!
SOOSH
NIGHT...
I'VE NEVER SEEN HIM LOOK SO SAD.

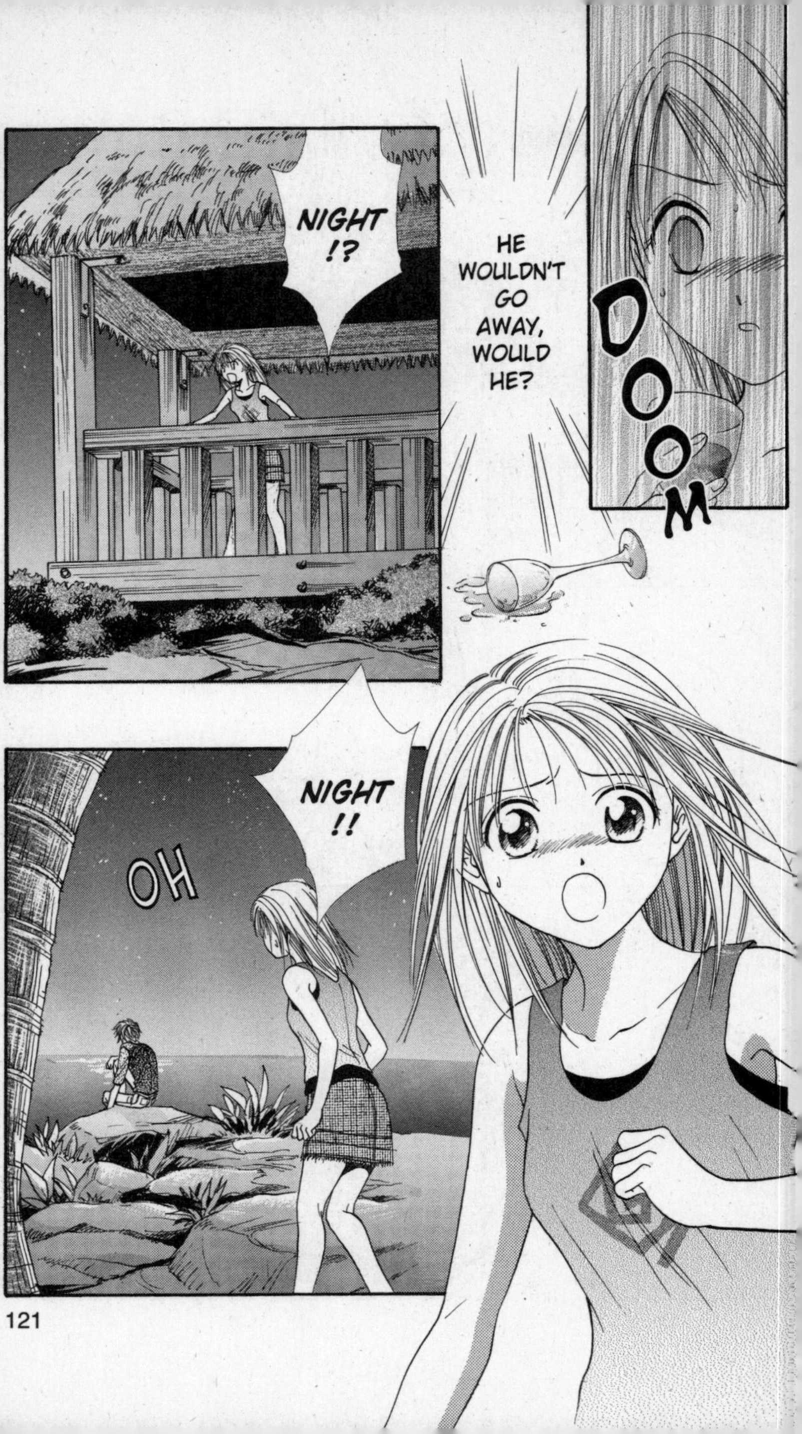
DOOM
HE WOULDN'T GO AWAY, WOULD HE?
NIGHT !?
NIGHT !!
OH

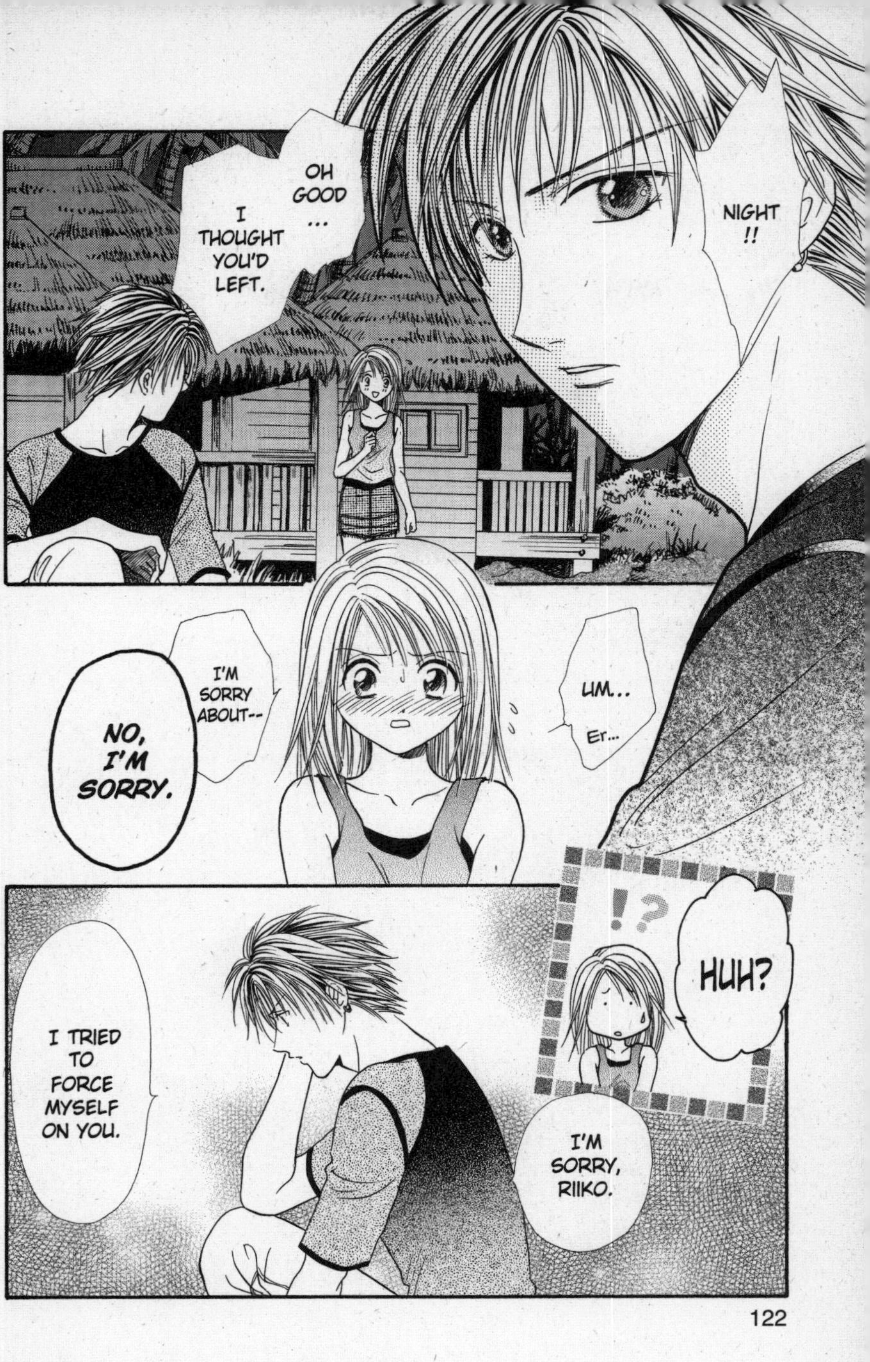
NIGHT !!
OH GOOD ...
I THOUGHT YOU'D LEFT.
UM..
Er...
I'M SORRY ABOUT--
NO, I'M SORRY.
!?
HUH?
I'M SORRY, RIIKO.
I TRIED TO FORCE MYSELF ON YOU.

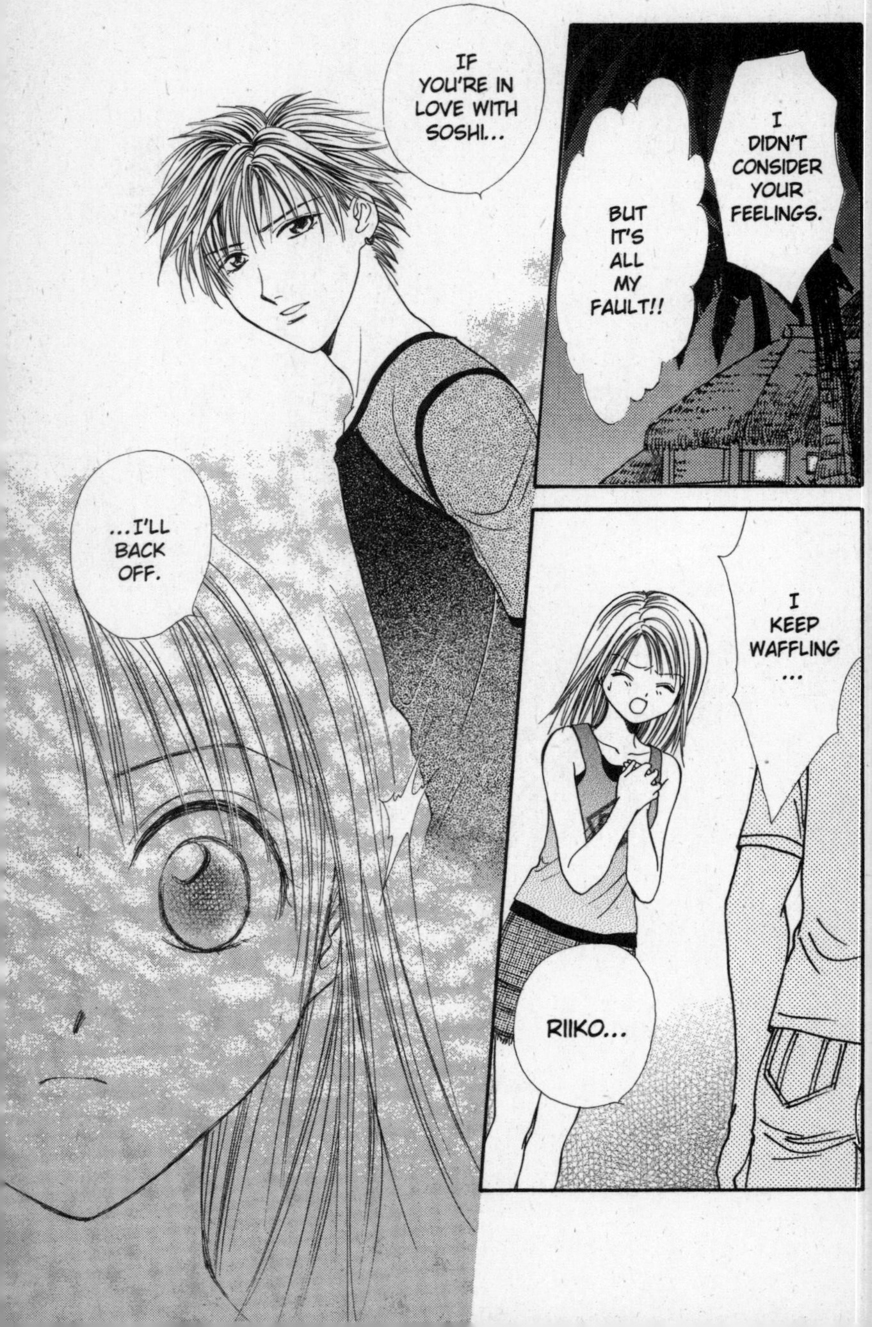
I DIDN'T CONSIDER YOUR FEELINGS.
BUT IT'S ALL MY FAULT!!
I KEEP WAFFLING...
RIIKO...
IF YOU'RE IN LOVE WITH SOSHI...
...I'LL BACK OFF.

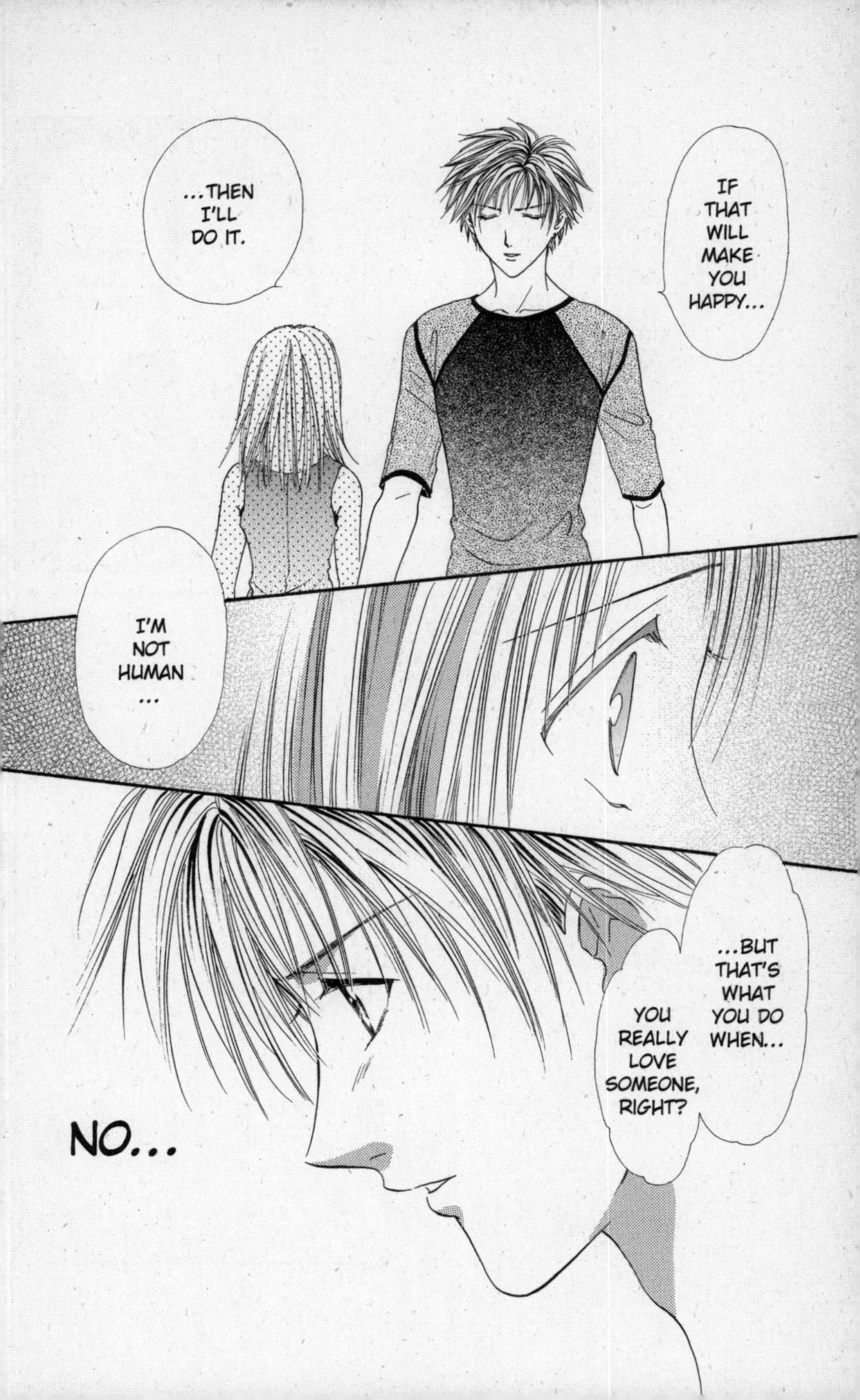
IF THAT WILL MAKE YOU HAPPY...
...THEN I'LL DO IT.
I'M NOT HUMAN ...
...BUT THAT'S WHAT YOU DO WHEN...
YOU REALLY LOVE SOMEONE, RIGHT?
NO...

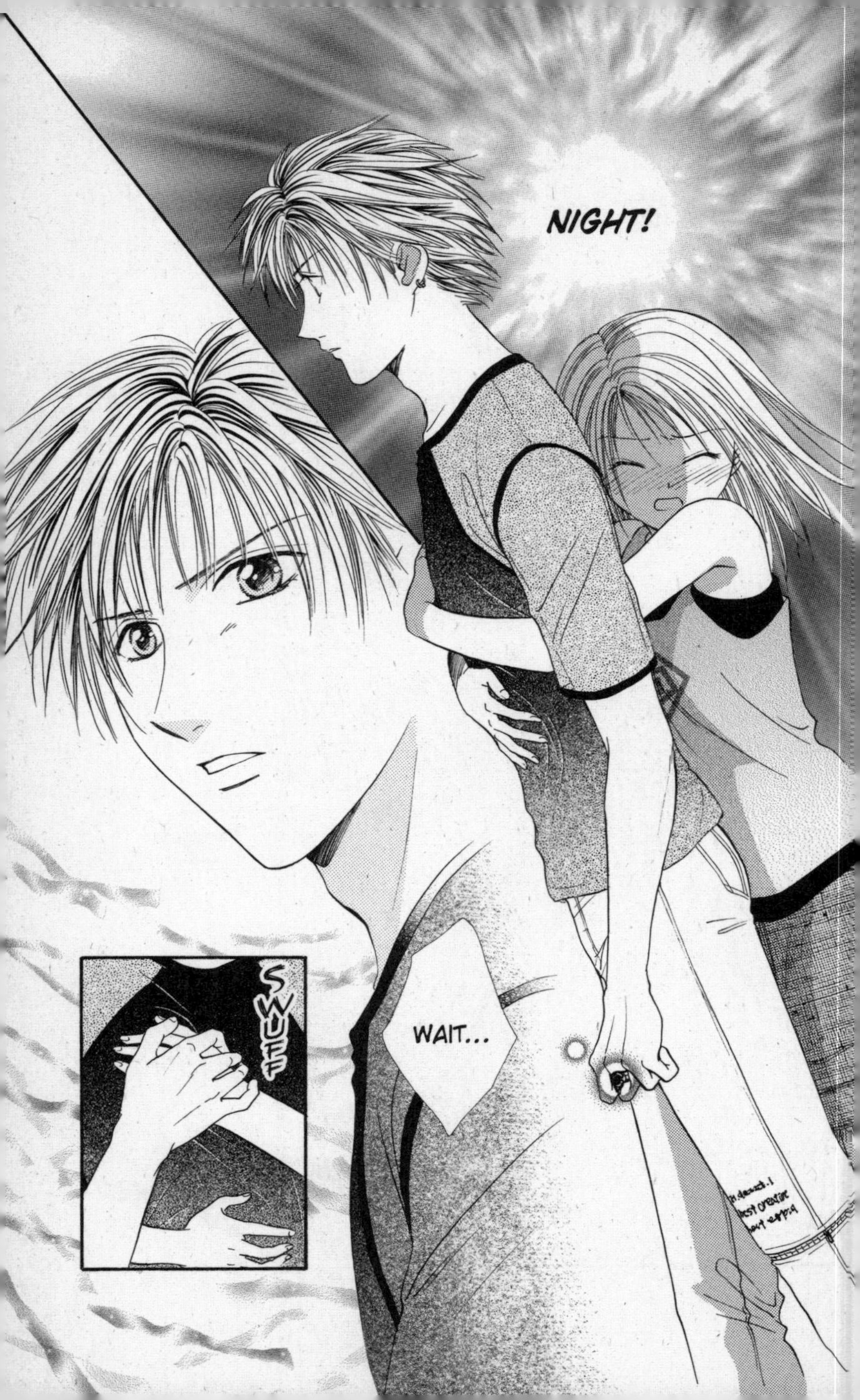
NIGHT!
WAIT...
SWUFF

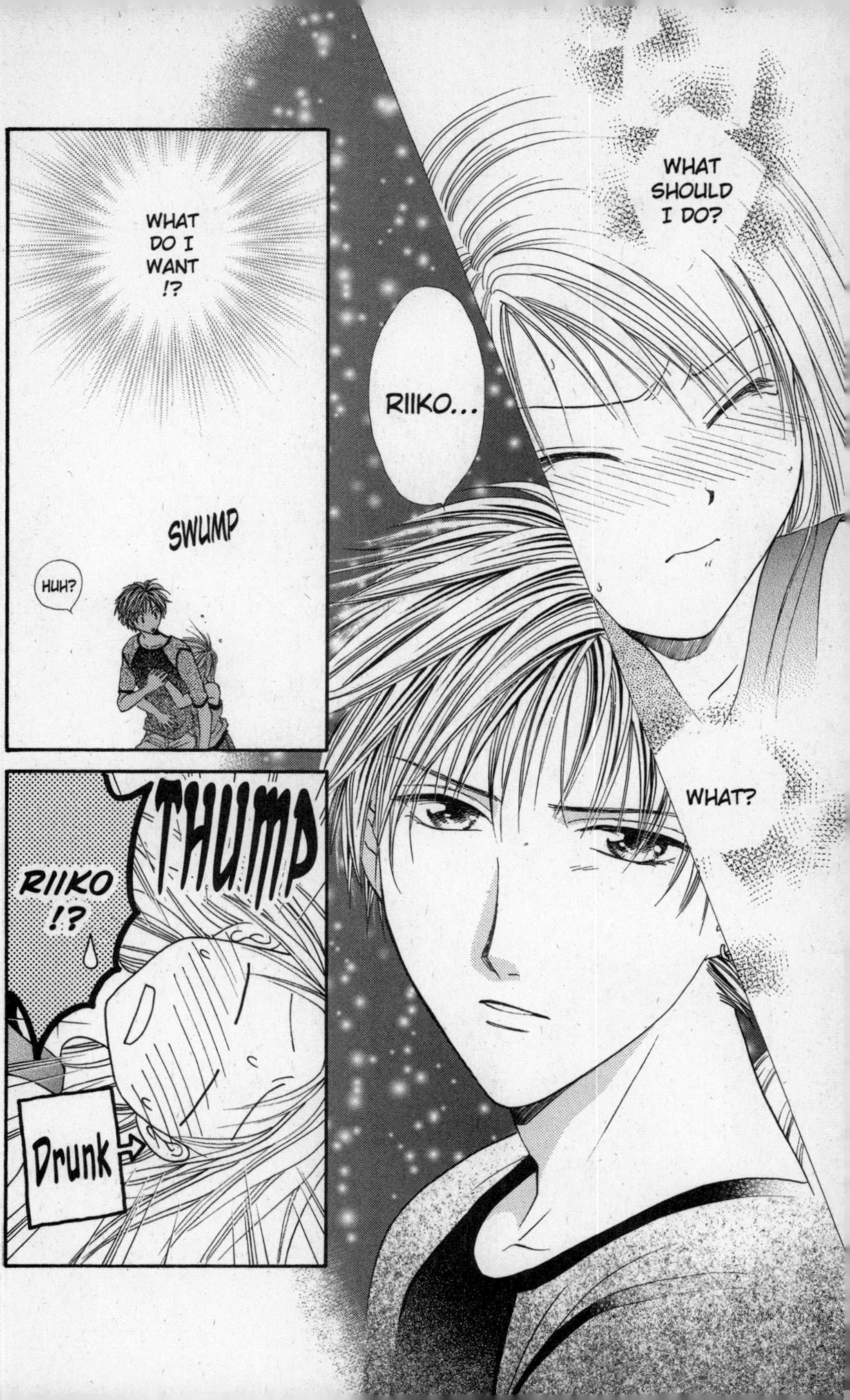
WHAT SHOULD I DO?
RIIKO...
WHAT?
WHAT DO I WANT !?
SWUMP
HUH?
THUMP
RIIKO !?
Drunk

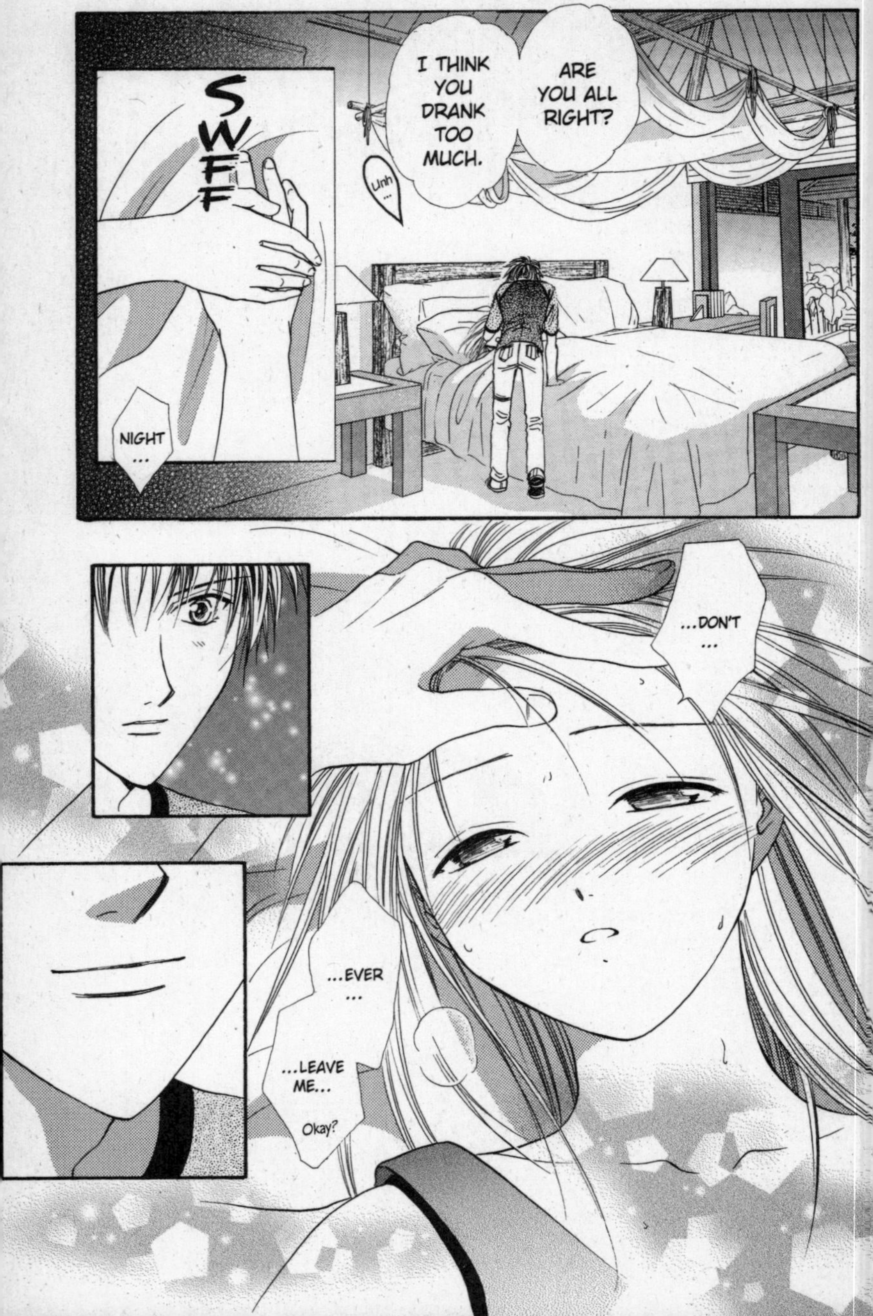
ARE YOU ALL RIGHT?
I THINK YOU DRANK TOO MUCH.
Unh...
SWFF
NIGHT...
...DON'T...
...EVER...
...LEAVE ME...
Okay?

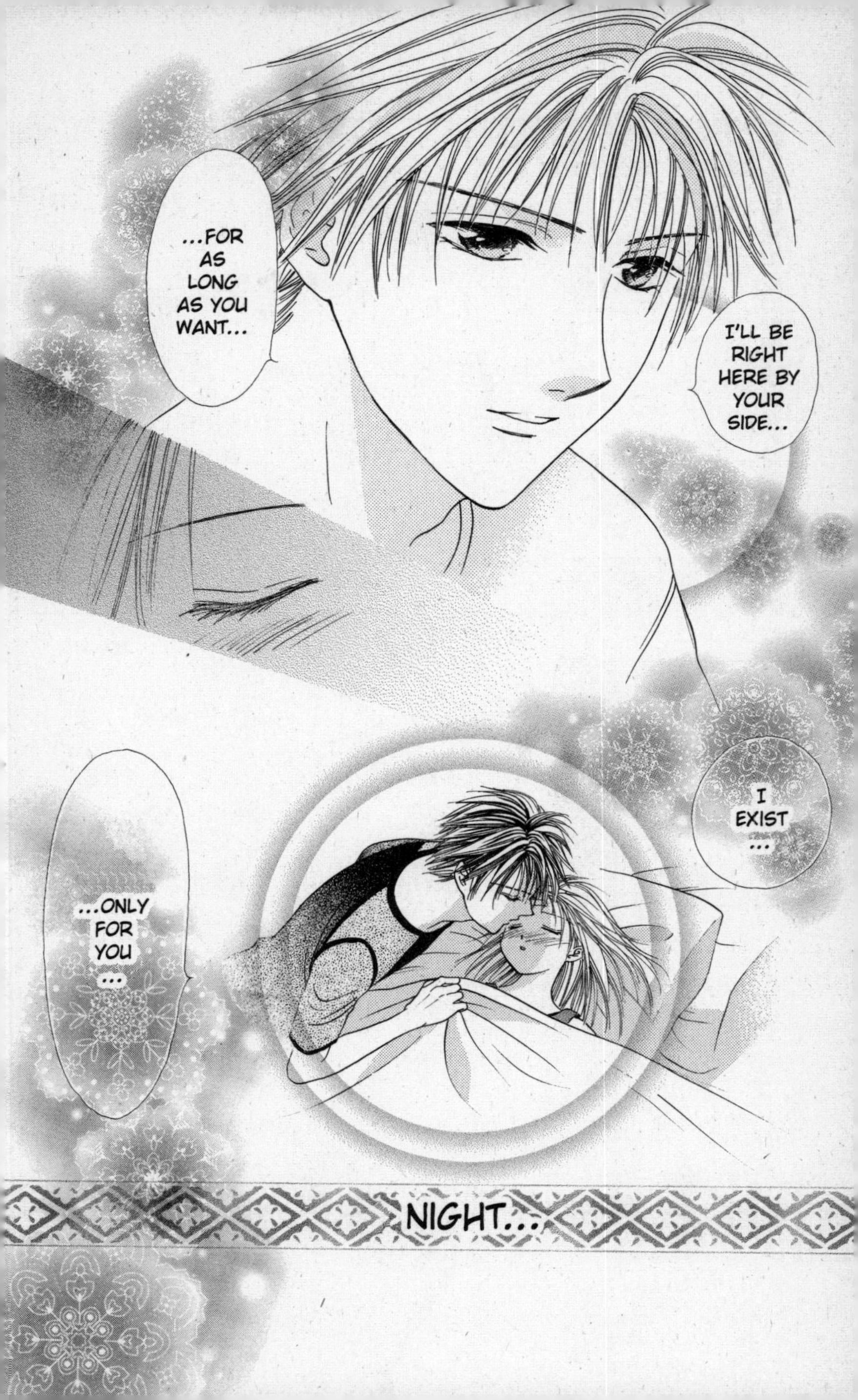
I'LL BE RIGHT HERE BY YOUR SIDE...
...FOR AS LONG AS YOU WANT...
I EXIST...
...ONLY FOR YOU...
NIGHT...

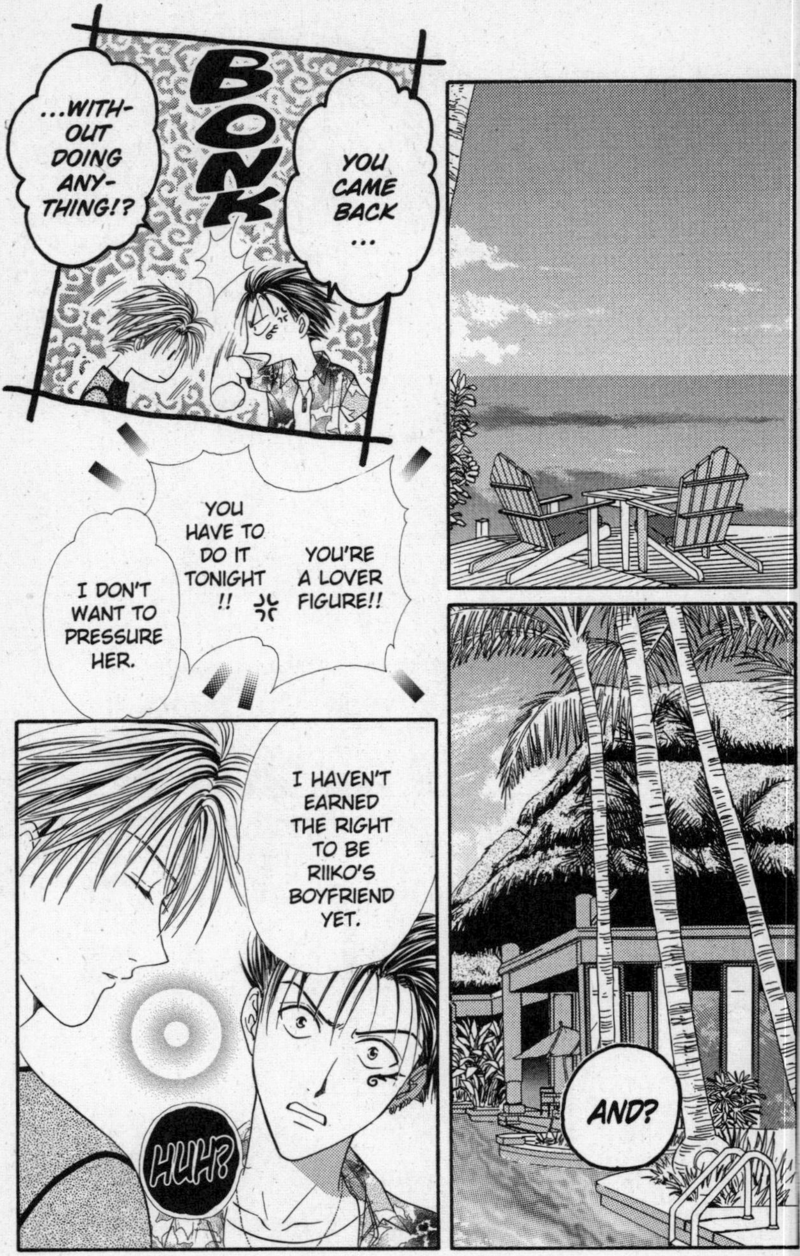
AND?
YOU CAME BACK ...
...WITH-OUT DOING ANY-THING!?
BONK
YOU'RE A LOVER FIGURE!!
YOU HAVE TO DO IT TONIGHT !!
I DON'T WANT TO PRESSURE HER.
I HAVEN'T EARNED THE RIGHT TO BE RIIKO'S BOYFRIEND YET.
HUH?

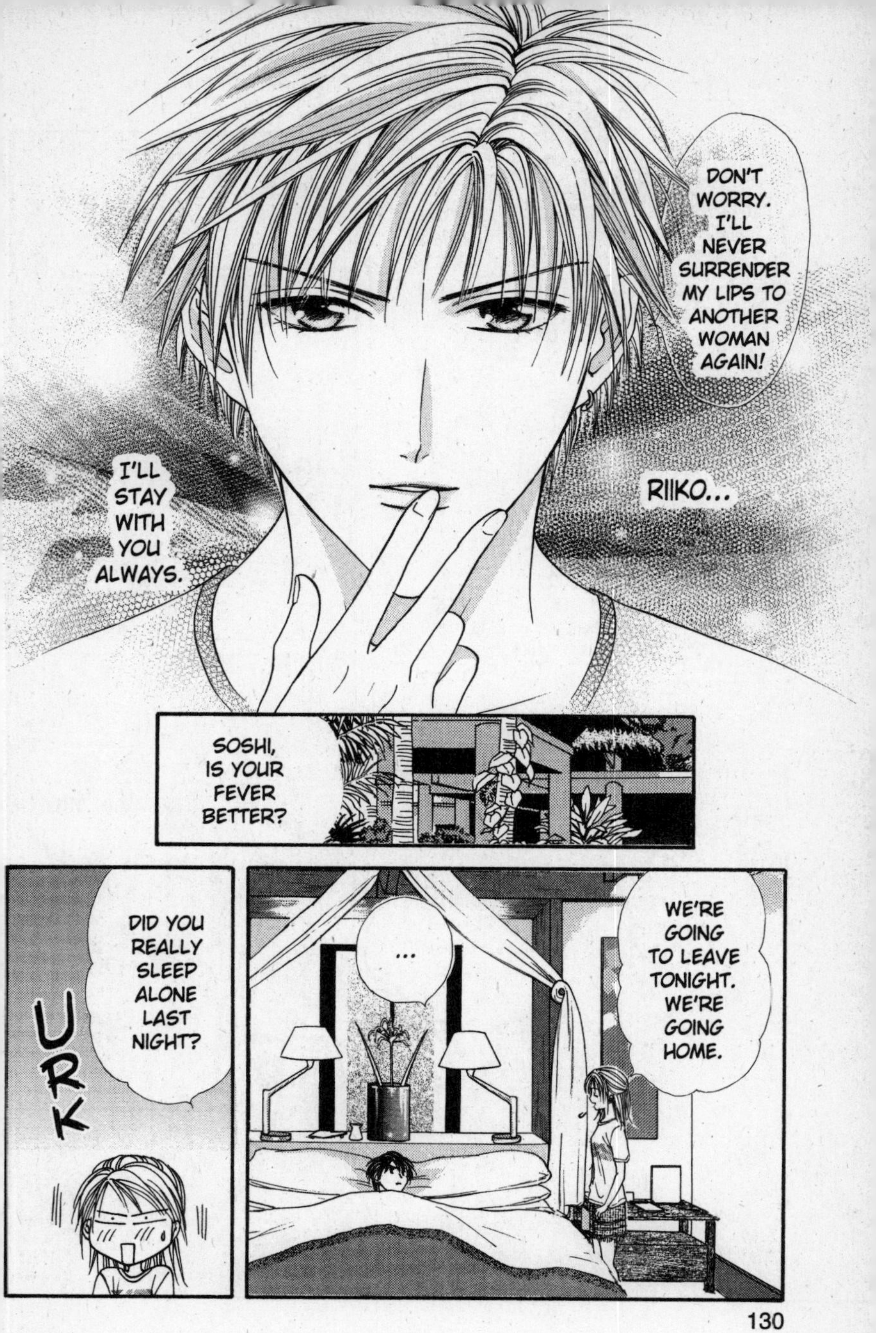
DON'T WORRY. I'LL NEVER SURRENDER MY LIPS TO ANOTHER WOMAN AGAIN!
RIIKO...
I'LL STAY WITH YOU ALWAYS.
SOSHI, IS YOUR FEVER BETTER?
WE'RE GOING TO LEAVE TONIGHT. WE'RE GOING HOME.
...
DID YOU REALLY SLEEP ALONE LAST NIGHT?
URK

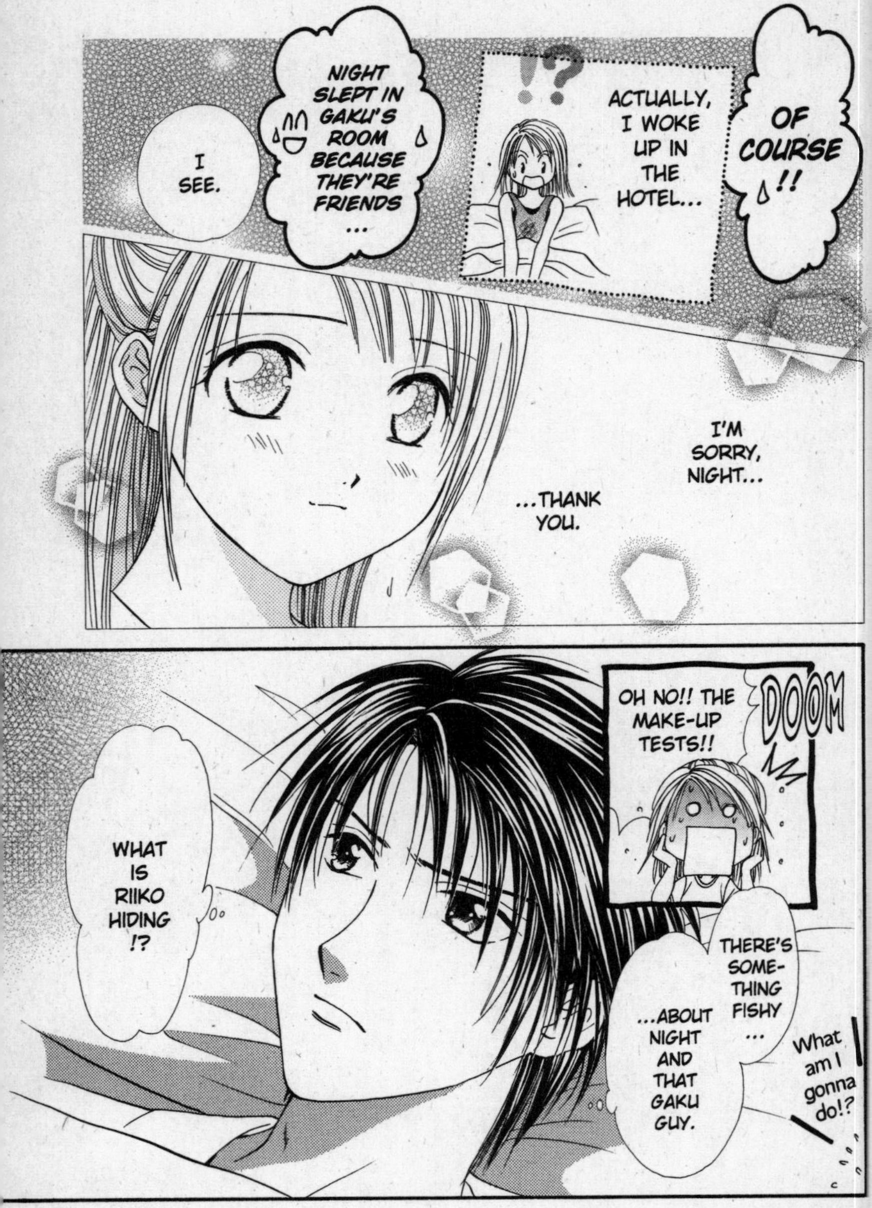
OF COURSE!!
ACTUALLY, I WOKE UP IN THE HOTEL...
!?
NIGHT SLEPT IN GAKU'S ROOM BECAUSE THEY'RE FRIENDS...
I SEE.
I'M SORRY, NIGHT...
...THANK YOU.
DOOM
OH NO!! THE MAKE-UP TESTS!!
What am I gonna do!?
THERE'S SOME-THING FISHY...
...ABOUT NIGHT AND THAT GAKU GUY.
WHAT IS RIIKO HIDING!?

Absolute Boyfriend

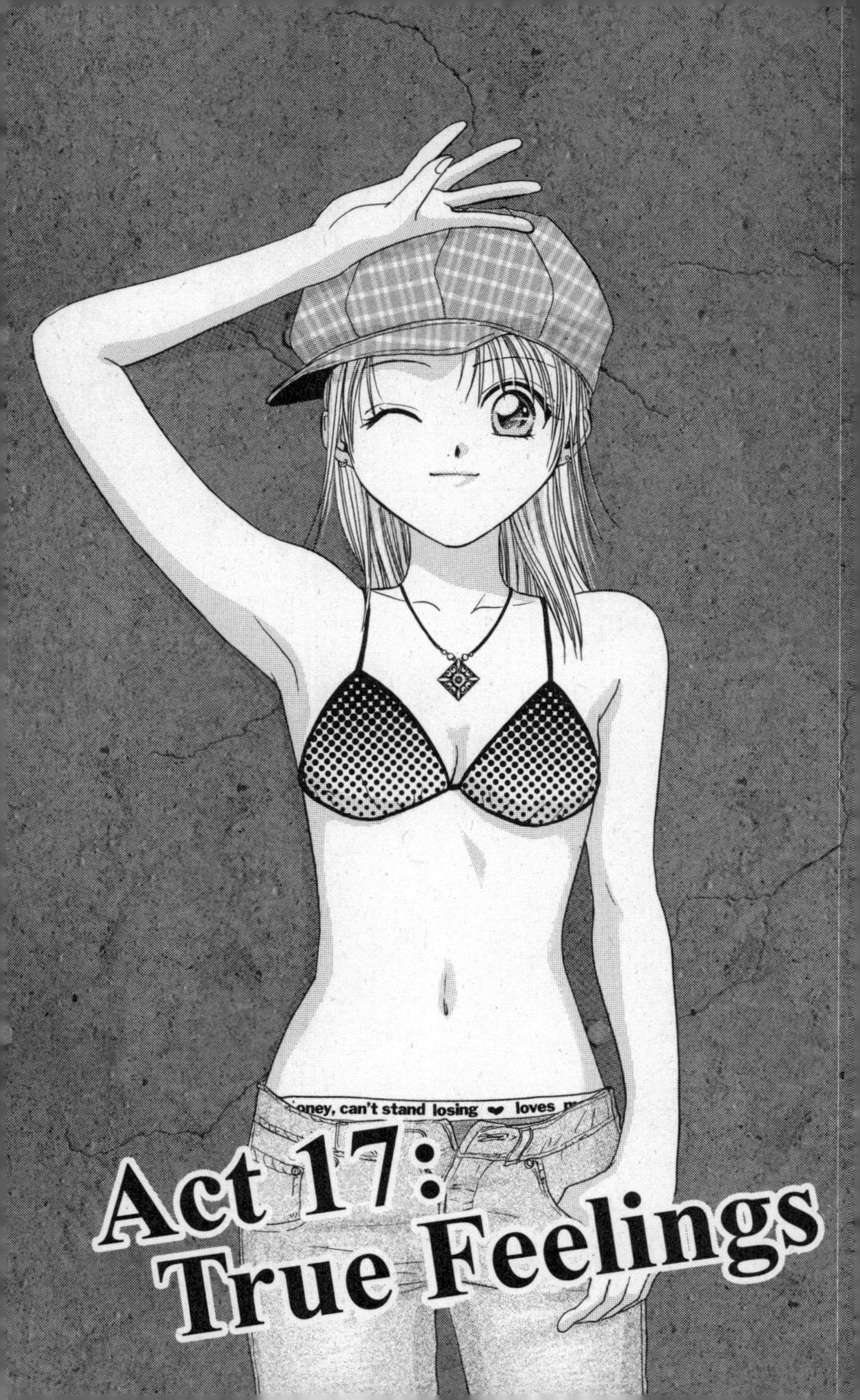
oney, can't stand losing ❤ loves
Act 17:
True Feelings

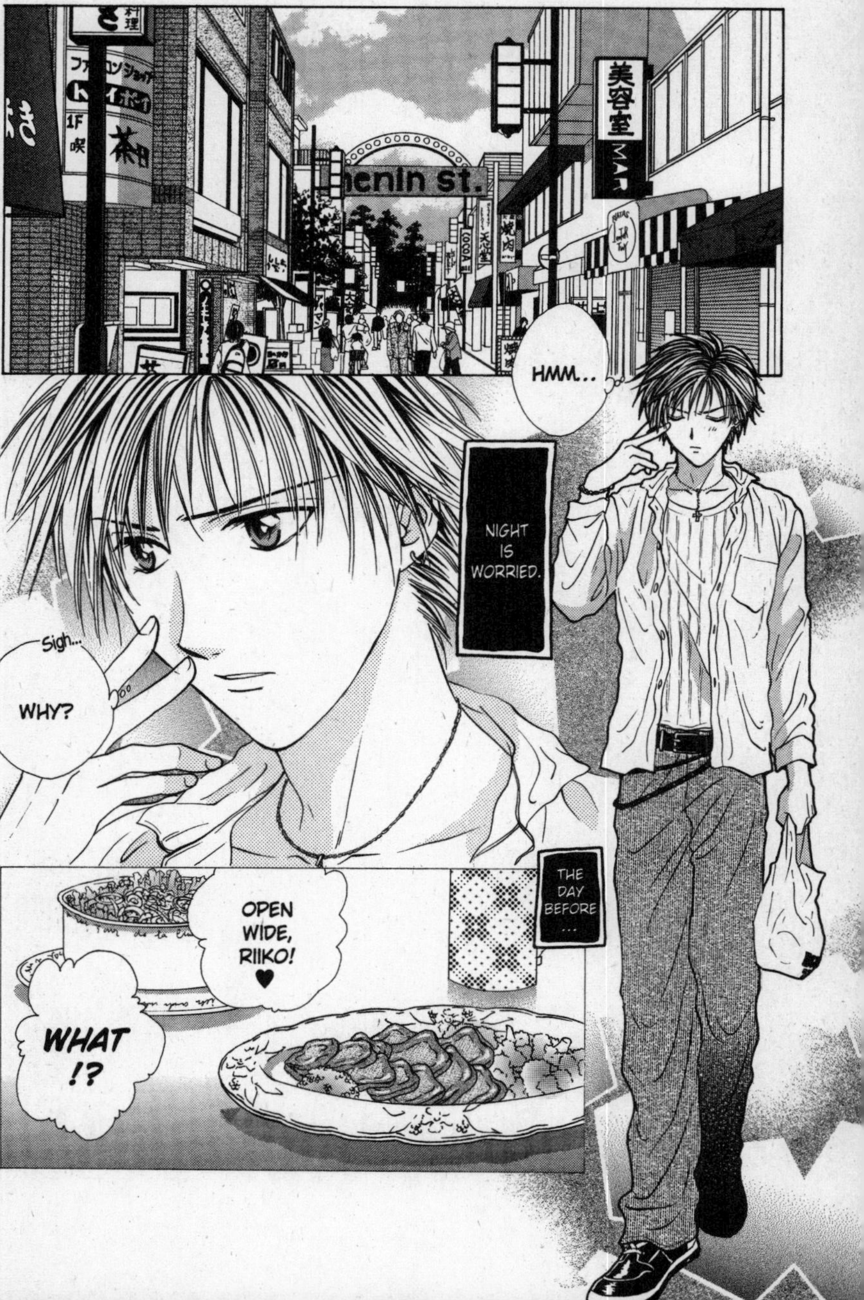
美容室
HMM...
NIGHT IS WORRIED.
Sigh...
WHY?
THE DAY BEFORE...
OPEN WIDE, RIIKO! ♥
WHAT!?

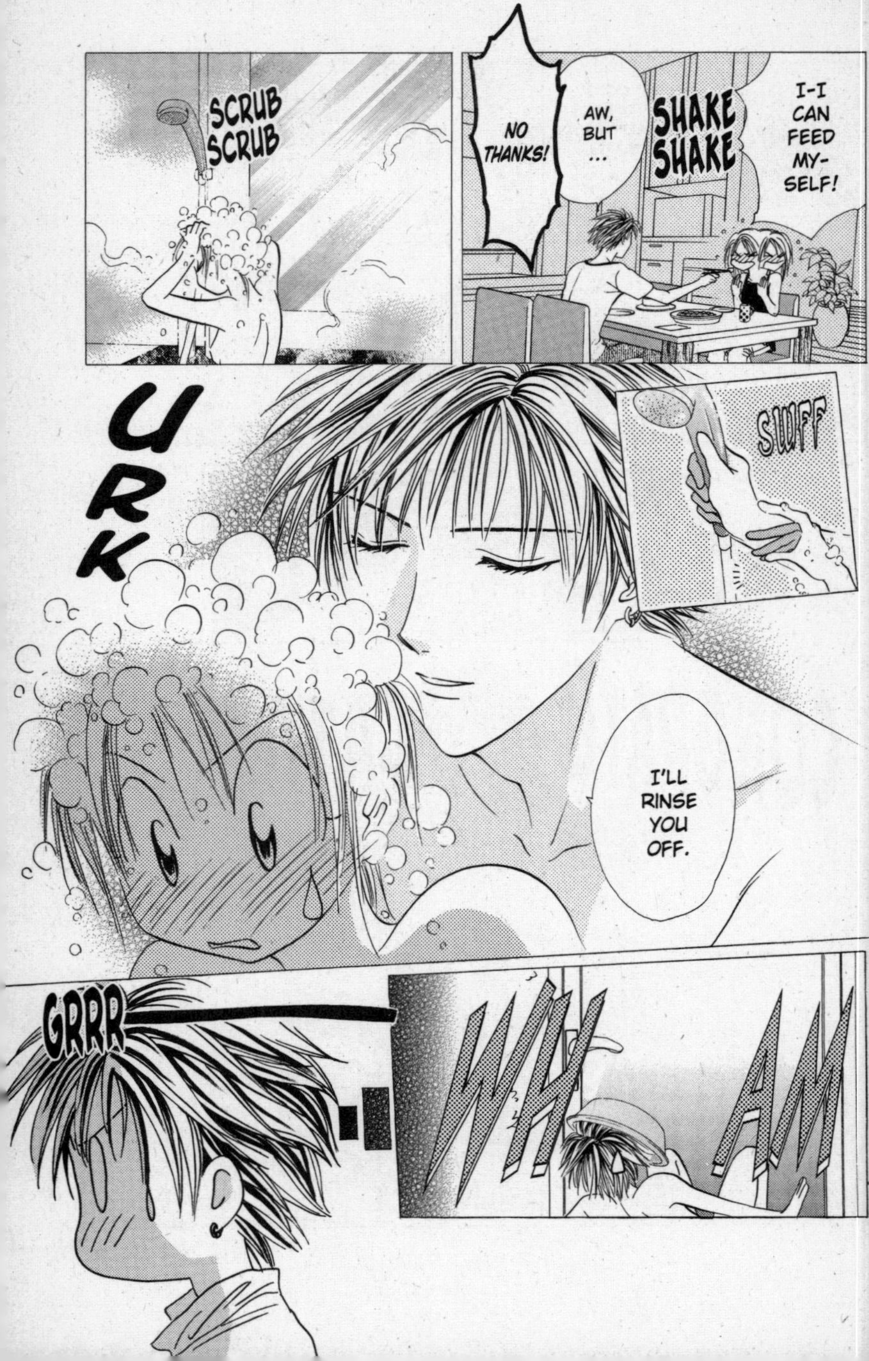
I-I CAN FEED MY-SELF!
SHAKE SHAKE
AW, BUT ...
NO THANKS!
SCRUB SCRUB
SWFF
I'LL RINSE YOU OFF.
URK
WHAM
GRRR

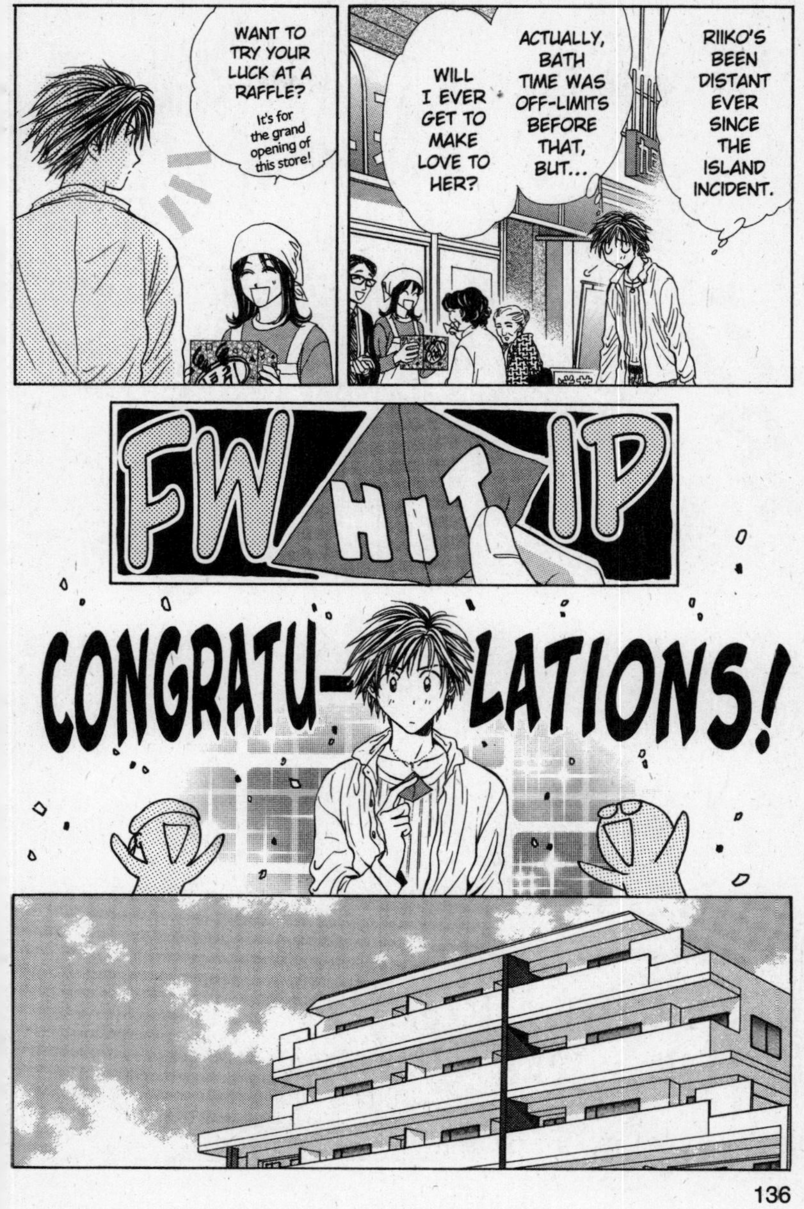
RIIKO'S BEEN DISTANT EVER SINCE THE ISLAND INCIDENT.
ACTUALLY, BATH TIME WAS OFF-LIMITS BEFORE THAT, BUT...
WILL I EVER GET TO MAKE LOVE TO HER?
WANT TO TRY YOUR LUCK AT A RAFFLE?
It's for the grand opening of this store!
FWIP
HIT
CONGRATU-LATIONS!

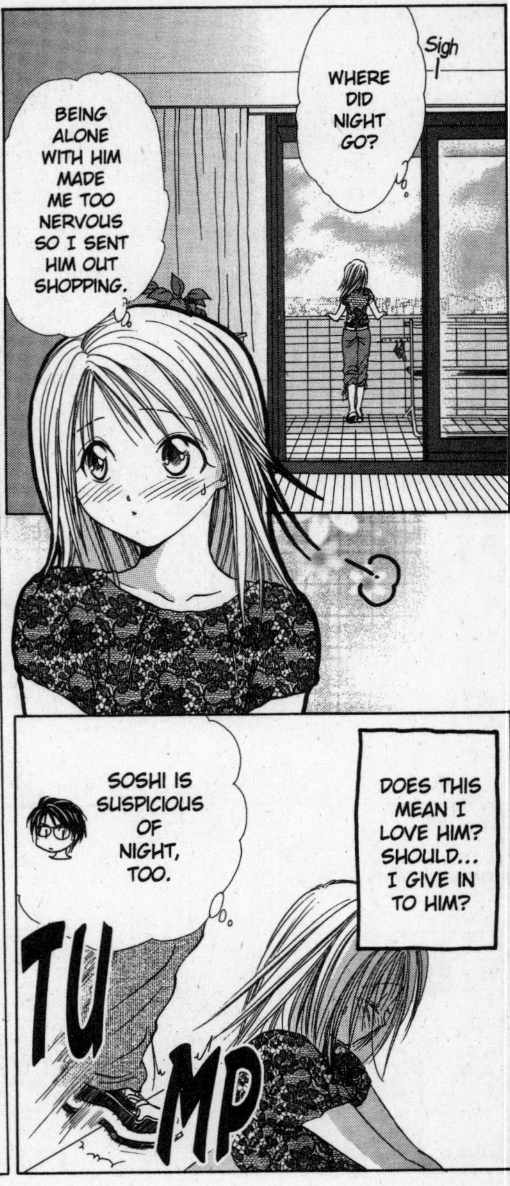
Sigh
WHERE DID NIGHT GO?
BEING ALONE WITH HIM MADE ME TOO NERVOUS SO I SENT HIM OUT SHOPPING.
DOES THIS MEAN I LOVE HIM? SHOULD... I GIVE IN TO HIM?
SOSHI IS SUSPICIOUS OF NIGHT, TOO.
TUMP

Hmm, I've been doing this for 16 years. I'm currently trying to streamline my art more. I used to go crazy and stick screentone all over the place. Now looking at the latter half of *Fushigi Yugi* or *Ceres* makes my eyes hurt. I'm amazed I did all that. But it's okay because I loved doing it at the time. Now I wish I could do away with screentone altogether and just do black-and-white line art (smile). (But that's probably unlikely.) Working for a commercial publication is always a race against time, so I have to sacrifice some of the details... It's not that I'm cutting corners, there's just no point in getting hung up on details if I can't make my deadlines. But I'd prefer to be really obsessive about them. It's sad to think that I could do more when I was younger and had more stamina. I've redirected my perfectionism into other aspects of my work, so the problem is how to do it all within the time constraints. There's so much I wish I could do!! But there's no point talking about it (smile). It's better to conserve my energy. But do I even have any to conserve? I can never be fully satisfied with my work. Are all artists like that? I can't believe I totally forget how to do all the screentone effects once a title ends. I look through my old stuff and I'm like, "Huh!? How'd I do that!?" Seriously. I even forget how to draw after every title!? Come on!!

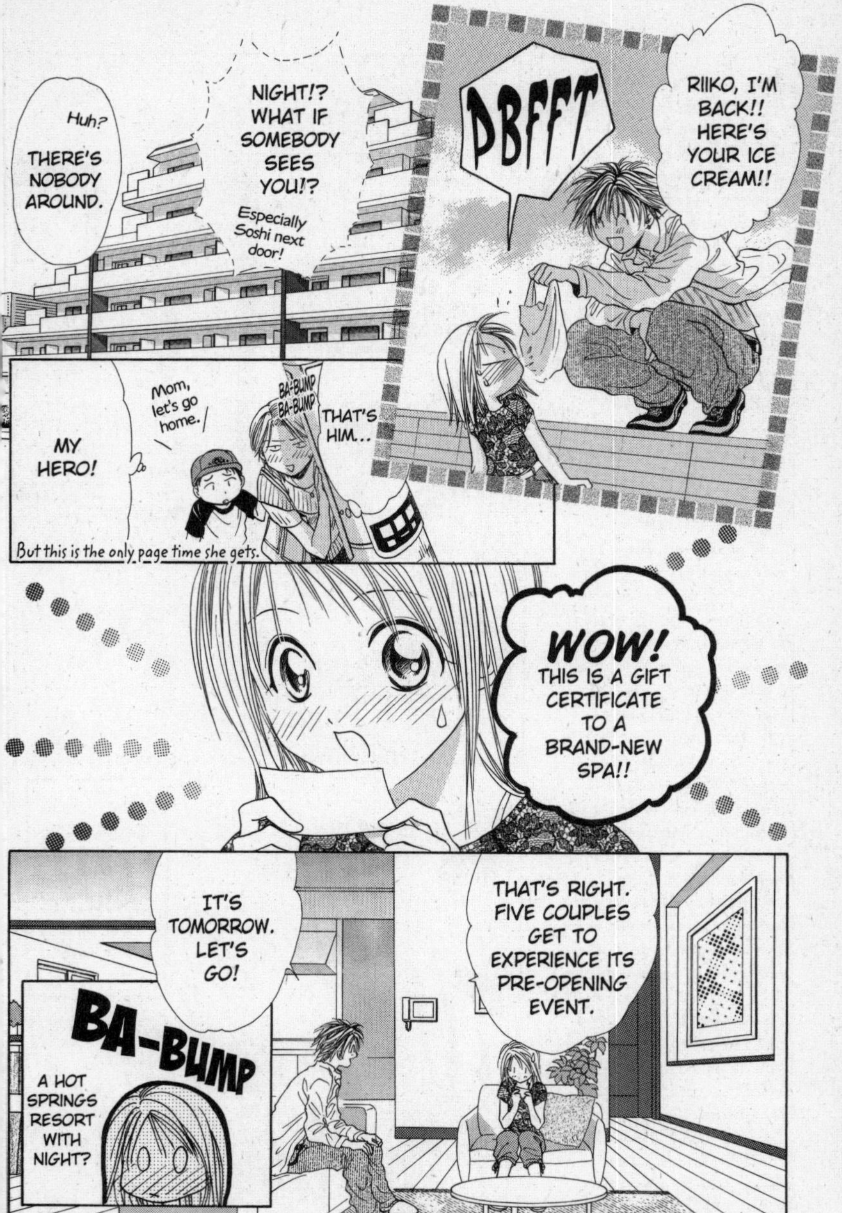
RIIKO, I'M BACK!! HERE'S YOUR ICE CREAM!!
PBFFT
NIGHT!? WHAT IF SOMEBODY SEES YOU!?
Especially Soshi next door!
Huh?
THERE'S NOBODY AROUND.
THAT'S HIM...
BA-BUMP BA-BUMP
Mom, let's go home.
MY HERO!
But this is the only page time she gets.
WOW!
THIS IS A GIFT CERTIFICATE TO A BRAND-NEW SPA!!
THAT'S RIGHT. FIVE COUPLES GET TO EXPERIENCE ITS PRE-OPENING EVENT.
IT'S TOMORROW. LET'S GO!
BA-BUMP
A HOT SPRINGS RESORT WITH NIGHT?

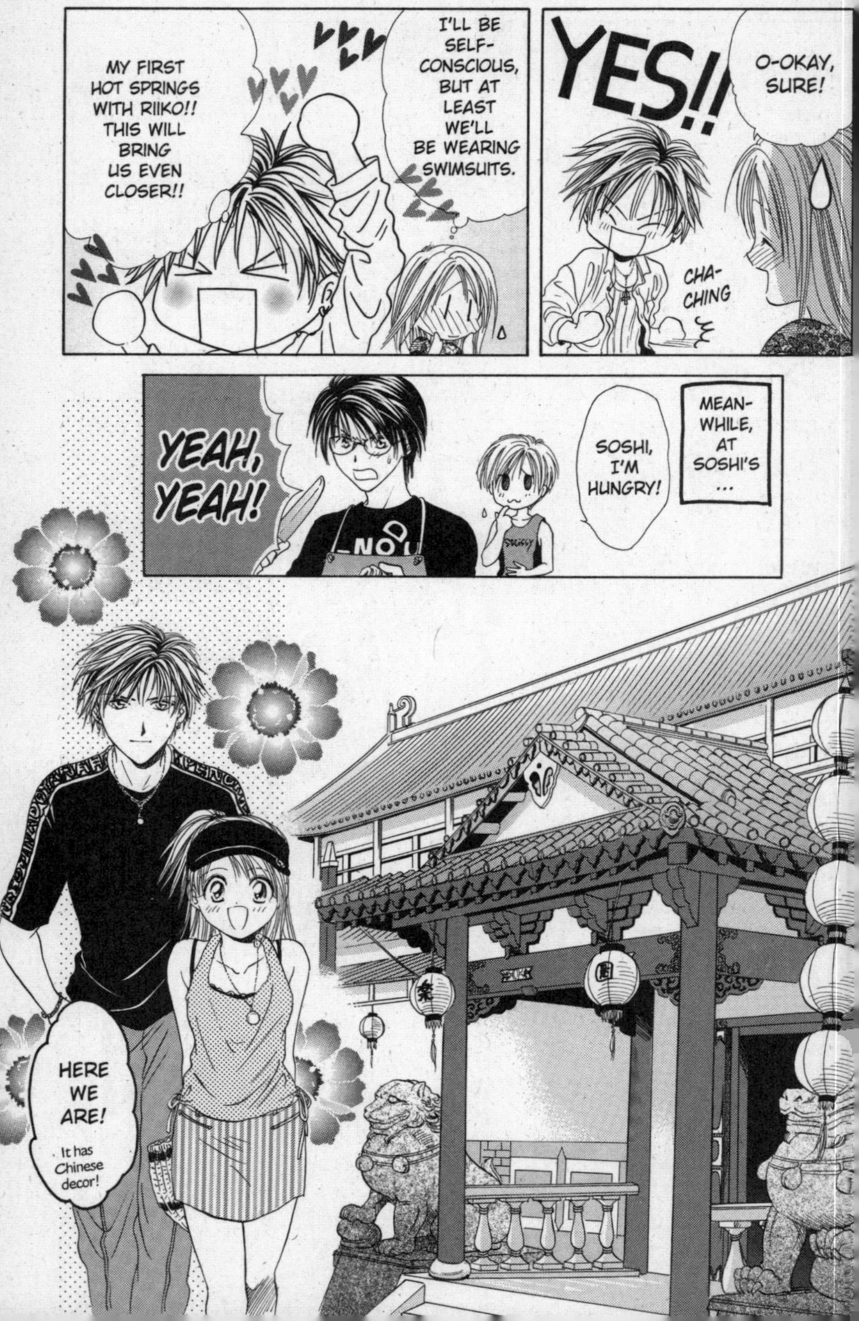
O-OKAY, SURE!
YES!!
CHA-CHING
I'LL BE SELF-CONSCIOUS, BUT AT LEAST WE'LL BE WEARING SWIMSUITS.
MY FIRST HOT SPRINGS WITH RIIKO!! THIS WILL BRING US EVEN CLOSER!!
MEAN-WHILE, AT SOSHI'S ...
SOSHI, I'M HUNGRY!
YEAH, YEAH!
HERE WE ARE!
It has Chinese decor!

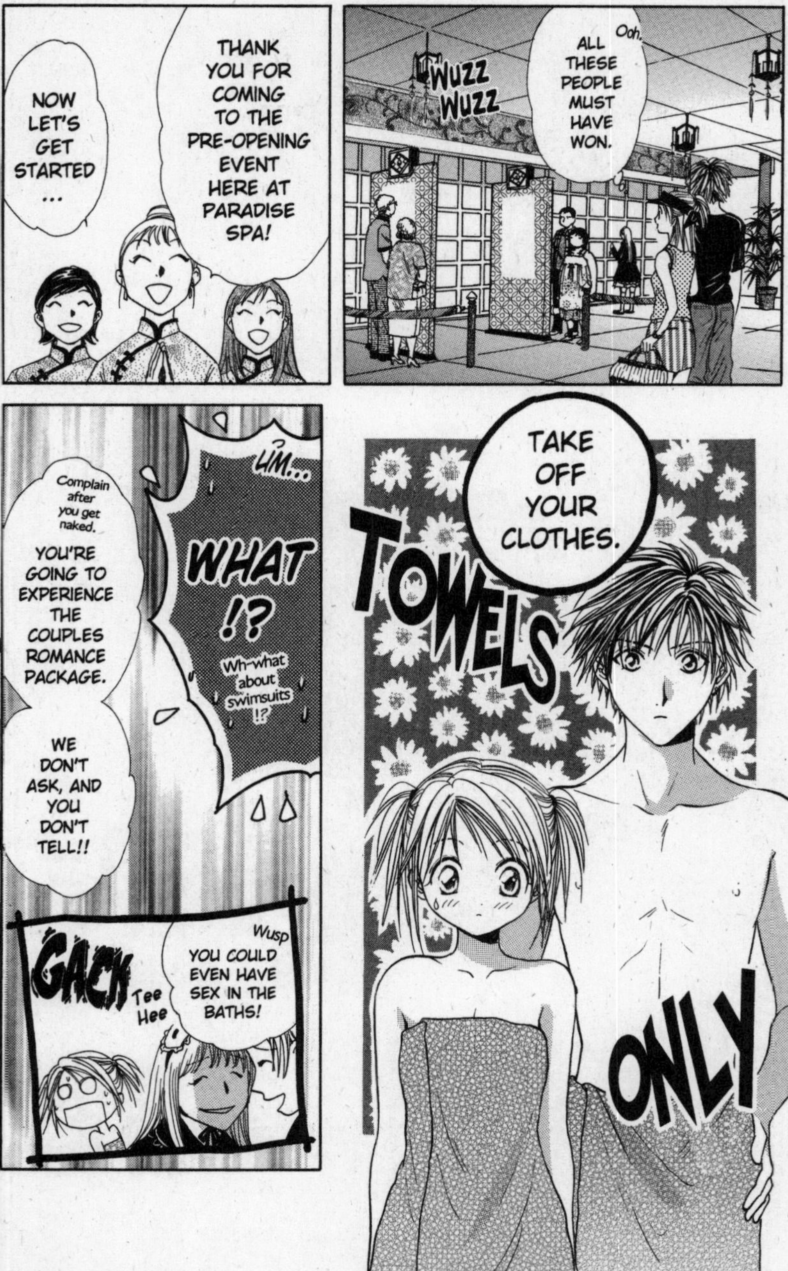
WUZZ WUZZ
Ooh.
ALL THESE PEOPLE MUST HAVE WON.
THANK YOU FOR COMING TO THE PRE-OPENING EVENT HERE AT PARADISE SPA!
NOW LET'S GET STARTED...
TAKE OFF YOUR CLOTHES.
TOWELS ONLY
UM...
WHAT!?
Wh-what about swimsuits!?
Complain after you get naked.
YOU'RE GOING TO EXPERIENCE THE COUPLES ROMANCE PACKAGE.
WE DON'T ASK, AND YOU DON'T TELL!!
Wusp
YOU COULD EVEN HAVE SEX IN THE BATHS!
Tee Hee
GACK

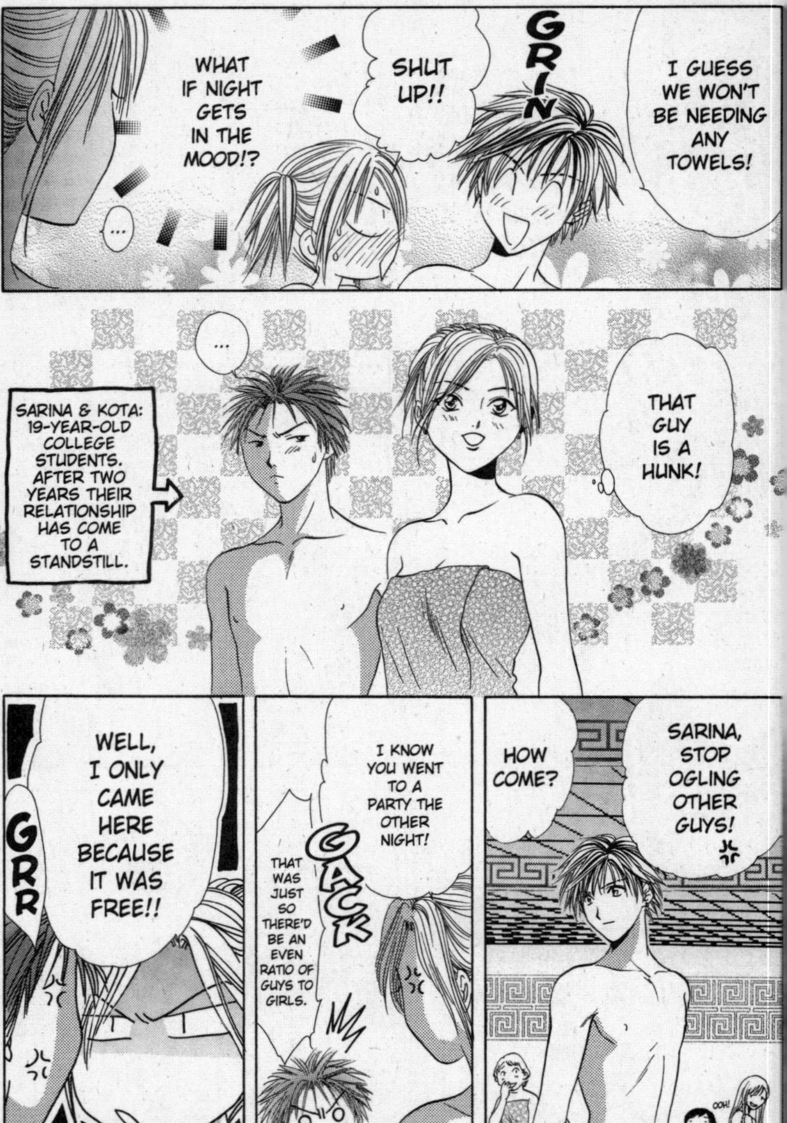
I GUESS WE WON'T BE NEEDING ANY TOWELS!
GRIN
SHUT UP!!
WHAT IF NIGHT GETS IN THE MOOD!?
...
THAT GUY IS A HUNK!
...
SARINA & KOTA: 19-YEAR-OLD COLLEGE STUDENTS. AFTER TWO YEARS THEIR RELATIONSHIP HAS COME TO A STANDSTILL.
SARINA, STOP OGLING OTHER GUYS!
HOW COME?
OOH!
I KNOW YOU WENT TO A PARTY THE OTHER NIGHT!
GACK
THAT WAS JUST SO THERE'D BE AN EVEN RATIO OF GUYS TO GIRLS.
WELL, I ONLY CAME HERE BECAUSE IT WAS FREE!!
GRR

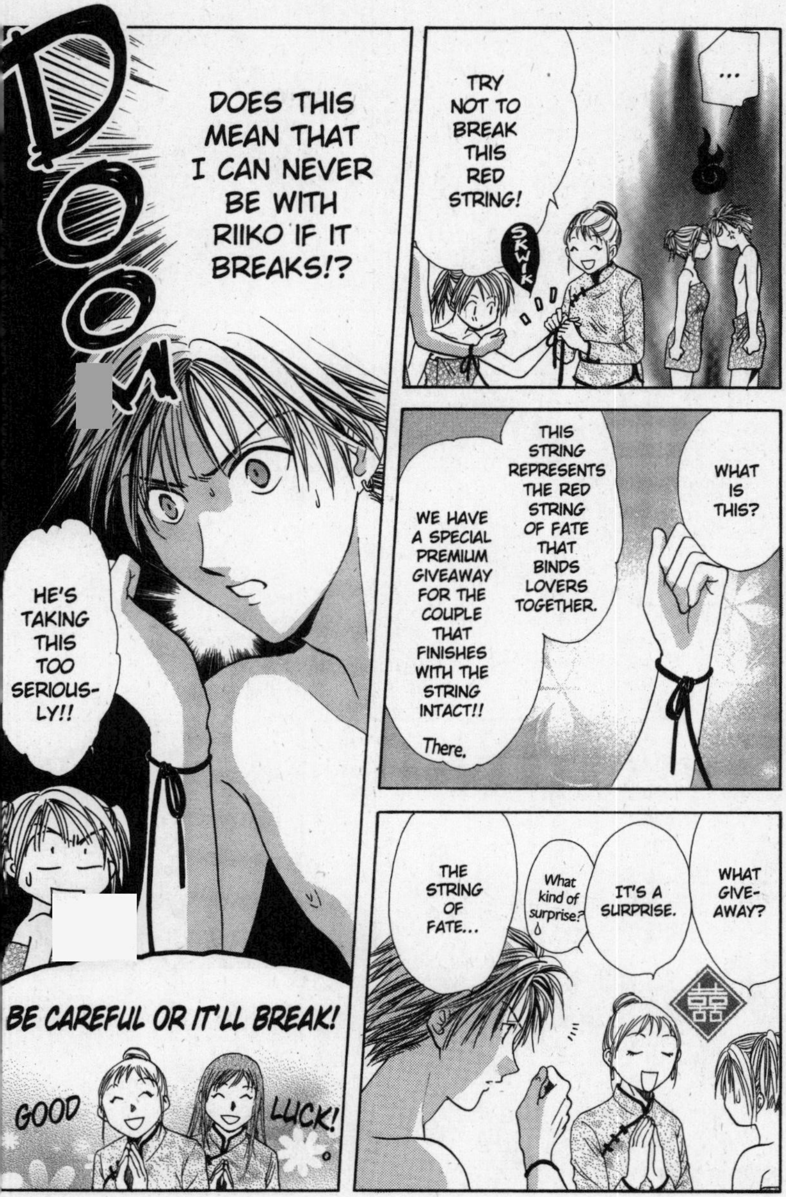
...
TRY NOT TO BREAK THIS RED STRING!
SKWIK
WHAT IS THIS?
THIS STRING REPRESENTS THE RED STRING OF FATE THAT BINDS LOVERS TOGETHER.
WE HAVE A SPECIAL PREMIUM GIVEAWAY FOR THE COUPLE THAT FINISHES WITH THE STRING INTACT!!
There.
WHAT GIVE-AWAY?
IT'S A SURPRISE.
What kind of surprise?
THE STRING OF FATE...
DOOOM
DOES THIS MEAN THAT I CAN NEVER BE WITH RIIKO IF IT BREAKS!?
HE'S TAKING THIS TOO SERIOUS-LY!!
BE CAREFUL OR IT'LL BREAK!
GOOD LUCK!

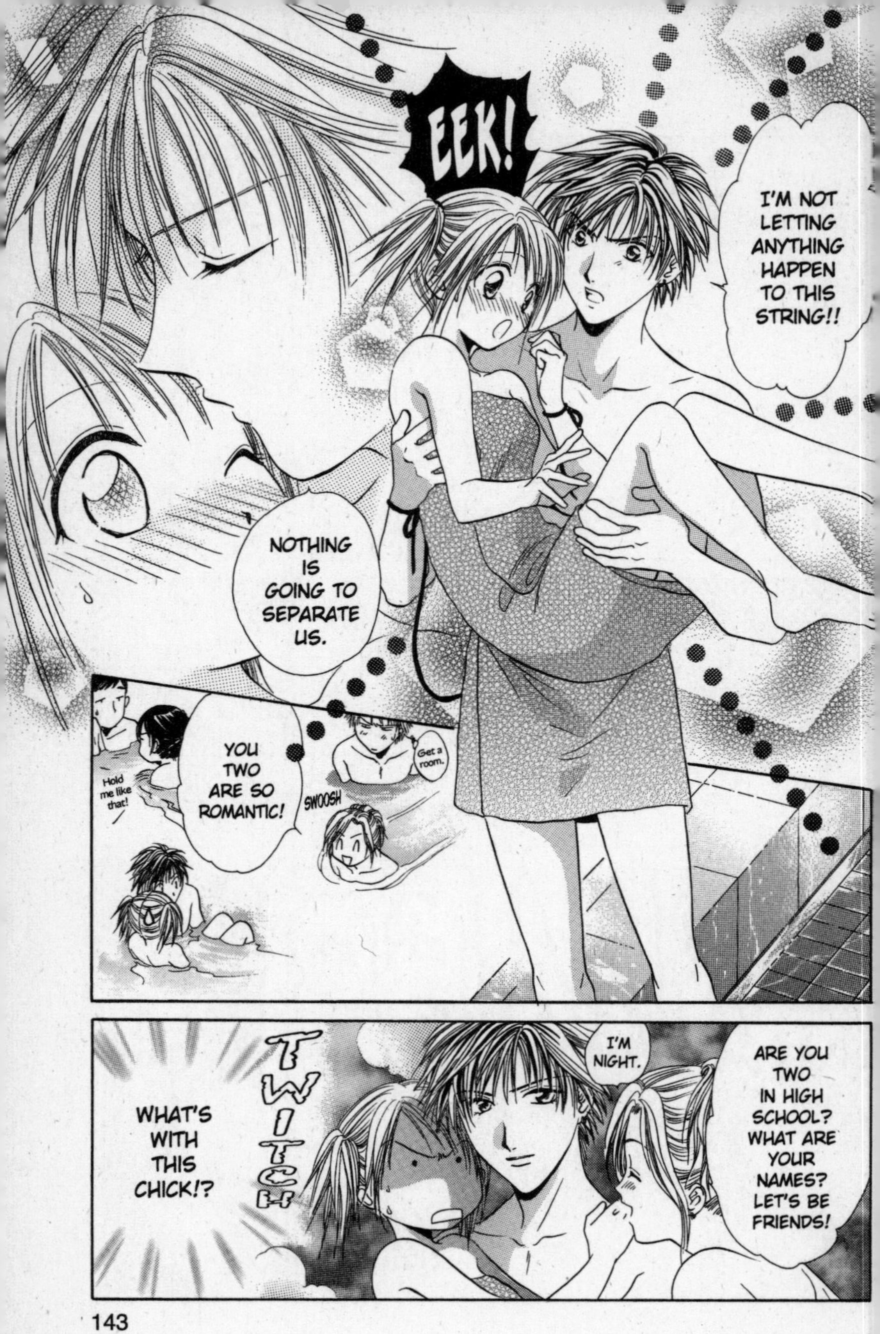
EEK!
I'M NOT LETTING ANYTHING HAPPEN TO THIS STRING!!
NOTHING IS GOING TO SEPARATE US.
Get a room.
YOU TWO ARE SO ROMANTIC!
Hold me like that!
SWOOSH
ARE YOU TWO IN HIGH SCHOOL? WHAT ARE YOUR NAMES? LET'S BE FRIENDS!
I'M NIGHT.
TWITCH
WHAT'S WITH THIS CHICK!?

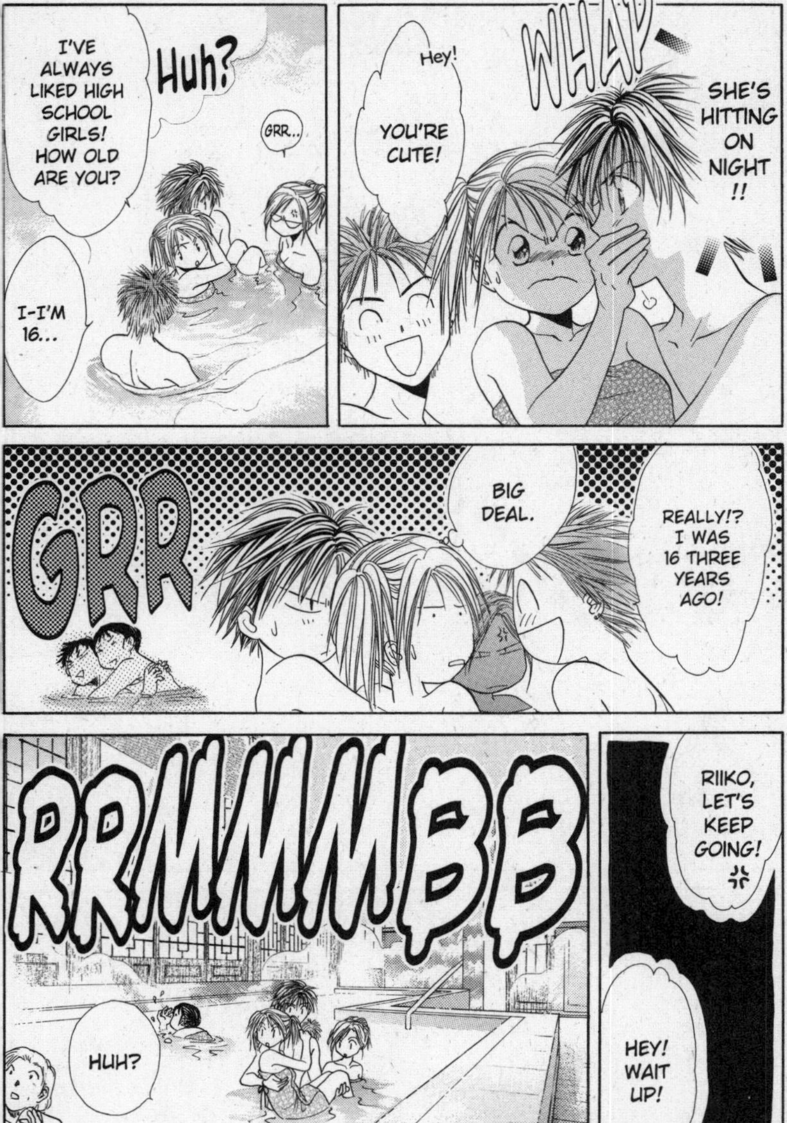
Hey!
YOU'RE CUTE!
WHAP
SHE'S HITTING ON NIGHT!!
I'VE ALWAYS LIKED HIGH SCHOOL GIRLS! HOW OLD ARE YOU?
Huh?
GRR...
I-I'M 16...
REALLY!? I WAS 16 THREE YEARS AGO!
BIG DEAL.
GRR
RIIKO, LET'S KEEP GOING!
HEY! WAIT UP!
RRMMMBB
HUH?

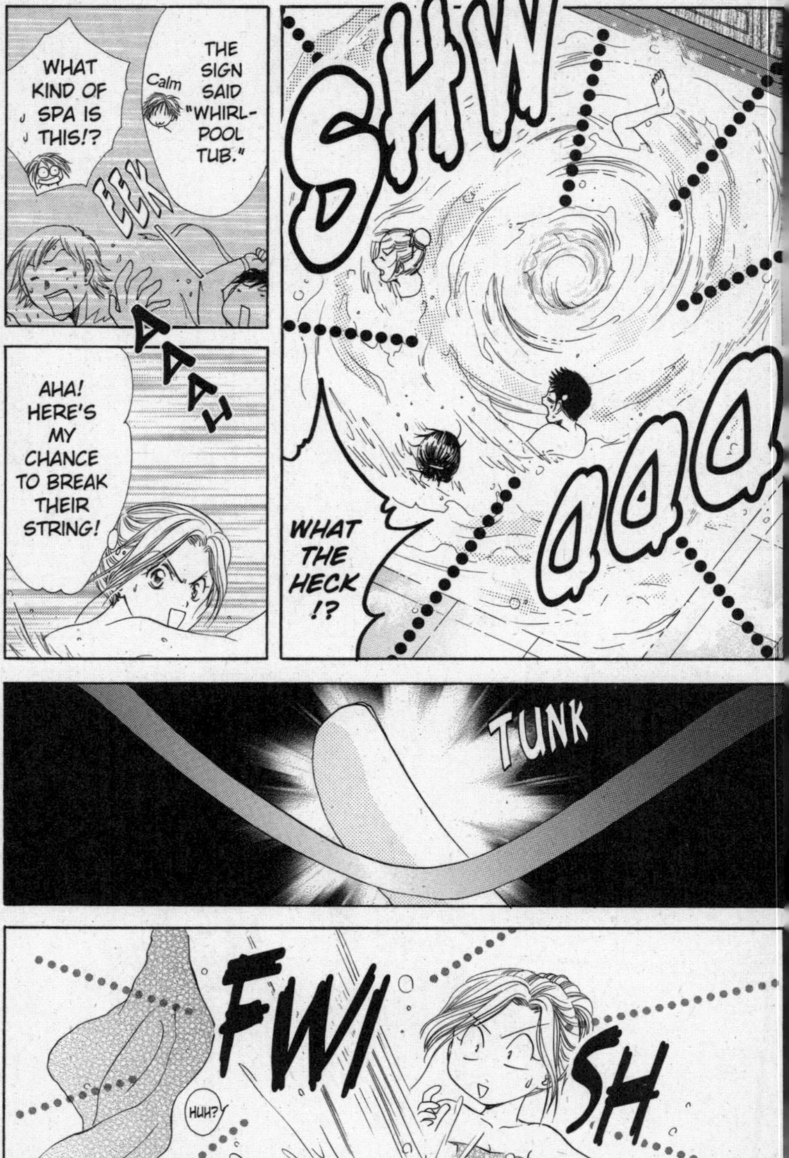
SHWAAA
WHAT THE HECK!?
Calm
THE SIGN SAID "WHIRLPOOL TUB."
WHAT KIND OF SPA IS THIS!?
EEK
AHA! HERE'S MY CHANCE TO BREAK THEIR STRING!
TUNK
FWISH
HUH?

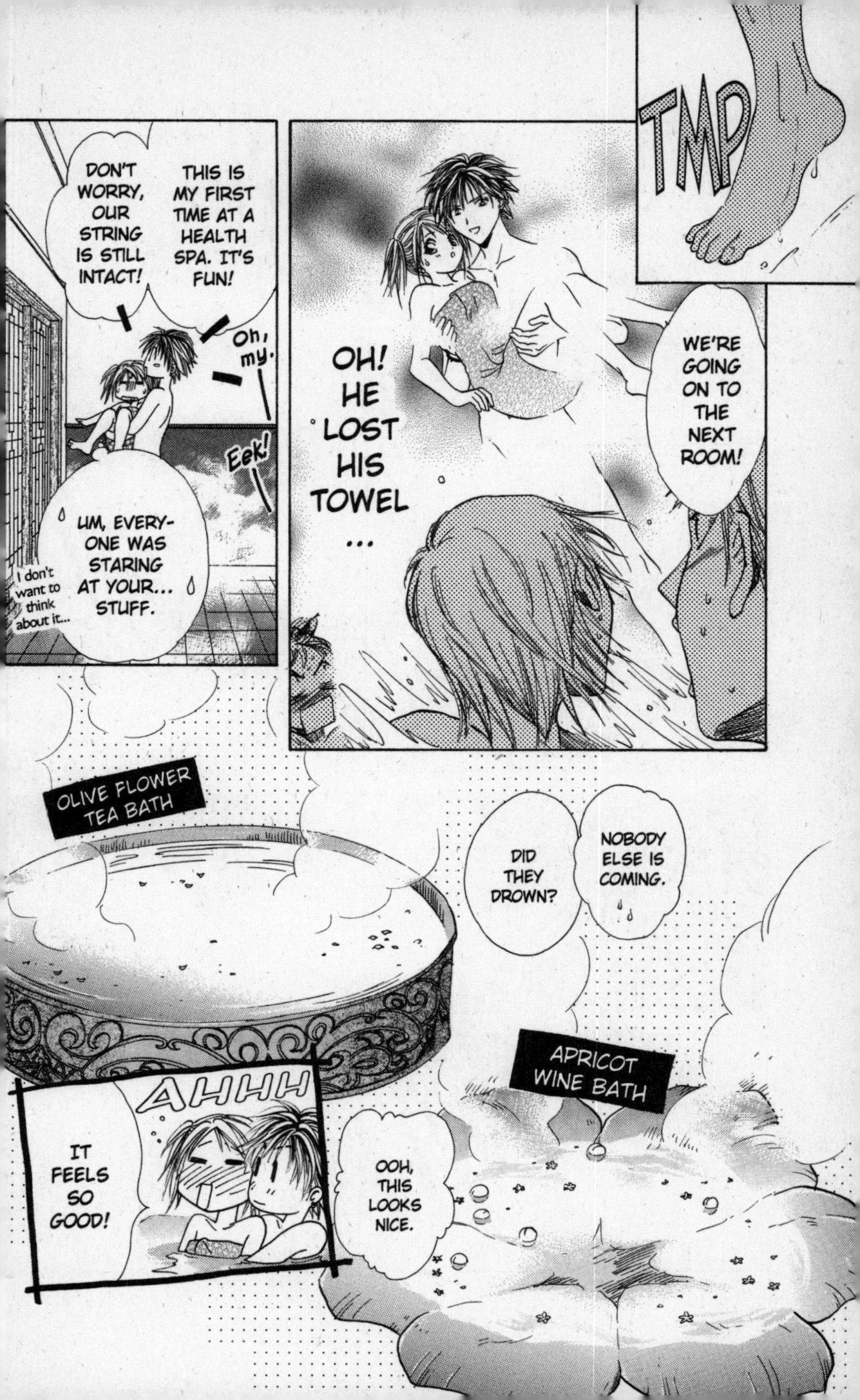
TMP
WE'RE GOING ON TO THE NEXT ROOM!
OH! HE LOST HIS TOWEL...
THIS IS MY FIRST TIME AT A HEALTH SPA. IT'S FUN!
DON'T WORRY, OUR STRING IS STILL INTACT!
Oh, my.
Eek!
UM, EVERYONE WAS STARING AT YOUR... STUFF.
I don't want to think about it...
NOBODY ELSE IS COMING.
DID THEY DROWN?
OLIVE FLOWER TEA BATH
APRICOT WINE BATH
OOH, THIS LOOKS NICE.
AHHH
IT FEELS SO GOOD!

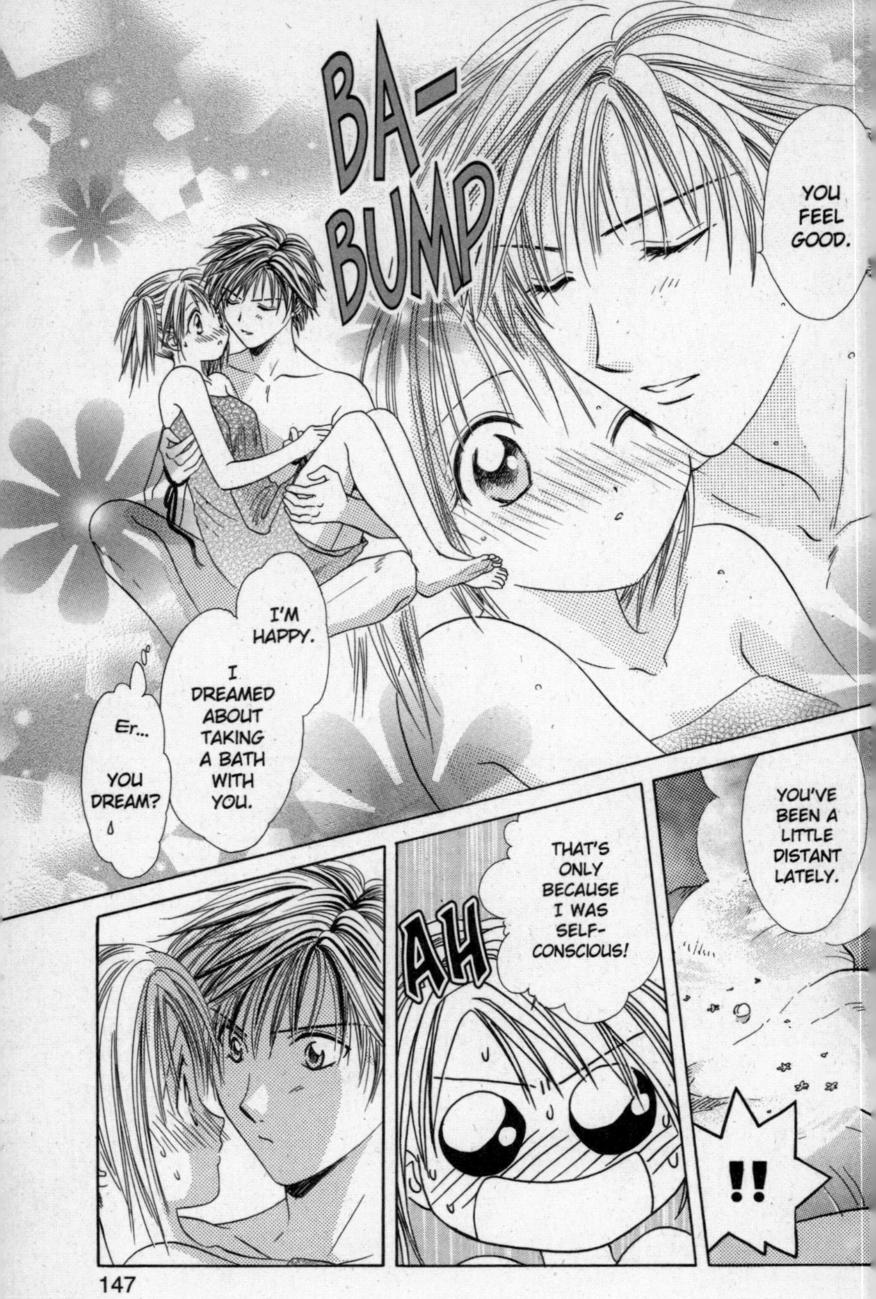
YOU FEEL GOOD.
BA-BUMP
I'M HAPPY.
I DREAMED ABOUT TAKING A BATH WITH YOU.
Er...
YOU DREAM?
YOU'VE BEEN A LITTLE DISTANT LATELY.
!!
THAT'S ONLY BECAUSE I WAS SELF-CONSCIOUS!
AH

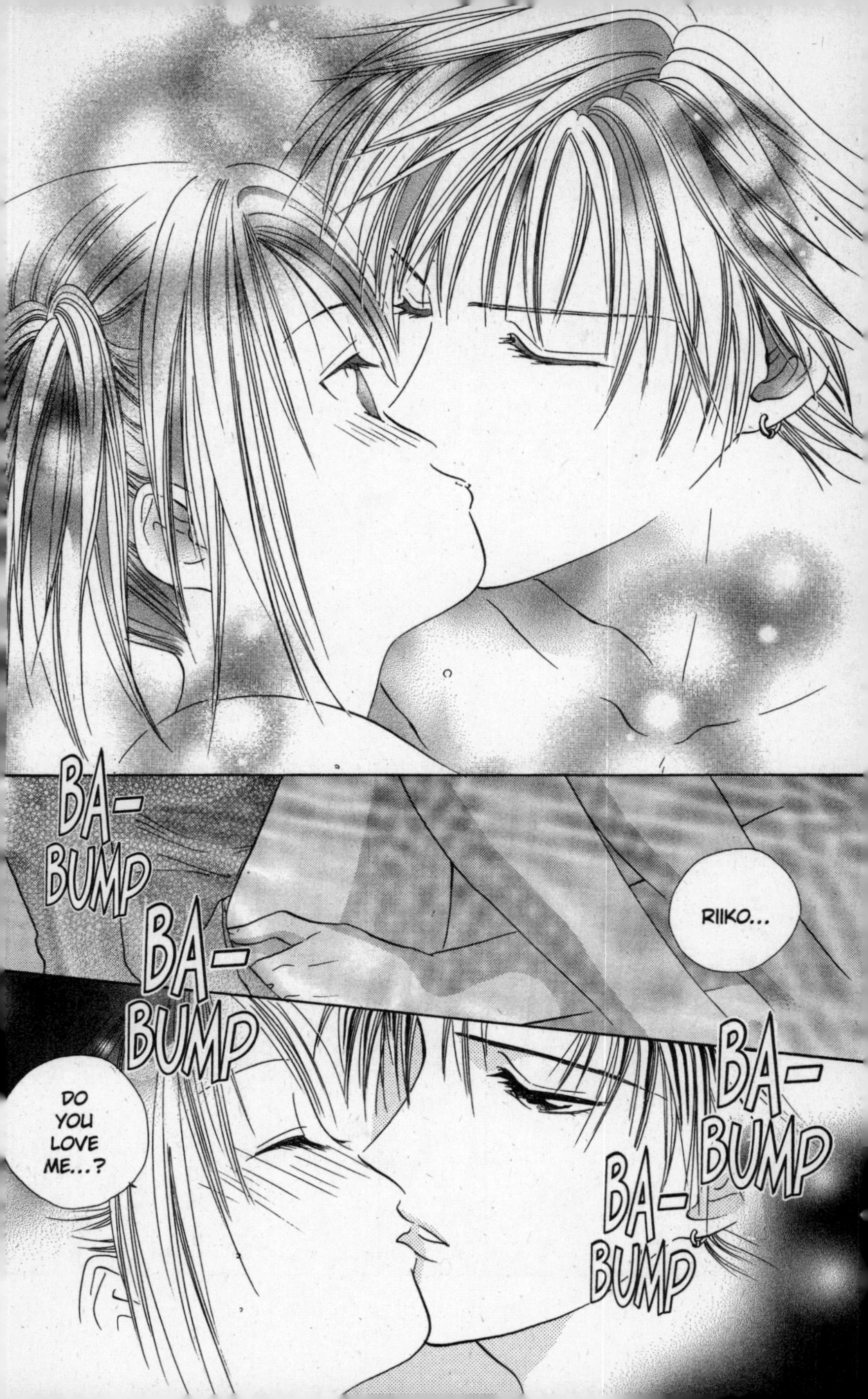
RIIKO...
BA-BUMP
BA-BUMP
BA-BUMP
BA-BUMP
DO YOU LOVE ME...?

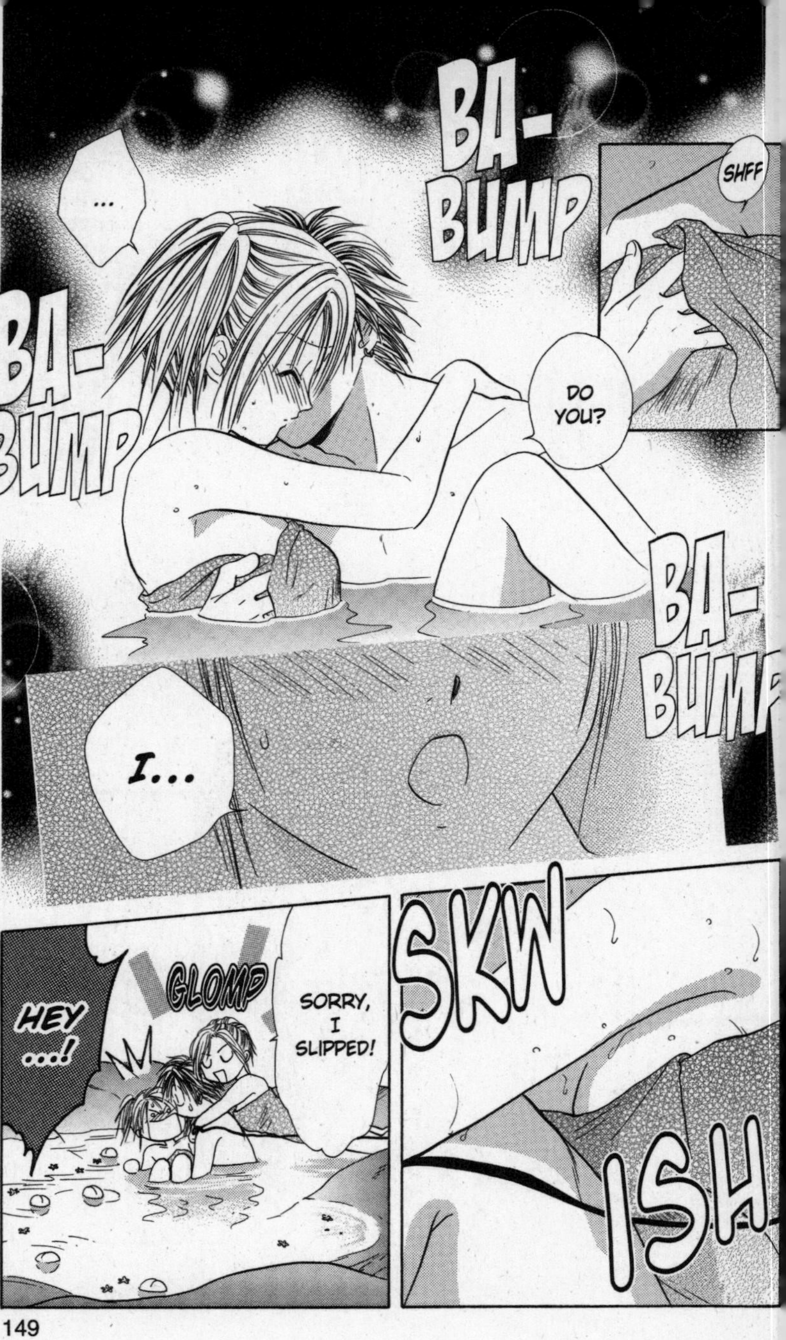
SHFF
BA-BUMP
DO YOU?
...
BA-BUMP
BA-BUMP
I...
SKWISH
SORRY, I SLIPPED!
GLOMP
HEY ...!

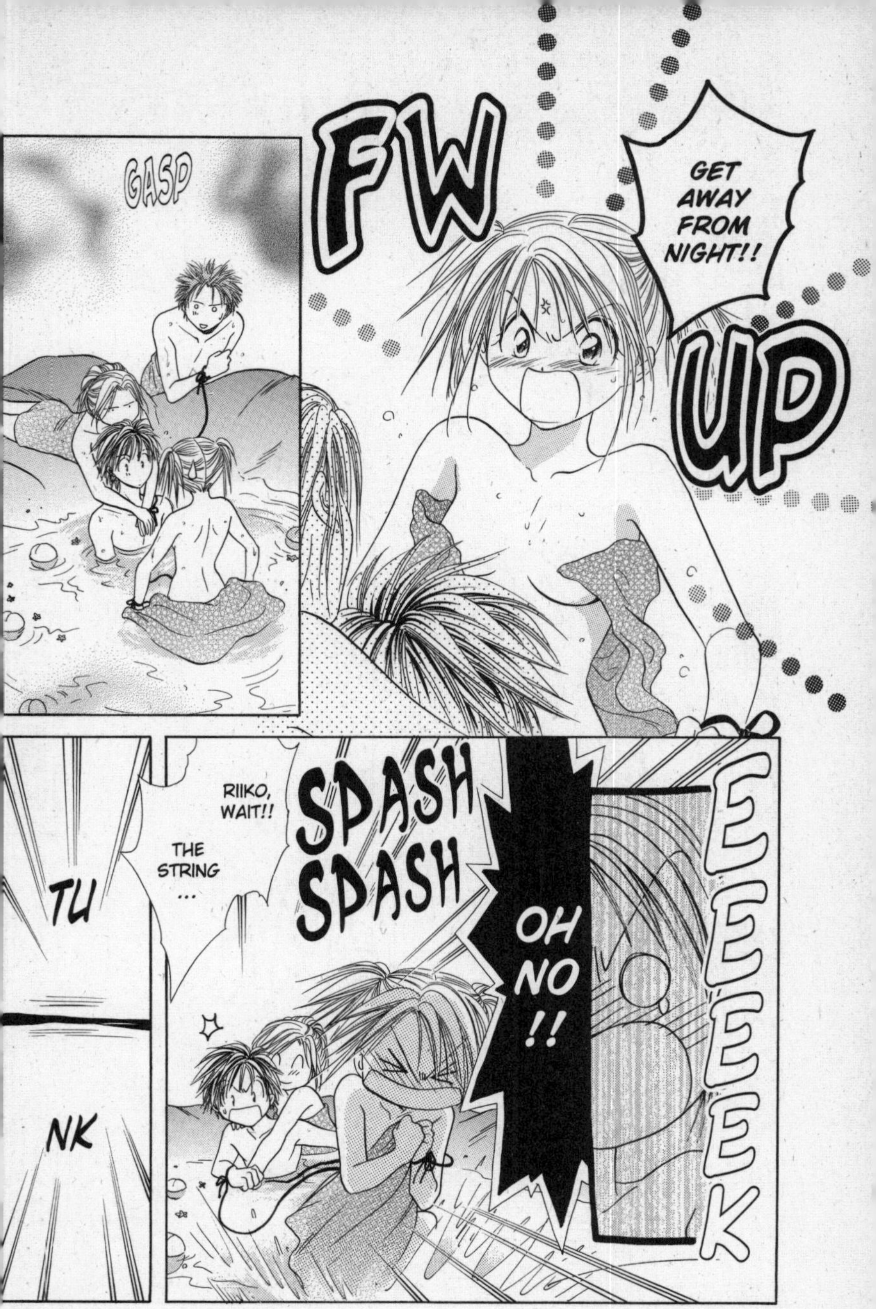
FW
UP
GET AWAY FROM NIGHT!!
GASP
EEEEEEK
SPASH SPASH
RIIKO, WAIT!!
THE STRING ...
OH NO !!
TU
NK

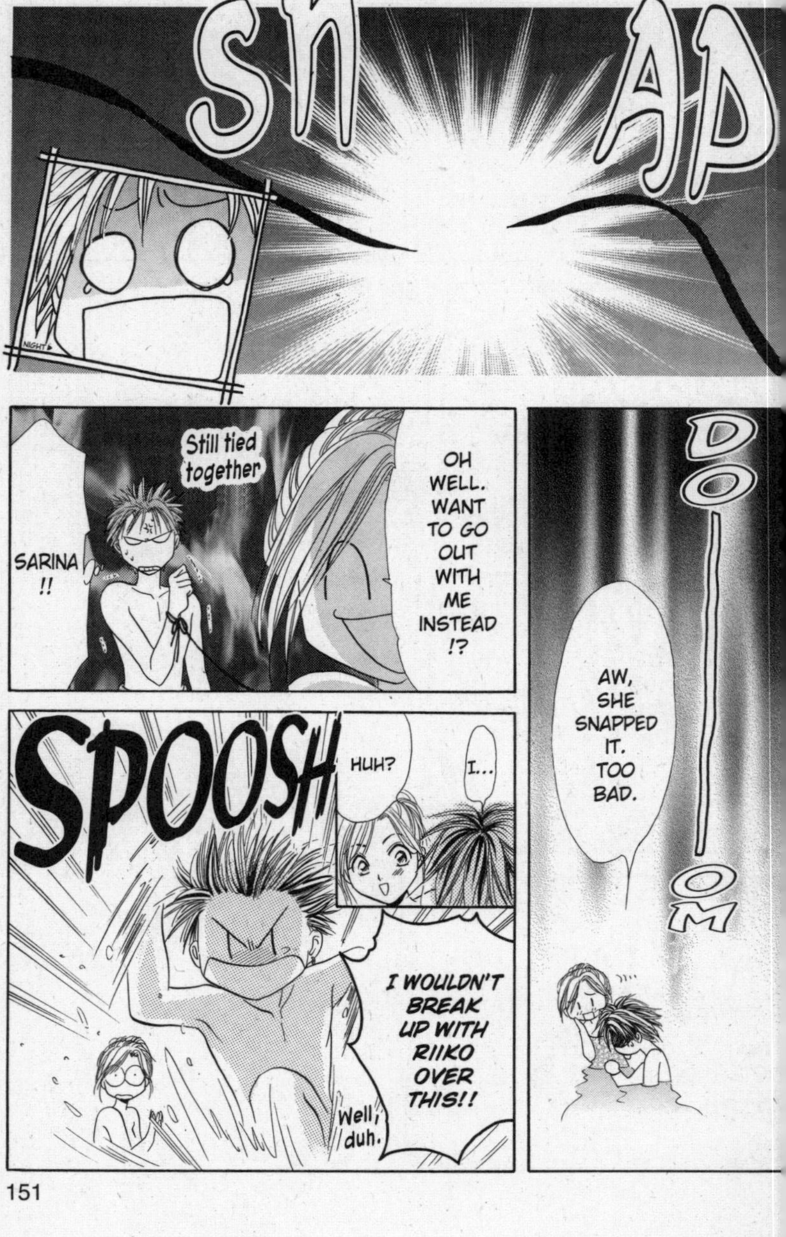
SNAP
NIGHT
DOOM
AW, SHE SNAPPED IT. TOO BAD.
OH WELL. WANT TO GO OUT WITH ME INSTEAD!?
Still tied together
SARINA!!
I...
HUH?
SPOOSH
I WOULDN'T BREAK UP WITH RIIKO OVER THIS!!
Well, duh.

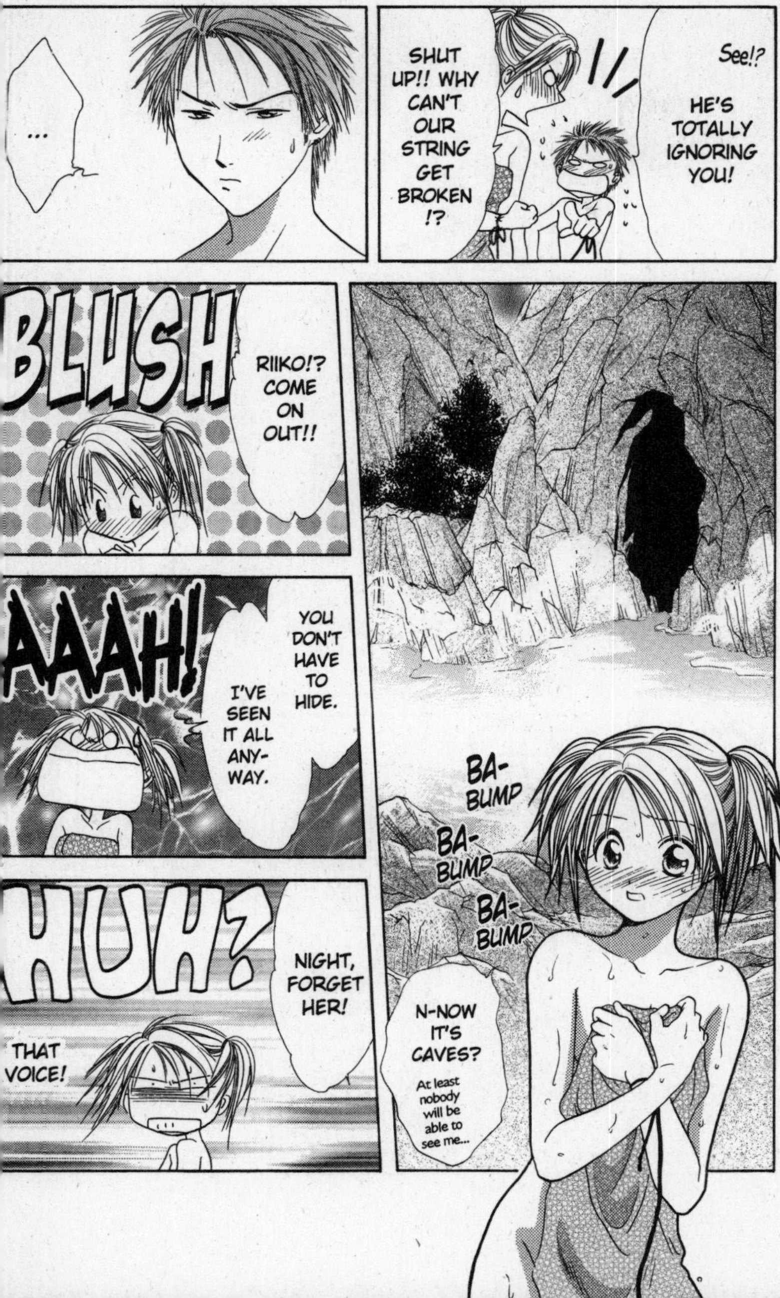
See!?
HE'S TOTALLY IGNORING YOU!
SHUT UP!! WHY CAN'T OUR STRING GET BROKEN!?
...
BA-BUMP
BA-BUMP
BA-BUMP
N-NOW IT'S CAVES?
At least nobody will be able to see me...
RIIKO!? COME ON OUT!!
BLUSH
YOU DON'T HAVE TO HIDE.
I'VE SEEN IT ALL ANY-WAY.
AAAH!
NIGHT, FORGET HER!
HUH?
THAT VOICE!

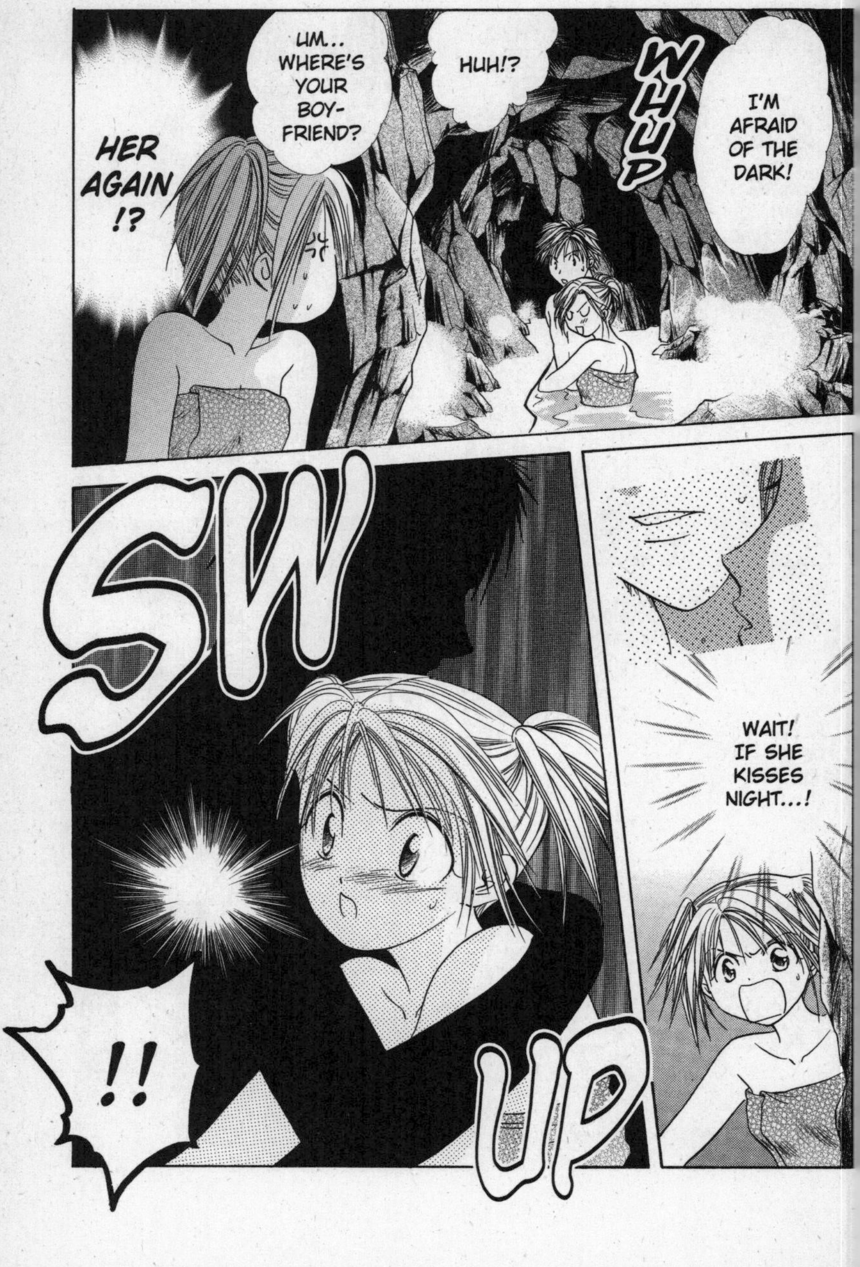
I'M AFRAID OF THE DARK!
WHUP
HUH!?
UM.. WHERE'S YOUR BOY-FRIEND?
HER AGAIN !?
WAIT! IF SHE KISSES NIGHT...!
SW
UP
!!

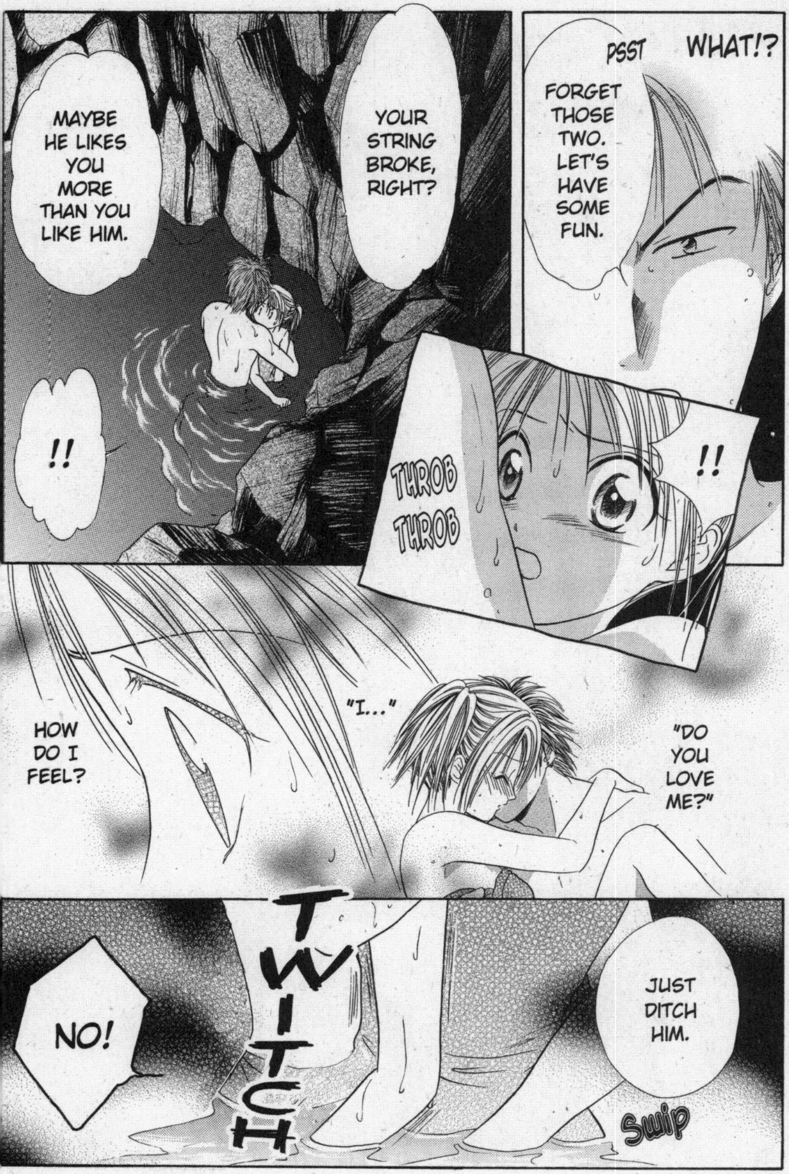
WHAT!?
PSST
FORGET THOSE TWO. LET'S HAVE SOME FUN.
YOUR STRING BROKE, RIGHT?
MAYBE HE LIKES YOU MORE THAN YOU LIKE HIM.
!!
!!
THROB THROB
"DO YOU LOVE ME?"
"I..."
HOW DO I FEEL?
JUST DITCH HIM.
Swip
TWITCH
NO!

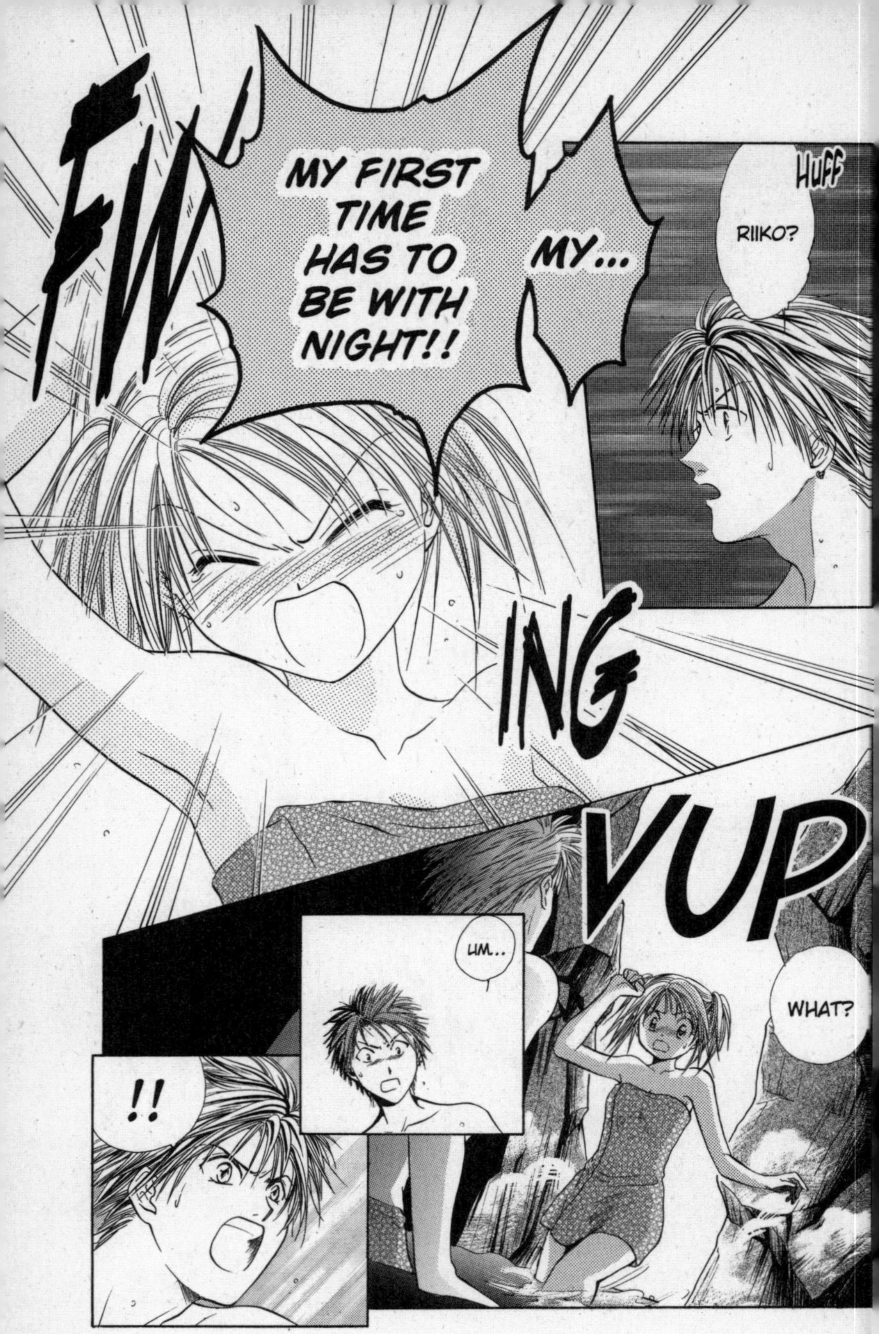
HUFF
RIIKO?
MY...
MY FIRST TIME HAS TO BE WITH NIGHT!!
FWING
VUP
WHAT?
UM...
!!

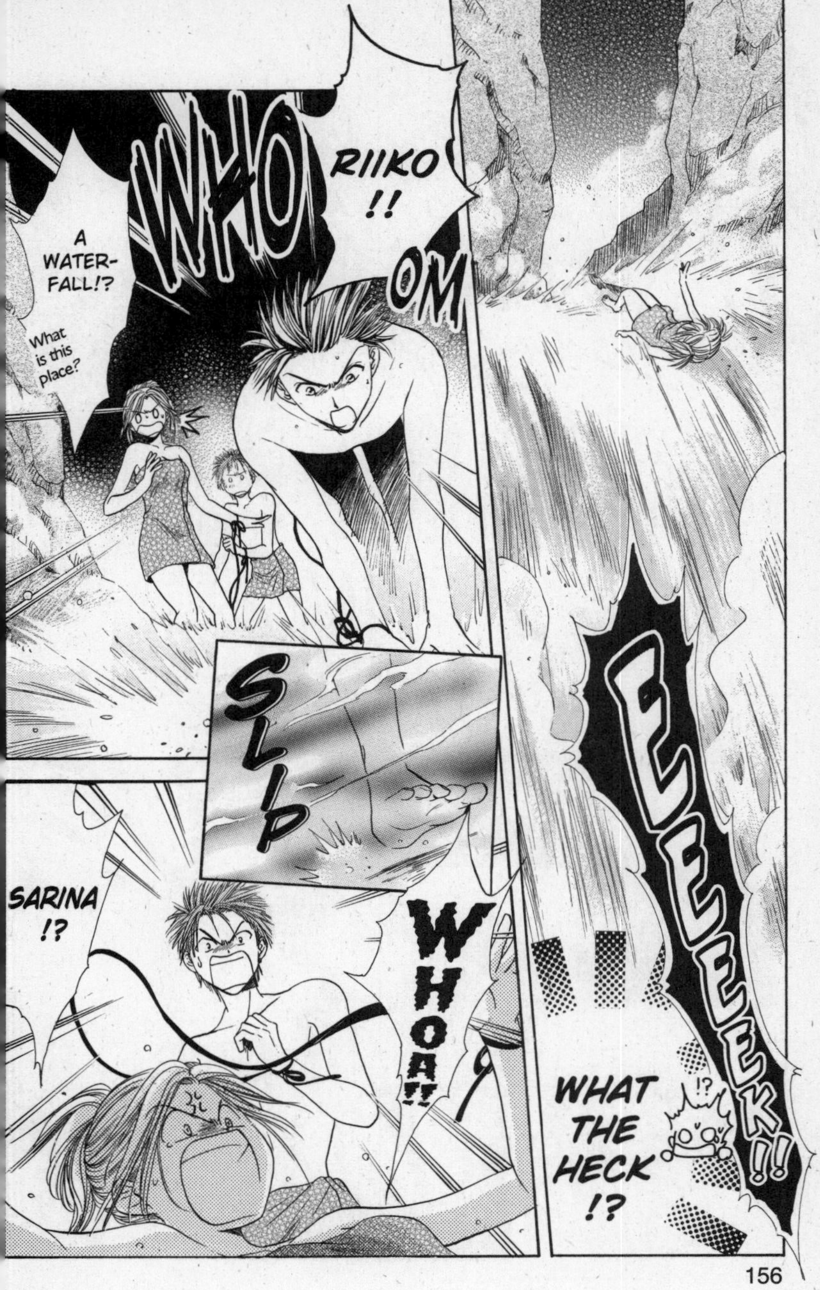
EEEEEK!!
WHAT THE HECK !?
!?
RIIKO !!
WHOOM
A WATERFALL!?
What is this place?
SLIP
WHOA!!
SARINA !?

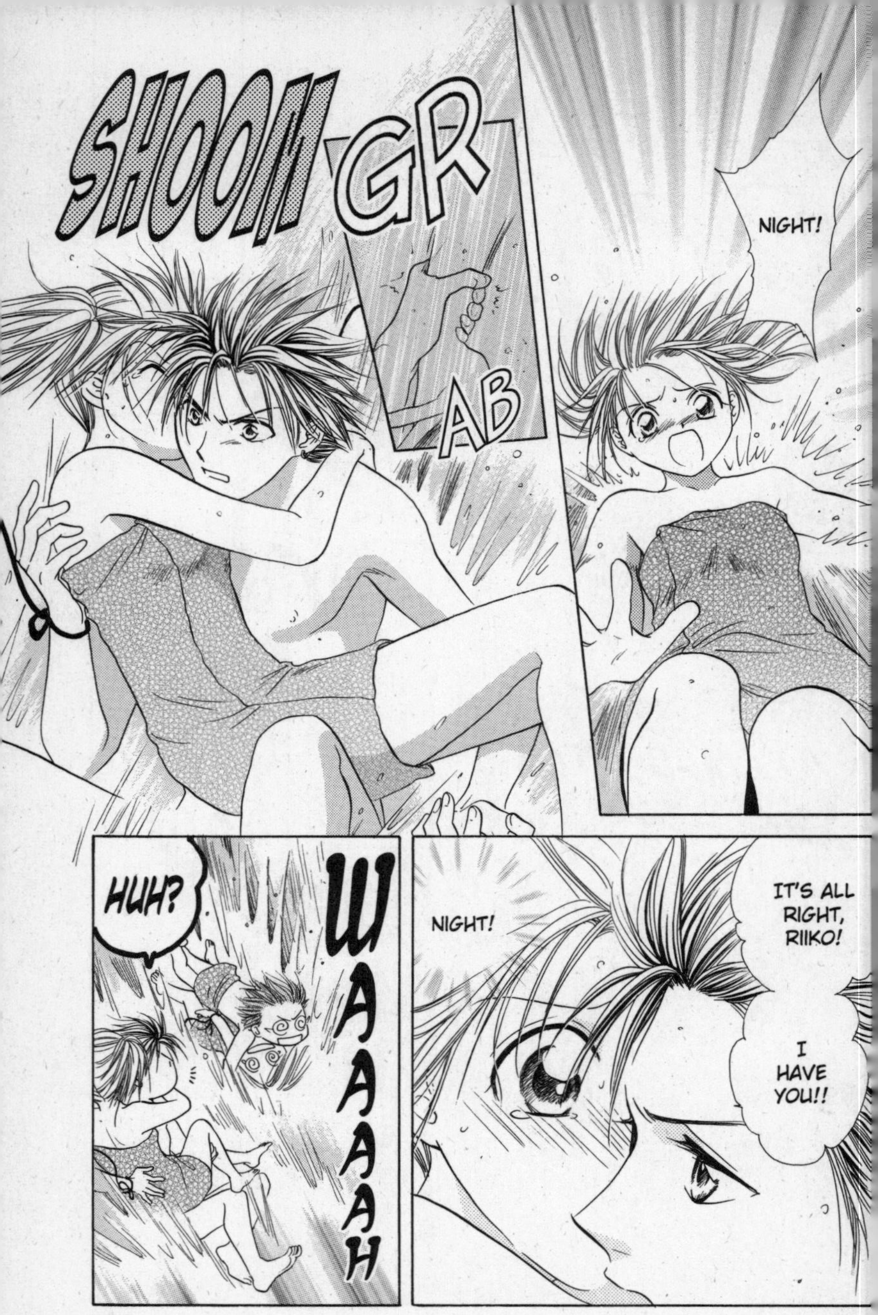
NIGHT!
GRAB
SHOOM
IT'S ALL RIGHT, RIIKO!
I HAVE YOU!!
NIGHT!
WAAAAAAH
HUH?

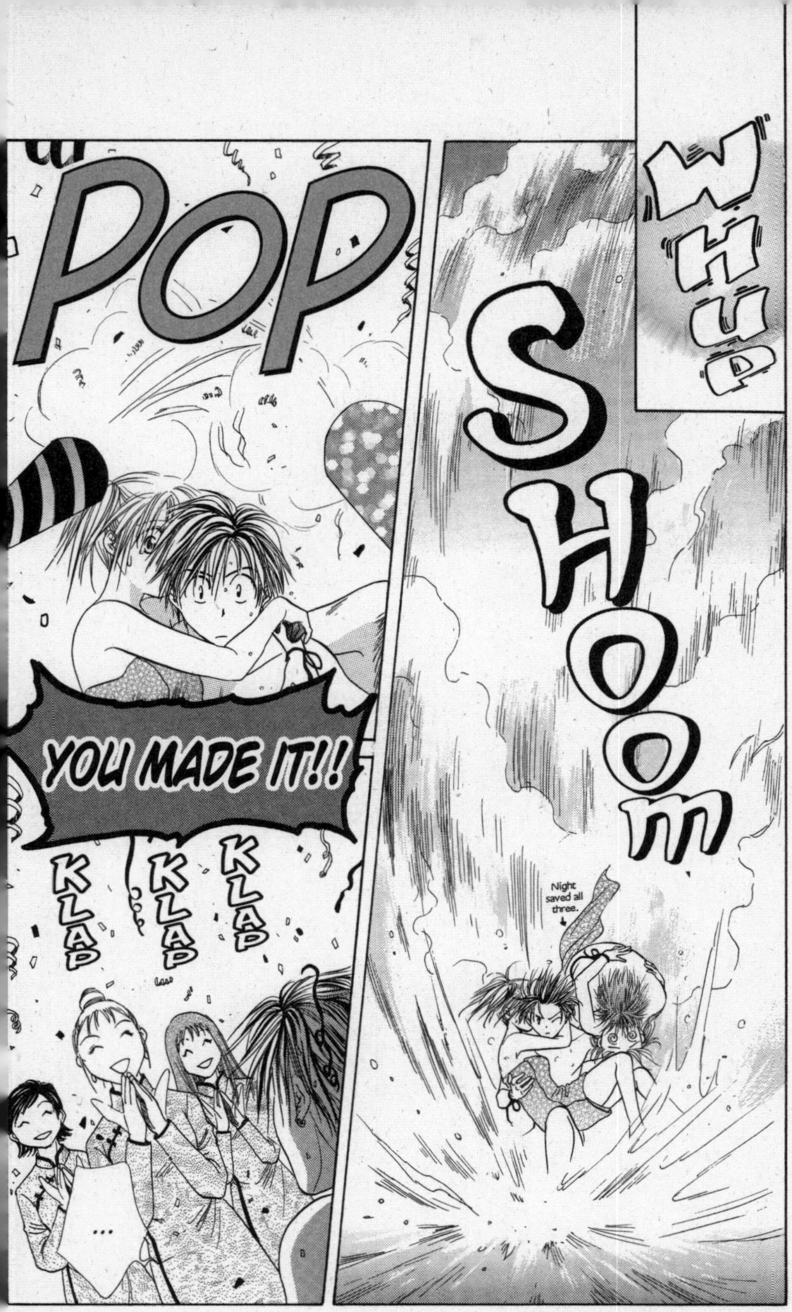
WHUP
SHOOM
Night saved all three.
POP
YOU MADE IT!!
KLAP
KLAP
KLAP
...

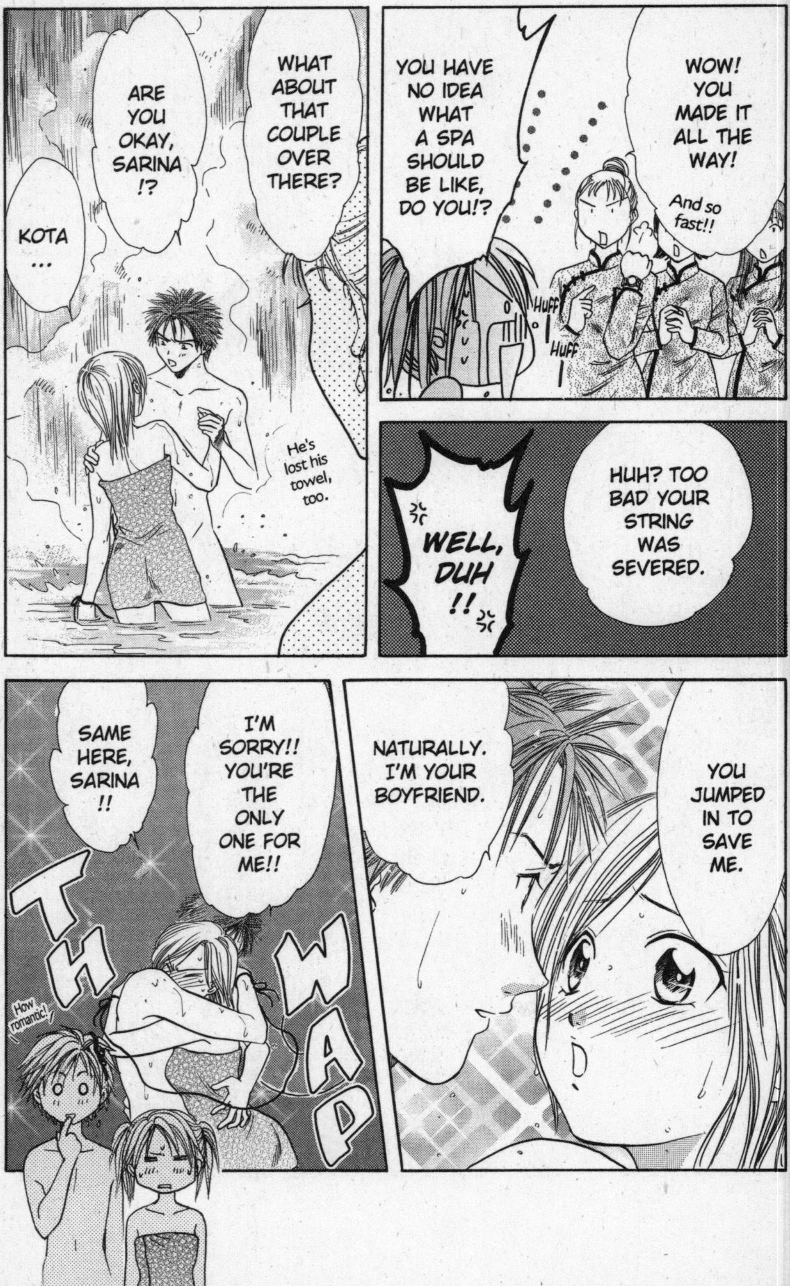
WOW! YOU MADE IT ALL THE WAY!
And so fast!!
YOU HAVE NO IDEA WHAT A SPA SHOULD BE LIKE, DO YOU!?
Huff
Huff
HUH? TOO BAD YOUR STRING WAS SEVERED.
WELL, DUH!!
WHAT ABOUT THAT COUPLE OVER THERE?
ARE YOU OKAY, SARINA!?
KOTA...
He's lost his towel, too.
YOU JUMPED IN TO SAVE ME.
NATURALLY. I'M YOUR BOYFRIEND.
I'M SORRY!! YOU'RE THE ONLY ONE FOR ME!!
SAME HERE, SARINA!!
THWAP
How romantic!

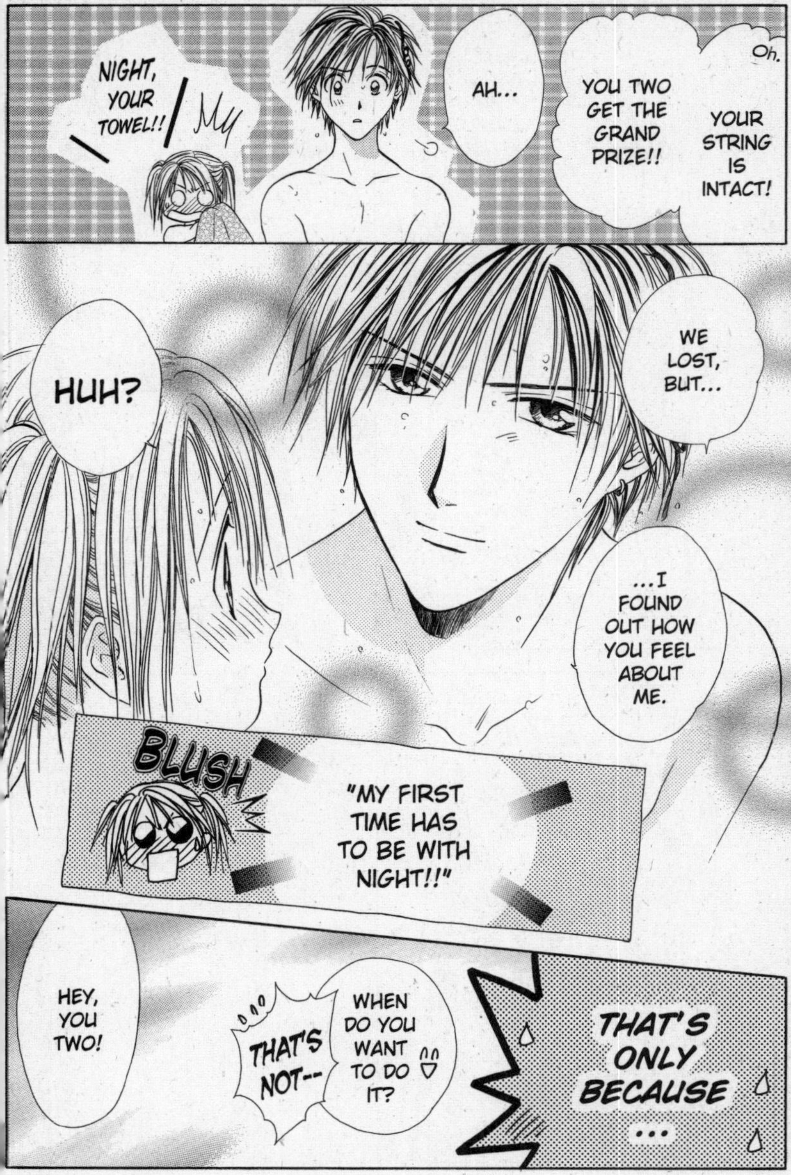
Oh.
YOUR STRING IS INTACT!
YOU TWO GET THE GRAND PRIZE!!
AH...
NIGHT, YOUR TOWEL!!
WE LOST, BUT...
...I FOUND OUT HOW YOU FEEL ABOUT ME.
HUH?
BLUSH
"MY FIRST TIME HAS TO BE WITH NIGHT!!"
THAT'S ONLY BECAUSE ...
WHEN DO YOU WANT TO DO IT?
THAT'S NOT--
HEY, YOU TWO!

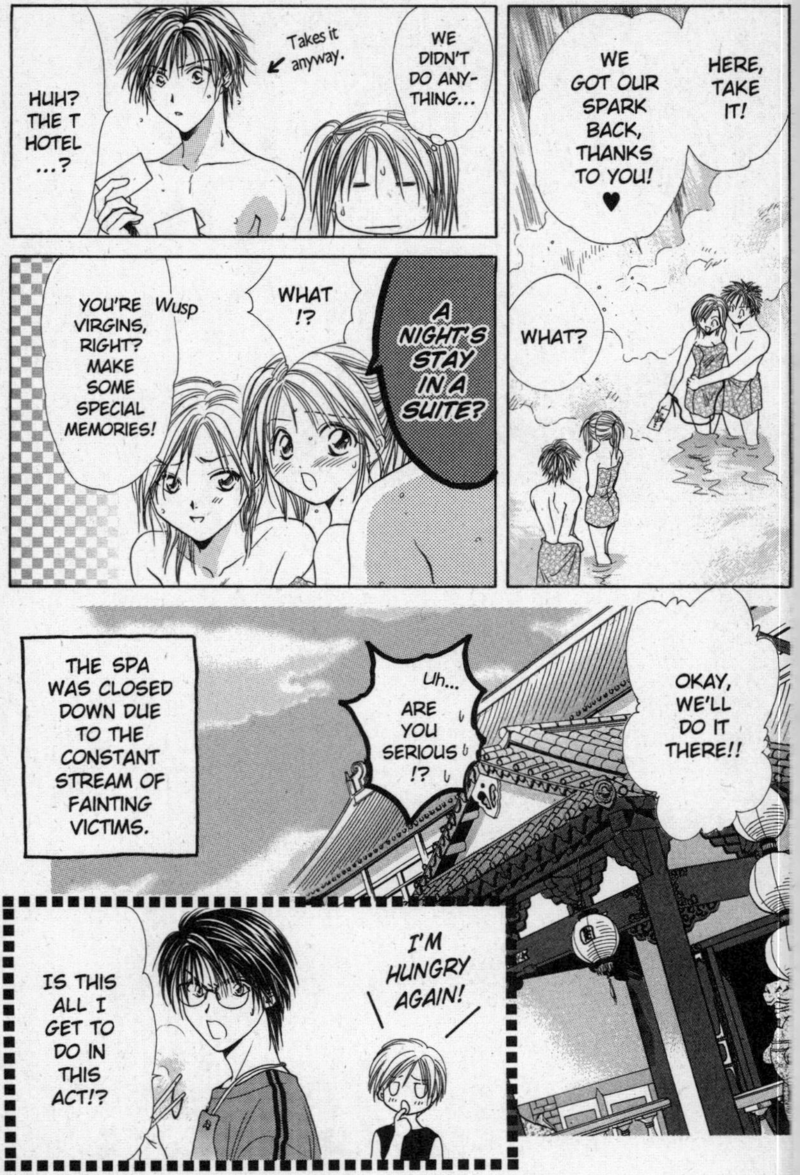
HERE, TAKE IT!
WE GOT OUR SPARK BACK, THANKS TO YOU! ♥
WHAT?
WE DIDN'T DO ANY-THING...
Takes it anyway.
HUH? THE T HOTEL ...?
A NIGHT'S STAY IN A SUITE?
WHAT !?
Wusp
YOU'RE VIRGINS, RIGHT? MAKE SOME SPECIAL MEMORIES!
OKAY, WE'LL DO IT THERE!!
Uh... ARE YOU SERIOUS !?
THE SPA WAS CLOSED DOWN DUE TO THE CONSTANT STREAM OF FAINTING VICTIMS.
I'M HUNGRY AGAIN!
IS THIS ALL I GET TO DO IN THIS ACT!?

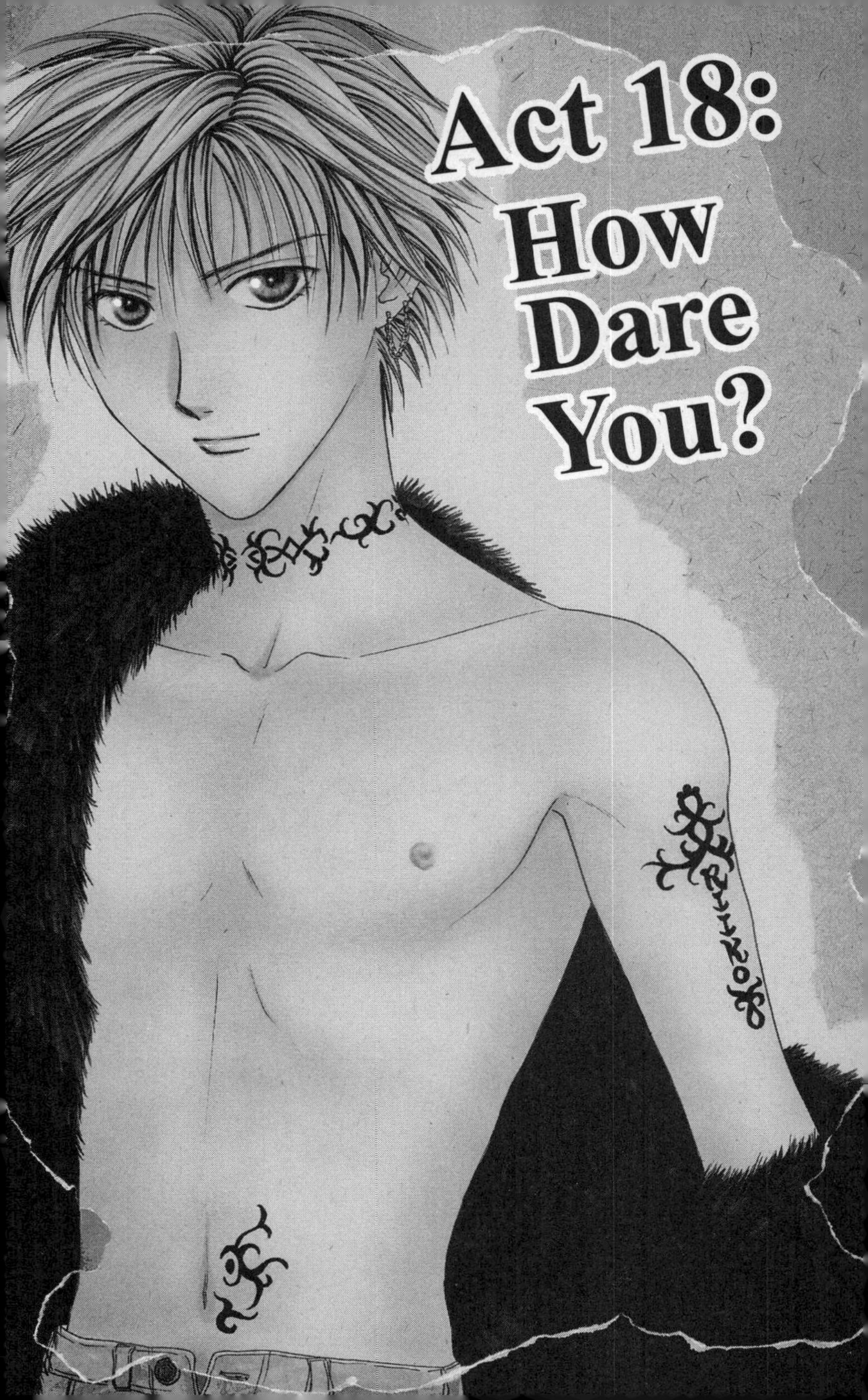
Act 18:
How
Dare
You?

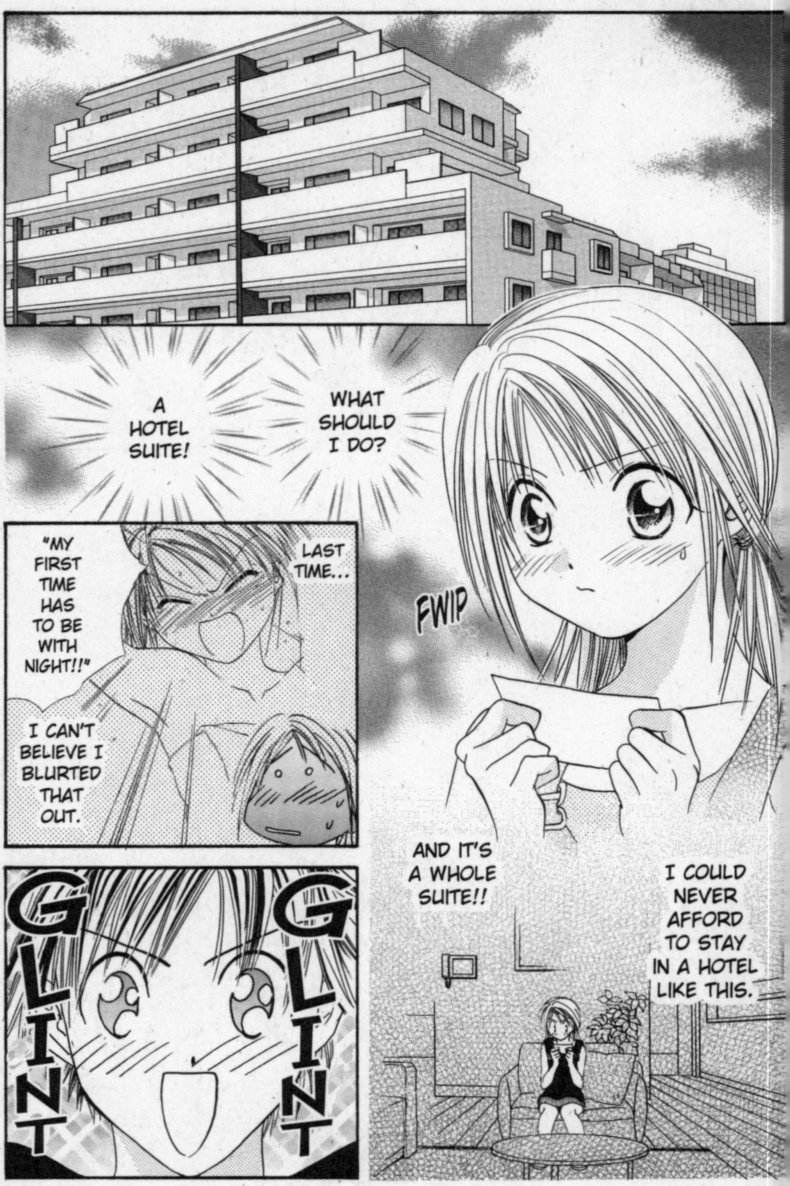
WHAT SHOULD I DO?
A HOTEL SUITE!
FWIP
I COULD NEVER AFFORD TO STAY IN A HOTEL LIKE THIS.
AND IT'S A WHOLE SUITE!!
LAST TIME...
"MY FIRST TIME HAS TO BE WITH NIGHT!!"
I CAN'T BELIEVE I BLURTED THAT OUT.
GLINT
GLINT

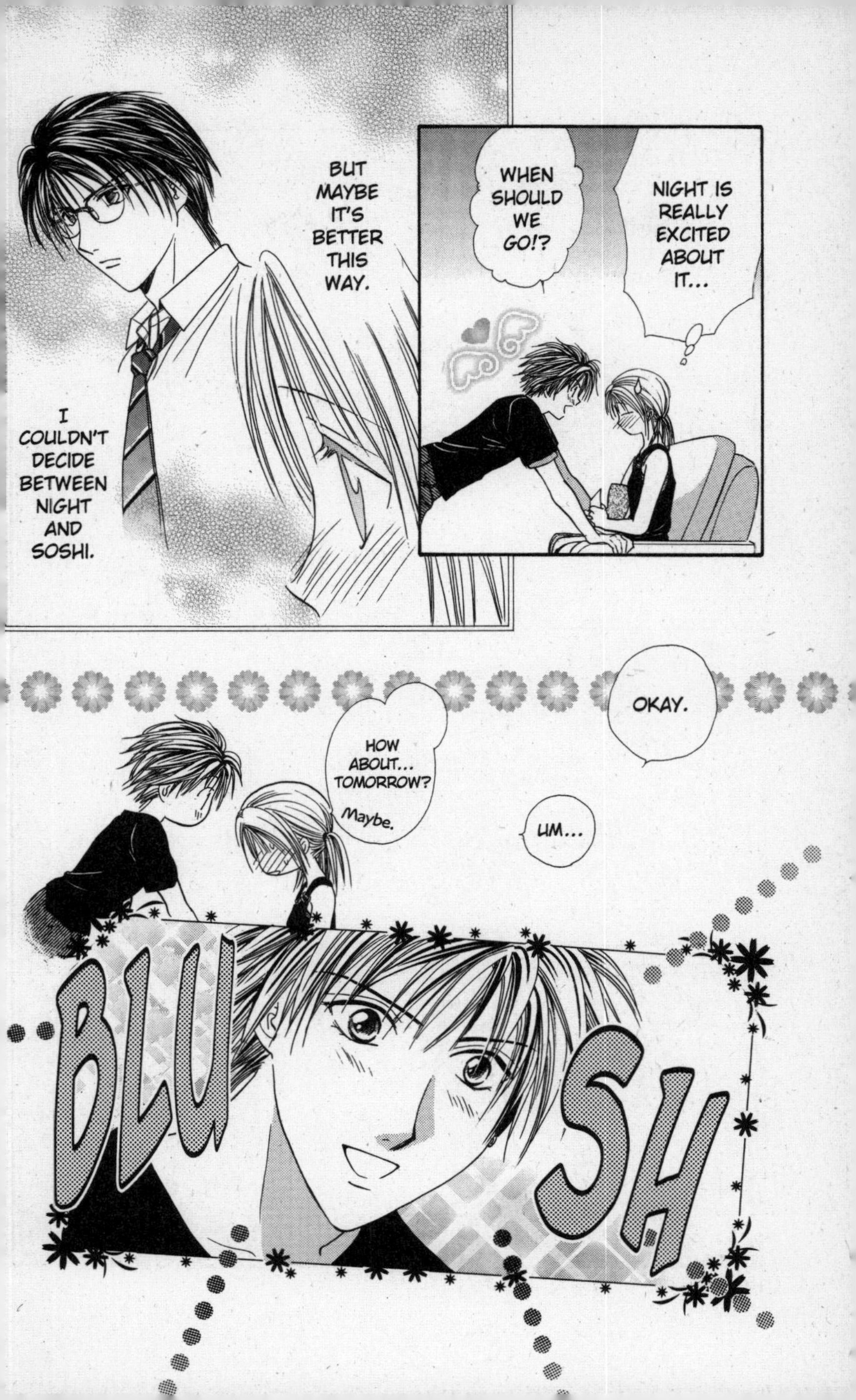
NIGHT IS REALLY EXCITED ABOUT IT...
WHEN SHOULD WE GO!?
BUT MAYBE IT'S BETTER THIS WAY.
I COULDN'T DECIDE BETWEEN NIGHT AND SOSHI.
OKAY.
HOW ABOUT... TOMORROW?
Maybe.
UM...
BLUSH

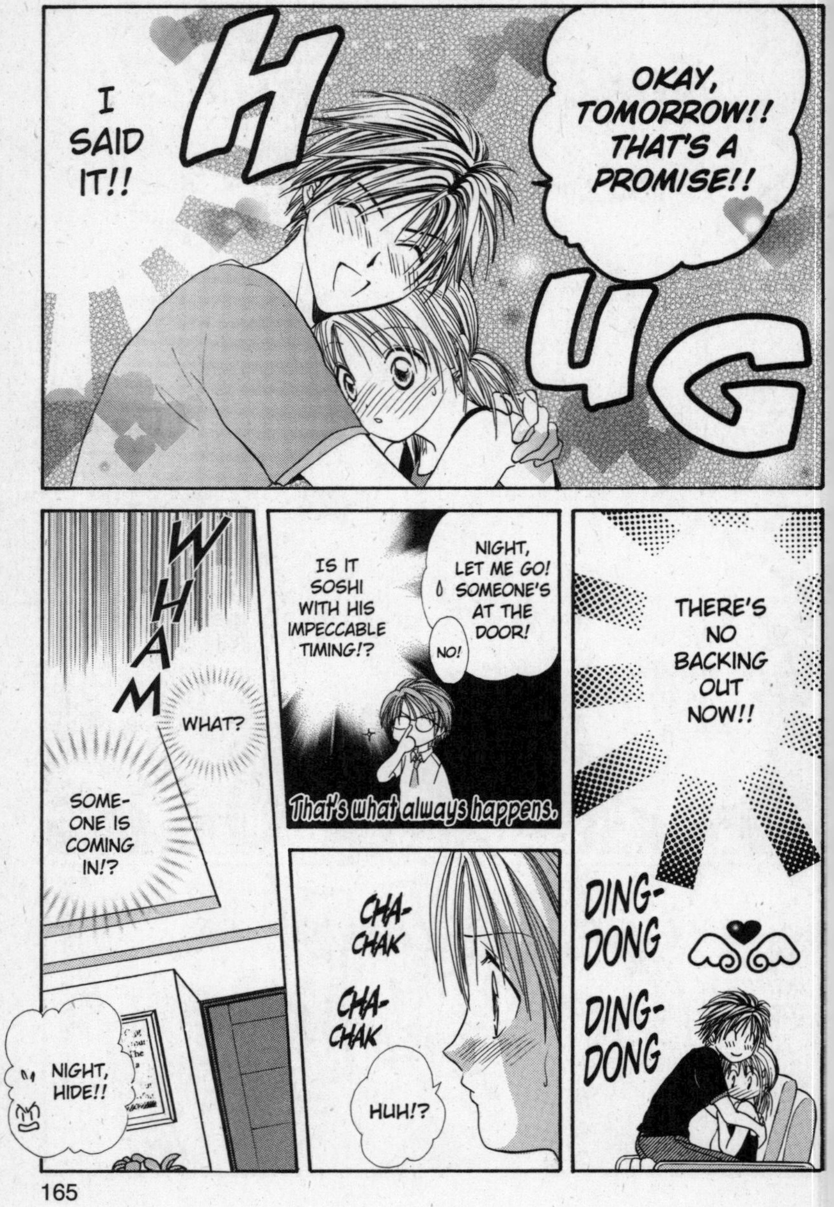
OKAY, TOMORROW!! THAT'S A PROMISE!!
HUG
I SAID IT!!
THERE'S NO BACKING OUT NOW!!
DING-DONG
DING-DONG
NIGHT, LET ME GO! SOMEONE'S AT THE DOOR!
NO!
IS IT SOSHI WITH HIS IMPECCABLE TIMING!?
That's what always happens.
CHA-CHAK
CHA-CHAK
HUH!?
WHAM
WHAT?
SOME-ONE IS COMING IN!?
NIGHT, HIDE!!

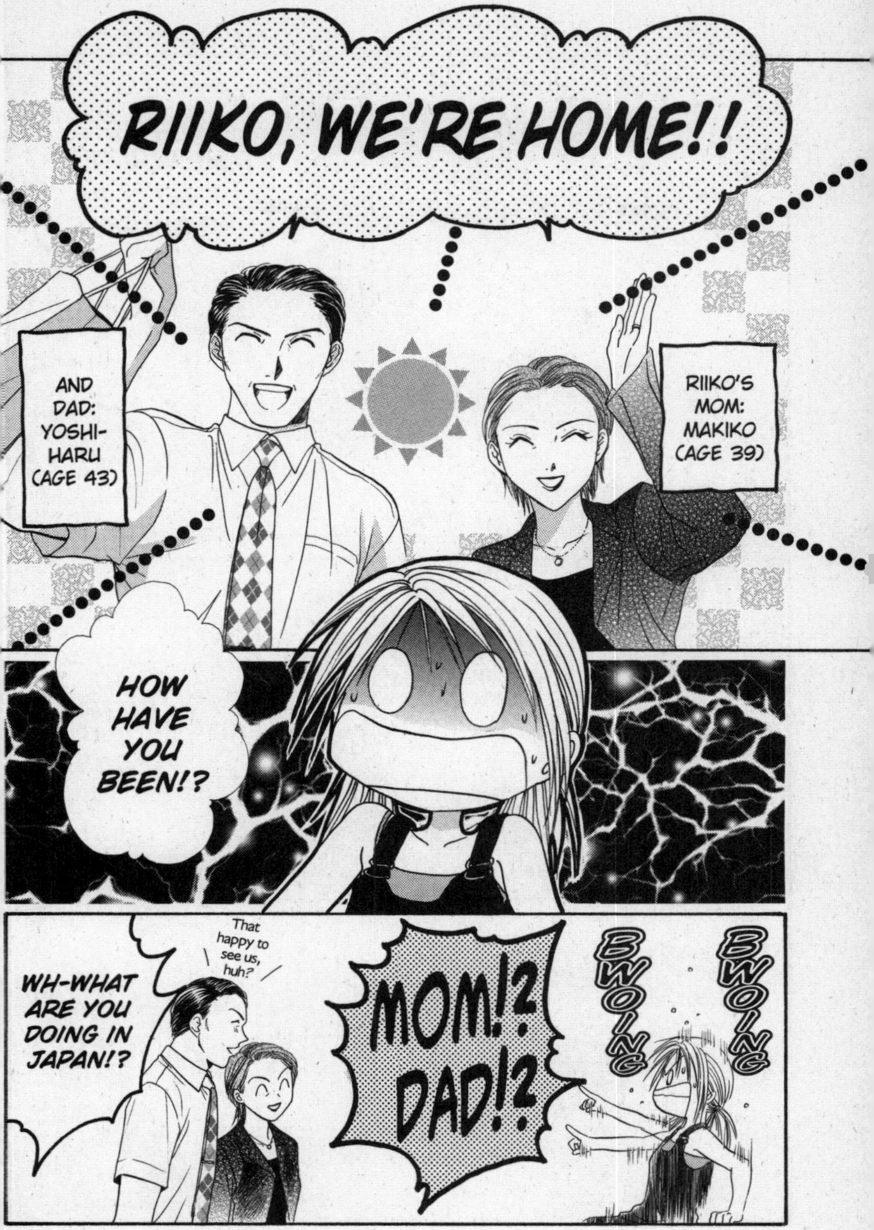
RIIKO, WE'RE HOME!!
RIIKO'S MOM: MAKIKO (AGE 39)
AND DAD: YOSHI-HARU (AGE 43)
HOW HAVE YOU BEEN!?
BWOING BWOING
MOM!? DAD!?
That happy to see us, huh?
WH-WHAT ARE YOU DOING IN JAPAN!?

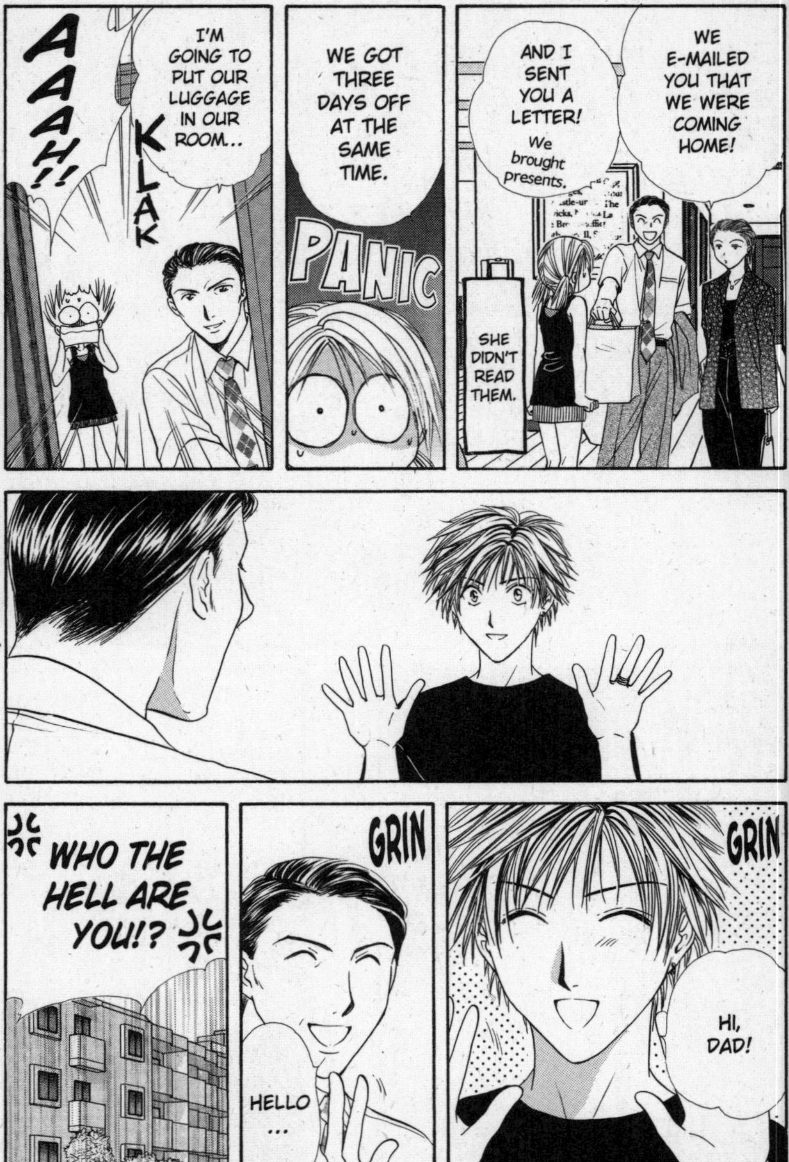
WE E-MAILED YOU THAT WE WERE COMING HOME!
AND I SENT YOU A LETTER!
We brought presents.
SHE DIDN'T READ THEM.
WE GOT THREE DAYS OFF AT THE SAME TIME.
PANIC
I'M GOING TO PUT OUR LUGGAGE IN OUR ROOM...
KLAK
AAAAH!!
GRIN
HI, DAD!
GRIN
HELLO ...
WHO THE HELL ARE YOU!?

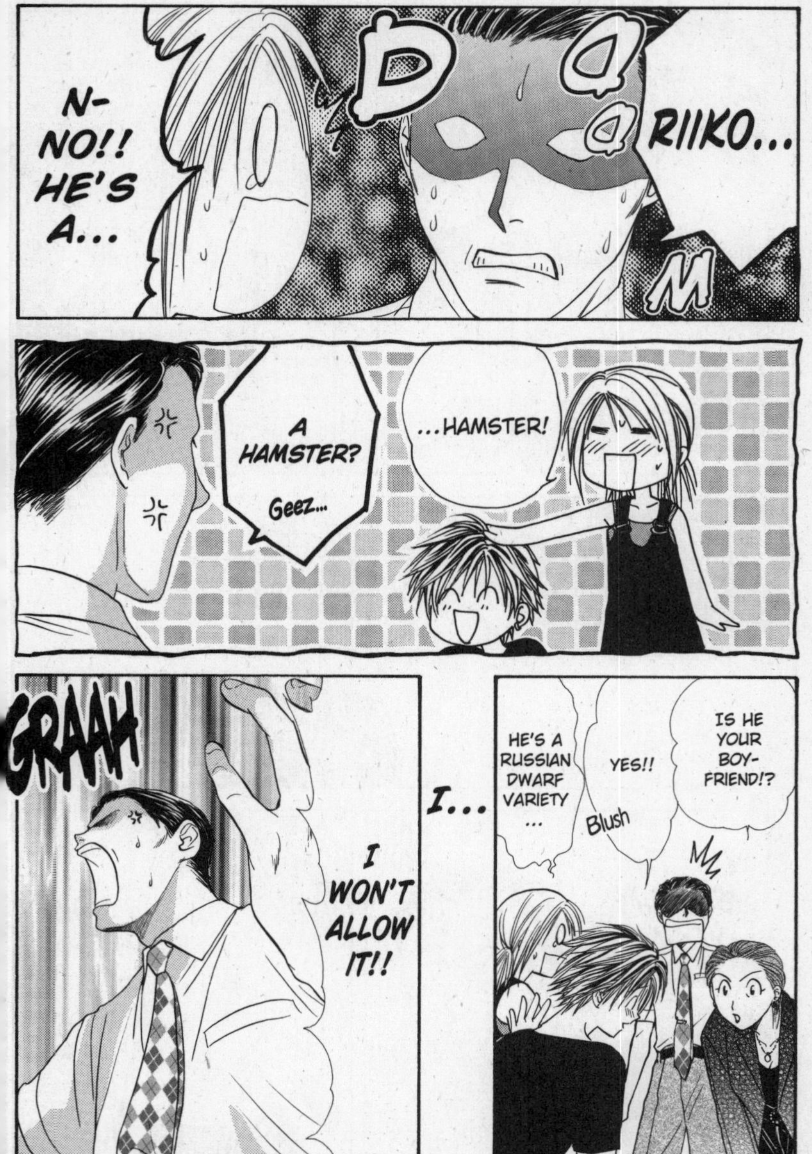
RIIKO...
DOOM
N-NO!! HE'S A...
...HAMSTER!
A HAMSTER?
Geez...
IS HE YOUR BOY-FRIEND!?
YES!!
Blush
HE'S A RUSSIAN DWARF VARIETY ...
I...
I WON'T ALLOW IT!!
GRAAH

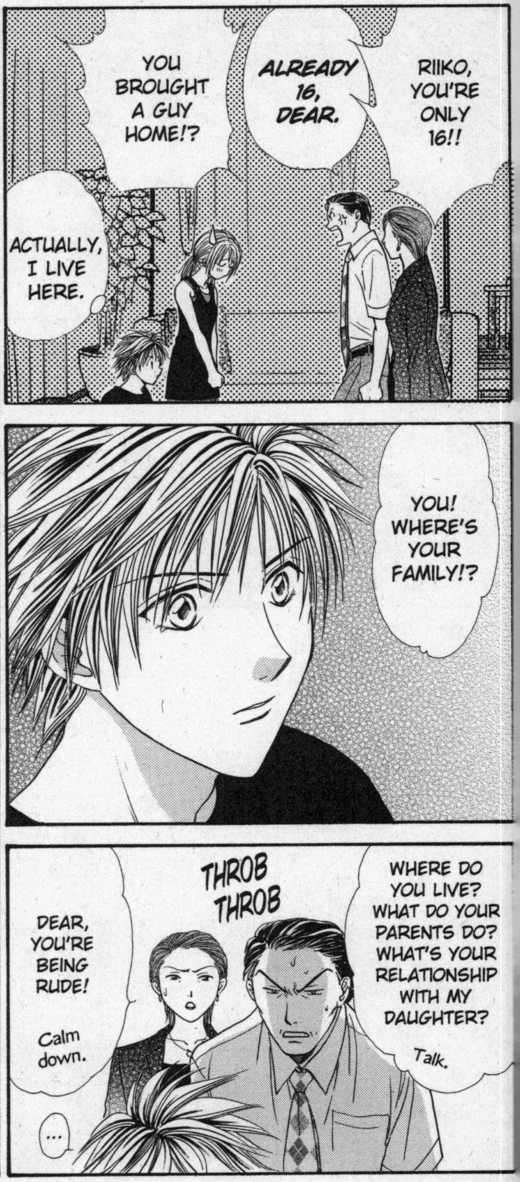
RIIKO, YOU'RE ONLY 16!!
ALREADY 16, DEAR.
YOU BROUGHT A GUY HOME!?
ACTUALLY, I LIVE HERE.
YOU! WHERE'S YOUR FAMILY!?
WHERE DO YOU LIVE? WHAT DO YOUR PARENTS DO? WHAT'S YOUR RELATIONSHIP WITH MY DAUGHTER?
Talk.
THROB THROB
DEAR, YOU'RE BEING RUDE!
Calm down.
...

I don't have much to say about *Absolute Boyfriend* (well, I do, but not about this volume). There isn't much to say about a romantic comedy. Three volumes already. They're also releasing a drama CD. I'm not very familiar with voice actors these days, but they're all good, so check it out! ♥ (smile) More details in the next volume, maybe? *FY: Genbu Kaiden* will be out, as well as the special edition *FY* anthology. This anthology is entirely Yuu Watase. I wasn't paying much attention during the planning stages, but this is kind of awesome. (It doesn't feel real yet.) It's the same size as a regular anthology. It comes with all sorts of extras, and there are 100 pages of *Genbu Kaiden*!! 100 pages!? I haven't even started it yet.
I have to do the cover and the color pages, too...
I'm looking forward to the features. The Suzaku/Seiryu stuff is in there, too, for all the old *FY* fans. It's like this entire book is the Universe of the Four Gods itself. I wonder how long it'll continue? (smile) It'll keep going as long as it sells. Please buy it. You won't regret it. (I'm shameless.) This is really going to wear me out. It could kill me, but I won't let it. I have to go all the way to the Byakko story arc. But I never thought would get its own magazine. It'll support me for the rest of my life (smile). You can understand why I'm so wired.
I'm actually anemic...
I'm looking forward to the *Absolute Boyfriend* drama CD.
I'll give it my all! Good luck, me! (I'm my own cheerleader.) See you next time, when Night gets a rival!!
Ting-a-ling ~♪

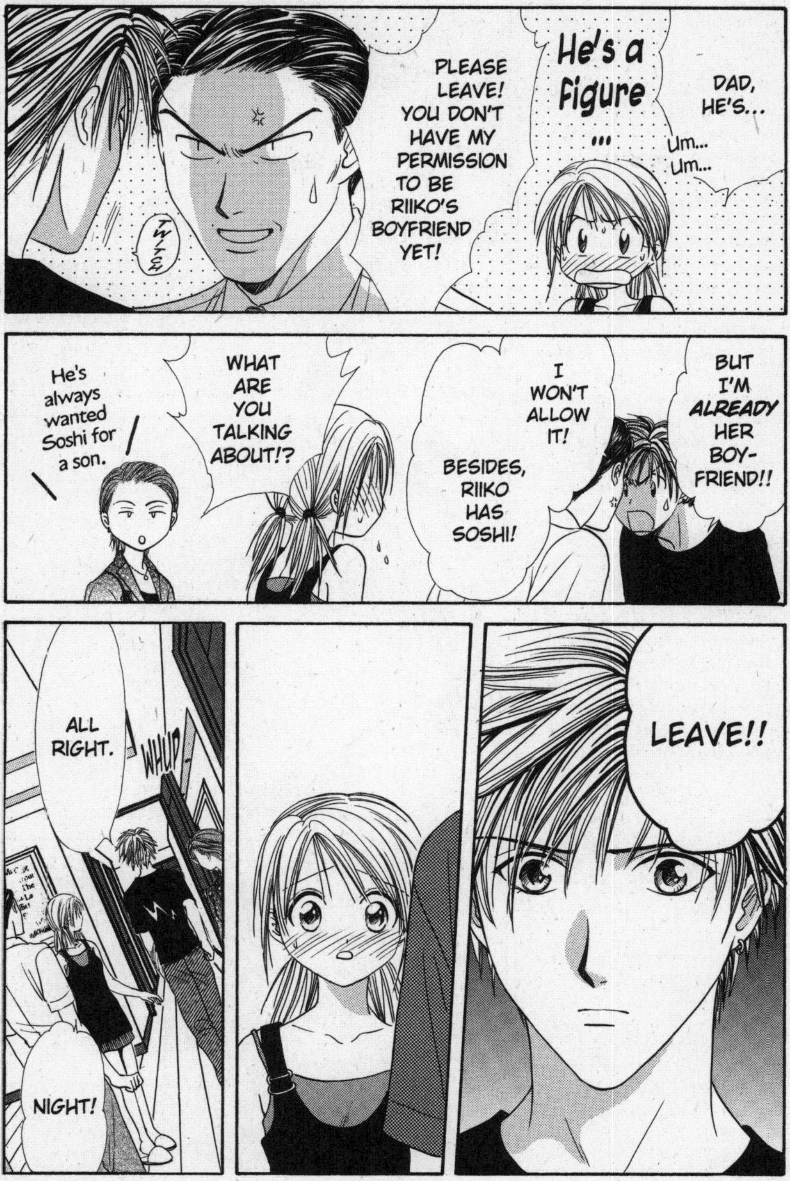
DAD, HE'S...
Um... Um...
He's a figure ...
PLEASE LEAVE! YOU DON'T HAVE MY PERMISSION TO BE RIIKO'S BOYFRIEND YET!
TWITCH
BUT I'M *ALREADY* HER BOY-FRIEND!!
I WON'T ALLOW IT!
BESIDES, RIIKO HAS SOSHI!
WHAT ARE YOU TALKING ABOUT!?
He's always wanted Soshi for a son.
LEAVE!!
ALL RIGHT.
WHUP
NIGHT!

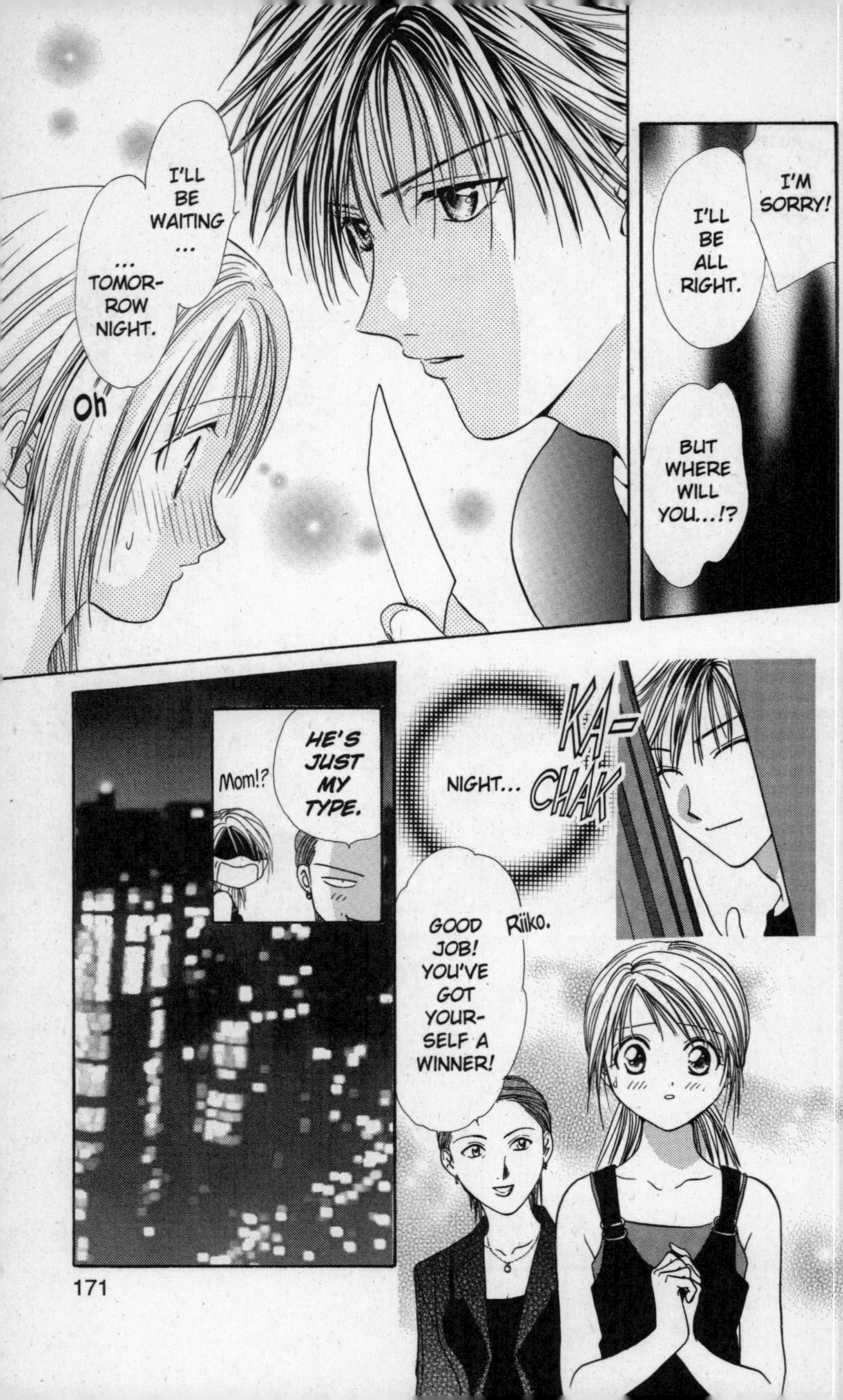
I'M SORRY!
I'LL BE ALL RIGHT.
BUT WHERE WILL YOU...!?
I'LL BE WAITING ...
... TOMORROW NIGHT.
Oh
KA-CHAK
NIGHT...
Riiko.
GOOD JOB! YOU'VE GOT YOURSELF A WINNER!
HE'S JUST MY TYPE.
Mom!?

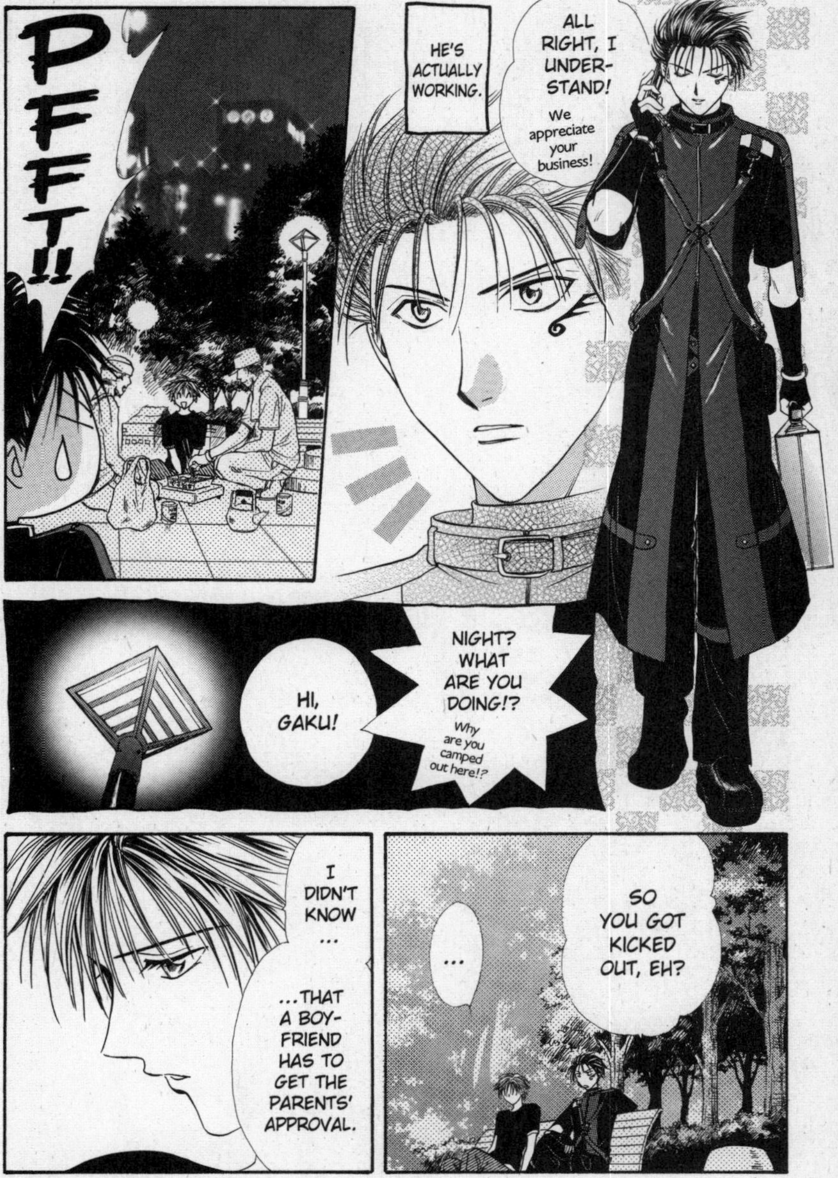
ALL RIGHT, I UNDERSTAND!
We appreciate your business!
HE'S ACTUALLY WORKING.
PFFT!!
NIGHT? WHAT ARE YOU DOING!?
Why are you camped out here!?
HI, GAKU!
SO YOU GOT KICKED OUT, EH?
...
I DIDN'T KNOW...
...THAT A BOY-FRIEND HAS TO GET THE PARENTS' APPROVAL.

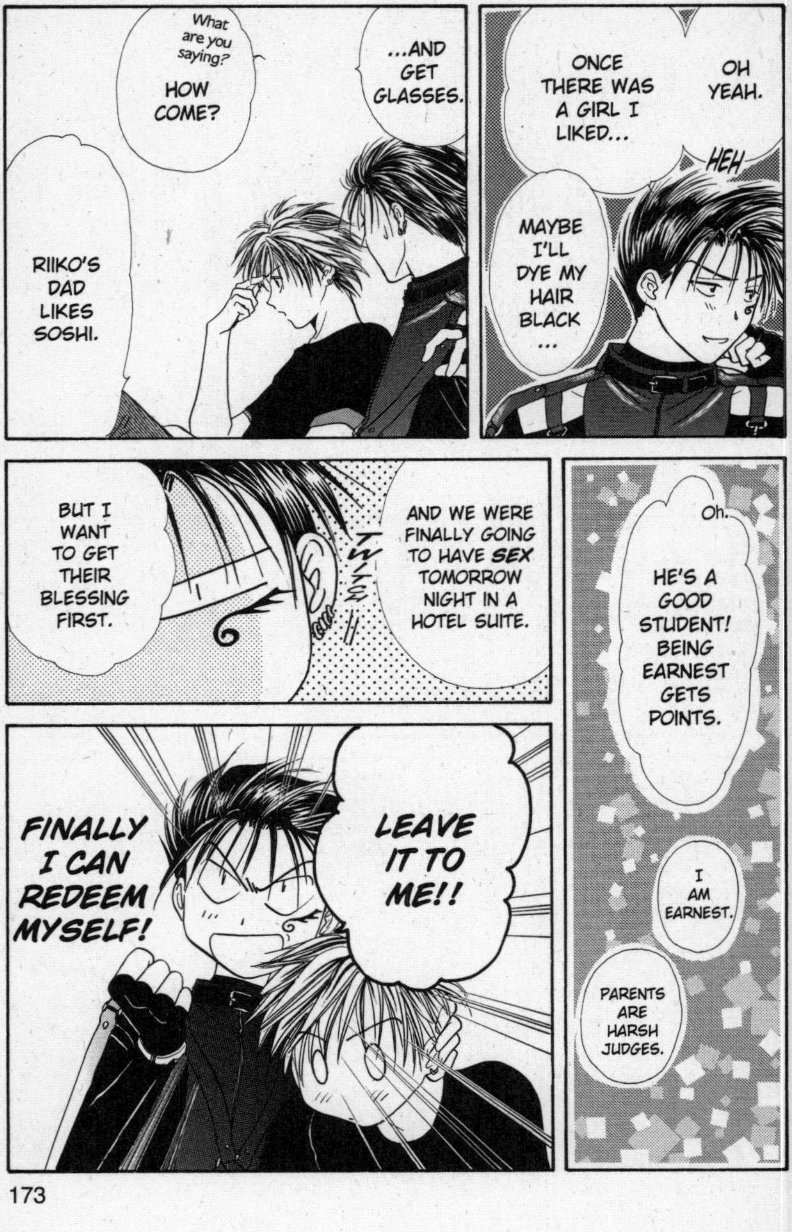
OH YEAH.
HEH
ONCE THERE WAS A GIRL I LIKED...
MAYBE I'LL DYE MY HAIR BLACK...
...AND GET GLASSES.
What are you saying?
HOW COME?
RIIKO'S DAD LIKES SOSHI.
Oh.
HE'S A GOOD STUDENT! BEING EARNEST GETS POINTS.
I AM EARNEST.
PARENTS ARE HARSH JUDGES.
AND WE WERE FINALLY GOING TO HAVE SEX TOMORROW NIGHT IN A HOTEL SUITE.
TWITCH
BUT I WANT TO GET THEIR BLESSING FIRST.
LEAVE IT TO ME!!
FINALLY I CAN REDEEM MYSELF!

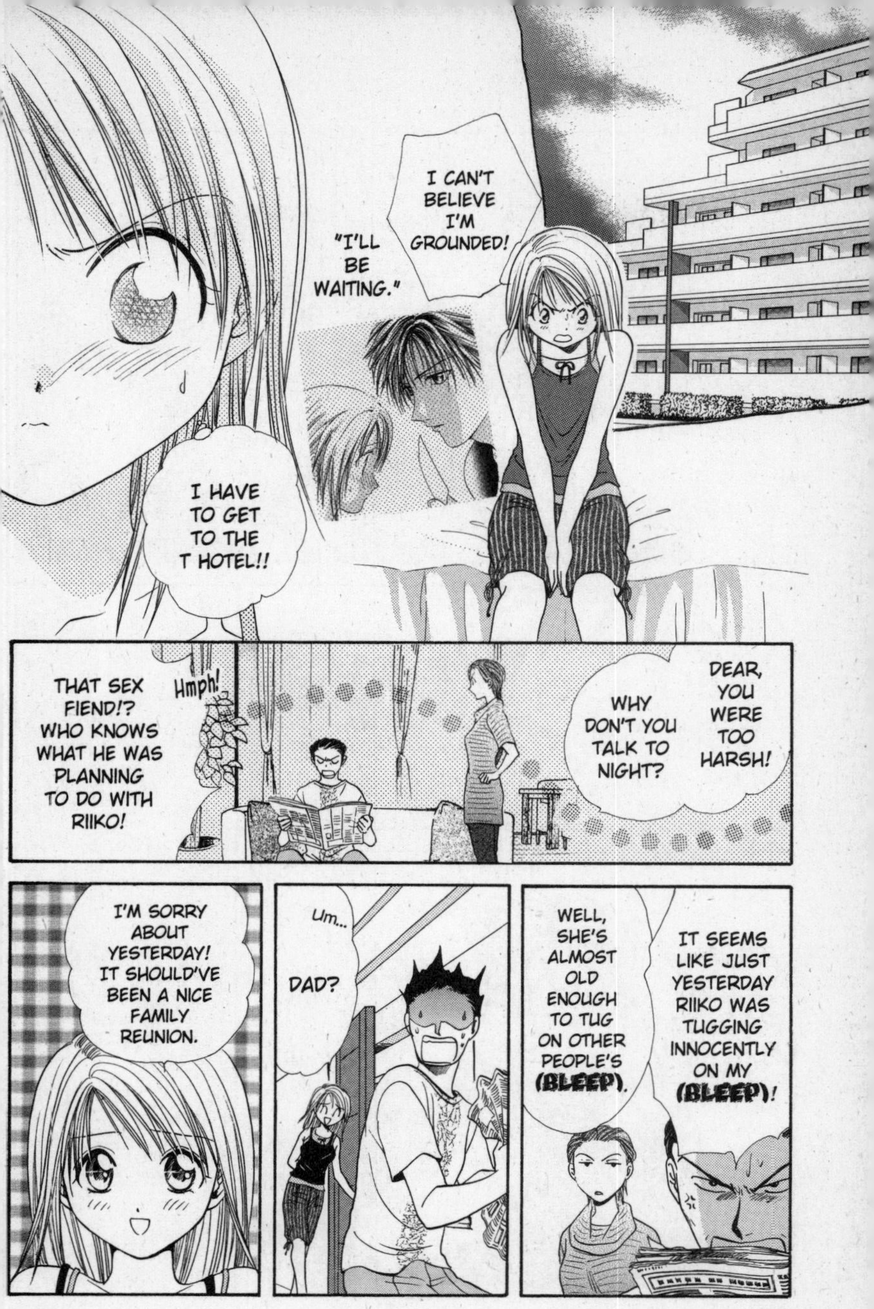
I CAN'T BELIEVE I'M GROUNDED!
"I'LL BE WAITING."
I HAVE TO GET TO THE T HOTEL!!
DEAR, YOU WERE TOO HARSH!
WHY DON'T YOU TALK TO NIGHT?
Hmph!
THAT SEX FIEND!? WHO KNOWS WHAT HE WAS PLANNING TO DO WITH RIIKO!
IT SEEMS LIKE JUST YESTERDAY RIIKO WAS TUGGING INNOCENTLY ON MY (BLEEP)!
WELL, SHE'S ALMOST OLD ENOUGH TO TUG ON OTHER PEOPLE'S (BLEEP).
Um...
DAD?
I'M SORRY ABOUT YESTERDAY! IT SHOULD'VE BEEN A NICE FAMILY REUNION.

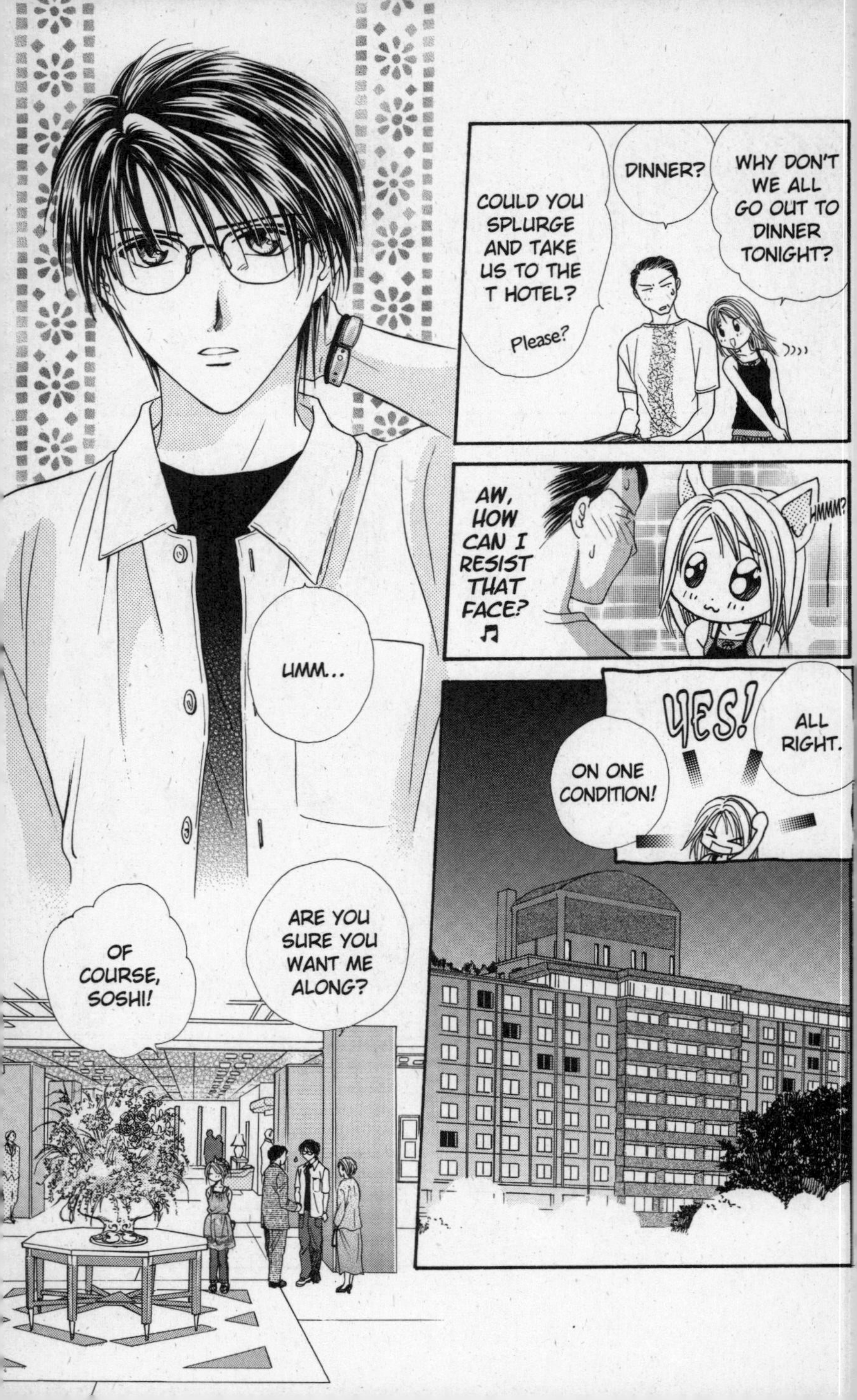
WHY DON'T WE ALL GO OUT TO DINNER TONIGHT?
DINNER?
COULD YOU SPLURGE AND TAKE US TO THE T HOTEL?
Please?
HMMM?
AW, HOW CAN I RESIST THAT FACE? ♫
ALL RIGHT.
YES!
ON ONE CONDITION!
UMM...
ARE YOU SURE YOU WANT ME ALONG?
OF COURSE, SOSHI!

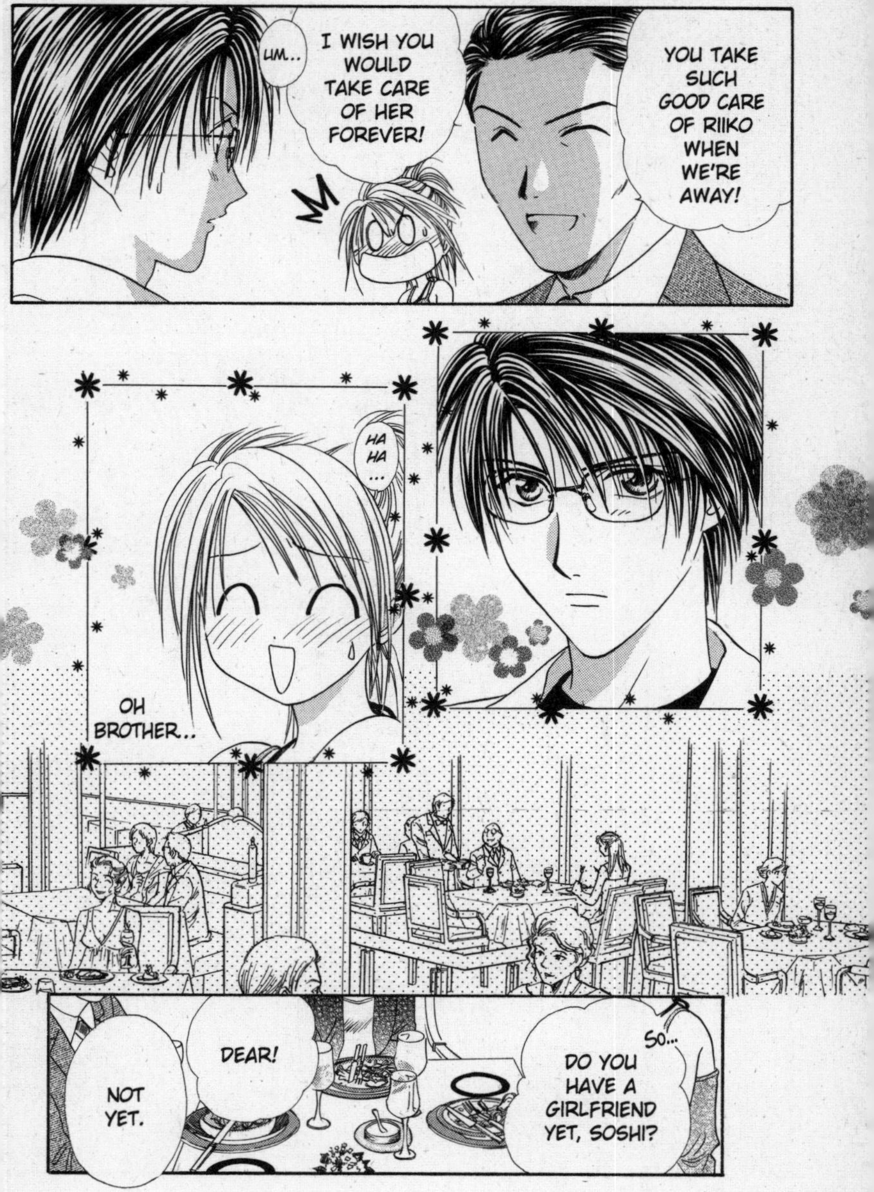
YOU TAKE SUCH GOOD CARE OF RIIKO WHEN WE'RE AWAY!
I WISH YOU WOULD TAKE CARE OF HER FOREVER!
UM..
HA HA ...
OH BROTHER..
SO...
DO YOU HAVE A GIRLFRIEND YET, SOSHI?
DEAR!
NOT YET.

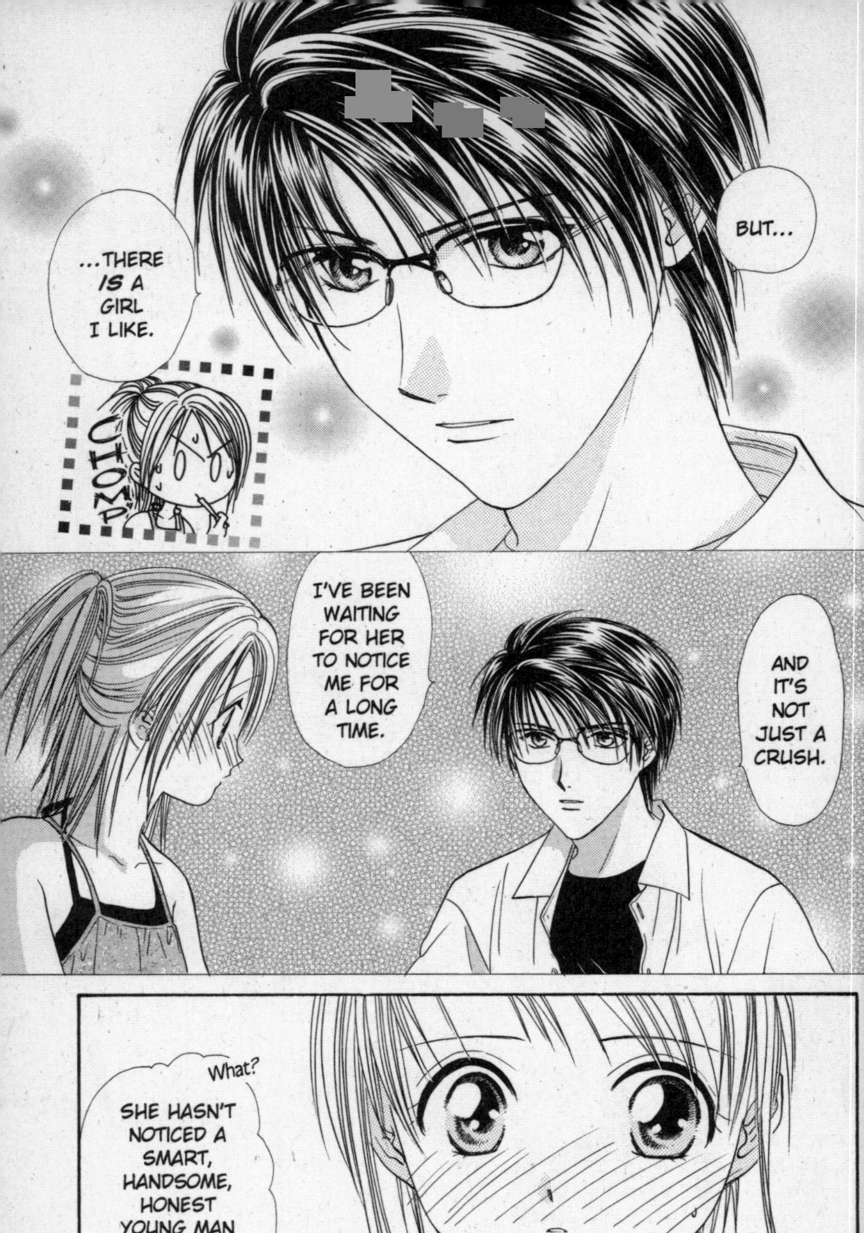
BUT...
...THERE IS A GIRL I LIKE.
CHOMP
AND IT'S NOT JUST A CRUSH.
I'VE BEEN WAITING FOR HER TO NOTICE ME FOR A LONG TIME.
What?
SHE HASN'T NOTICED A SMART, HANDSOME, HONEST YOUNG MAN LIKE YOU?

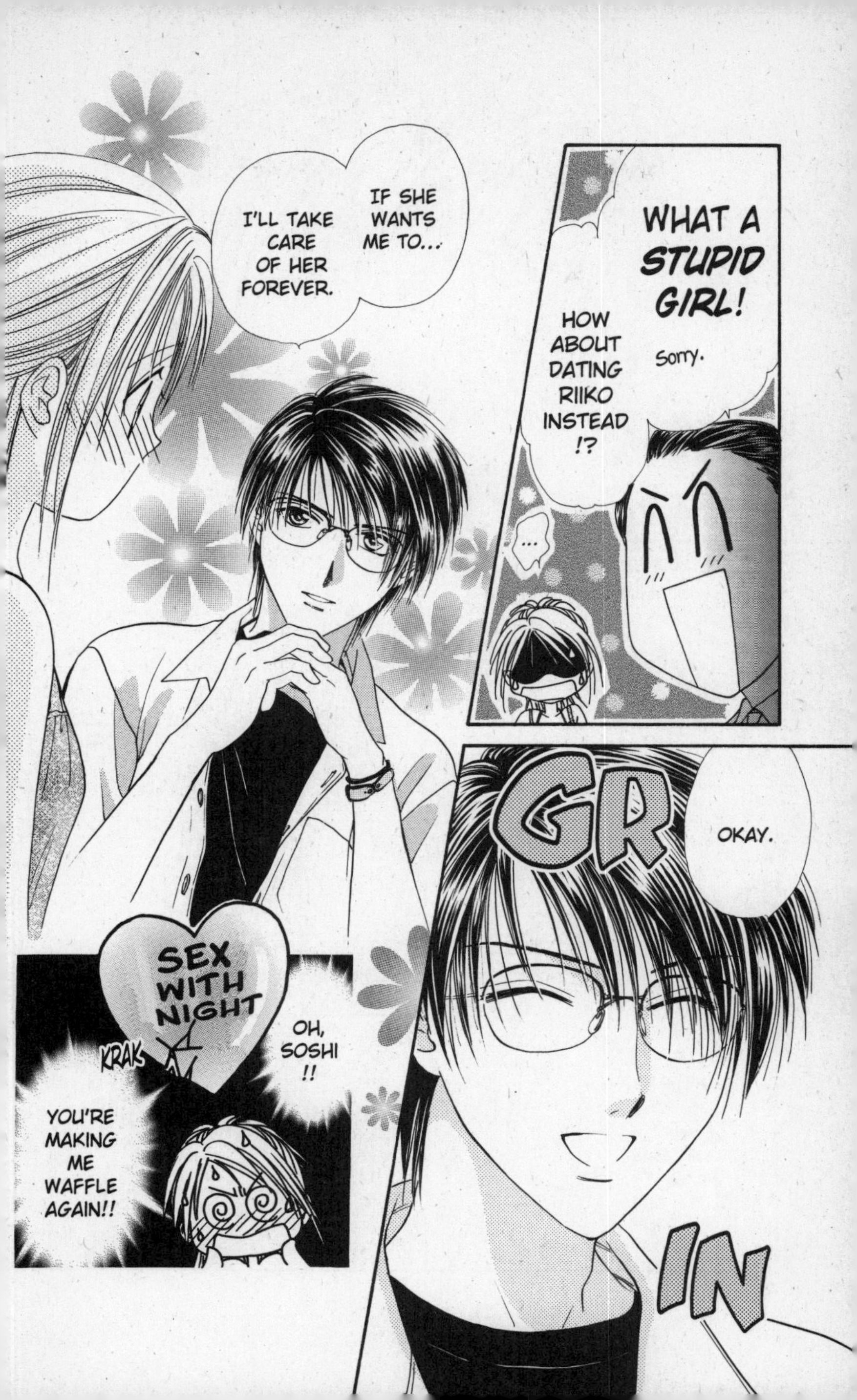
IF SHE WANTS ME TO...
I'LL TAKE CARE OF HER FOREVER.
WHAT A STUPID GIRL!
HOW ABOUT DATING RIIKO INSTEAD !?
Sorry.
...
GR
OKAY.
IN
SEX WITH NIGHT
KRAK
OH, SOSHI !!
YOU'RE MAKING ME WAFFLE AGAIN!!

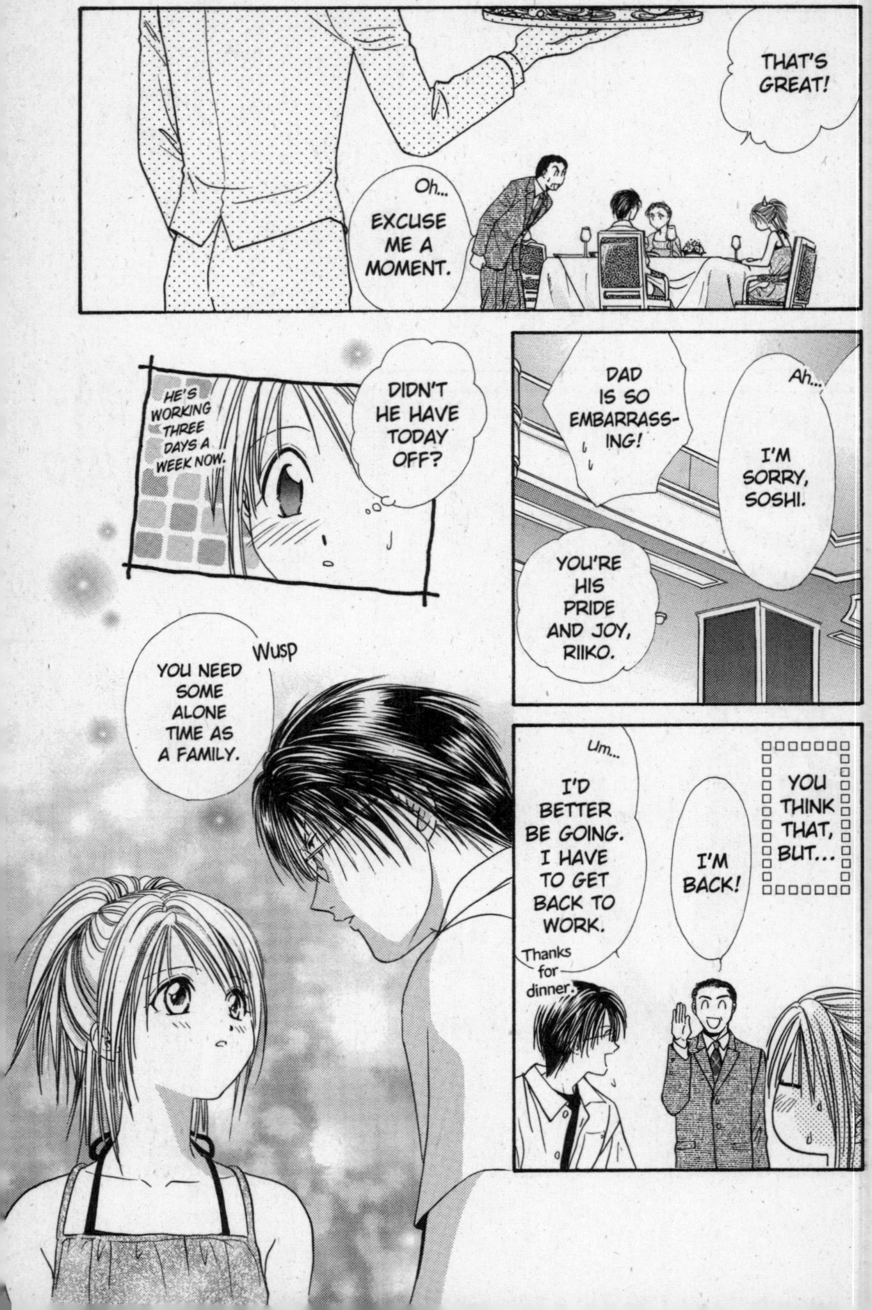
THAT'S GREAT!
Oh... EXCUSE ME A MOMENT.
Ah... I'M SORRY, SOSHI.
DAD IS SO EMBARRASSING!
YOU'RE HIS PRIDE AND JOY, RIIKO.
DIDN'T HE HAVE TODAY OFF?
HE'S WORKING THREE DAYS A WEEK NOW.
YOU THINK THAT, BUT...
I'M BACK!
Um... I'D BETTER BE GOING. I HAVE TO GET BACK TO WORK.
Thanks for dinner.
Wusp
YOU NEED SOME ALONE TIME AS A FAMILY.

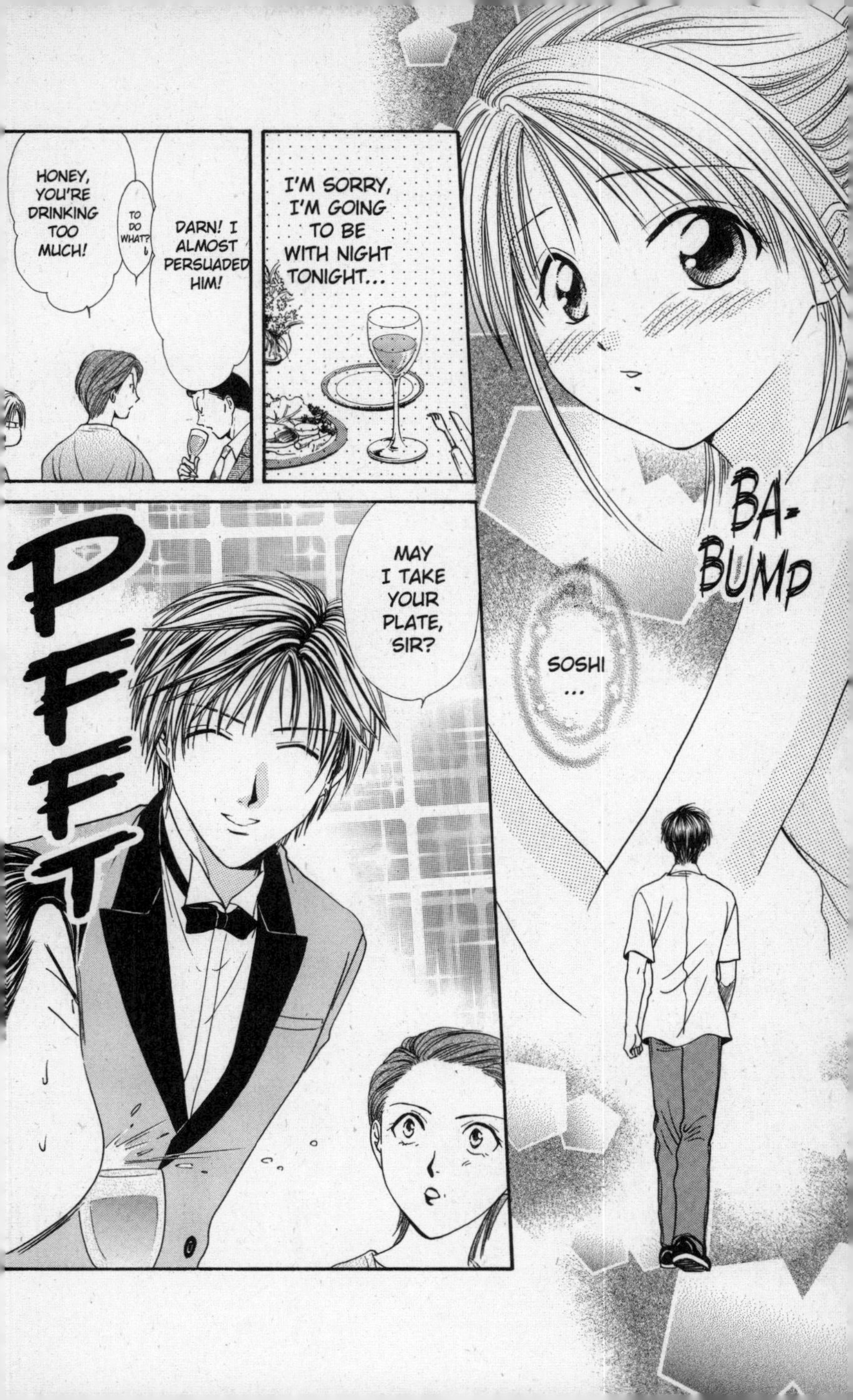
BA-BUMP
SOSHI...
I'M SORRY, I'M GOING TO BE WITH NIGHT TONIGHT...
DARN! I ALMOST PERSUADED HIM!
TO DO WHAT?
HONEY, YOU'RE DRINKING TOO MUCH!
MAY I TAKE YOUR PLATE, SIR?
PFFT

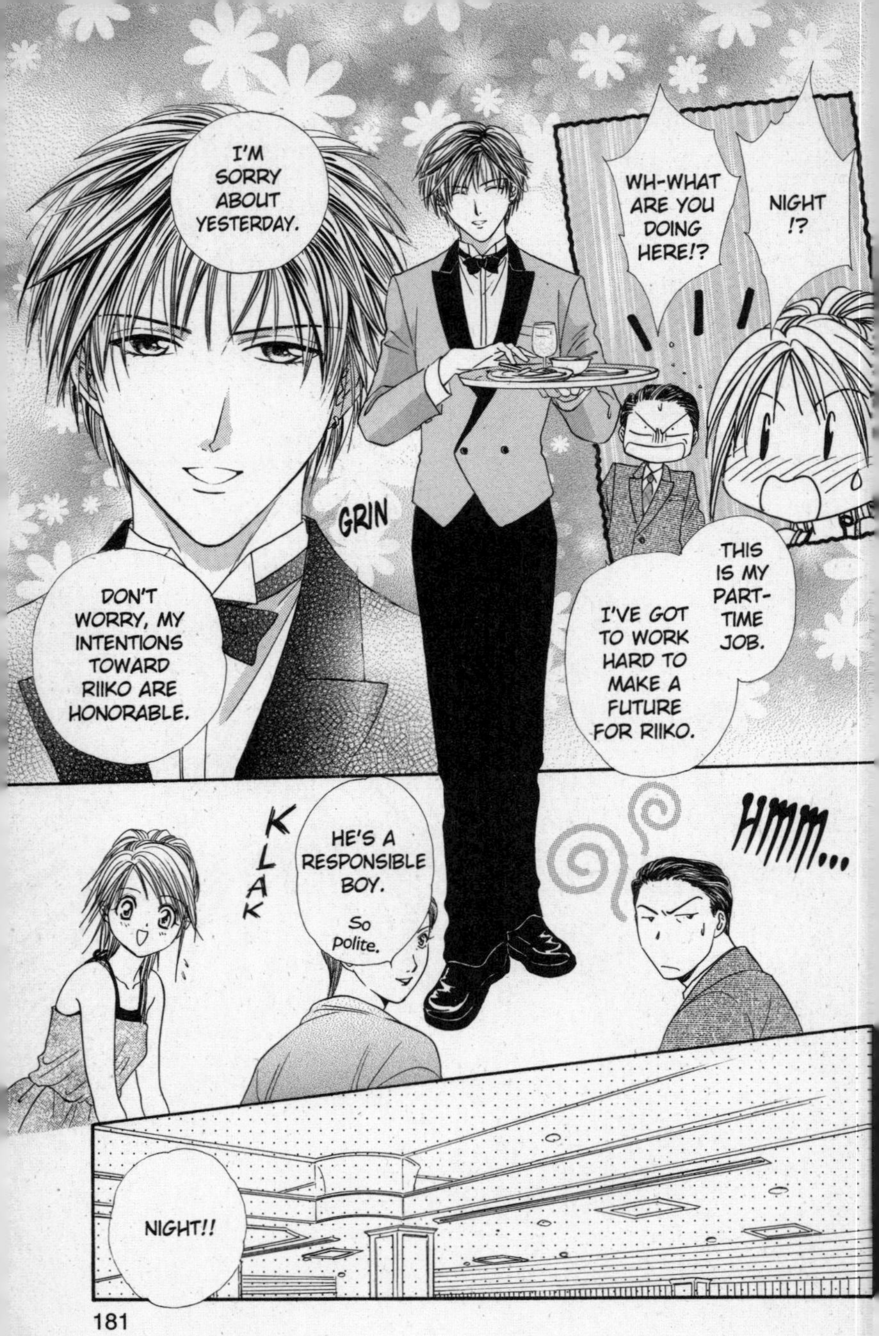
NIGHT !?
WH-WHAT ARE YOU DOING HERE!?
I'M SORRY ABOUT YESTERDAY.
GRIN
THIS IS MY PART-TIME JOB.
I'VE GOT TO WORK HARD TO MAKE A FUTURE FOR RIIKO.
DON'T WORRY, MY INTENTIONS TOWARD RIIKO ARE HONORABLE.
HMMM...
HE'S A RESPONSIBLE BOY.
So polite.
KLAK
NIGHT!!

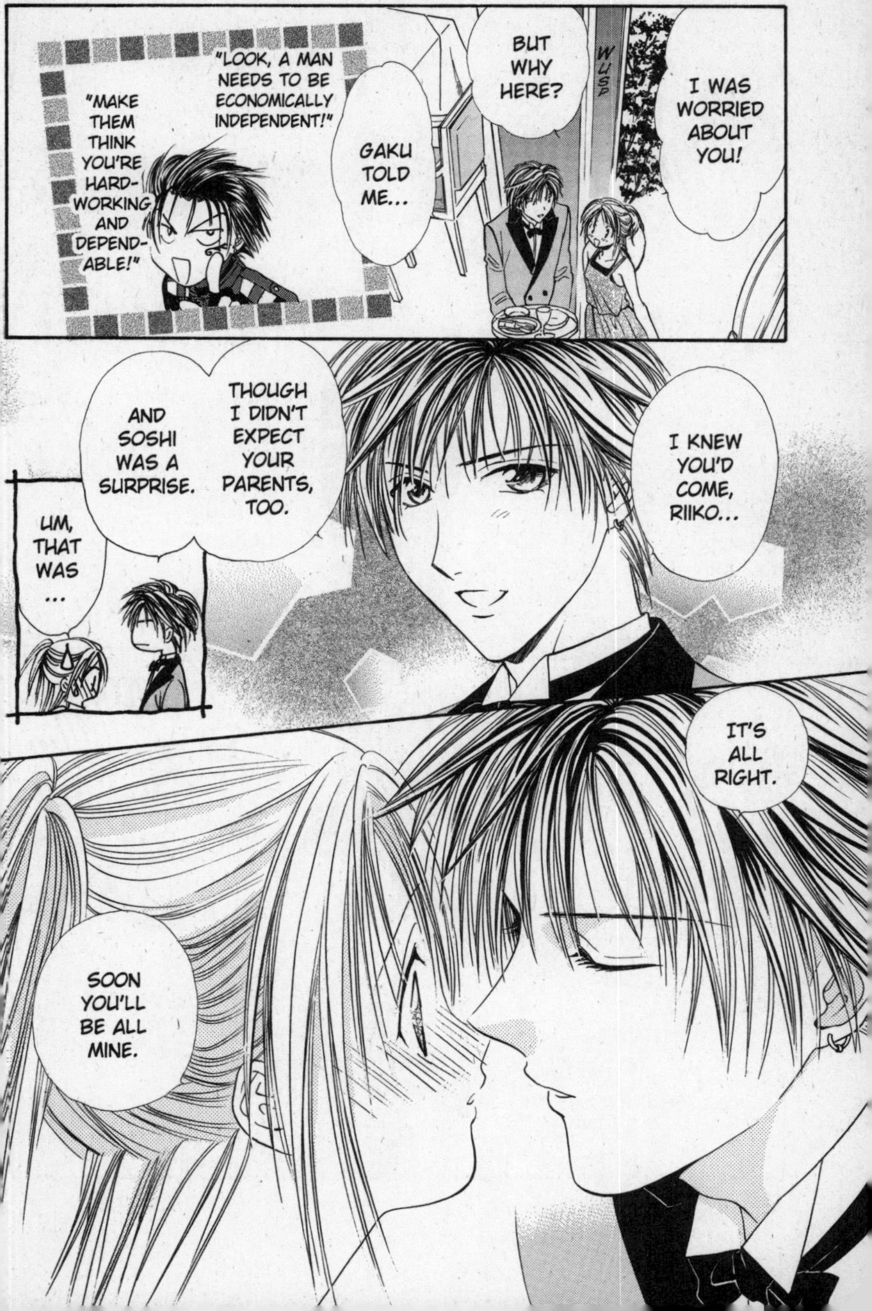
I WAS WORRIED ABOUT YOU!
BUT WHY HERE?
GAKU TOLD ME...
"LOOK, A MAN NEEDS TO BE ECONOMICALLY INDEPENDENT!"
"MAKE THEM THINK YOU'RE HARD-WORKING AND DEPENDABLE!"
I KNEW YOU'D COME, RIIKO...
THOUGH I DIDN'T EXPECT YOUR PARENTS, TOO.
AND SOSHI WAS A SURPRISE.
UM, THAT WAS ...
IT'S ALL RIGHT.
SOON YOU'LL BE ALL MINE.

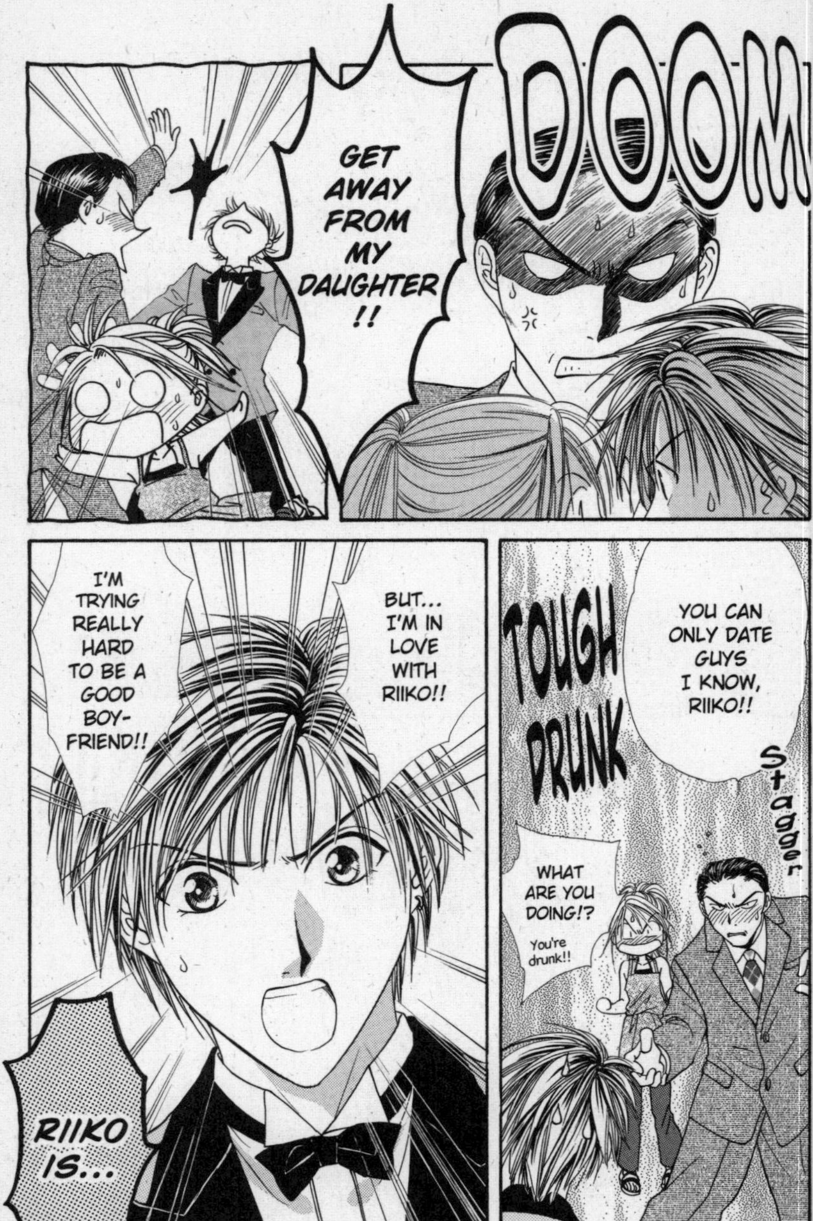
DOOM
GET AWAY FROM MY DAUGHTER!!
YOU CAN ONLY DATE GUYS I KNOW, RIIKO!!
TOUGH DRUNK
Stagger
WHAT ARE YOU DOING!?
You're drunk!!
I'M TRYING REALLY HARD TO BE A GOOD BOY-FRIEND!!
BUT... I'M IN LOVE WITH RIIKO!!
RIIKO IS...

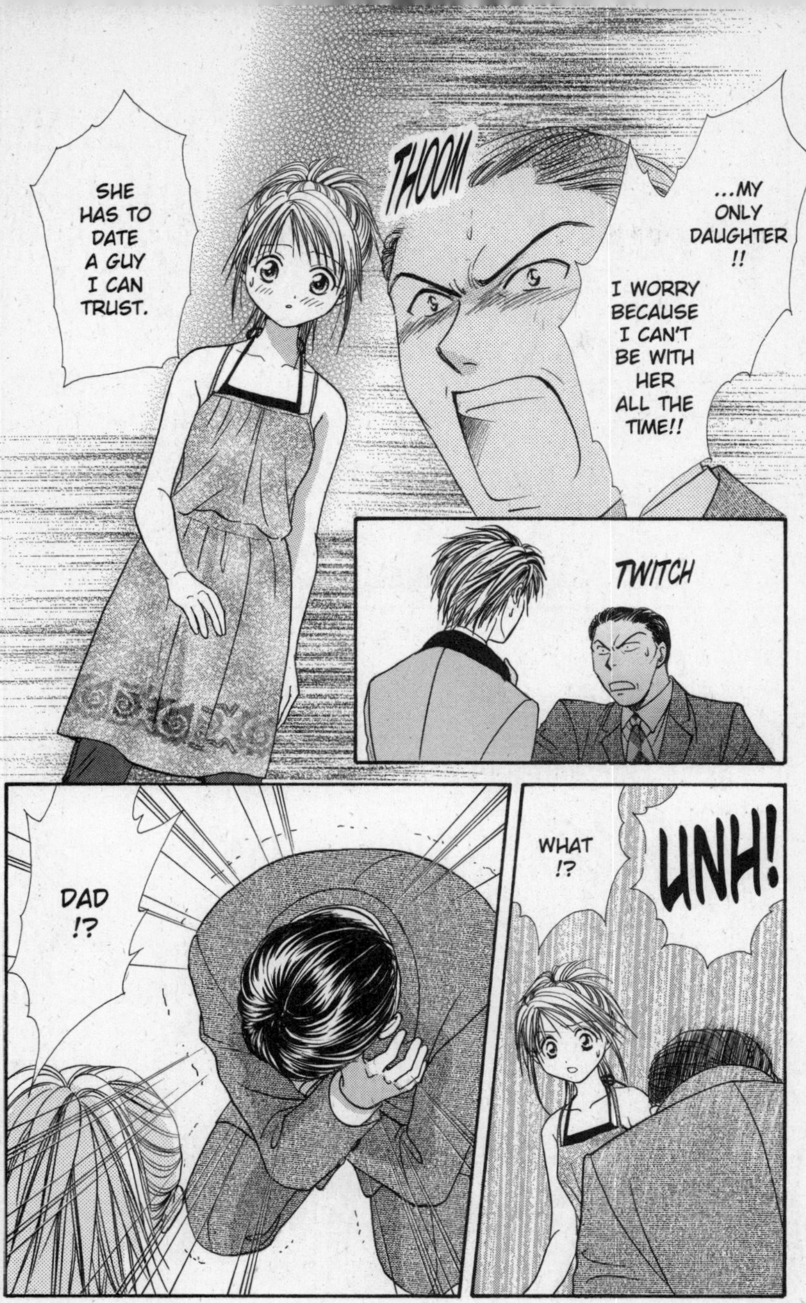
...MY ONLY DAUGHTER !!
I WORRY BECAUSE I CAN'T BE WITH HER ALL THE TIME!!
THOOM
SHE HAS TO DATE A GUY I CAN TRUST.
TWITCH
UNH!
WHAT !?
DAD !?

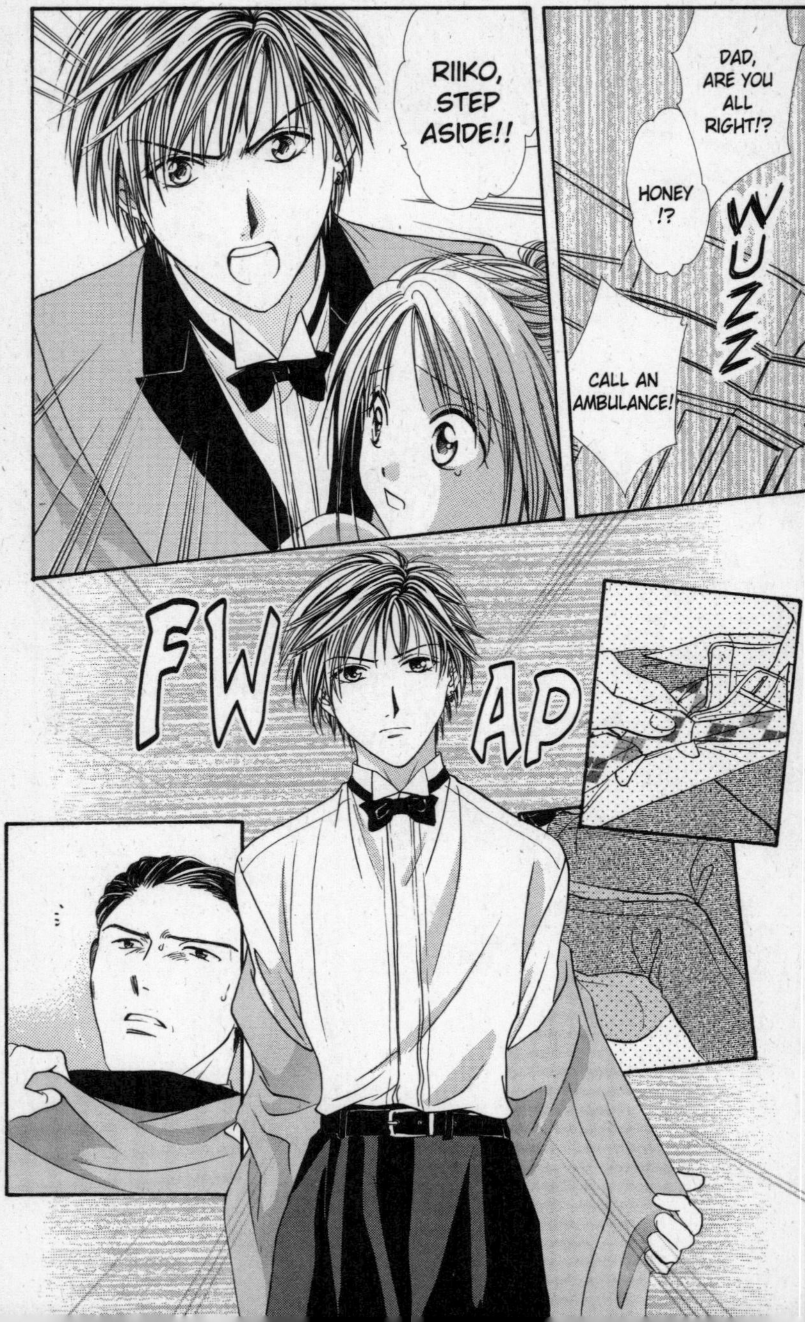
DAD, ARE YOU ALL RIGHT!?
HONEY !?
WUZZ
CALL AN AMBULANCE!
RIIKO, STEP ASIDE!!
FWAP

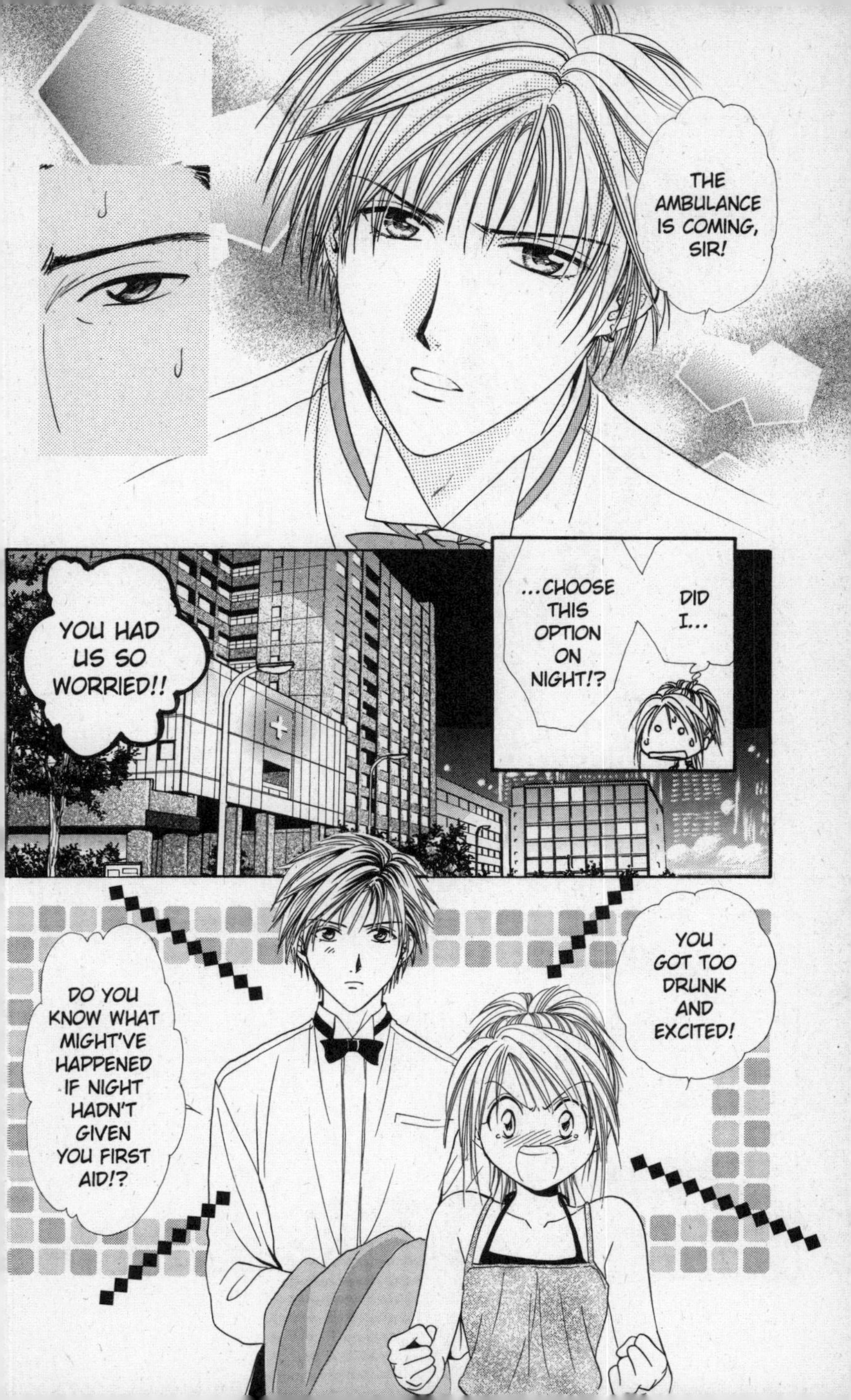
THE AMBULANCE IS COMING, SIR!
DID I...
...CHOOSE THIS OPTION ON NIGHT!?
YOU HAD US SO WORRIED!!
YOU GOT TOO DRUNK AND EXCITED!
DO YOU KNOW WHAT MIGHT'VE HAPPENED IF NIGHT HADN'T GIVEN YOU FIRST AID!?

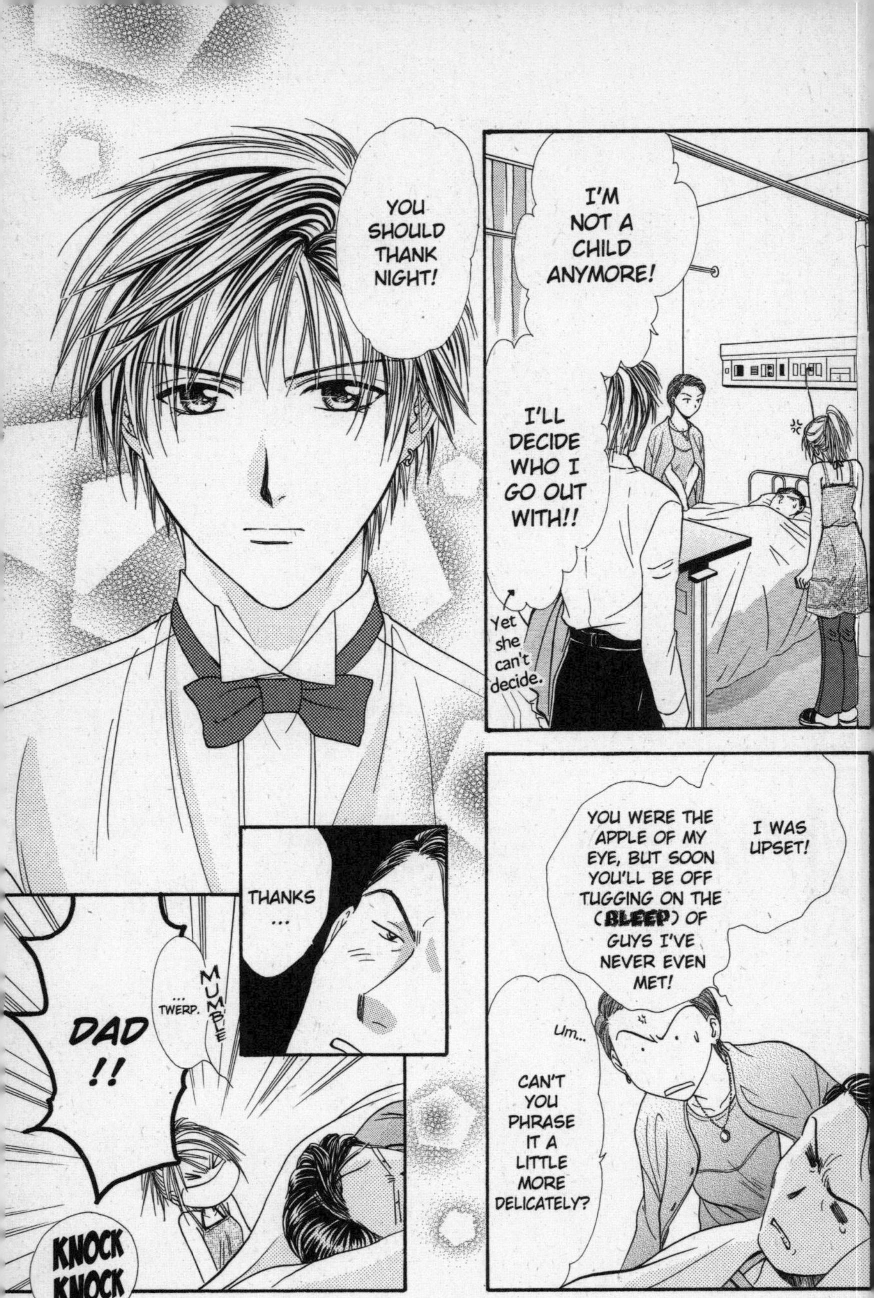
I'M NOT A CHILD ANYMORE!
I'LL DECIDE WHO I GO OUT WITH!!
Yet she can't decide.
I WAS UPSET!
YOU WERE THE APPLE OF MY EYE, BUT SOON YOU'LL BE OFF TUGGING ON THE (BLEEP) OF GUYS I'VE NEVER EVEN MET!
Um...
CAN'T YOU PHRASE IT A LITTLE MORE DELICATELY?
YOU SHOULD THANK NIGHT!
THANKS ...
MUMBLE
... TWERP.
DAD !!
KNOCK KNOCK

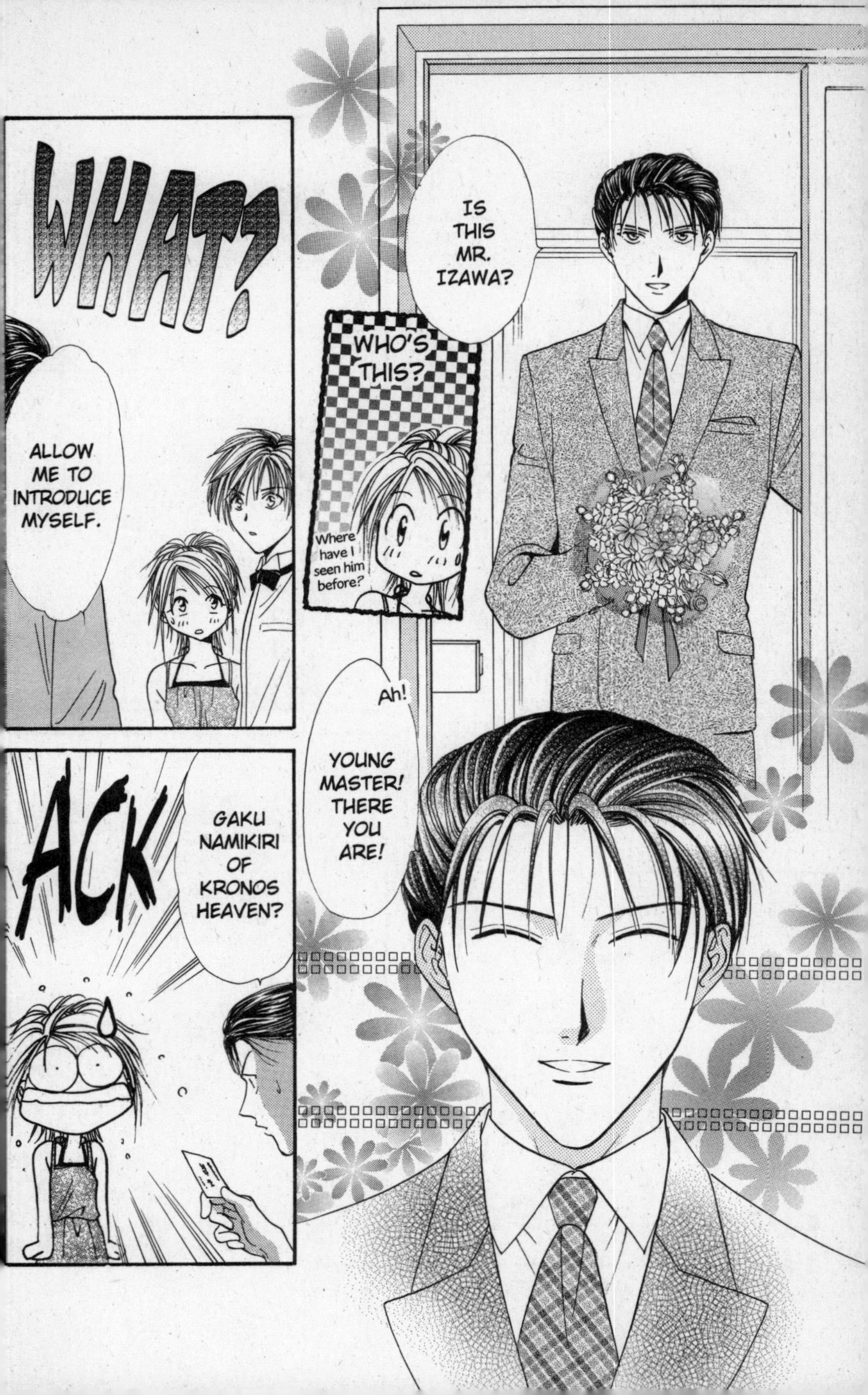
IS THIS MR. IZAWA?
WHO'S THIS?
Where have I seen him before?
Ah!
YOUNG MASTER! THERE YOU ARE!
WHAT?
ALLOW ME TO INTRODUCE MYSELF.
GAKU NAMIKIRI OF KRONOS HEAVEN?
ACK

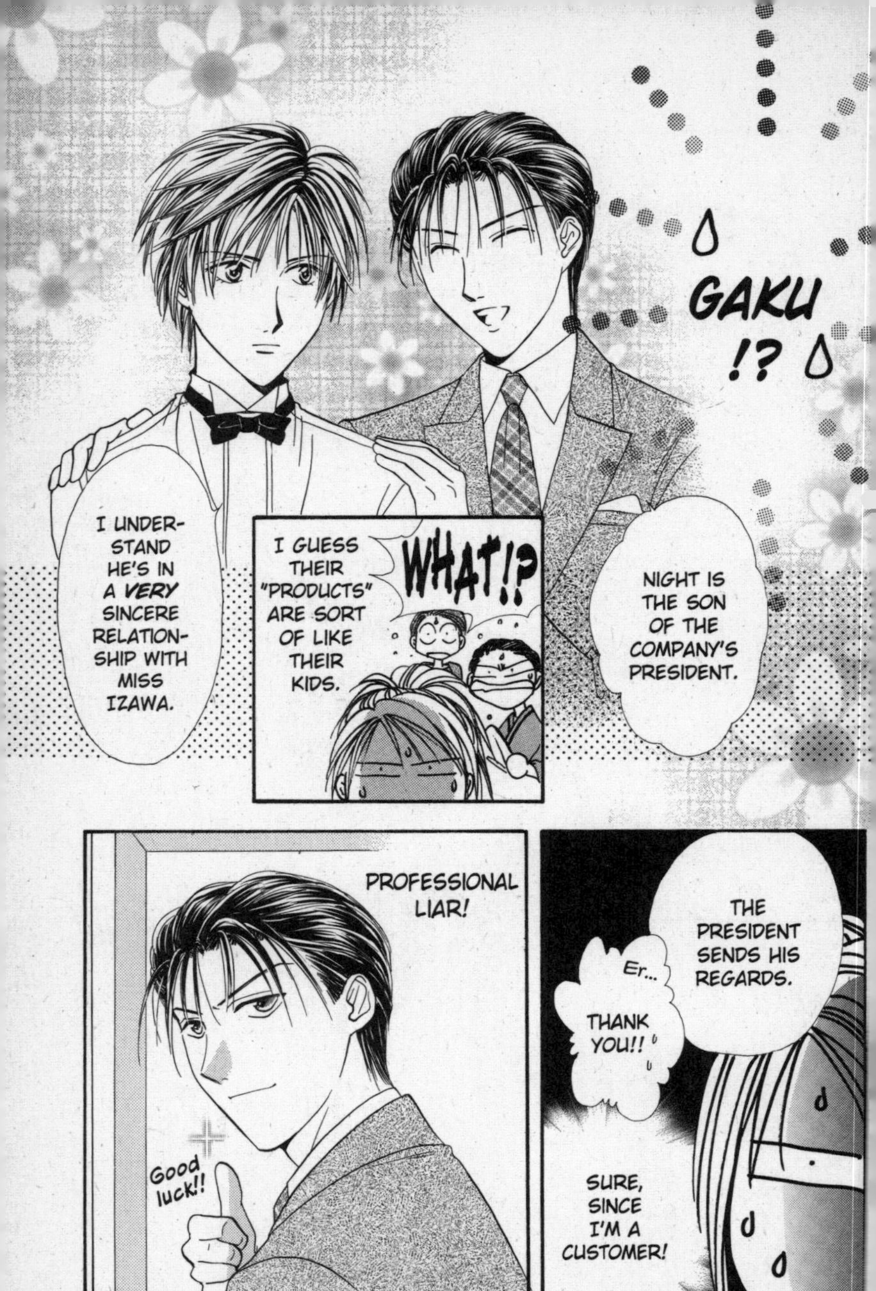
GAKU !?
NIGHT IS THE SON OF THE COMPANY'S PRESIDENT.
I UNDERSTAND HE'S IN A *VERY* SINCERE RELATIONSHIP WITH MISS IZAWA.
WHAT!?
I GUESS THEIR "PRODUCTS" ARE SORT OF LIKE THEIR KIDS.
THE PRESIDENT SENDS HIS REGARDS.
Er...
THANK YOU!!
SURE, SINCE I'M A CUSTOMER!
PROFESSIONAL LIAR!
Good luck!!

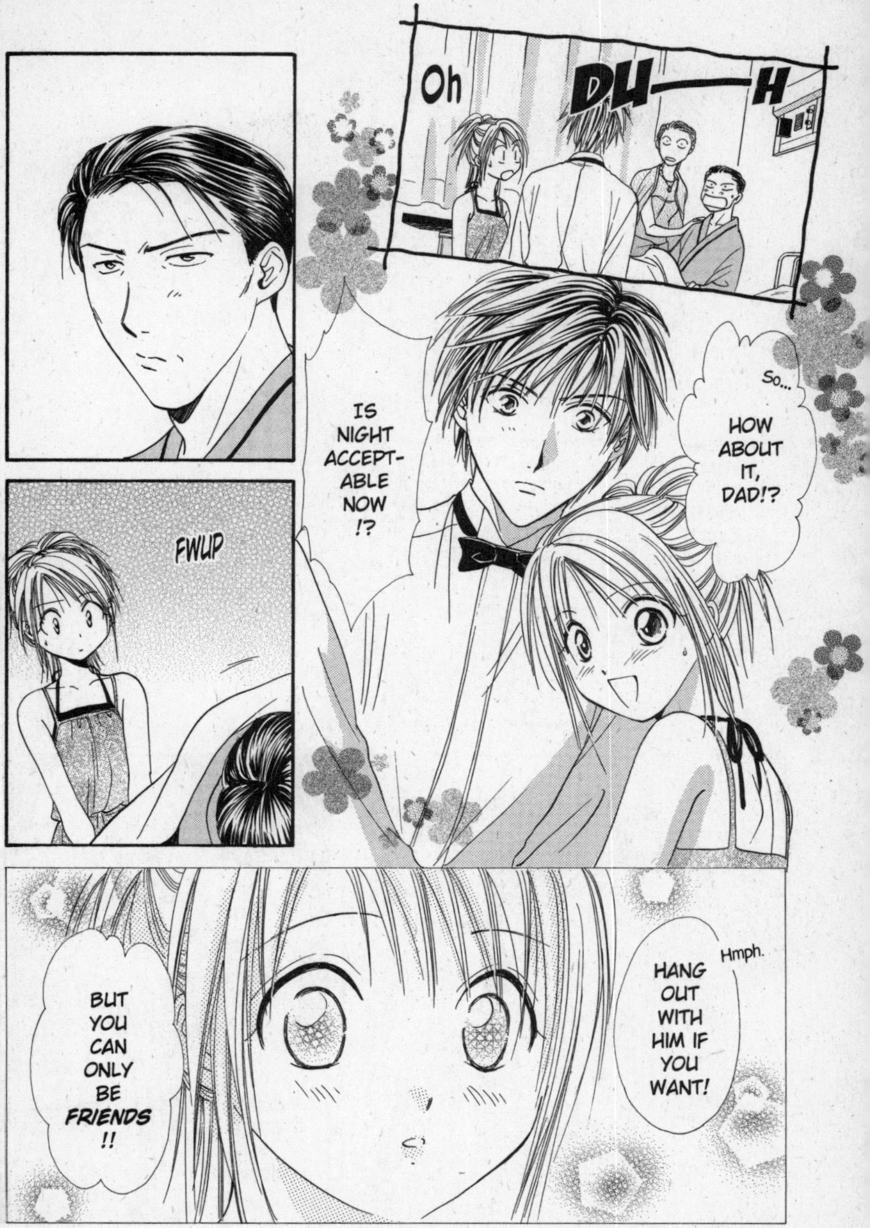
Oh
DUH—H
So...
HOW ABOUT IT, DAD!?
IS NIGHT ACCEPTABLE NOW!?
FWUP
Hmph.
HANG OUT WITH HIM IF YOU WANT!
BUT YOU CAN ONLY BE FRIENDS!!

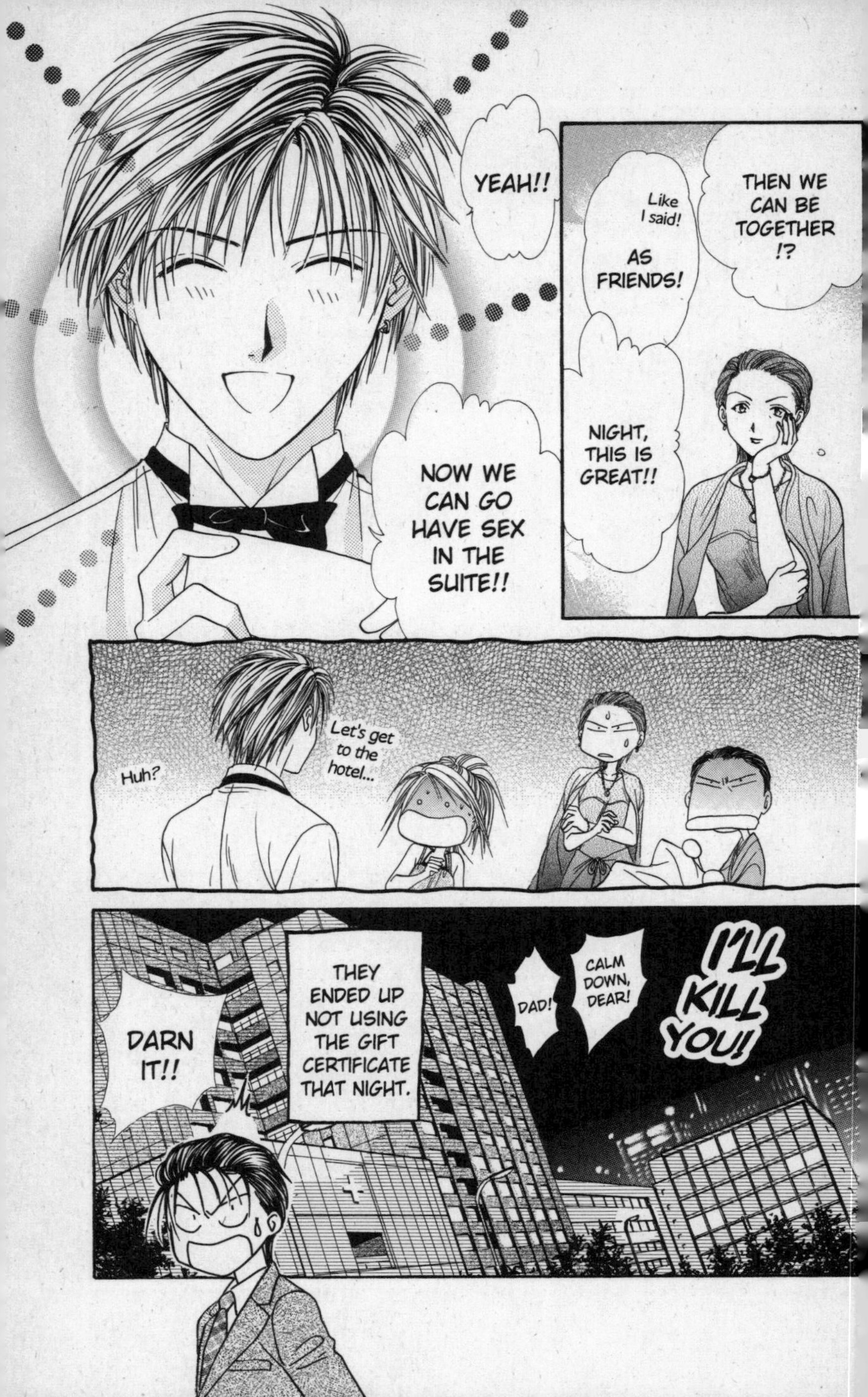
THEN WE CAN BE TOGETHER !?
Like I said!
AS FRIENDS!
NIGHT, THIS IS GREAT!!
YEAH!!
NOW WE CAN GO HAVE SEX IN THE SUITE!!
Let's get to the hotel...
Huh?
I'LL KILL YOU!
CALM DOWN, DEAR!
DAD!
THEY ENDED UP NOT USING THE GIFT CERTIFICATE THAT NIGHT.
DARN IT!!

i received a gift pack of organic black tea. i'm generally a coffee drinker so i was never really into black tea, but this tastes really mild! it's not bitter at all! i don't usually use milk or sugar personally, but this is delicious without it. Try it if you get a chance.

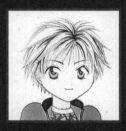

Yuu Watase

Birthday: March 5 (Pisces)

Blood type: B

Born and raised in Osaka.

Hobbies: listening to music, reading. Likes most music besides *enka* (traditional Japanese ballads) and heavy metal. Lately into health and wellness, like massage, mineral waters and wheat grass juice. But her job is her biggest "hobby"!

Debut title: *Pajama de Ojama* (An intrusion in Pajamas) (*Shojo Comics*, 1989, No. 3)

ABSOLUTE BOYFRIEND
Volume 3
Shojo Beat Edition

Story and Art by
YUU WATASE

© 2003 Yuu WATASE/Shogakukan
All rights reserved.
Original Japanese edition "ZETTAI KARESHI"
published by SHOGAKUKAN Inc.

English Adaptation/Lance Caselman
Translation/Lillian Olsen
Touch-up Art & Lettering/Freeman Wong
Design/Courtney Utt
Editor/Nancy Thistlethwaite

Printed in Canada

Published by VIZ Media, LLC
P.O. Box 77010
San Francisco, CA 94107

10 9 8 7 6 5 4
First printing, February 2007
Fourth printing, October 2010

PARENTAL ADVISORY
ABSOLUTE BOYFRIEND is rated T+ for Older Teen and is recommended for ages 16 and up. This volume contains suggestive themes.
ratings.viz.com

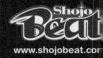

www.viz.com

www.shojobeat.com

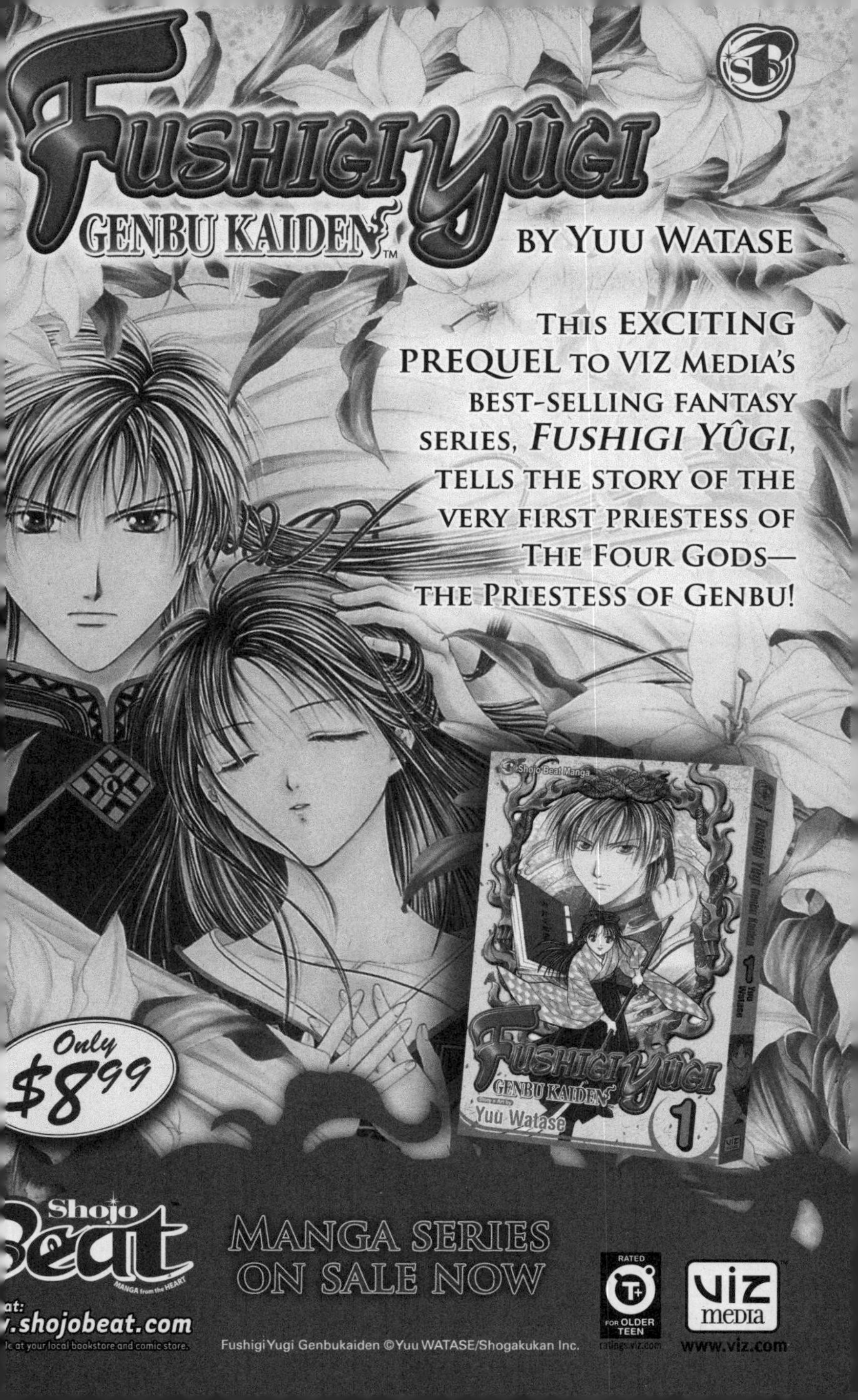
Fushigi Yûgi
Genbu Kaiden™
By Yuu Watase
This EXCITING PREQUEL to VIZ Media's best-selling fantasy series, *Fushigi Yûgi*, tells the story of the very first priestess of The Four Gods—the Priestess of Genbu!
Only $8.99
Shojo Beat Manga
Fushigi Yûgi Genbu Kaiden
Yuu Watase
1
Shojo Beat
MANGA from the HEART
at:
.shojobeat.com
le at your local bookstore and comic store.
MANGA SERIES ON SALE NOW
RATED T+ FOR OLDER TEEN
ratings.viz.com
viz media
www.viz.com
FushigiYugi Genbukaiden ©Yuu WATASE/Shogakukan Inc.

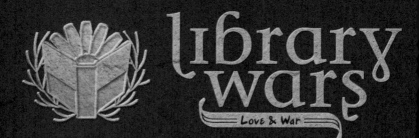
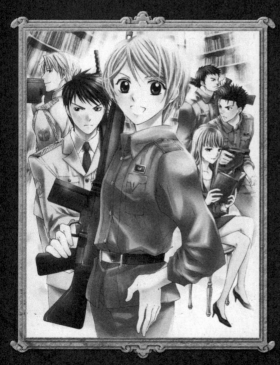

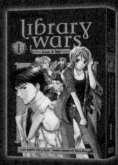

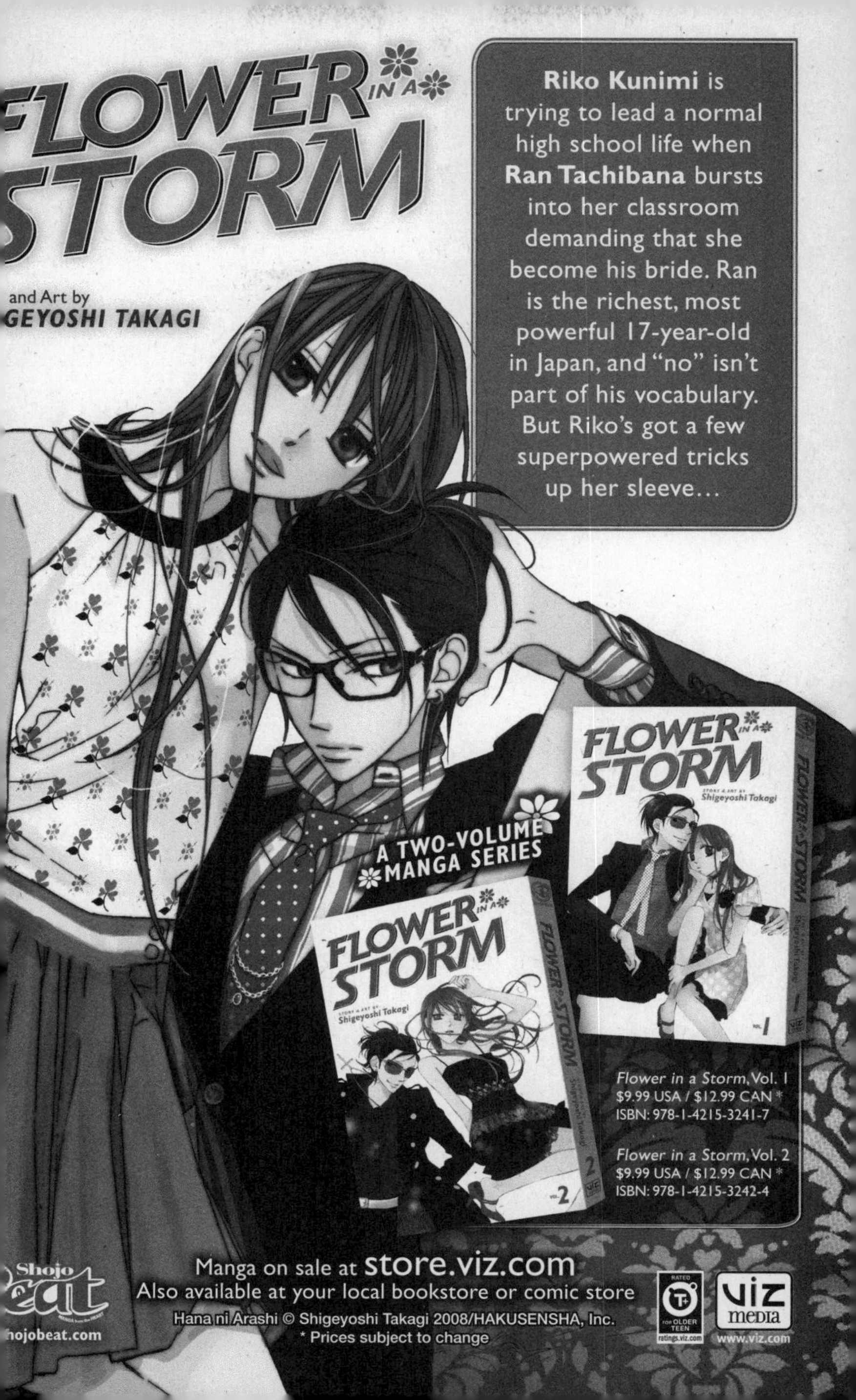

FLOWER IN A STORM
and Art by
GEYOSHI TAKAGI
Riko Kunimi is trying to lead a normal high school life when **Ran Tachibana** bursts into her classroom demanding that she become his bride. Ran is the richest, most powerful 17-year-old in Japan, and "no" isn't part of his vocabulary. But Riko's got a few superpowered tricks up her sleeve...
A TWO-VOLUME MANGA SERIES
FLOWER IN A STORM
Shigeyoshi Takagi
Flower in a Storm, Vol. 1
$9.99 USA / $12.99 CAN *
ISBN: 978-1-4215-3241-7
Flower in a Storm, Vol. 2
$9.99 USA / $12.99 CAN *
ISBN: 978-1-4215-3242-4
Manga on sale at store.viz.com
Also available at your local bookstore or comic store
Hana ni Arashi © Shigeyoshi Takagi 2008/HAKUSENSHA, Inc.
* Prices subject to change
Shojo Beat
shojobeat.com
RATED T+ FOR OLDER TEEN
ratings.viz.com
VIZ MEDIA
www.viz.com

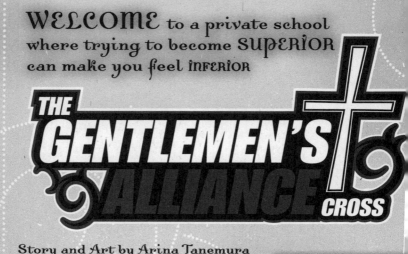
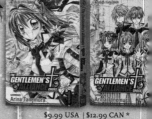

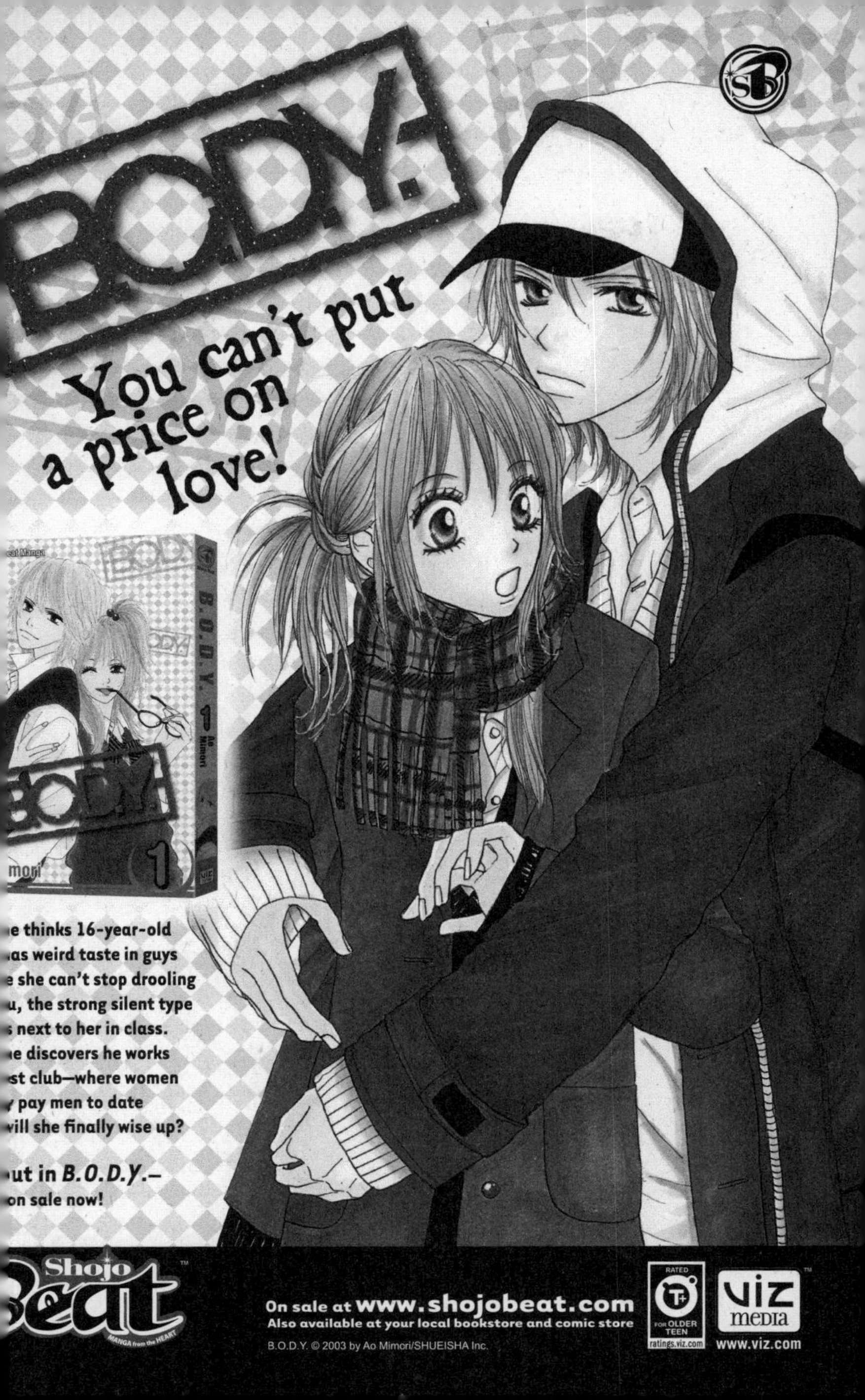
B.O.D.Y.
You can't put a price on love!
B.O.D.Y.
1
Ao Mimori
...e thinks 16-year-old
...as weird taste in guys
...e she can't stop drooling
...u, the strong silent type
...s next to her in class.
...e discovers he works
...st club—where women
...y pay men to date
...will she finally wise up?
...ut in *B.O.D.Y.*–
on sale now!
Shojo Beat
MANGA from the HEART
On sale at www.shojobeat.com
Also available at your local bookstore and comic store
B.O.D.Y. © 2003 by Ao Mimori/SHUEISHA Inc.
RATED T+ FOR OLDER TEEN
ratings.viz.com
VIZ media
www.viz.com

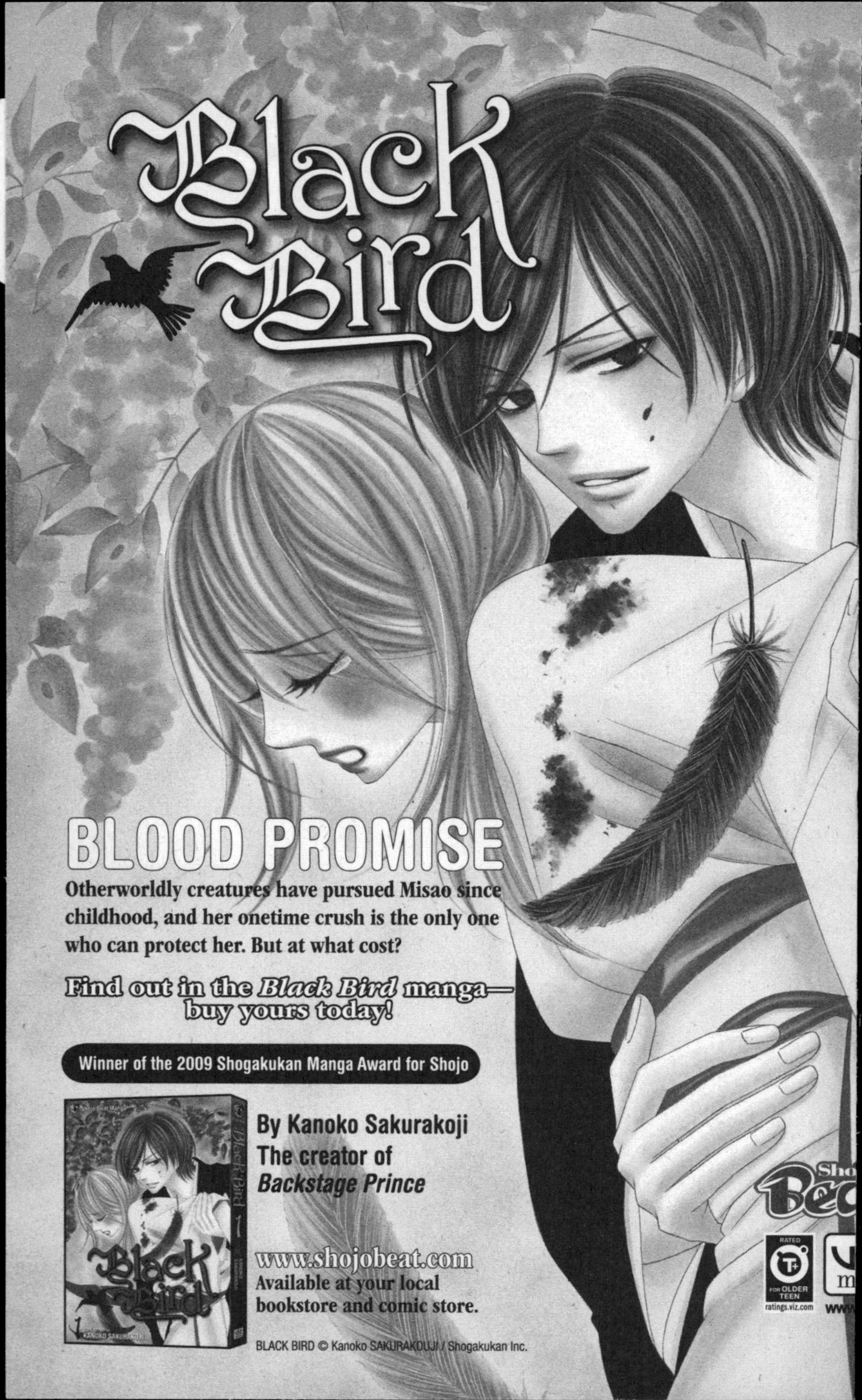
Black Bird
BLOOD PROMISE
Otherworldly creatures have pursued Misao since childhood, and her onetime crush is the only one who can protect her. But at what cost?
Find out in the Black Bird manga—buy yours today!
Winner of the 2009 Shogakukan Manga Award for Shojo
By Kanoko Sakurakoji
The creator of
Backstage Prince
www.shojobeat.com
Available at your local bookstore and comic store.
RATED T+ FOR OLDER TEEN
ratings.viz.com
BLACK BIRD © Kanoko SAKURAKOUJI / Shogakukan Inc.

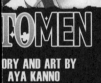
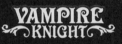